BANKRUPTCY CRIMES

THIRD EDITION

To Steve and Erika,

May your bikes and hikes be many, and your crimes be few.

Warm regards,
Stephanie

BANKRUPTCY CRIMES

Third Edition

By

Stephanie Wickouski

Beard Books
Washington, D.C.

ISBN 1-58798-272-2

Printed in the United States of America

To Robert M. Viles
1939–1999

Bankruptcy \(ban-krupt-tse) *n* [from Old Italian *banca* bank or bench + *rotta* broken} **1:** a federal judicial proceeding initiated by a person who is liable to creditors and seeks relief from his debts **2:** impoverishment; destitution <moral bankruptcy>

The word **bankruptcy** is derived from the Italian *banka rotta*, meaning broken table. In the Middle Ages, creditors would break the counters of debtors who failed to pay their debts.

FOREWORD

Bankruptcy law provides one of those unique intersections where different disciplines of the law should, but don't always, come together. Bankruptcy has its own clear, but distinct, criminal and civil components. Oftentimes, practitioners who focus on bankruptcy law do not have the criminal law background to appreciate the consequences of certain conduct nor recognize the techniques and process used by prosecutors investigating that conduct. Conversely, white collar criminal practitioners almost never have the background in bankruptcy law, its regulations and nuances, to understand or appreciate potential defenses that may arise. Similarly, prosecutors, when they investigate offenses arising out of a bankruptcy situation, often resort to charging other offenses with which they are more familiar and comfortable, rather than using the Bankruptcy Criminal Code. Fraud, perjury, bribery, embezzlement, money laundering, and destruction of records are easily recognizable to white collar defense attorneys and prosecutors, but may be treated very differently in a bankruptcy context.

The immediate and obvious value of this book as I read it is that Stephanie Wickouski understands both sides of the bankruptcy issue. For years there has been a need for a treatise that explains criminal law and process to bankruptcy lawyers, and bankruptcy law to criminal practitioners. This book does exactly that. Whether explaining the elements of criminal offenses or outlining the statutory intricacies of bankruptcy law, Ms. Wickouski takes the reader, whatever his or her background going in, and explains the situation from all perspectives. The pitfalls of parallel proceedings become clear and understandable to the practitioner reading this book.

Having known Stephanie Wickouski for nearly 15 years, it was easy for me to understand how she could take different perspectives on bankruptcy, some of which are contradictory and many of which are confusing, and explain them so that all could understand. If I were a lawyer involved in a bankruptcy matter, whether civil or criminal, and had only one reference work that I could rely upon, it would be this book.

E. Lawrence Barcella, Jr.
Paul, Hastings, Janofsky & Walker LLP
Washington, D.C.

PREFACE

No two topics provoke more heated debate than the criminal justice system and bankruptcy. A common perception is that the criminal justice system protects the guilty at the expense of the innocent, and bankruptcy is nothing short of legalized stealing.

Of course, life is not that simple. The good guys and bad guys cannot be distinguished by hat color. Having toiled many years in the field, I have seen the full spectrum of circumstances which can lead to a bankruptcy. Debtors — and creditors for that matter — come in all varieties: those victimized by circumstances beyond their control, and those whose problems are self-inflicted by negligence, greed, or outright dishonesty.

Needless to say, our system is not foolproof in its mission to punish the guilty and vindicate the innocent. Like most lawyers, I am frequently taken to task by non-lawyers because of the irrational contradictions and sometimes perverse results of the legal system. Thus I find myself in the role of apologist for both my areas of practice: bankruptcy and criminal justice.

By representing each client diligently, without value judgments based on innocence or culpability, we are protecting more than just that client. Our legal system is founded on the premise that a fair adversarial process, in which each side is vigorously represented, leads to truth, insures that justice is done, and protects the rights of all. Lawyers are committed to safeguarding that process, a commitment that overrides individual ends in any given case. Both the bankruptcy system and the criminal justice system are on the cutting edge of this principle.

It is easy to rail against an "unjust" result in a particular case and to ignore the collective benefits created by the bankruptcy and criminal justice systems. Some foreign bankruptcy systems are corrupt, slow, or ineffectual. These defects can have a disastrous effect on the economies — and societies — affected. The American system is considered a model around the world because of the clarity of the law, the efficiency of the courts, and the integrity of the judges. None of these should be taken for granted.

The bankruptcy system is the safety valve of our economy. Without a fair and effective bankruptcy system, the risk inherent in business ventures would deter entrepreneurial initiative, and thereby retard growth and productivity. Without the availability of bankruptcy relief, business owners would be saddled permanently with the consequences of an unprofitable venture. Resources would never be redirected from losing ventures to potentially profitable ones.

Bankruptcy is the inevitable analog of commerce. Our bankruptcy system is not perfect, but its goals are pure. The flaws of the process have been the subject of ongoing reform. As a result, the system evolves and improves with each passing decade.

The public perceives the criminal justice system as more fraught with inequities and less susceptible to reform than the bankruptcy system. One needs only to consider the alternatives to our system to be reminded of its merits. Some criticism of both the bankruptcy system and the criminal justice system is warranted; enforcement is often lax and almost always uneven. Significantly, the recent federal enforcement initiative in the area of bankruptcy crime has had a positive effect on public perception of both the bankruptcy and criminal justice systems.

I wrote this book because I believe in the need for criminal sanctions against bankruptcy fraud and for consistent, effective enforcement of those sanctions. Just as the participants in the civil bankruptcy system, the debtor and creditors, must abide by the rules of that system, the participants in the criminal system, the prosecution and defense, must not abuse their respective rights and power. It is my hope that this work will assist the participants in discerning those limits.

ACKNOWLEDGMENTS

Many family members, colleagues, and friends contributed to the writing of this book, and I am grateful to all of them. My most significant collaborator was my husband, David Fletcher. Faced with a house cluttered with the raw materials of a book in progress, David responded with an abundance of humor, encouragement, and good ideas. My sister, Sheila Wickouski, is herself a published author. She first taught me how to write and has been the source of excellent editorial advice and inspiration ever since. My mother, Mary L. Wickouski, fostered my independence, energy, and professional pursuits, including my legal career and this book. I am also grateful to my late father, Edward C. Wickouski, for urging me to pursue law as a profession and bankruptcy as a specialty.

Special thanks are owed to my terrific editor, Nina Novak, and legal assistant, Daniel D. Northrop, who worked on this project with me on a daily basis, and whose efforts were invaluable to its successful completion. Special thanks are also owed to attorney Jennifer E. Martella, who contributed substantially to this work. This book was enhanced by the extraordinary talent which Nina, Daniel and Jennifer each brought to this project. Thanks are also due to my colleagues Kristin K. Going and Daniel Morse.

I am indebted to my colleagues who supported my endeavor enthusiastically; in particular, my partner Harold L. Kaplan and my former partners, the late William O. Bittman, Nancy Luque and Judge Henry Hudson, who were my mentors in criminal law.

I am grateful to my revered committee, JT, Anthony, and Therese. They always responded to my requests, no matter how hopeless, difficult, or ordinary.

I must acknowledge the part that all of my clients, colleagues, and opposing counsel have contributed to this book. I have been delighted by some of these individuals and frustrated by others. The most annoying and difficult of people have fostered my growth in the law no less than the most gracious and easy. I am grateful to all of them for their contribution to my continuing legal education, and to the experience which created this book.

LIST OF ABBREVIATIONS

ABA	American Bar Association
Bankruptcy Code	Title 11, United States Code § 101, *et seq.*
Bankruptcy Criminal Code	Title 18, United States Code, chapter 9 (§§ 151-157)
DOJ	United States Department of Justice
FBI	Federal Bureau of Investigation
Fed. R. Bankr. P.	Federal Rules of Bankruptcy Procedure
Fed. R. Civ. P.	Federal Rules of Civil Procedure
Fed. R. Crim. P.	Federal Rules of Criminal Procedure
Fed. R. Evid.	Federal Rules of Evidence
Federal Criminal Code	Title 18, United States Code
IRS	Internal Revenue Service
RICO	Racketeer Influenced and Corrupt Organization Act
USSG	United States Sentencing Guidelines

ABOUT THE AUTHOR

Stephanie Wickouski is a partner at Drinker Biddle & Reath in New York, NY. She specializes in business bankruptcy, insolvency, and commercial litigation. Her articles have appeared in *The National Law Journal*, *The American Bar Association's Litigation* Magazine, *Legal Times*, *Washington Business Journal*, and official publications of the District of Columbia, New Jersey, and Pennsylvania State Bar Associations. She was selected by her peers for inclusion in *The Best Lawyers in America*, and by *Washingtonian* Magazine in its "Top Lawyers" issue. She also has been named as one of twelve nationally recognized Outstanding Restructuring Lawyers by *Turnarounds & Workouts*.

She taught creditors' rights at the Catholic University School of Law and was formerly a law clerk to the Hon. Roger M. Whelan, former U.S. Bankruptcy Judge for the District of Columbia. Prior to entering private practice, she was a trial attorney with the Civil Division of the U.S. Department of Justice. She served as a panel trustee for the U.S. Bankruptcy Court for the Eastern District of Virginia and as a mediator for the U.S. District Court for the District of Columbia and the U.S. Bankruptcy Court for the Southern District of New York.

Ms. Wickouski can be reached at swickous@aol.com.

CONTRIBUTOR

Jennifer E. Martella is an attorney with the Washington, D.C. office of Baker & McKenzie LLP, specializing in securities, corporate and banking.

CONTENTS

Foreword ix
Preface xi
Acknowledgments xiii
List of Abbreviations xiv
About the Author xv
Contributor xvi

Part 1: Introduction and History 1
1. Overview 1
2. Historical summary 5
3. Common fraud schemes 10
4. Due process and the interpretation of criminal statutes 14

Part 2: Analysis of Title 18, United States Code, Chapter 9 17
5. Overview 17
6. Concealment of assets: 18 U.S.C. § 152(1) 28
7. False oaths, accounts and declarations: 18 U.S.C. § 152(2) and 152(3) 40
8. False claims: 18 U.S.C. § 152(4) 50
9. Receiving property with the intent to defeat the Bankruptcy Code and bribery: 18 U.S.C. § 152(5) and (6) 54
10. Fraudulent prebankruptcy transfers: 18 U.S.C. § 152(7) 63
11. Concealment or destruction of records: 18 U.S.C. § 152(8) and (9) and § 1519 67
12. Embezzlement against estates: 18 U.S.C. § 153 71
13. Adverse interest and conduct of officers: 18 U.S.C. § 154 74
14. Fee agreements in cases under title 11 and receiverships: 18 U.S.C. § 155 78
15. Bankruptcy petition preparer fraud: 18 U.S.C. § 156 82
16. Bankruptcy fraud: 18 U.S.C. § 157 87

Part 3: Related offenses 91
17. Statutory overlap and multiplicity 91
18. Aiding and abetting: 18 U.S.C. § 2; principals and accessories: 18 U.S.C. § 3; and misprision: 18 U.S.C. § 4 95

19. Conspiracy: 18 U.S.C. § 371 101
20. False statements: 18 U.S.C. §§ 1001, 1014, and 1032 108
21. Mail, wire or bank fraud: 18 U.S.C. § 1341-1344 116
22. Obstruction of justice: 18 U.S.C. § 1503 121
23. Perjury: 18 U.S.C. §§ 1621-23 126
24. Racketeer Influenced and Corrupt Organizations Act: 18 U.S.C. § 1962 135
25. Money laundering: 18 U.S.C. § 1956 140
26. Other related provisions 146

Part 4 : Prosecution and defense 147
27. Investigation 147
28. Indictment 153
29. Overview of defenses 157
30. Statute of limitations 162
31. Advice of counsel 166
32. Attorney-client privilege 169
33. The Fifth Amendment privilege 175

Part 5 : Penalties 182
34. Federal Sentencing Guidelines 182
35. Restitution, fines and forfeitures 195
36. Plea agreements 200

Part 6 : Civil and collateral issues 202
37. Relationship between civil and criminal proceedings 202
38. Ethics and professional responsibility 205

Appendix A Excerpts from Title 11, United States Code (The Federal Bankruptcy Code) 216
Appendix B Excerpts from Title 18, United States Code (Crimes and Criminal Procedure) 258
Appendix C Excerpts from The Federal Rules of Bankruptcy Procedure (effective December 1, 2005) 283
Appendix D Excerpts from The Federal Rules of Evidence 294
Appendix E Form 1 Voluntary Petition 295
Appendix F List of Creditors Holding 20 Largest Unsecured Claims 301
Appendix G Schedules 302
Appendix H Statement of Financial Affairs 323
Appendix I Proof of Claim 334
Appendix J Excerpts from The ABA Model Rules of Professional Conduct 339
Appendix K Excerpts from The U.S. Sentencing Guidelines Manual, as amended and effective November 1, 2004 360

Table of Authorities 386

General Statutory Materials 395

Index 399

PART 1

INTRODUCTION AND HISTORY

1. Overview

The American bankruptcy system is hailed by foreign legal scholars but scorned by the American public. Public cynicism toward the bankruptcy system has grown steadily over the past few decades as the number and size of corporate and individual filings have increased. In 2005, over 2 million cases were filed – a record high. The amount of debt that was extinguished, reduced, or otherwise affected in these cases totals in the billions.

High profile bankruptcy cases have destroyed public confidence in the bankruptcy system. In many cases, debtors discharge huge liabilities and emerge wealthy. The common perception is that the system is seriously flawed, if not outright corrupt. Fraud is seen not as the exception but as the rule.

Experts estimate that approximately ten percent of all bankruptcy cases involve abuse or fraud. If such an approximation is accurate, the number of such cases in 2005 was over 200,000. Some experts have opined that the incidence of fraud is on the rise recently, due to a confluence of social, economic, and legal factors.

Until recently, however, criminal prosecutions arising from bankruptcy cases received little attention or publicity. The increased volume of bankruptcy filings in the past decade brought about a heightened interest in criminal enforcement. In 1992, the United States Department of Justice (DOJ) made the aggressive prosecution of bankruptcy crime a high priority. Subsequently, DOJ launched "Operation Total Disclosure," declaring enforcement of the criminal bankruptcy statutes a nationwide priority. Operation Total Disclosure is an extensive, nationally coordinated law enforcement effort spearheaded by the Attorney General and United States attorneys and supported by the United States trustee system, the Criminal and Tax Divisions of DOJ, the Federal Bureau of Investigation, the United States Postal Inspection Service, the Offices of Inspector General, and the Social Security Administration. Since the launching of this law enforcement initiative, the consequent investigations have resulted in hundreds of indictments. Former Attorney General Janet Reno stated that the ensuing bankruptcy crime prosecutions were part of DOJ's ongoing effort to deter fraud, protect the integrity of the bankruptcy system, and enhance public confidence in the system.

Ms. Reno's statement underscores the fact that the law does not seek to redress the rights of individual creditors, but to protect the system as a whole. In many instances, violations can occur even if there is no benefit to the defendant and no injury to any creditor. Since Operation Total Disclosure was launched, prosecutors have focused increasingly on conduct that defrauds the judicial process, as opposed to conduct that causes identifiable losses to creditors.

> The reach of the bankruptcy system extends far beyond those directly involved in the process. The bankruptcy system is designed to be society's safety valve. The availability of bankruptcy relief encourages entrepreneurs to invest energy, money, and resources into the marketplace without the risk of permanent liability for a failed venture. The bankruptcy system depends on voluntary disclosure and compliance. In order for such a system to work properly and justly, debtors, lawyers, and trustees need to be truthful with the court, the creditors, and each other. It is essential that everybody play by the rules. Criminal bankruptcy laws are intended to protect the integrity *of* the process by demanding integrity of everyone *in* the process.
>
> In the past, the government would target certain predictable schemes for prosecution. While these old schemes are still the subject of many investigations and indictments, federal prosecutors, in their recent focus on bankruptcy fraud, are also targeting conduct that many lawyers might not even recognize as criminal. Consider the following examples:
>
> - a man files bankruptcy using the wrong Social Security number
> - a lawyer files a personal bankruptcy case on his own behalf, but does not list his interest in bank accounts that are held in the name of a corporation
> - a creditor receives payments from a bankruptcy debtor, which were not approved by the bankruptcy court

- a non-lawyer collects fees from an individual to file a bankruptcy petition on that individual's behalf; the petition is filed without the required information, or is not filed at all
- a debtor's lawyer files a disclosure with the court which contains an incomplete disclosure of the law firm's representation of other clients, some of which are creditors in the case

All of these were actual cases in which defendants either pled or were found guilty of bankruptcy fraud. All received jail sentences, in some cases as long as six years.

These incidents may not seem that shocking. So why were they prosecuted? All prosecutions begin with an investigation, usually triggered by a report of a suspected crime from a United States bankruptcy judge or by a United States trustee. Bankruptcy judges and trustees must report any suspected bankruptcy crime to one of the nation's United States attorneys.[1] Once the suspected crime has been investigated, usually by the FBI in coordination with the United States attorney, the decision to prosecute bankruptcy fraud is made by the United States attorney.

The United States attorney is a presidential appointee whose job is to further the objectives of the current president's administration. The United States attorney may or may not have prior prosecutorial experience. His mission is not to prosecute cases personally, but to make judgment calls as to which cases should be prosecuted. The decision to prosecute is often intended as a message to the community that certain conduct will not be tolerated.

The criteria considered in the exercise of prosecutorial discretion includes: (1) is the loss or injury substantial? (2) is the evidence sufficient? (3) is the law clear? The United States attorney must consider not just whether a potential defendant will be convicted, but whether he should be. One significant consideration in the decision of whether or not to prosecute is the existence of an adequate noncriminal alternative. In a bankruptcy fraud situation, the civil penalties for fraud are often so grave that they may be adequate as both punishment and deterrent.

Ironically, the factors considered by the prosecution in bringing a case are the very same questions that defense counsel often ask when developing a defense. Both prosecutors and defense counsel require an understanding of the statutory bankruptcy criminal provisions[2] and their use and interpretation, as

---

[1] 18 U.S.C. § 3057.

[2] Title 18, United States Code, chapter 9 (the "Bankruptcy Criminal Code").

well as the relationship between those provisions and other federal law, including civil bankruptcy law (the Federal Bankruptcy Code[3]), other federal criminal statutes,[4] and the Federal Sentencing Guidelines.[5] There is considerable overlap between the Bankruptcy Criminal Code and other federal criminal statutes, such as money laundering, wire, mail and bank fraud, and perjury.

The chapters that follow analyze the Bankruptcy Criminal Code within the context of federal criminal law and practice, as well as civil bankruptcy law and practice. The prosecution and defense of a bankruptcy crime is examined from "soup to nuts," from the commencement of an investigation through sentencing. The associated problems of parallel civil and criminal proceedings are also discussed. Lastly, the ethical and professional responsibilities of the practitioner are addressed.

---

[3] Title 11, United States Code (the "Bankruptcy Code").
[4] These statutes are found primarily in title 18, United States Code.
[5] *See* chapter 34.

2. Historical summary

Modern American bankruptcy law, like most of the American legal system, has its origins in English common law. Bankruptcy law, however, did not originate in England. The earliest bankruptcy statutes are said to have been enacted in Rome under Julius Caesar. The term "bankruptcy" is derived from the Italian term "banca rotta,"[6] or broken table, which referred to a medieval practice of breaking the money table of a tradesman who failed to pay his debts. Many early bankruptcy laws were criminal in nature: debtors were incarcerated for not paying debts.

Italian city-states were among the first jurisdictions to move toward civil alternatives, and enacted some of the earliest civil bankruptcy laws. Among the earliest of such reform initiatives occurred in Padua in the thirteenth century. Fernando Bulhom, a Portuguese émigré, spiritual leader and social reformer, lobbied the Paduan magistrates to adopt a law providing debtors with an alternative to prison — surrendering their assets to their creditors. The Edict of Padua, passed on March 15, 1231, was one of the earliest civil bankruptcy laws.[7]

The earliest English bankruptcy laws were enacted in the sixteenth century under King Henry VIII and were criminal in nature, but the penalties under the bankruptcy statute of 1543 were primarily monetary. In 1604, the penalty for perjury was increased to include standing on the public pillory and the nailing of an ear. Incredible as it seems today, in the early eighteenth century, concealment and other bankruptcy fraud became capital crimes. In actual practice, the death penalty for a bankruptcy crime was relatively rare, and probably less than half a dozen executions occurred.

As is the case with much modern legislation, the driving force behind early bankruptcy reform was not the humane but the practical. Loss of personal freedom does not benefit creditors as much as taking a debtor's assets or requiring him to dedicate future earnings to repay debts.

---

[6] The Latin term was "Bancus ructus."

[7] Within a year of his death in 1231, Fernando Bulhom was declared a saint by Pope Gregory IX, and is now known as St. Anthony of Padua.

Bankruptcy was not essentially decriminalized until the eighteenth century. The most significant philosophical change in the English bankruptcy laws occurred with the first law providing for a discharge of debts. The bankruptcy statutes were amended several times during the nineteenth century, and debtors' prison was abolished completely in 1869. However, absconding to evade creditors was still punishable by hard labor.

Early American bankruptcy law

The predicate for American bankruptcy law is found in the bankruptcy clause to the Constitution, which empowers Congress to pass uniform laws on the subject of bankruptcy.[8] The bankruptcy clause was first proposed to the Constitutional Convention by Charles Pinkney in 1787. There was general consensus in support of the bankruptcy clause, with only one state, Connecticut, voting against. The first bankruptcy statute was enacted by Congress in 1800 but was repealed three years later. This law criminalized perjury with respect to assets in a bankruptcy case. A subsequent act, which was passed in 1841 and repealed two years later, had similar perjury provisions. The next act, which was passed in 1857, contained many criminal provisions which conceptually resembled the current Bankruptcy Criminal Code.

The next major bankruptcy legislation, the Bankruptcy Act of 1898, remained in effect until 1979. Most of the current Bankruptcy Criminal Code, particularly § 152, resembles the criminal provisions of the Bankruptcy Act of 1898. Interestingly, the criminal provisions in the earliest laws were contained in the bankruptcy statutes rather than in the criminal statutes.

Congress enacted amendments to the bankruptcy law in 1926 and 1937. The 1937 legislation was in large part a response to corrupt practices in equity receiverships and business bankruptcies during the Great Depression of the 1930's. The 1937 amendments included the Borah Act, which prohibited fee fixing agreements in bankruptcies and receiverships. The Borah Act was contained in title 28 and was the predecessor of § 155 of the Bankruptcy Criminal Code.

The Bankruptcy Commission

The bankruptcy law was completely overhauled in 1978, after almost a decade of intensive investigation and analysis. In 1970, Congress established the Commission on the Bankruptcy Laws of the United States (the Bankruptcy Com-

---

[8] U.S. CONST. art. I, § 8, cl. 4.

mission),[9] a federal commission charged with rewriting the Bankruptcy Act. The Bankruptcy Commission issued its report in July 1973. In its report, which was delivered to the president, Congress, and the chief justice of the Supreme Court, the Bankruptcy Commission noted that in the first half of the twentieth century, there were widespread abuses and corruption in the bankruptcy system:

> [T]he administration of the bankruptcy law was characterized by serious abuses and malpractices on the part of attorneys, receivers, trustees, appraisers, custodians, auctioneers, and other persons and associations. [In 1929] the bulk of the bankruptcy practice in New York City was concentrated in the hands of approximately 21 law firms. . . . Counsel for the petitioning creditors would suggest that the court appoint a certain person as receiver, and the receiver would then select counsel for the petitioning creditors as his attorney; thereafter the process would continue when the receiver was elected or appointed trustee and counsel for the petitioning creditors was chosen as his attorney. . . . These abuses led to others and to conflicts; outright theft occurred. Twelve attorneys were indicted; one absconded and then committed suicide; two pleaded guilty and received jail sentences.[10]

The Bankruptcy Commission described numerous factors which led to these conditions, factors which in large part had not been addressed by prior bankruptcy reform. Some of these factors were the inefficiencies of the Bankruptcy Act, the fact that the criminal provisions had become largely ineffective, and the dual administrative and adjudicative roles of the bankruptcy courts.

The Bankruptcy Commission recommended a sweeping overhaul of the law and the bankruptcy system, including the establishment of a Federal Bankruptcy Commissioner to oversee bankruptcy cases and supervise trustees, separate from the court, whose role should be strictly adjudicative. The Bankruptcy Commission recommended that the administrative functions of the commissioner include investigation of complaints of fraud and abuse, and monitoring

---

[9] The late Dean Robert M. Viles, to whom this book is dedicated, was one of the five staff members of the Bankruptcy Commission and served as its research director. The other four members were Frank R. Kennedy (executive director), Walter Ray Phillips, Philip Shuchman, and Gerald Smith (deputy directors).

[10] Report of the Commission on the Bankruptcy Laws of the United States, H. R. Doc. 93-137, 93d Cong., 1st Sess. (App. Pt. 4-350-1).

of the enforcement of criminal provisions.[11] This concept eventually became reality, with the creation of the United States Trustee program launched in the Bankruptcy Reform Act of 1978.

The Bankruptcy Reform Act of 1978

The Bankruptcy Commission's recommendations led to the enactment of a completely rewritten bankruptcy code eight years later. In 1978, Congress enacted the Bankruptcy Reform Act of 1978 (the "1978 Act"), which took effect on October 1, 1979. The 1978 Act removed the administrative role from the bankruptcy court, addressing the major problem highlighted by the Bankruptcy Commission. The 1978 Act established a pilot program of United States trustees in selected judicial districts. The program eventually became permanent and was expanded nationwide. One of the primary missions of the United States Trustee program was to prevent fraud and abuse in the bankruptcy system. This one aspect of the 1978 Act, more than any other reform, has been widely credited with reducing corruption and abuse by trustees and lawyers within the bankruptcy system. Several amendments to the Bankruptcy Criminal Code were also made in the 1978 Act. The Bankruptcy Code and Bankruptcy Criminal Code were again amended in 1994.

Bankruptcy legislation, both civil and criminal, is often a response to a prevailing social or economic problem. The Borah Act of 1937 sought to curb and punish fee fixing in equity receiverships, a practice that was widespread during the Great Depression. The primary goal of the 1978 Act was to remedy problems where the existing law had failed. The 1978 Act was aimed at making the process more effective, particularly in business reorganizations, less incestuous, and less corruption-prone. The criminalization of bankruptcy petition preparer fraud in § 156 in 1994 sought to address the prevalence of bankruptcy mills, which have been fueled by the record-high levels of consumer debt during the last two decades.

Bankruptcy crime today

Throughout the course of American history and a series of bankruptcy reform measures, some bankruptcy crimes have changed little. Concealment in a bankruptcy has been a crime for four and a half centuries; perjury, for almost four centuries. Certain patterns of conduct seem to recur decade after decade (if not century after century). New schemes, and new crimes, develop, but the old

---

[11] Report of the Commission on the Bankruptcy Laws of the United States, H. R. Doc. 93-137, 93d Cong., 1st Sess. (App. Pt. 4-353).

ones, particularly asset concealment and perjury, are still common. These "traditional" crimes are as serious as ever.

Modern criminal bankruptcy law represents the most sophisticated response to bankruptcy fraud to date. Throughout much of human history, the response to insolvency has been punitive, not remedial. This fact alone suggests that, in a moral sense, while we may not regard bankruptcy as wrong, we do not see it as right. There are many aspects of insolvency that may be viewed as morally questionable: abuse of credit; living beyond one's means; lack of any honest intention to repay one's debts; failure to manage one's personal finances or business. Someone who consumes at the expense of others has less than scrupulous rectitude.

The premise of early bankruptcy law was that the failure to pay debt was equivalent to fraud, for which the debtor should be punished. The forms of punishment in prior centuries included not only seizure of property, which is akin, in principle, to civil bankruptcy today, but also physical punishment, imprisonment, and execution. In modern American society, where many citizens regard execution for even the most heinous murders to be morally wrong, execution for failure to pay debt is unthinkable. Yet, the decriminalization of bankruptcy took centuries to accomplish and was not easy at that. In many instances, reform was spearheaded by spiritual rather than political leaders.

Over time, the scope of criminal conduct was narrowed and more specifically defined. Dishonesty and concealment have always been and probably always will be regarded as crimes. New crimes are defined because, as the civil bankruptcy system becomes more sophisticated, new forms of bankruptcy abuse emerge.

The role of criminal sanctions in insolvency situations has evolved drastically since the inception of bankruptcy law. Bankruptcy has legal, social and moral aspects. Society's evaluation of the social and moral aspects of bankruptcy determines whether the conduct will fall within the purview of the civil bankruptcy system or the criminal justice system.

3. Common fraud schemes

The ways in which fraud can be committed are virtually endless, but certain patterns recur. Four of the most common traditional schemes are popularly known as the "bustout," the "bleedout," "looting," and "skimming." There are also several schemes of recent vintage, the fastest growing of which is the "bankruptcy mill."

The bustout

The bustout is one of the best known bankruptcy frauds. Bustouts are planned and executed over a protracted period of time. The scheme begins with the formation of a seemingly legitimate and financially sound business, an entity which is almost always a corporation. The principal (an owner, shareholder, or manager) develops a favorable credit rating, sometimes but not always using false credit references or false financial statements. On behalf of the corporation, he orders inventory and pays for it promptly, thereby lulling suppliers to ship larger and larger amounts of merchandise on credit. Once a large inventory is in place, the bustout begins. The business sells the inventory at prices which are substantially below market value, and perhaps are even below cost. Sometimes inventory is hidden in a related company. The principal, once a "good" customer, tells the creditors that the company is having a temporary cash flow problem, perhaps even blaming the problem on his own slow paying customers. In so doing, the principal persuades his creditors to hold off on taking legal action. By the time the creditors realize they have been duped, the assets (and the principal) are gone.

Sometimes the bustout involves a "take-down" man. In this type of scheme, the owners in a sham sales transaction transfer the business to the take-down man, who then tells creditors for the first time that there are financial problems, which he blames on the "former" owner. The take-down man lulls the creditors into forbearing, possibly into extending further credit. Of course, all the while, the take-down man is part of the owner's scheme.

The bleedout

A variation on the bustout is the bleedout. A bleedout involves a depletion of assets over a period of time in a more subtle manner than a bustout. While a bustout typically involves a company with a short life span, a bleedout often involves a company with a longer life span. The goal of a bleedout is to drain the company of value for as long a period as possible. Insider transactions, particularly capital infusion characterized as loans, and complicated corporate transactions, are two of the common warning signs. Use of pension funds or trust fund taxes is not uncommon in a bleedout. By the time the creditors realize what is happening, it is, of course, too late.

Looting

Another recurring scheme is looting. Looting begins with a failing company and a principal who wants to move the company's assets to a new business, one which is not plagued with debt (at least, not at this point). The principal obtains a straw buyer to act secretly on his behalf and purchase the failing company's assets at a low price. The effect is to swindle the creditors who, of course, would never have released their claims against the assets at such a low price if had they known that the debtor's principal was the true buyer. Sometimes, one or more of the creditors collude with the debtor in a looting scheme.

Looting can occur in or out of a bankruptcy case. Looting can take place right under the nose of the judge and the trustee, sometimes with the unwitting approval of both. When it occurs in a bankruptcy case, the scenario unfolds in a predictable way. First, the debtor seeks court approval on an expedited or emergency basis to sell substantially all the debtor's assets to a purchaser, whom the debtor represents to the court to be a disinterested party. The terms of the proposed sale, however, are hardly at arms-length. While the price may seem adequate on its face, the terms of the contract favor the purchaser in a manner most unusual in a bankruptcy case. For example, the sale contract may provide for transfer of all cash, deposits, and causes of action to the seller; "no-shop" provisions, which preclude the debtor from advertising the sale or soliciting other potential purchasers; and an unusually high termination fee.

Bankruptcy sales are always subject to court approval, and the process usually allows parties interested in buying the assets the opportunity to make an offer at or prior to the hearing on the sale. A termination fee is a fee which a debtor agrees to pay a proposed purchaser if the purchaser is ultimately outbid by another bidder. A termination fee may only be paid in a bankruptcy case if the amount of the fee, and the terms under which it would be paid, are approved by the bankruptcy court. Termination fees are often included among so-called bid protection orders. Through such orders, a debtor will seek to establish and structure the bidding process, often in a manner favoring one bidder.

There is nothing illegal *per se* about a no-shop provision, a termination fee, bid protections, or even a sale to a related party. What separates a looting scheme from a legitimate sale is the undisclosed relationship between the debtor and buyer. The buyer is, in fact, just a mere shell. Nondisclosure of that fact is at the heart of the looting scheme.

Skimming

Another common scheme is skimming. Skimming has a number of variations, but the basic idea is to drain cash flow while not paying the mortgage or third party creditors. Skimming can occur either before or after a bankruptcy case is filed. In either instance, skimming gives rise to a number of bankruptcy crimes. Skimming is most frequently seen in the commercial real estate context. The owner does not make mortgage payments despite the fact the property is generating rental income. Often, the property or an interest in the property will be transferred to a new entity, which will in turn file bankruptcy. Equity skimming schemes sometimes involve numerous pieces of property or numerous bankruptcy filings.

Modern schemes

In recent years, the profile of the typical bankruptcy crime has changed. The old fashioned schemes are still prevalent, but several new ones have emerged as well. One of the most popular modern bankruptcy crimes is the bankruptcy mill scheme. This scheme can take on endless variations, but the basic fraud is the filing of bankruptcy petitions, either voluntary or involuntary, for a number of individual debtors, each of which is on the verge of foreclosure or eviction. In the typical scheme, the mill solicits business by advertising that it can stop foreclosures fast.

The fraud lies in the fact that the bankruptcy mill charges the prospective debtor a fee but misrepresents what it will actually provide. The debtor may not even realize that a bankruptcy petition is being filed. Sometimes, the debtor is told that refinancing will be arranged or provided. The mill does not actually accomplish this, and in most cases, has no intention of obtaining refinancing for the debtor. The petition is filed without schedules or other required documents. The mill's client usually does not realize the consequences of a defective bankruptcy filing. Ultimately, the bankruptcy court dismisses the petition or lifts the automatic stay to permit the mortgage holder to foreclose, and the hapless debtor loses his home.

Bankruptcy fraud schemes harm individual victims in myriad ways that are both serious and heartwrenching. The most severe and permanent damage, however, is that to the judicial process. Such fraud schemes diminish confidence in the legal system itself. The key to restoring the public's faith in the bankruptcy process is effective enforcement of sanctions against bankruptcy fraud.

4. Due process and the interpretation of criminal statutes

Criminal statutes are interpreted and applied according to certain key principles that derive from fundamental rights. The key principles governing statutory interpretation are based on due process and separation of powers.

The Fifth Amendment of the Constitution provides, in pertinent part:

> No person shall be deprived of life, liberty or property without due process of law.[12]

Due process is a fundamental right that entitles an ordinary citizen to notice of what is required and what is prohibited.[13] The Due Process Clause prohibits the government from imposing criminal liability for conduct where an individual would have no reason to know that such conduct would result in the loss of life, liberty or property. Notice and fair warning are essential in the criminal justice system. Punishment of crimes that are not clearly defined is perceived as fundamentally unfair.

The right of every citizen to notice and fair warning in the area of criminal law is the basis of three key principles governing the interpretation of criminal statutes. These doctrines are legality, void for vagueness, and lenity. All three doctrines are based on the fundamental principles of due process and separation of powers.

Legality (also called "the rule of law")[14] prohibits the creation of retroactive crimes. *Ex post facto* crimes are prohibited in our legal system.[15] Stated differently, Congress cannot pass a criminal statute and make it retroactive. This principle dovetails with the doctrines of void for vagueness and lenity, which also insure that conduct is not criminalized after the fact.

---

[12] U.S. CONST. amend. V.

[13] *See, e.g., United States v. Harriss,* 347 U.S. 612 (1954).

[14] The term "rule of law" is one of the most misused and misinterpreted terms in jurisprudence. In the past few years, the words "rule of law" became political buzzwords. The popular connotation of this term is completely at odds with its traditional meaning.

[15] U.S. CONST. art. I, § 9.

The doctrine of void for vagueness requires that legislative crime definition be precise. A criminal statute may not permit a "standardless sweep [that] allows policemen, prosecutors and juries to pursue their personal predilections."[16] Society as a whole has an interest in criminal conduct being clearly defined. If the law is not clear, it fails to have a deterrent effect.

Lenity requires that ambiguities in criminal statutes are to be resolved in favor of the defendant.[17] As the Supreme Court stated in *Dunn v. United States*:

> [T]his Court's long established practice of resolving questions concerning the ambit of a criminal statute in favor of lenity . . . reflects not merely a convenient maxim of statutory construction. Rather, it is rooted in the fundamental principles of due process which mandate that no individual be forced to speculate, at peril of indictment, whether his conduct is prohibited . . . [T]o ensure that a legislature speaks with clarity when marking the boundaries of criminal conduct, courts must decline to impose punishment for actions that are not "plainly and unmistakably" proscribed. (citations omitted).[18]

Lenity prohibits courts from adopting innovative interpretations of criminal statutes. The strict construction rule, however, does not require nullification of the evident purpose of the statute, nor does it require that the statute be given its narrowest meaning. As the United States Court of Appeals for the District of Columbia stated, "[T]he statute is not to be construed so strictly as to defeat the intention of the legislature."[19]

The Court, in a later case, stated:

> [The rule of lenity] is founded on two policies that have long been part of our tradition. First, "a fair warning should be given to the world in language that the common world will understand, of what the law intends to do if a certain line is passed. To make the warning fair, so far as possible the line should be clear." . . . Second, because of the seriousness of criminal penalties, and because criminal punishment usually represents the moral condemnation of the community, legislatures and not courts should define criminal activity. This policy

---

[16] *Kolender v. Lawson*, 461 U.S. 352, 358 (1983) (citation omitted).
[17] *See, e.g.*, *Dunn v. United States*, 442 U.S. 100 (1979); *United States v. Nofziger*, 878 F.2d 442 (D.C. Cir. 1989).
[18] *Dunn*, 442 U.S. at 112-13.
[19] *United States v. Moore*, 613 F.2d 1029, 1044 (D.C. Cir. 1979).

> embodies "the instinctive distaste against men languishing in prison unless the lawmaker has clearly said they should." (citations omitted)[20]

The rule of lenity *ensures* fair warning by requiring that courts resolve ambiguity in a criminal statute so as to apply the statute only to conduct clearly covered.[21]

These three basic doctrines are rooted not only in the Due Process Clause, but also in the constitutional principle of separation of powers. The role of each of the three branches of government in the criminal justice system must be separate: the legislative branch defines the law; the executive branch enforces the law; and the judicial branch interprets and applies the law. Separation of powers dictates that neither the executive branch (*e.g.*, the prosecutor) nor the judicial branch (*e.g.*, the judge) defines crime. That role is exclusively the province of the legislative branch — Congress.

The Bankruptcy Criminal Code is not vague, but several provisions are ambiguous. In some instances, ambiguities arise because the Bankruptcy Criminal Code defines conduct that is prohibited in bankruptcy cases but uses terminology that differs from the terminology used in the Bankruptcy Code. In cases in which the conflicting terminology is the basis for a defense argument that no crime was committed, courts have generally interpreted the Bankruptcy Criminal Code broadly. This tendency would appear to fly in the face of the rule of lenity. One explanation for this departure is that due process and lenity arguments are rarely argued in such cases. Another explanation is the judicial view that a debtor's entry into the bankruptcy process provides fair warning of both the letter and the spirit of law. This view appears to underlie many of the decisions which broadly construe Bankruptcy Criminal Code provisions. This approach, however, is not completely consistent with lenity.

Legality (or the rule of law) is rarely an issue in bankruptcy criminal cases. The law has changed very little in the past few decades. In fact, some aspects of the law have remained substantially unchanged for over a century. Where the law has changed, the differences are often technical and there is often little benefit for a defendant in invoking an earlier version of the law.

In some instances, the case law interpreting the Bankruptcy Criminal Code is sparse. Where interpretation of an ambiguity in such a provision is critical, the defendant may be well advised to invoke basic due process principles in urging a narrow interpretation.

---

[20] *Nofziger*, 878 F.2d at 452.

[21] *United States v. Lanier*, 520 U.S. 259 (1997).

PART 2

ANALYSIS OF TITLE 18, UNITED STATES CODE, CHAPTER 9

5. Overview

Bankruptcy crimes are defined in chapter 9 (the "Bankruptcy Criminal Code") of title 18 of the United States Code (the "Federal Criminal Code"), §§ 151 through 157. Most violations are Class D felonies and carry statutory penalties of up to five years imprisonment and a $250,000 fine,[22] as well as mandatory restitution under the Federal Sentencing Guidelines.[23]

Fundamental bankruptcy policy

Each provision of chapter 9 is aimed at protecting the federal bankruptcy system through enforcement of the Bankruptcy Code's underlying principles, policies, and procedures. The primary policy objectives of the Bankruptcy Code are:

1. To provide a fresh start and financial rehabilitation to honest debtors. This is accomplished through the granting of a discharge.[24]
2. To provide equality of distribution of the debtor's assets to creditors. This is accomplished through *pro rata* treatment of similarly situated creditors and disgorgement of fraudulent and preferential transfers.[25]

---

[22] The most frequently utilized provision of chapter 9, § 152, provides for a fine of $250,000. 18 U.S.C. § 3571(b)(3). The fine is increased to $500,000 if the defendant is an organization. 18 U.S.C. § 3571(c)(3). The fine may be up to twice the pecuniary gain or loss involved in the crime under certain circumstances. 18 U.S.C. § 3571(d).

[23] 18 U.S.C. § 3663-4; USSG § 5E1.1. *See* chapter 35 (Restitution).

[24] *Local Loan Co. v. Hunt*, 292 U.S. 234, 244 (1934).

[25] *Begier v. I.R.S.*, 496 U.S. 53, 58 (1990).

These policies serve public as well as private interests.[26] The availability of bankruptcy relief allows individuals, in exchange for surrendering their assets, to be released from the consequences of financial misfortunes. With the help of a fresh start, debtors are able to work productively. Bankruptcy serves the public interest because:

> [I]t gives to the honest but unfortunate debtor who surrenders for distribution the property which he owns at the time of bankruptcy, a new opportunity in life and a clear field for future effort, unhampered by the pressure and discouragement of pre-existing debt. (citations omitted).[27]

Civil bankruptcy law, as codified in the Bankruptcy Code,[28] is a comprehensive framework designed with this goal in mind.

The bankruptcy system rests on full and accurate disclosure by all debtors, and voluntary compliance with the law and rules by all creditors, trustees, and other officers of the court. An effective and just bankruptcy system requires the following:

1. The debtor must disclose all his assets and liabilities to the court and the creditors, and must not conceal or transfer assets which are property of his bankruptcy estate.
2. The creditors and the debtor must follow the bankruptcy process for distribution from the estate.
3. The debtor must tell the truth, the whole truth, and nothing but the truth to the court, the trustee, and the creditors.
4. The debtor and creditors must not evade the bankruptcy requirements through bribery or fraud.
5. The debtor's lawyer must act ethically and must not facilitate any fraud upon the court or the creditors.

Equally important as the policy of a fresh start is the principle of equality of distribution to creditors. This is the other fundamental policy objective of the bankruptcy laws. The principle of equality is not literal. It does not mean that each creditor in a bankruptcy case is entitled to receive the same amount, or even the same percentage distribution on its claim, as every other creditor.

---

[26] *Local Loan Co.*, 292 U.S. at 244.

[27] *Local Loan Co.*, 292 U.S. at 244.

[28] Title 11, United States Code, § 101, *et seq.*

The Bankruptcy Code establishes priorities for different categories of claims. In most cases, because of statutory priorities, some creditors receive payment of all or part of their claims, while other creditors may receive less, if they receive anything at all. Equality means that the treatment and distribution is equitable, in that each claim receives the same treatment as other claims with the same priority and legal rights.[29] Several provisions of the Bankruptcy Criminal Code are directed at ensuring that the statutory mandates for equitable distribution are followed and not altered through fraud or bribery.

Bankruptcy crimes are all rooted in a violation of a duty, restriction, or requirement of the Bankruptcy Code, the Federal Rules of Bankruptcy Procedure, a bankruptcy court order, or the direction of a trustee. Often the distinction between using and abusing the law is unclear. Even less clear is the distinction between abusing the law and breaking it.

The role of counsel further complicates this question. Counsel has an ethical duty to represent a client zealously, within the bounds of the law.[30] This now means stretching the bounds of the law as far as possible. The line between an innovative strategy to protect a client's assets from creditors and a conspiracy with a client to conceal his assets is often gray. To complicate matters further, the distinction between an aggressive strategy and a criminal scheme often rests on the grayest factor of them all: intent.

Intent

A necessary element of all felonious bankruptcy fraud is criminal intent. All bankruptcy crimes under §§ 152, 153, and 155 contain the element of "knowing and fraudulent" intent. The intent element of § 154 is only "knowing" and of § 157, only "fraudulent." Fraudulent intent as an element of a bankruptcy crime generally means an intent to deceive a creditor, trustee, or bankruptcy judge. Intent in the strict sense, a criminal state of mind, is difficult if not impossible to prove directly. The prosecution rarely has direct evidence of the defendant's state of mind (such as a statement from the defendant that he intended to defraud creditors), and therefore this element is usually proven circumstantially. In practice, the evidence threshold required to prove intent is low. A debtor's lack of candor with the court and the trustee is often sufficient for the government to make a *prima facie* showing of intent. In addition, stealth is sometimes considered incriminating. "Persons whose intention is to shield

---

[29] *See, e.g., Begier*, 496 U.S. at 58.

[30] This mandate has been supplanted in many jurisdictions by the duty to represent a client diligently. ABA Model Rule 1.3.

their assets from creditor attack while continuing to derive the benefit of those assets rarely announce their purpose."[31]

Concealing assets from creditors is perhaps the most common bankruptcy crime. This is hardly surprising. The reason why most debtors file bankruptcy is to keep assets from creditors. Most debtors seek to do so through legitimate means.

The desire to protect assets is not limited to persons with financial problems. Many clients, whether or not they have financial difficulties, consult counsel to advise and assist them in protecting their wealth from the reach of creditors. Entrepreneurs who incur personal liability in connection with business ventures sometimes engage in "asset planning," which may include transferring assets to spendthrift trusts or family partnerships, shifting wealth to exempt assets, or prepaying mortgage loans on property held as tenants by the entirety. All of these steps render assets difficult or impossible for creditors to reach. While each of these actions may not be fraudulent *per se*, a systematic pattern would certainly demonstrate the intent to deter creditors, even if not to defraud them.

Where is the line drawn between the prudent and the illegal? The major difference between aggressive but legitimate asset protection tactics (even bad faith tactics) and bankruptcy fraud is the element of deceit, deception, or dishonesty. Bad faith connotes conduct which was unwarranted or even improperly motivated, but not dishonest.

The sophistication of the defendant in business and legal matters is a factor upon which a finder of fact can rely in divining intent. Courts have upheld jury findings of fraudulent intent on the part of businessmen or accountants, in circumstances where the same inference would not be drawn from the same conduct by members of the medical profession or housewives not involved in business. The latter are presumed to have less knowledge about legal and financial matters.

The bankruptcy "debtor"

Obviously, not every fraud on creditors will constitute a crime. For a bankruptcy crime to occur, a debtor or a case under title 11 must exist. Bankruptcy cases are commenced by the filing of a petition with the bankruptcy court. Petitions may be voluntary (*i.e.*, filed by the debtor) or involuntary (*i.e.*, filed by a creditor). Most cases are commenced by voluntary petitions. In a voluntary petition, the debtor, whether an individual or business entity, will elect a

---

[31] *United States v. Goodstein*, 883 F.2d 1362, 1370 (7th Cir. 1989) (citations omitted).

chapter of the Bankruptcy Code under which relief is sought: chapter 7 (liquidation); chapter 9 (municipalities); chapter 11 (reorganization); chapter 12 (family farmers); or chapter 13 (wage earner plans).[32]

For purposes of the Bankruptcy Criminal Code, a "debtor" is defined as "a debtor concerning whom a petition has been filed under title 11."[33] For this reason, the determination of what or who is or may be a debtor is significant. A "debtor" is defined in § 101(13) of the Bankruptcy Code, which provides that a "debtor" means a "person or municipality concerning which a case under this title has been commenced."[34]

Section 109 of the Bankruptcy Code, entitled "Who May Be A Debtor," limits the eligibility to be a debtor in several ways. First, a debtor must be a "person," which includes an individual, partnership, and corporation.[35] Certain categories of persons are ineligible to be debtors under certain chapters of title 11. Railroads, insurance companies, banks, and most other financial institutions may not be chapter 7 debtors.[36] Only insolvent municipalities authorized by law to file under chapter 9 of the Bankruptcy Code, and who have met certain creditor conditions, may be chapter 9 debtors.[37] Only a debtor who may be a chapter 7 debtor, excepting a stock broker or commodity broker, or a railroad, may be a chapter 11 debtor.[38]

Who may be a debtor under chapter 13 is limited to an individual with regular income whose noncontingent, liquidated, unsecured debts are less than $307,675,[39] and whose noncontingent, unliquidated and secured debts are less than $922,975.[40] Only a family farmer with regular annual income may be a debtor under chapter 12.[41]

Finally, certain factors within the 180 days immediately prior to the filing of a bankruptcy case will render a person ineligible to be a debtor under any title. Such factors include dismissal of a prior case for failure to abide by court orders, or to appear before the court in proper prosecution of the case, or dismissal of a prior bankruptcy case at the debtor's request following the filing of a request for relief from stay.[42]

---

[32] Chapter 13 is only available to individual debtors. 11 U.S.C. § 109(e).

[33] 18 U.S.C. § 151.

[34] 11 U.S.C. § 101(13).

[35] 11 U.S.C. § 101(41).

[36] 11 U.S.C. § 109(b).

[37] 11 U.S.C. § 109(c).

[38] 11 U.S.C. § 109(d).

[39] The ceiling for cases commenced prior to April 1, 2004 was $290,525.

[40] The ceiling for cases commenced prior to April 1, 2004 was $871,550.

[41] 11 U.S.C. § 109(f).

[42] 11 U.S.C. § 109(g).

While the definition of debtor set forth in § 151 of the Bankruptcy Criminal Code on its face is literally coextensive with the Bankruptcy Code's definition of a debtor, the use of the word "debtor" in the Bankruptcy Criminal Code cannot be reconciled entirely with the Bankruptcy Code definition. Under the Bankruptcy Code, a "debtor" is limited to a person eligible to be a debtor under § 109. In practical terms, a bankruptcy case can be commenced by or against an ineligible person, whose case may ultimately be dismissed by the bankruptcy court because that person could not be a "debtor." On its face, § 151 would exclude such a person from the definition of "debtor." An argument could be made, however, that the use of the word "debtor" in § 151 is broader and includes all persons who are the subject of a bankruptcy petition. The remainder of chapter 9 suggests such a definition. This question has not been addressed or resolved by the courts, leaving open a defense based on the nonexistence of a debtor in a case where the subject of the bankruptcy petition was ultimately determined ineligible to be a debtor.

The trustee

Another definitional issue presented in chapter 9 is the meaning of the word "trustee." Under the Bankruptcy Code, the term has several different meanings. The traditional meaning of a "trustee in bankruptcy" is a fiduciary appointed to administer the assets of a debtor's estate. In a chapter 7 case, the word "trustee" has its traditional meaning. A trustee is always appointed in a chapter 7 case to administer the debtor's estate. In chapter 12 (family farmer) and chapter 13 (wage earner) cases, a trustee is appointed only for the purpose of collecting and distributing to creditors funds paid by the debtor under a confirmed repayment plan. In these cases, unlike chapter 7, the debtor remains in control of his assets, and the trustee is neither charged with nor empowered to liquidate them.

In a chapter 11 case a trustee is not automatically appointed. Chapter 11 trustees are the exception rather than the rule. Unless the court orders the appointment of a chapter 11 trustee for cause (which includes fraud, incompetence, or gross mismanagement), the debtor remains in possession of the assets and business during the bankruptcy case. A debtor in possession under chapter 11 has all the rights, powers, and duties of a trustee.[43] Thus, the word "trustee" in the Bankruptcy Code means and includes the debtor in possession in a chapter 11 case.

---

[43] 11 U.S.C. § 1107(a).

Further, the word "trustee" is frequently also used to mean the United States trustee and his assistants. The United States trustee system was established under the Bankruptcy Reform Act of 1978 and took effect as a pilot program in 1979, and later made a permanent program in all but two judicial districts. The United States trustees are officials of the United States Department of Justice with administrative and oversight responsibility over bankruptcy cases. There are 21 regional United States trustees. While the United States trustee is part of the executive as opposed to the judicial branch, the United States trustees perform functions that were previously handled by the bankruptcy courts prior to the Bankruptcy Reform Act of 1978. The United States trustees select, appoint, and supervise bankruptcy trustees, who are typically private lawyers; they review applications for compensation and reimbursement filed by professionals employed in bankruptcy cases; they monitor plans, disclosure statements, financial reporting requirements, schedules, fees, and other bankruptcy filing requirements; and they select committees of creditors to serve in chapter 11 cases. The United States trustees also have an important role in reporting and investigating suspected bankruptcy crime.[44]

Disclosure

Many bankruptcy crimes are rooted in the failure to comply with the duty to disclose an asset liability, transfer, or transaction. Full disclosure is at the heart of the bankruptcy process. A debtor is required to disclose all assets and liabilities on schedules filed with the bankruptcy court under unsworn declaration.[45] Section 521[46] of the Bankruptcy Code provides:

> The Debtor shall -
>
> (1) file a list of creditors; and unless the court orders otherwise –
> a schedule of assets and liabilities;
> a schedule of current income and current expenditures;
> a statement of financial affairs, . . .
>
> (4) if a trustee is serving in the case or an auditor serving under section 586(f) of title 28, surrender to the trustee all property of the estate and any recorded information, including books, documents, records, and papers, relating to property of the estate[.]

---

[44] *See* chapter 27.

[45] Official Bankruptcy Form 6 (Appendix G).

[46] This section is applicable in all bankruptcy cases. 11 U.S.C. § 103(a).

11 U.S.C. § 521. The form of the lists and schedules are prescribed in Fed. R. Bankr. P. 1007.[47] Pursuant to Fed. R. Bankr. P. 1008, bankruptcy petitions, lists, schedules, statements, and any amendments thereto must be verified or contain an unsworn declaration as provided by 28 U.S.C. § 1746.[48]

Shortly after the commencement of the bankruptcy case, the debtor must testify under oath at a creditors' meeting convened under § 341 of the Bankruptcy Code.[49] If ordered by the court, the debtor must submit to an oral examination requested by a party in interest, with respect to his acts, conduct, assets, liabilities, financial condition, and any other matter concerning the administration of the estate.[50] A trustee or chapter 11 debtor in possession, if required by the Court, must file a number of reports, including monthly statements of receipts and disbursements.[51] Filing of monthly operating reports of financial transactions occurring during the bankruptcy case is required by the United States trustee under standard, court-ordered procedures in effect in virtually every judicial district. Every one of these requirements presents an opportunity for concealment, false oath or declaration, or a false account, each of which is a violation of § 152.

Failure to disclose assets (or potential assets, such as prebankruptcy transfers or preferences) in the various requisite filings or upon questioning by the trustee, may constitute concealment. Such nondisclosure is perhaps the most common form of the crime. The same nondisclosure, if it occurs on bankruptcy schedules or other documents signed under oath or declared under penalty of perjury, will constitute a false oath or declaration, respectively. Failure to disclose assets in sworn testimony at a § 341 meeting, Fed. R. Bankr. P. 2004 examination, deposition, or hearing will create still other instances of false oaths.

Property of the estate

Obviously, defining the universe of assets which must be disclosed is significant both from a civil and criminal standpoint. The filing of a bankruptcy petition creates an "estate"[52] which, loosely speaking, comprises the assets which are subject to the jurisdiction of the court and administration by the trustee, and potentially available to produce a distribution to creditors. The definition of property of the estate in the Bankruptcy Code encompasses:

---

[47] Official Bankruptcy Form 4, 6 (Appendixes F, G).

[48] Section 1746 permits unsworn declarations to be made in lieu of sworn statements. *See* chapter 7.

[49] 11 U.S.C. § 341; *see* Fed. R. Bankr. P. 4002(1).

[50] Fed. R. Bankr. P. 2004.

[51] Fed. R. Bankr. P. 2015.

[52] 11 U.S.C. § 541(a).

> (a) . . . the following property, wherever located and by whomever held:
>
> (1) . . . all legal or equitable interests of the debtor in property as of the commencement of the case. . . .
>
> (6) Proceeds, product, offspring, rents, or profits of or from property of the estate, except such as are earnings from services performed by an individual debtor after the commencement of the case.
>
> (7) Any interest in property that the estate acquires after the commencement of the case.[53]

The scope of this section is broad. Property of the estate includes all kinds of property, both tangible and intangible. The interests of the debtor in property includes not only legal title to property but also other interests such as beneficial, equitable, or leasehold interests.[54]

While the existence of a debtor or a bankruptcy case is not usually an area of dispute in a criminal case, whether the property in question is within the reach of the statute often is. The language used in the Bankruptcy Criminal Code ("property of the debtor" or "property belonging to the estate of a debtor"[55]) is not identical to the operative term used and defined in the Bankruptcy Code ("property of the estate"[56]). To complicate matters further, the Bankruptcy Code also uses, but does not define, "property of the debtor."[57] The inconsistency of the statutory language creates a potential ambiguity, and thus becomes a basis for both defense[58] and prosecution arguments, where the Bankruptcy Code language does not fit the case.

As broad as the scope of property under the Bankruptcy Code is, the scope of similar but not identical terms in the Bankruptcy Criminal Code can sometimes be even more expansive. Consider the case in which the debtor is an individual who owns a corporation (not in bankruptcy) which is the debtor's alter ego. From a civil bankruptcy standpoint, unless and until the corporate veil is pierced,[59] the debtor is required only to list his ownership interest (*i.e.*,

---

[53] 11 U.S.C. § 541(a).

[54] *See United States v. Whiting Pools, Inc.*, 462 U.S. 198 (1983).

[55] *See, e.g.*, 18 U.S.C. § 152.

[56] 11 U.S.C. § 541.

[57] 11 U.S.C. § 543(a).

[58] *See* chapter 4.

[59] To obtain such a determination, the trustee (or a creditor in certain circumstances) must commence an adversary proceeding, the equivalent of a civil action in a non-bankruptcy court. Like civil actions, adversary proceedings are initiated by the filing of a complaint. *See* Fed. R. Bankr. P. 7003. Adversary proceedings proceed the same way as other civil actions and are adjudicated similarly, through dispositive motion or trial. Unless and until a ruling is entered in the context of such an action, the corporate veil stands.

his stock) in the corporation on his bankruptcy schedules, not the assets of the corporation itself. Similarly, a transfer of the assets of the corporation, unlike a transfer of his individually-held assets, would be outside the jurisdiction of the bankruptcy court and would not require notice to creditors or court approval.

Criminal courts, however, have not drawn such technical distinctions in upholding convictions of debtors engaged in such schemes. In some cases, indirect ownership, and transfers of assets in which the debtor has no direct legal ownership, have triggered criminal liability. Criminal culpability has been based on theories which cannot always be squared with civil bankruptcy law.

While a common thread among most bankruptcy crimes is the violation of a civil bankruptcy mandate, coupled with criminal intent to deceive or defraud creditors, not all civil violations trigger a crime. Conversely, a crime may exist in the absence of a violation of the Bankruptcy Code. Because the definitions in the criminal and civil bankruptcy laws differ, it is technically possible for conduct which does not violate the Bankruptcy Code to constitute a crime under the Bankruptcy Criminal Code. One example is an aborted attempt to sell an asset outside the ordinary course of business without court approval. If the sale is not accomplished, (civil) § 363,[60] which requires court approval of a sale of property of the estate outside the ordinary course of business, is not violated because no actual sale has taken place. Under some circumstances, however, the actions involved in such unsuccessful attempt can constitute a violation of (criminal) § 152. From a practical standpoint, however, this is the most difficult case for the government to prove, unless the defendant's conduct is egregious. What constitutes egregious conduct becomes apparent from an examination of the case law.

An example of actions that arguably did not technically violate the Bankruptcy Code, but constituted an offense under the Bankruptcy Criminal Code, is described in *United States v. Goodstein.*[61] Goodstein, a bankruptcy lawyer, acquired a business which subsequently experienced serious financial problems. After placing the company into bankruptcy, he merged it with another corporation, a merger accomplished through a transfer of his individually-owned stock in the debtor. Goodstein moved the debtor's equipment and assets to the other corporation's location, thereby jeopardizing the perfection of the debtor's secured party's security interest. The transaction was later approved retroac-

---

[60] Section 363(b)(1) of the Bankruptcy Code provides:

The trustee, after notice and a hearing, may use, sell, or lease, other than in the ordinary course of business, property of the estate, ...

[61] *Goodstein*, 883 F.2d 1362.

tively by the bankruptcy court. Goodstein was charged with a bankruptcy crime under § 152 for "transfer(ring) and conceal(ing) the property of the corporation with intent to defeat the bankruptcy laws."[62] Goodstein argued that he was free to transfer his own stock, which was not an asset of the debtor, without notice to creditors or approval by the bankruptcy court. He also argued that moving the assets was in the ordinary course of business and neither notice to creditors nor court approval was required.

While Goodstein's arguments were plausible enough under a literal reading of the Bankruptcy Code, the court of appeals rejected his defenses. The court acknowledged that the case presented a difficult problem because the transfer of Goodstein's stock was not encompassed by the literal language of the Bankruptcy Code. The court, however, viewed the stock transfer as non-routine because it resulted in a merger and change of control. The court deemed that the transaction was an indirect disposition of property done with fraudulent intent, constituting a transfer under the Bankruptcy Code and violative of § 152.

Courts applying the Bankruptcy Criminal Code do not ask whether some specific section of the Bankruptcy Code was violated, but rather, whether the bankruptcy process as a whole was violated. Whether Goodstein violated § 363 of the Bankruptcy Code by selling his stock or moving the debtor's assets without court approval is debatable, but the fact that his conduct violated the bankruptcy process is not. Abuse of the bankruptcy process by deception is the crux of the offense.

---

[62] *Goodstein,* 883 F.2d 1365.

6. Concealment of assets: 18 U.S.C. § 152(1)

Section 152(1) of title 18, Unites States Code, states:

> A person who-
>
> (1) knowingly and fraudulently conceals from a custodian, trustee, marshall, or other officer of the court charged with the control or custody of property, or, in connection with a case under title 11, from creditors, or the United States trustee, any property belonging to the estate of a debtor; . . .
>
> shall be fined under this title[63], imprisoned not more than 5 years, or both.

Asset concealment is considered the most common bankruptcy crime. Like most other bankruptcy crimes, concealment is a Class D felony. The crime of concealment requires four elements: (1) a concealment (2) which is knowing and fraudulent (3) of property of the estate of a debtor (4) in a bankruptcy case. The definition of concealment under prior law (the Bankruptcy Act of 1898) meant secreting, falsifying, and mutilating.[64] Concealment also encompasses hiding or withdrawing from observation, or covering or keeping from sight.[65] The concealment section has been substantially unchanged since the now repealed Bankruptcy Act of 1898. Accordingly, the definition of concealment as interpreted by courts under the 1898 law is still applicable. The definition under current law is broad, and includes the actions defined under prior law. Concealment includes any actions that impede a bankruptcy trustee's ability to distribute assets of the debtor to the debtor's creditors.[66]

---

[63] Section 152 carries a fine of $250,000. 18 U.S.C. § 3571(b)(3). The fine is increased to up to $500,000 if the defendant is an organization. 18 U.S.C. § 3571(c)(3). Under certain circumstances, the fine may be twice the pecuniary gain or loss involved in the crime. 18 U.S.C. § 3571(d).

[64] *Coghlan v. United States*, 147 F.2d 233 (8th Cir. 1945); *United States v. Schireson*, 116 F.2d 881, 884 (3d Cir. 1940).

[65] *United States v. Mathies*, 203 F. Supp. 797 (W.D. Pa. 1962).

[66] *United States v. Wagner*, 382 F.3d 598 (6th Cir. 2004).

The principal objective of this section is to prevent and punish efforts by a debtor to avoid distribution of any part of his bankruptcy estate.[67] Persons who are not debtors, however, may also be prosecuted for concealment under this section.[68]

Concealment of property belonging to the estate of a debtor from a trustee, custodian, marshall, or other officer of the court can take a number of forms, including hiding or failure to disclose an asset during a bankruptcy case, as well as transferring an asset prior to bankruptcy with the intent of defrauding creditors. Concealment is not limited to physical secretion.[69] Section 152(1) was intended to cover all methods a person may use to defeat distribution of assets to creditors in a bankruptcy.[70] The term is construed broadly and includes preventing discovery or withholding knowledge by refusal or failure to divulge information.[71] For instance, it would be impossible for a debtor to physically hide real estate he owned, such as an office building or shopping center. A debtor could, however, conceal these assets by writing "none" on Bankruptcy Schedule A (Real Estate), thus not disclosing his ownership of the assets.

Failure to list an asset on the bankruptcy schedules is the most obvious instance of concealment. Misleading or vague descriptions of an asset can also be deemed concealment where the description is written in such a way to camouflage an asset.[72] An example is listing a rare and valuable Patek Philippe in need of an overhaul as an "old broken watch," thus suggesting an item of little or no value as opposed to an item potentially worth thousands, if not hundreds of thousands, of dollars.

Concealment under this section necessarily involves property of a bankruptcy estate or of the debtor. If there is no bankruptcy or if the property does not belong to the estate or the debtor, the statutory elements of concealment are not present. It is not always clear, however, what constitutes property within the definition of the statute. An example is the situation presented in *United States v. Goodstein.*[73] In *Goodstein*, transfer of stock in the debtor, which was owned not by the debtor but by its principal shareholder, triggered a bankruptcy offense based on an expansive view of what constituted property of the debtor. The court viewed the change of control of the debtor as being an indirect disposition, *i.e.*, functional equivalent of transfer of property of the debtor.

---

[67] *Stuhley v. Hyatt*, 667 F.2d 807 (9th Cir. 1982).
[68] *United States v. Fraidin*, 63 F. Supp. 271 (D. Md. 1945).
[69] *Coghlan*, 147 F.2d 233.
[70] *Wagner*, 382 F.3d at 608.
[71] *Coghlan*, 147 F.2d at 236.
[72] *United States v. Grant*, 971 F.2d 799 (1st Cir. 1992).
[73] *United States v. Goodstein*, 883 F.2d 1362 (7th Cir. 1989); *see* chapter 5.

The result of decisions such as *Goodstein* is to expand the definition of "property of the estate" for criminal purposes.

Intent

As is the case with all other bankruptcy crimes, criminal intent is a key element of the crime. Intent is usually proven circumstantially. The concealment must be "knowing and fraudulent." Knowing means not accidentally. A concealment which occurred because of an innocent mistake is not a crime. An example of an innocent mistake would be that the page of the schedules (which listed the rare watch) was lost in the attorney's copying machine.

If the concealment was not accidental, it is presumed to be knowing and willful.[74] Signing bankruptcy schedules which fail to disclose assets is rarely an accident. What of the debtor who signs the schedules without reading them, later claiming he relied on his lawyer to prepare them? The jury is sometimes instructed that willful blindness does not negate intent.[75] Stated differently, deliberately not reading the "false" bankruptcy schedules so as to create a defense that the concealment was not "knowing," is considered "knowing."[76] The sophisticated businessman who does not read the schedules, claiming he relied on his lawyer, may be "willfully blind" and therefore "knowing." Consider, on the other hand, the housewife of a businessman who is not involved in the family business and has no personal knowledge of the assets, and who signs schedules in a joint bankruptcy filing with her husband, trusting her husband to make sure the papers are in order. The housewife who did not read the schedules and relied on her husband may have a plausible defense.[77]

The determination of what is "fraudulent" intent is somewhat more complicated. Fraudulent means an intent to deceive.[78] A specific intent to defraud the bankruptcy court or obstruct the bankruptcy process is not necessarily required.[79] Some knowledge of a bankruptcy case, however, is necessary to con-

---

[74] *Bartkus v. United States*, 21 F.2d 425 (7th Cir. 1927).

[75] This is sometimes called the "ostrich instruction," as was stated in *United States v. Ramsey*, 785 F.2d 184, 190 (7th Cir. 1986):

> You may infer knowledge from a combination of suspicion and indifference to the truth. If you find that a person had a strong suspicion that things were not what they seemed or that someone had withheld some important facts, yet shut his eyes for fear of what he would learn, you may conclude that he acted knowingly, as I have used the word.

[76] *United States v. Defazio*, 899 F.2d 626, 635-36 (7th Cir. 1990).

[77] *United States v. McCormick*, 72 F.3d 1404 (9th Cir. 1995); *United States v. White*, 879 F.2d 1509 (7th Cir. 1989).

[78] *United States v. Diorio*, 451 F.2d 21, 23 (2d Cir. 1971).

[79] *See* chapter 7 (Fraudulent intent).

stitute a fraudulent concealment.[80] The defendant will not be exonerated where he willfully remained ignorant of the existence of a bankruptcy case or of the appointment of a trustee.[81]

This issue is sometimes raised in a situation where a chapter 11 case has been converted to a case under chapter 7, or where the appointment of a trustee is ordered by the court. Once the court has ordered the appointment of a trustee, the selection of a trustee is made by the United States trustee. Sometimes there is a short time lag between the time the bankruptcy court orders the conversion (and hence the automatic appointment of a chapter 7 trustee) or the appointment of a chapter 11 trustee, and the selection of the trustee. The trustee is also required to "qualify," *e.g.*, establish the requisite bond in his fiduciary role for the estate. This time lag can be hours, days, or sometimes weeks. Defendants have argued that their disposition of property in this interim period does not constitute concealment from a trustee, since one was technically not in place. The argument has also been raised that until the debtor has notice of the selection and qualification of the individual trustee, the intent element of the crime is not met.

Prosecution under the concealment section of a defendant who disposes of an asset in the interim period between the entry of a court order appointing a trustee, and the trustee's actual appointment, is particularly problematic. It is conceivable that some transfers or expenditures during this time period could be nonfraudulent, for example, paying expenses in the ordinary course of business. Transactions which have no purpose other than to keep funds or assets away from the trustee's administration, however, will have § 152(1) implications.

Property

Legal title is not determinative of whether the property belongs to the debtor or bankruptcy estate for purposes of a § 152(1) violation. Failure to disclose equitable ownership of property on the schedules will constitute concealment.[82] This was the case under the Bankruptcy Act of 1898 and it remains the case under the Bankruptcy Code. The Bankruptcy Code definition of "property of the estate" includes "all legal or equitable interests of the debtor in property as of the commencement of the case."[83] For instance, funds held in a bank ac-

---

[80] *United States v. Tashjian*, 660 F.2d 829, 841-42 (1st Cir. 1981).

[81] *United States v. Yasser*, 114 F.2d 558 (3d Cir. 1940).

[82] *Duggins v. Heffron*, 128 F.2d 546 (9th Cir. 1942); *Schireson*, 116 F.2d 881; *see also* 11 U.S.C. § 541(a)(property of the estate, as defined by the 1978 amendments to the Bankruptcy Code, includes all legal or equitable interests of the debtor in property as of the commencement of the case).

[83] 11 U.S.C. § 541(a)(1).

count not in the debtor's name, such as an attorney's escrow account or an account held by an affiliated entity, are property of the debtor's estate.[84]

Conversely, where the debtor holds a legal interest but no beneficial interest, failure to disclose constitutes concealment. One example is property held jointly by a debtor and ex-spouse where the equity will be paid to the ex-spouse under a property settlement agreement, or where the property is completely encumbered.[85]

If neither legal title nor beneficial ownership is determinative, where precisely is the line drawn as to what constitutes the debtor's property? No one factor is determinative. Beneficial ownership, in particular, is often hard to discern.

Numerous bankruptcy fraud prosecutions have been brought involving vehicles, usually expensive ones, which were used or purportedly used for business purposes, and where either the company or its principal ultimately files a bankruptcy petition. The vehicle will not be listed on the bankruptcy schedules, and the principal will claim that the car really belongs to him (if the company is in bankruptcy) or to the company (if the principal is in bankruptcy). Courts uniformly have declined to apply a bright line test in these situations. Numerous factors are considered, no one of which is controlling: Who paid for the vehicle? Who holds the title to the vehicle? Who claims depreciation on, or expenses for, the vehicle for tax purposes? Who uses the vehicle? Who pays the insurance premiums, fuel expenses, and repair bills? Was the vehicle transferred to a friendly third party, such as a spouse or child when the debtor's financial troubles ensued? Was the car listed on personal financial statements or on the company balance sheets?

While courts give particular weight to the source of funds to purchase the vehicle, no one factor is dispositive. The totality of the circumstances will determine whether the debtor's interest in the vehicle was sufficient to trigger the duty to schedule the asset.

If there is legal uncertainty as to whether an asset is estate property, a debtor's liability for omission of the asset is far from clear. Some courts have held that omitting an asset from the schedules, the legal ownership of which is unclear, will not be considered knowing and fraudulent.[86] Other courts, however, have held that the debtor must disclose the existence of assets whose status in uncertain, even if the assets are held ultimately not to be property of the estate.[87] As the court stated in *United States v. Grant*:

---

[84] *United States v. Cardall*, 885 F.2d 656, 678 (10th Cir. 1989).

[85] *See United States v. Rowe*, 144 F.3d 15 (1st Cir. 1998).

[86] *United States v. Collins*, 424 F. Supp. 465 (E.D. Ky 1977).

[87] *United States v. Cherek*, 734 F.2d 1248 (7th Cir. 1984).

> If the debtor's schedules omit or camouflage an asset, the chapter 7 trustee is disabled from exercising an informed judgment as to whether the debtor had sufficient legal, equitable, or possessory interest to permit and warrant its liquidation for the benefit of creditors.[88]

While there is no bright line test articulated here, a plausible distinction between these two lines of cases[89] is whether the status of the law, as opposed to the status of the asset, is uncertain. For instance, where the law is unclear as to whether the debtor has a claim for back wages upon reinstatement to his government job, the uncertainty may bear on whether his omission of the potential claim for back pay was knowing and fraudulent.[90] On the other hand, where the debtor is uncertain as to whether the asset is property of the estate, the debtor may not preempt the bankruptcy court's determination in that regard by failing to report the asset.[91] A good faith belief that the assets at issue were not property of the debtor or the estate, will likely negate intent. An example would be the debtor who did not know that his father left him the rare and valuable Patek.

Materiality

The value of property concealed is irrelevant as far as § 152(1) is concerned.[92] Concealment has no materiality element.[93] Conviction for concealment of assets worth $100 in an estate with $3,000,000 worth of assets has been upheld.[94] Failure to disclose assets that would have been subject to exemption if they had been scheduled constitutes concealment.[95] The reason is that property which is claimed as exempt is nevertheless property of the estate. Such property only becomes exempt if it is listed on the schedules and no objection is filed (or an objection is overruled).[96] The offense in failing to list an "exempt" asset lies in the debtor's attempt to retain or conceal property which would otherwise be subject to administration by the trustee, whether or not

---

[88] *Grant*, 971 F.2d at 805.
[89] *Compare Collins*, 424 F. Supp. at 465, with *Grant*, 971 F.2d at 805.
[90] *Collins*, 424 F. Supp. 465.
[91] *Cherek*, 734 F.2d at 1254.
[92] *Mathies*, 203 F. Supp. at 800.
[93] *Grant*, 971 F.2d 799.
[94] *Grant*, 971 F.2d at 808-09.
[95] *See United States v. Shadduck*, 112 F.3d 523 (1st Cir. 1997).
[96] *Shadduck*, 112 F.3d 523.

such property would have ultimately been removed from administration through exemption or abandonment.[97] The overriding purpose of the section is to deter and punish conduct which would interfere with the trustee's role in evaluating and liquidating assets:

> Section 152 promotes efficient bankruptcy administration and an equitable allocation of assets of debtor estates by criminalizing efforts to preempt a neutral and informed assessment by the trustee as to the status and value of the debtor's legal, equitable and possessory interests in property at the commencement of the case.[98]

A possible loophole, however, may exist where the property is of *de minimus* value, or where the estate is solvent.[99]

Overlap with other sections

Section 152(1) is intended principally to cover actions relating to the disclosure of assets and affairs of debtors, as opposed to outright theft or embezzlement, which are crimes covered under separate sections.[100] In many instances, however, conduct which falls within the ambit of § 152(1) may also be criminal under several other provisions, or may be part of a scenario where several offenses may be charged.

For instance, transferring legal title to property prior to a bankruptcy filing while retaining a secret interest constitutes concealment.[101] An example is conveying a deed to real property to a friendly party for a purchase price (real or purported) with an implicit, usually unwritten agreement, to reconvey the property to the debtor after bankruptcy. Filing bankruptcy schedules which, in turn, fail to list the debtor's interest in the property, also constitutes a violation of § 152(2) or (3) (false oath, account, or declarations).[102] Another example of conduct that constitutes more than one offense is transfer of ownership and control of a debtor corporation after bankruptcy without notice to creditors or bankruptcy court approval. This could trigger criminal liability for concealment under § 152(1),[103] but could also be a violation of § 152(5), which forbids transfers with the intent to defeat title 11. If the proceeds of the sale are

---

[97] *See Shadduck*, 112 F.3d at 531.
[98] *Grant*, 971 F.2d at 805.
[99] *Grant*, 971 F.2d at 809, n.19.
[100] *United States Trustee v. Repp* (*In re Sheehan*), 187 B.R. 669 (Bankr. D. Ariz. 1995).
[101] *Stuhley v. Hyatt*, 667 F.2d 807 (9th Cir. 1982).
[102] *See United States v. Center*, 853 F.2d 568 (7th Cir. 1988), discussed in chapter 7.
[103] *Goodstein*, 883 F. 2d 1362.

not reported on monthly operating reports, an additional concealment charge may arise,[104] in addition to a false account or declaration charge.

Concealment is often committed simultaneously with the offense of making a false oath or declaration. As a practical matter, the omission of an asset from the schedules effectively hides the underlying fraud, and the debtor's interest in the asset that was fraudulently conveyed, from discovery by the trustee, creditors and court.[105] For instance, when a debtor files his bankruptcy schedules intentionally omitting an asset, so as to keep his trustee from discovering it, and the schedules are signed under oath, both §§ 152(1) and 152(2)(false oaths) are violated.[106] Thus, failing to schedule an asset may constitute both concealment and making a false oath or declaration.[107] If a false oath also effectuates a concealment, prosecution for both crimes does not constitute double punishment.[108] As the Third Circuit in *United States v. Schireson* stated:

> [A] man may frequently suffer two penalties for the same act if that act is the means of committing two offenses. If he kills two birds with one stone he can well be punished for killing each bird, if killing birds is an offense.[109]

Concealment and false oath or declaration offenses are often committed in tandem. Failure to schedule an asset may easily lead to other actions to prevent discovery of the asset. For instance, Debtor X is asked by his bankruptcy lawyer, who is preparing X's bankruptcy schedules, what personal property he owns. X tells his counsel he owns a family heirloom, a rare and valuable antique rug, with which he could not bear to part. Counsel puts on the schedules: "household furnishings — value unknown." X purposefully does not read the schedules before he signs it under penalty of perjury. When asked under oath at the creditors' meeting convened under § 341 of the Bankruptcy Code about his "household furnishings," he says, "I don't have anything but an old, used rug." When the trustee, having received a tip from an angry creditor, sends an appraiser to Debtor X's house, the Debtor (also on a tip) sends the rug out for cleaning. The conduct described gives rise to numerous violations, including

---

[104] A reasonable argument may be made that only one concealment charge lies for concealment of both the assets and the proceeds. *See* chapter 17, note 5.

[105] *United States v. Shapiro*, 101 F.2d 375, 378 (7th Cir. 1939).

[106] *Duggins*, 128 F.2d 546.

[107] *Coghlan*, 147 F.2d 233.

[108] *Schireson*, 116 F.2d at 884.

[109] *Schireson*, 116 F.2d at 884.

concealment, making a false declaration, and making a false oath. What started with grandmother's rug ends up with a stiff fine, a jail term, and, in the case of counsel, suspension or disbarment, if not criminal charges.[110] Sometimes an asset is transferred fraudulently prior to bankruptcy, and subsequently the asset is not listed on the bankruptcy schedules. This also gives rise to both concealment and false declaration charges.[111]

Another example is the failure to disclose assets or the misrepresentation of their value in a disclosure statement. The Bankruptcy Code requires the proponent of a chapter 11 plan (usually the debtor) to file a disclosure statement which must be approved by the court as containing "adequate information" which is defined as:

> [I]nformation of a kind, and in sufficient detail as far as is reasonably practical in light of the nature and history of the debtor's books and records, including a discussion of the potential material Federal tax consequences of the plan to the debtor, any successor to the debtor, and a hypothetical investor typical of the holders of claims or interests in the case, that would such a hypothetical investor ... to make an informed judgment about the plan[.][112]

The case of *In re Scott*, a civil case involving denial of discharge and not a criminal prosecution, is instructive. In *Scott*, the debtors filed disclosure statements that did not identify or separately value their specific ownership interests in over 70 business entities, lumping their interests in these entities into one single line. Later, it was determined that the debtors had received large amounts of cash from one partnership, which was not previously disclosed, and that thousands of intercompany transactions had occurred throughout the case which were impossible to reconstruct. The Seventh Circuit found that the disclosure statement, which contained material omissions and which was distributed to all creditors with a request for court approval, was equivalent to a false unsworn, oral statement. The court stated that, given the significance of the value of the debtor's business interests to the creditor's consideration of the debtor's plan

---

[110] Conviction of an attorney for concealment or for making a false oath under § 152(2) in connection with a bankruptcy case is grounds for disbarment. *See, e.g., In re Masterson*, 280 N.Y.S.2d 936 (N.Y. 1967). An attorney's participation in a bankruptcy crime raises numerous issues (the attorney may be charged as a principal or as an aider or abettor) (*see* chapter 18) and has implications with respect to the attorney client privilege (*see* chapter 32). Such conduct has serious professional and ethical ramifications as well. *See* chapter 38.

[111] *See Center*, 853 F.2d 568; *see also Cardall*, 85 F.2d at 678.

[112] 11 U.S.C. § 1125(a)(1).

and the debtor's duty as a fiduciary to furnish financial information as requested by creditors, the debtor's failure to make full and accurate disclosure of interests in business entities constituted concealment.[113]

Since disclosure statements are not filed under oath or penalty of perjury, omissions and misstatements in a disclosure statement would not constitute a false oath under § 152(2) or a false declaration under § 152(3). In some instances, however, such disclosure statement transgressions could give rise to a false account charge under § 152(2). For instance, a fraudulent liquidation analysis or balance sheet could be encompassed by the term "account."[114]

Continuing offense

Concealment is a continuing offense.[115] As the Fifth Circuit stated:

> . . . [C]oncealment by its nature is an act which goes on until detected or its consequences are purged. Its purpose is not merely to remove or withdraw assets from the control of the Court, but to do that in a way that the existence of the assets is not known or their withdrawal detected.[116]

The acts can be done before or after bankruptcy. As a result, concealment that occurs prior to the commencement of the case can form the basis for criminal liability. This is illustrated in the case of *United States v. Levine*.[117] Prior to filing bankruptcy, the Levines secreted large amounts of cash in trust accounts set up by their lawyers and accountants. In their bankruptcy, the Levines did not disclose the assets they had transferred prior to bankruptcy, thus the concealment crime was completed once the case was underway.

Examples of concealment

Concealment crimes can vary greatly in their nature and seriousness. Crimes of concealment may be colorful, even comical. Other concealment cases are dramatic, even heart breaking. The pattern of modern bankruptcy crimes often follows prevailing social and economic trends. Two examples are *United States*

---

[113] *In re Scott*, 172 F.3d 959 (7th Cir. 1999).

[114] The term "account" is not defined either in the Bankruptcy Code or Federal Criminal Code. *See* chapter 7.

[115] *Sultan v. United States*, 249 F.2d 385 (5th Cir. 1957); *see also* 18 U.S.C. § 3284 (statute of limitations for concealment does not begin to run until discharge is granted or denied); *see* chapter 30.

[116] *Sultan*, 249 F.2d at 386.

[117] *United States v. Levine*, 970 F.2d 681 (10th Cir. 1992). This case is discussed further in chapter 31.

v. Grant[118] and *United States v. Yagow,*[119] cases involving a Bostonian investment advisor/art collector and a North Dakotan farmer, respectively. John Grant and Merlyn Yagow have probably never met, but if they did, they would have little in common besides the fact that they both were convicted of bankruptcy fraud.

John Grant, a nonpracticing lawyer, owned a financial and investment planning company. He and his company filed chapter 11 cases, both of which were later converted to chapter 7. Prior to the bankruptcy cases, Grant purchased nine prints by artist John Stobart from the Stobart Gallery in Boston. The criminal charges against Grant stemmed from incidents allegedly occurring shortly after his personal and corporate chapter 11 cases were converted to chapter 7. Counsel for the creditors committee, upon visiting Grant's corporate offices at 92 State Street in Boston, noticed that some prints appeared to be missing. The trustee attempted to schedule an immediate "home visit" with Grant. Grant unsuccessfully tried to put off the trustee's visit for a few days. Grant was able to buy only a few hours of time by arranging to meet the trustee that afternoon in Grant's office in Boston, from which they would go to Grant's home together. Grant then raced home and loaded the Stobart prints in his van, drove it to the MBTA station, parked it, and then took the MBTA back to Boston, to meet the trustee as agreed. Unfortunately for Grant, one of his creditors saw Grant as he was taking items out of his house. The creditor "dropped the dime" on Grant — with a phone call to the FBI. As Grant returned home later that day, he was met by an FBI agent.

Yagow, the North Dakota farmer, filed a chapter 11 case to stay a creditor's repossession of his farm machinery and equipment. Eventually Yagow lost the rights to his farm assets, under a creditor-proposed liquidation plan confirmed by the bankruptcy court.

Yagow fought the loss of his farm property to the bitter end. He refused to cooperate with the liquidating trustee and was jailed for contempt of court. His efforts to thwart repossession of his assets included digging a trench around his property to make it difficult for anyone to come on his land. He also asked neighbors to store his machinery for him. When indicted, he disappeared for almost a year until arrested by the FBI. At his arraignment, he refused to comply with the proceedings and had to be brought into court lying on a cart. Yagow lied repeatedly under oath that he did not know where the assets were and that he had done nothing to conceal them.

---

118 *Grant*, 971 F.2d 799.

119 *United States v. Yagow*, 953 F.2d 427 (8th Cir. 1992).

These two cases are noteworthy for several reasons. First, the nature and significance of the assets concealed in each case were dramatically different. In *Grant*, the debtor concealed artwork, a luxury which was hardly essential to the debtor's livelihood or physical welfare. Further, its value was questionable. The court's opinion suggests that the value could have been as little as a few hundred dollars. In *Yagow*, the debtor concealed farm equipment, which was his only means to a livelihood and was of significant value both to him and the creditors. Grant seemed to act impulsively, as contrasted with Yagow, who engaged in a systematic pattern of frustrating creditors over an extended period of time. From an objective standpoint, the crime in *Yagow* was far more serious than the crime in *Grant*. Yagow concealed property worth thousands rather than hundreds; the fraud was committed systematically over several years rather than in the course of a day.

The pathos of Yagow and the self-indulgence of Grant were reflected in the ultimate disposition in each case.[120] Grant was convicted of concealment and received a sentence of twelve months probation. The relatively light sentence is commensurate with the impulsive, almost anecdotal nature of his conduct. Yagow was convicted on eleven counts of bankruptcy fraud, including concealment, false declarations and false oaths, and was sentenced to 21 months in prison, followed by two years of supervised release. While Yagow's conduct itself was egregious, the fact that his punishment was not far more severe obviously reflects mitigating circumstances, if not outright sympathy for his situation.

[120] Sentencing for most bankruptcy crimes is governed by the Federal Sentencing Guidelines (*see* chapter 38).

7. False oaths, accounts and declarations: 18 U.S.C. § 152(2) and 152(3)

Section 152(2) of title 18, United States Code, states:

> A person who -
>
> knowingly and fraudulently makes a false oath or account in or in relation to any case under title 11. . . .
>
> shall be fined under this title,[121] imprisoned not more than five years, or both.

Making a false oath or account is a class D felony. The false oaths provision has not been substantially changed since the prior Bankruptcy Act of 1898. Accordingly, the case law interpreting and applying the pre-1978 law is still relevant.

The crime requires the following four elements: (1) a knowing and fraudulent, (2) false, (3) oath or account, (4) in or in relation to a case under title 11. The language "in or in relation to any case under title 11" is broad, encompassing statements made in a bankruptcy case or in cases arising from a bankruptcy case.[122] "Accounts" typically mean accountings filed with the court, including monthly operating reports required by the United States trustee, as well as accountings filed by bankruptcy trustees.

Section 152(2) must be considered in conjunction with § 152(3), which states that a person commits a crime who:

> Knowingly and fraudulently makes a false declaration, certificate, verification, or statement under penalty of perjury as permitted under section 1746 of title 28, in or in relation to any case under title 11[;].

[121] Section 152 carries a fine of $250,000. 18 U.S.C. § 3571(b)(3). The fine is increased to up to $500,000 if the defendant is an organization. 18 U.S.C. § 3571(c)(3). Under certain circumstances, the fine may be equal to twice the pecuniary gain or loss involved in the crime. 18 U.S.C. § 3571(d).

[122] *See United States v. Yagow*, 953 F.2d 427, 433 (8th Cir. 1992).

Section 1746 allows unsworn declarations to be made instead of sworn statements:

> Wherever, under any law of the United States or under any rule, regulation, order, or requirement made pursuant to law, any matter is required or permitted to be supported, evidenced, established, or proved by the sworn declaration, verification, certificate, statement, oath, or affidavit, in writing of the person making the same (other than a deposition, or an oath of office, or an oath required to be taken before a specified official other than a notary public), such matter may, with like force and effect, be supported, evidenced, established, or proved by unsworn declaration, certificate, verification, or statement, in writing of such person which is subscribed by him, as true under penalty of perjury, and dated, in substantially the following form:
> (2) If executed within the United States, its territories, possessions, or commonwealths: "I declare (or certify, verify, or state) under penalty of perjury that the foregoing is true and correct. Executed on (date).
>
> (Signature)."[123]

Section 152(3) closes a potential loophole to § 152(2) in situations where a § 1746 declaration is made instead of an oath.

A bankruptcy case presents numerous opportunities for the making of an oath or declaration. The first such opportunity is the filing of the bankruptcy petition.[124] The bankruptcy schedules, statement of financial affairs, and lists required by Fed. R. Bankr. P. 1008 must be filed shortly after the petition. The petition, lists, schedules, and statement must be signed under penalty of perjury. The debtor is required to appear through a designated representative who must testify under oath at the meeting of creditors prescribed by statute.[125] The debtor must appear and be examined under oath if an examination is ordered by the Court under Fed. R. Bankr. P. 2004, typically at the request of a creditor. Testimony at depositions and hearings in bankruptcy court are under oath.[126]

---

[123] Added Pub.L.94-550, § 1(a), Oct. 18, 1976, 90 Stat. 2534.
[124] Official Bankruptcy Form 1; *see* Appendix E.
[125] 11 U.S.C. § 341.
[126] *See* Fed. R. Evid. 101, 603.

Fraudulent intent

Like every other subsection of § 152, subsections (2) and (3) contain the element that the proscribed act be "knowing" and "fraudulent." This element was recently considered by the Seventh Circuit in a highly publicized case involving the conviction of a bankruptcy lawyer, a partner in a large New York City firm, for violation of § 152. John Gellene was charged and convicted of knowingly and fraudulently making a false material declaration in a chapter 11 case in which his firm was counsel to the debtor. The declaration which Gellene filed in connection with his firm's retention under Fed. R. Bankr. P. 2014[127] did not disclose the firm's concurrent representation of one of the debtor's major creditors and an individual who managed that creditor. Subsequently, the declaration was amended, but it still failed to disclose the firm's connection with the creditor. At a hearing on the firm's fee application, Gellene testified concerning the declarations but still did not disclose the firm's representation of the creditor. The representation was eventually discovered by another major creditor, who then sought disgorgement of $1.8 million in fees which the firm had been awarded. Several months thereafter, Gellene finally filed a third amended declaration disclosing the representations of the creditor and the individual.

At Gellene's trial, the district court instructed the jury that "[a] statement is fraudulent if known to be untrue and made with intent to deceive." On appeal, Gellene argued that "fraudulently" requires not merely intent to deceive, but intent to defraud, *i.e.*, the defendant must intend to deprive someone of some right, interest or property by deceit, not merely mislead. The court rejected this argument:

> We cannot accept Mr. Gellene's narrowly circumscribed definition of "intent to defraud" or "fraudulently." Mr. Gellene would limit exclusively the statute's scope to false statements that deprive the debtor of his property or the bankruptcy estate of its assets. In our view, such a parsimonious interpretation was not intended by Congress. First, the plain wording of the statute suggests no such limited scope. Rather, the plain wording of the statute punishes making a false statement "knowingly and fraudu-

[127] Fed. R. Bankr. P. 2014 states, in pertinent part:

(a) Application for an Order of Employment

. . . The application shall be accompanied by a verified statement of the person to be employed setting forth the person's connections with the debtor, creditors, or any other party in interest, their respective attorneys and accountants, the United States trustee, or any person employed in the office of the United States trustee.

> lently." The common understanding of the terms "fraudulently" includes the intent to deceive.[128]

The court held that the term "fraudulent" includes statements made with the intent to defraud, but is not so limited and includes

> [A]ll the possible methods by which a debtor or any other person may attempt to defeat the intent and effect of the Bankruptcy Code and that the expansive scope of the statute 'reaches beyond the wrongful sequestration of a debtor's property and also encompasses the knowing and fraudulent making of false oaths and declarations in the context of a bankruptcy proceeding.' (citations omitted)[129]

Literal truth

An answer to a question is not fraudulent if there is an objectively reasonable interpretation of the question under which the answer is not false.[130] Questions on a bankruptcy schedule, however, must be construed in light of the purpose of the schedule. This may mean construing "or" as encompassing "and" where an answer in the conjunctive is warranted.[131]

An example of these principles at work is the case of *United States v. Rowe.*[132] At the time Robert Rowe filed his chapter 7 petition, he owned a half interest in a residence with his ex-wife and rented another house in which he lived. The monthly rent of over $1,800 on Rowe's residence was paid by a construction company which was formed by Rowe but owned by a friend. On his bankruptcy Schedule A (Real Property) he listed "NONE." On his Schedule J (Current Expenditures of Individual Debtor(s)), in response to the item "Rent on home mortgage payment," Rowe answered, "$395."

Rowe's defense to charges of making false statements on his bankruptcy schedules was that (a) he had no beneficial interest in the house owned with his ex-wife because it was completely encumbered by mortgages and attachments, and he had an agreement with his ex-wife that she would receive any equity; (2) his answer to the disjunctive question was truthful because he was paying $395 in monthly mortgage payments on the house he owned with his ex-wife, and the question asked for rent *or* mortgage payment, not both; and (3) since

---

[128] *United States v. Gellene,* 182 F.3d 578, 586 (7th Cir. 1999).

[129] *Gellene,* 182 F.3d at 586-87.

[130] *United States v. Rowe,* 144 F.3d 15, 21 (1st Cir. 1998).

[131] *Rowe,* 144 F.3d at 21.

[132] *Rowe,* 144 F.3d at 15.

he was not personally making the rental payments on his residence, he was not required to list them. The prosecution argued that Rowe's answer, even if it was literally true, was deceptive because by not listing his rental payment, he sought to hide the fact that he was the true owner of the construction company, which was paying his rent.

The court agreed in part but disagreed in part with Rowe's arguments:

> [I]n a false statement prosecution, an answer to a question is not fraudulent if there is an objectively reasonable interpretation of the question under which the answer is not even false.[133]

The court distinguished the case before it from this general rule, relying on rules of statutory construction, which provides that "or" can mean "and" where the clear purpose requires such a construction.[134] Even though it rejected Rowe's "disjunctive" argument, the court did find Rowe's explanation, that he did not list the rent payments because he was not making them, plausible. The court reversed Rowe's conviction on that count, stating that an objectively reasonable interpretation of the "expenditure" schedule would be to exclude payments by non-debtor parties. The court came to this result not completely without misgivings, noting that the government had not argued that the construction company was Rowe's alter ego, notwithstanding evidence to that effect.

The "literal truth" defense to a charge under § 152(2) has its limits.[135] Signing schedules that are true, but true only because a fraudulent transaction has occurred, is considered a false oath or declaration. This somewhat tautological doctrine is best illustrated by the case of *United States v. Center.*[136]

Mark Center was a bankruptcy lawyer who filed a chapter 11 case on behalf of Foxcliff, Inc. ("Foxcliff"), a corporation which owned a commercial real estate development. Foxcliff's principal shareholder also owned another company, Summit City Utilities, Inc. ("Summit") which owed $130,000 to Foxcliff. After the chapter 11 petition was filed, Center learned of a claim by

---

[133] *Rowe*, 144 F.3d at 21; *Cf. United States v. Bradstreet*, 135 F.3d 46, 51-52 (1st Cir.), *cert. denied*, 118 S. Ct. 1805 (1998).

[134] *Rowe*, 144 F.3d at 21.

[135] *See* chapter 23.

[136] *United States v. Center*, 853 F.2d 568 (7th Cir. 1988). Particularly shameful to the legal profession is the fact that in a number of landmark decisions on bankruptcy fraud, the defendants were lawyers. While it is often said that "hard cases make bad law," cases of bad lawyers make hard law. Many of these decisions "push the edge of the envelope" of the law. Such creative or expansive interpretations were arguably not intended by Congress but have been deemed by some courts as necessary to mete out justice in a given case.

Foxcliff against Summit. The claim against Summit was an asset of Foxcliff's chapter 11 estate. Foxcliff's shareholder assigned his personal claim against Foxcliff for paid-in capital to Summit, a transaction which was impermissible after bankruptcy. The effect of the transaction was to create an offset, effectively wiping out Foxcliff's claim against Summit. Center handled the documentation of the assignment, and prepared bankruptcy schedules for Foxcliff which did not list Foxcliff's claim against Summit.

Center was charged both with concealment and making a false entry in a document in a chapter 11 case.[137] The court held that Center's documentation of the transaction was a "false entry" because the transaction itself was fraudulent. Similarly, Center aided the making of a false declaration by assisting the debtor in filing schedules which reflected the end-result of the transaction. The court also held that the making of the entry of the fraudulent transaction was concealment. In rejecting Center's argument that the accounting entry, which reflects a fraudulent assignment, was not in itself false or fraudulent, the court stated:

> [Center]'s arguments . . . are ingenious but merely semantic gymnastics. An entry that accurately logs a fraudulent transaction is a fraudulent entry where the party making the entry is aware that he is recording a fraudulent transaction. There is no magic process of purification when the party directing the entry is the same party directing the concealment.[138]

Materiality

Unlike the crime of concealment, the courts have held that materiality is an element of crimes under §§ 152(2) and (3).[139] Materiality, however, is broadly construed.[140] Two commonly cited principles in determining materiality are: (1) matters pertaining to the extent, nature or history of the debtor's financial transactions, including income and employment; or (2) statements designed to secure adjudication by a particular bankruptcy court.[141]

---

[137] Center was charged under 11 U.S.C. § 2 (aiding and abetting). *See* chapter 18. It is not clear from the court's opinion whether Center was charged under § 152(2) (false oath or account) or § 152(8) (falsifying documents relating to a chapter 11 case). Based on the court's analysis, the conduct in the case would give rise to charges under either section. In any event, the *Center* decision has bearing on the interpretation of both of these sections.

[138] *Center*, 853 F.2d at 571.

[139] *United States v. Lindholm*, 24 F.3d 1078 (9th Cir. 1994); *Metheany v. United States*, 365 F.2d 90, 93 (9th Cir. 1966); *United States v. Key*, 859 F.2d 1257, 1261 (7th Cir. 1988).

[140] *Yagow*, 953 F.2d 427.

[141] *United States v. Phillips*, 606 F.2d 884 (9th Cir. 1979); *Yagow*, 953 F.2d at 433.

Failure to disclose under oath a relatively minor asset is not material,[142] but using a false Social Security number or address is.[143] Materiality is a question of law, not a fact question for the jury.[144]

An irrelevant opinion or response to an irrelevant question does not support a conviction under this section.[145] One example is where the trustee asks the debtor for his opinion on a question that requires a legal conclusion, such as a complex ownership issue, which the debtor is not qualified to give. "Knowing and fraudulent" means "an intentional untruth in a matter material to the issue which is itself material."[146] What is material in a bankruptcy case, however, is not limited to that which specifically relates to assets of the estate or directly affects the creditors. Materiality does not require showing [by the government] that the creditors were harmed by the false statements.[147] The impact on the creditors does not determine materiality.[148]

Consider the case of the debtor who falsely lists her Social Security number, prior addresses, and birthdate on her bankruptcy filings. Her Social Security number, prior addresses, and birthdate are obviously not assets or liabilities of the bankruptcy estate, nor are they directly related to the trustee's administration of assets. Such items are nevertheless considered material. While not direct misstatements about assets, such lies may impede the trustee's investigation of the debtor's financial history or even mislead the trustee and creditors as to the identity of the debtor. Failure to list prior addresses truthfully may have a bearing on prior financial transactions, such as a residence fraudulently conveyed prior to bankruptcy, or the diverted proceeds of a sale. Such misstatements may also have a bearing on venue, and thus be material, as they are potentially aimed to secure an adjudication by a specific tribunal.[149] Likewise, Social Security numbers and prior names would have a direct bearing on the debtor's eligibility to obtain a bankruptcy discharge,[150] available only every eight years.[151]

---

[142] *Key*, 859 F.2d 1257.
[143] *Phillips*, 606 F.2d 884.
[144] *Lindholm*, 24 F.3d 1078; *Metheany v. United States*, 390 F.2d 559 (9th Cir. 1968). In contrast, in a prosecution for making false statements under § 1001, materiality is a question of fact for the jury. *See* chapter 20.
[145] *United States v. Margolis*, 138 F.2d 1002 (3d Cir. 1943).
[146] *In re Slocum*, 22 F.2d 282, 285 (2d Cir. 1927) (citation omitted); *Phillips*, 606 F.2d 884.
[147] *Yagow*, 953 F.2d at 433.
[148] *In re Slocum*, 22 F.2d at 283.
[149] *Phillips*, 606 F.2d 884.
[150] *Phillips*, 606 F.2d 884.
[151] 11 U.S.C. § 727(a)(8).

Frequently a trustee or creditor at a § 341 meeting or Fed. R. Bankr. P. 2004 examination will ask a debtor about income earned and spent long before the bankruptcy case, or assets which were sold several years before the case was filed. Debtors are often questioned about transactions that occurred prior to bankruptcy, sometimes so long prior that those transactions could no longer be the subject of avoidance litigation[152] in the bankruptcy case. The question sometimes arises as to whether a debtor is obligated to respond to questions concerning assets outside the estate or a transfer beyond the "reachback" periods for voidable transfers.

The better view is that such questions are material because the creditors are entitled to inquire into what property passed through the debtor's hands prior to bankruptcy. Wide latitude is accorded to the trustee and creditors in this inquiry.[153] Even if the financial transaction occurred several years before the bankruptcy and the debtor derived no benefit from it, he must truthfully answer questions concerning such matters.

Section 152(2) and § 152(3) violations have occurred even when the misrepresentations on the schedules and false testimony did not have any effect on the outcome of the bankruptcy case, but were within the ambit of financial topics which are considered material. This principle is illustrated in *United States v. Key*.[154] Jeraldine Key and her husband Bobby Key owned and operated fast food restaurants and retail businesses. Bobby Key acquired a 51% interest in three corporations which the Keys formed. Three years later, in the face of ensuing financial problems, Bobby had his employees alter the corporate records to reflect that Jeraldine, not Bobby, was the original owner of the majority stock interest in the three corporations. Bobby's purpose was to shield his interest in the corporations from attachment by a judgment creditor.

The following year, the Keys filed a bankruptcy petition under chapter 11. The Keys' schedules listed that Jeraldine owned 51% of the stock of one corporation but not the other two. Bobby's schedules did not list any stock ownership in the three corporations. Under oath, Jeraldine testified that she owned the majority interest in all three corporations from their incorporation. Jeraldine's false testimony as to the date on which she acquired the stock, and the omission

---

[152] The trustee can avoid certain prebankruptcy transfers as voidable preferences or fraudulent conveyances, and recover the asset or funds that were transferred, and thus bring them into the estate for the benefit of the creditors collectively. *See* 11 U.S.C. § 544-549. The policy reason underlying these provisions is to insure equality of distribution to creditors. *See* chapter 5 (Fundamental bankruptcy policy).

[153] *In re Slocum*, 22 F.2d at 285.

[154] *Key*, 859 F.2d 1257.

of her interest in two of the Key's corporations on her bankruptcy schedules, became the basis of one of several bankruptcy fraud charges in her indictment.

Jeraldine argued that the three corporations were worthless and therefore misstatements about who owned them was immaterial. At Jeraldine's trial, the district judge instructed the jury as follows:

> [A]ny oath made as to what assets or property belonged or did not belong to a person who files a Chapter 11 proceeding in bankruptcy is material to such proceeding.[155]

The Court of Appeals, while upholding Jeraldine's conviction, suggested that "[t]his may be an overly broad statement of the legal standard for materiality."[156] The court noted that the government, at oral argument, in response to a question posed by one of the judges, conceded that a misstatement as to the ownership of a ream of paper in a case involving several million dollars would not be material for purposes of §§ 152(2) and (3). The court nevertheless upheld the district court's materiality instructions as to this case, stating:

> [M]ateriality does not require a showing that creditors are harmed by the false statements . . . Materiality is . . . established when it is shown that the inquiry bears a relationship to the bankrupt's business transactions or his estate, or concerns the discovery of assets, including the history of a bankrupt's financial transactions. (citations omitted).[157]

The court noted that "truthful disclosure of such transactions are important in enabling the trustee to trace the debtor's assets and/or to determine whether assets have been fraudulently transferred.[158]

In order to be material, the false statement need not be related to the estate's assets or pecuniary and property distribution issues. Misstatements in an attorney's Fed. R. Bankr. P. 2014 statement are material.[159] In *United States v. Gellene*, the Seventh Circuit rejected John Gellene's argument that his failure to divulge his firm's representation of a major secured creditor of the debtor was

---

[155] *Key*, 859 F.2d at 1261.
[156] *Key*, 859 F.2d at 1261.
[157] *Key*, 859 F.2d at 1261.
[158] *Key*, 859 F.2d at 1262.
[159] *Gellene*, 182 F.3d at 588.

not material because it was not intended to impact the distribution[160] of assets in a bankruptcy:

> We have no doubt that a misstatement in a Rule 2014 statement by an attorney about other affiliations constitutes a material misstatement. . . . [The procedures requiring court approval of employment of counsel by the debtor, and disclosure by the potential attorney] are not discretionary. The professionals "cannot pick and chose which connections are irrelevant or trivial." (citations omitted). . . . "[F]ailure to disclose is sufficient grounds to revoke an employment order and deny compensation." (citations omitted). . . [The] procedure is designed to ensure that a "disinterested person" is chosen to represent the debtor. This requirement goes to the heart of the integrity of the administration of the bankruptcy estate. The Code reflects Congress' concern that any person who might possess or assert an interest or have a predisposition that would reduce the value of the estate or delay its administration ought not to have a professional relationship with the estate.[161]

The rationale of the Seventh Circuit's ruling appears to be that a misstatement on a Fed. R. Bankr. P. 2014 statement is material because (1) it potentially impacts the estate, the administration of the case, and the creditors, even though it does not directly relate to an asset of the estate; and (2) it is aimed at securing a particular adjudication by the court, which is generally considered a test of materiality. On the last factor, the Court noted that Gellene apparently thought the omission was sufficiently important in order to obtain the desired result, which in itself is "a reliable index of materiality."[162]

---

[160] Another shortcoming of this argument is the fact that there are many ways in which an undisclosed conflict could impact the assets of the estate and the distribution to creditors. For instance, an undisclosed relationship between debtor's counsel and a creditor may impair the diligence and objectivity with which debtor's counsel investigates and pursues claims against that creditor, to the detriment of other creditors and the estate.

[161] *Gellene*, 182 F.3d at 588.

[162] *Gellene*, 182 F.3d at 588.

8. False claims: 18 U.S.C. § 152(4)

Section 152(4) of title 18, United States Code, states:

> A person who -
>
> knowingly and fraudulently presents any false claim for proof against the estate of a debtor, or uses any such claim in any case under title 11, in a personal capacity or as or through an agent, proxy, or attorney. . . shall be fined under this title,[163] imprisoned not more than five years, or both.[164]

The filing of a false proof of claim is a class D felony. Section 152(4) makes it a crime to knowingly and fraudulently present a false claim against a bankruptcy estate.

What constitutes a claim

The method by which a creditor normally asserts a claim in a bankruptcy case is by filing a proof of claim with the Bankruptcy Court. [165] If no objection is filed, the claim is deemed "allowed," which means that the amount of the claim for distributive purposes is established.[166] A proof of claim is not the only means by which a claim, a broadly defined term under the Bankruptcy Code,[167] is asserted. A claim, according to the Bankruptcy Code definition, is limited to a right arising before the petition. A right to payment arising after the filing of the petition is governed by Bankruptcy Code sections dealing with professional[168]

---

[163] Section 152 carries a fine of $250,000. 18 U.S.C. § 3571(b)(3). The fine is increased to up to $500,000 if the defendant is an organization. 18 U.S.C. § 3571(c)(3). Under certain circumstances, the fine may be equal to twice the pecuniary gain or loss involved in the crime. 18 U.S.C. § 3571(d).

[164] 18 U.S.C. § 152(4).

[165] 11 U.S.C. § 502(a). If an objection is filed, the Court determines the allowance and amount of the claim. 11 U.S.C. § 502(b).

[166] 11 U.S.C. § 502(a); Fed. R. Bankr. P. 3001-3005; Bankruptcy Official Form 10.

[167] 11 U.S.C. § 101(5).

[168] 11 U.S.C. § 326-331.

and administrative[169] expenses. Further, the filing of a proof of claim by a creditor is not required in a chapter 11 case if the creditor's debt is listed in the bankruptcy schedules and is not indicated to be disputed, unliquidated or contingent.[170]

The question of whether a violation of § 152(4) could occur in the absence of filing a proof of claim has not been addressed definitively in reported cases. The use of the words "presents any false claim for proof" would appear to limit culpability under § 152(4) to situations where an affirmative act has occurred that constitutes a "claim for proof." A passive omission, such as a creditor who does not file a claim where a debtor has erroneously listed that creditor's claim in an excessive amount on the schedules, would not fall within this section. The creditor has no duty to act in such a circumstance.

A more difficult question is whether the debtor's filing of schedules which intentionally overstate a claim would fall within § 152(4). Filing schedules containing entries which the debtor knows to be false would implicate § 152(3), but could also violate § 152(4), in light of § 1111(a) of the Bankruptcy Code, which makes listing a claim in the schedules tantamount to filing a proof of claim. While this question has not been addressed in the reported cases, the filing of schedules intentionally overstating a claim would arguably constitute the "presentment" of a "false claim for proof against the estate of the debtor."

A related issue is whether other means of asserting a claim in a bankruptcy case, such as filing a request for an administrative expense, would fall within § 152(4). Prosecution of a defendant who files a knowingly false request for an administrative expense would give rise to several statutory hurdles. First, an administrative expense is not a claim as defined in § 101(5) of the Bankruptcy Code. The latter term refers only to rights arising prior to the filing of a petition. An administrative expense is a right to payment arising after the petition. Second, an administrative expense is not sought by a proof of claim.[171] The language of § 152(4) uses the term "claim for proof," which implies the filing of a proof of claim. While Official Bankruptcy Form 10 carries a warning of criminal penalties for a false proof of claim, there is no official form for administrative claimants, and therefore they do not encounter the same warning. For these reasons, the rule of lenity would most likely preclude application of this section to an administrative claimant.[172]

---

[169] 11 U.S.C. § 503(a),(b).

[170] 11 U.S.C. § 1111(a).

[171] 11 U.S.C. § 503(b).

[172] *See* chapter 4.

Submitting a false administrative expense request in some respects is potentially more harmful to the other creditors and the estate, because administrative expenses enjoy priority in distribution over general unsecured creditors. On the other hand, there is less risk of actual harm because administrative expenses undergo a great degree of scrutiny. Such requests must meet the criteria set forth in § 503 of the Bankruptcy Code, and may only be allowed upon determination by the court. General unsecured claims, on the other hand, are deemed allowed automatically if no objection is filed, and thus there is often no judicial review or scrutiny as to their allowance.

Intent

To violate § 152(4), the presentment of the claim must be knowingly fraudulent. A good faith belief in the accuracy of the claim is a defense to this charge.[173] Creditors often file claims which overstate the amount actually owed. This is done for tactical reasons, *e.g.*, to leverage a settlement by forcing the debtor to object and thereby incur time and costs, or as a protective measure, *e.g.*, to preserve all the creditor's potential rights against the debtor's estate. Sometimes a creditor files an overstated claim with the intention of increasing its distributive share. None of these motives justify the filing of a claim that includes amounts not actually owed.

Where precisely is the line drawn between a colorable claim and a fraudulent one? Two reported decisions which involve defendants convicted of § 152(4) violations in connection with the same false proof of claim are instructive.[174] Daniel Overmyer was charged with filing, and Edmund Connery with aiding and abetting, a false bankruptcy claim. Connery was Overmyer's counsel. Overmyer owned a number of companies, including a warehouse business, an equipment leasing company, and a television station. All three companies became debtors in chapter 11 proceedings. The equipment leasing company filed a proof of claim in the bankruptcy case of the television station, which claim was overstated in at least three respects. First, the claim included charges for several months of lease payments for equipment not yet installed and for which no payments were owed. Second, the claim included installation charges for equipment not installed. Third, the claim was false because the station had, in fact, overpaid the lessor.

---

[173] *United States v. Connery*, 867 F.2d 929 (6th Cir. 1989).

[174] *Connery*, 867 F.2d 929; *United States v. Overmyer*, 867 F.2d 937 (6th Cir. 1989).

Neither Overmyer nor Connery actually prepared or signed the proof of claim that was the basis of their convictions. Overmyer orchestrated an elaborate set of transactions, including leases between the equipment leasing company and the television station, which were designed to mask or offset transfers made by the station to the leasing company. These transactions were the basis of the proof of claim. The *Overmyer* and *Connery* cases suggest that if a claimant sets up a sham transaction, which in turn becomes the basis for a claim, the claim is false. Further, the claimant may be liable for presenting a false claim even if he did not actually prepare or sign the claim. In order for the criminal culpability to arise, the defendant's involvement and participation in the scheme that is the basis of the claim, and in the filing of the proof of claim, must be pervasive. For instance, Overmyer instructed an employee to sign the claim, and the claim was signed in Connery's office. Overmyer told the employee who signed the claim that a substantial proof of claim needed to be filed in the bankruptcy case of the television station to "support" funds that had been removed from the station. Overmyer directed the employee to send a letter on behalf of the leasing company to the station stating these "costs."

Another question presented under § 152(4) is whether a claim filed for a debt which has been paid by a third party, is a false claim. The answer is unclear. If the payment did not release the principal obligation of the debtor to pay, then the claim should not be considered false.[175]

---

[175] *See United States v. Nill*, 518 F.2d 793 (5th Cir. 1975).

9. Receiving property with the intent to defeat the Bankruptcy Code and bribery: 18 U.S.C. § 152(5) and (6)

Section 152(5)

Section 152(5) of title 18, United States Code, states:

> A person who -
>
> knowingly and fraudulently receives any material amount of property from a debtor after the filing of a case under title 11, with intent to defeat the provisions of title 11[]
>
> shall be fined under this title[176], imprisoned not more than 5 years, or both.

The purpose of § 152(5) is to punish (and thus deter) creditors or other non-debtors from accepting property transferred outside of the parameters of the bankruptcy process. The section makes it a crime to accept payment on account of a debt or to buy assets from a debtor without court approval, unless permitted by the Bankruptcy Code. The section also criminalizes the acceptance of a bribe from a debtor, conduct which is also prohibited by § 152(6).

The section punishes parties, including creditors, who benefit from the debtor's evasion of the bankruptcy process, and in particular, the bankruptcy distribution process. Thus, receiving payments from a debtor on a legitimate debt may be illegal. Under the Bankruptcy Code, payments to creditors on account of claims arising before the filing of the bankruptcy petition may only be made as permitted by the Bankruptcy Code or as authorized by the court pursuant to provisions of the Bankruptcy Code. For instance, in a chapter 7 case, any interim and final distributions by the trustee in the case must be

---

[176] Section 152 carries a fine of $250,000. 18 U.S.C. § 3571(b)(3). The fine is increased to up to $500,000 if the defendant is an organization. 18 U.S.C. § 3571(c)(3). Under certain circumstances, the fine may be equal to twice the pecuniary gain or loss involved in the crime. 18 U.S.C. § 3571(d).

made in accordance with the priorities specified in § 726 of the Bankruptcy Code. In a chapter 11 case, except authorized by the Bankruptcy Code or the court,[177] payments to prepetition claimants may only be made under the terms of a plan confirmed under § 1129.[178] Thus, payments to creditors on account of such creditors' prepetition claims that are not in accordance with these provisions are violative of the Bankruptcy Code.

In addition to payment of creditors outside the Bankruptcy Code schemata, § 152(5) also encompasses violations of the Bankruptcy Code's restrictions on sale, use or lease of property. The debtor cannot use, sell or lease property of the estate outside the ordinary course of business without court approval and after notice and the opportunity for a hearing.[179] Use of cash collateral, funds in which a creditor holds a security interest, is subject to additional restrictions. Cash collateral cannot be used without the consent of the party with an interest in the cash collateral or court approval.[180] Non-debtor parties who knowingly receive money or property which is used, sold, or leased in violation of these restrictions may be held liable under § 152(5).

Ordinary course standard

Whether a sale, use or lease occurs in the ordinary course of business is of critical importance in determining if § 152(5) has been violated. If a sale to a buyer was made without court approval, but in the ordinary course of business, such sale could not be intended to "defeat the provisions of title 11" because title 11 expressly permits such a sale without court approval or notice to creditors. To complicate matters, the term "ordinary course of business" is not defined in the Bankruptcy Code.

Courts have defined "ordinary course" in the bankruptcy context by reference to two factors: (1) the vertical dimension; and (2) the horizontal dimension.[181] The vertical dimension asks the question: Was the transaction an "everyday" occurrence in the debtor's prepetition business? For example, if the debtor was a delicatessen prior to bankruptcy, selling sandwiches to customers at lunch time would be considered in the ordinary course of business. On the other hand, selling all of its kitchen equipment would not meet this test. A delicatessen is not in the business of selling kitchen equipment, although it might sell an item or two from time to time if it was not being used or was

---

[177] *See* 11 U.S.C. § 549.
[178] *See* 11 U.S.C. § 1129; 1141.
[179] 11 U.S.C. § 363(b)(1).
[180] 11 U.S.C. § 363(c)(2).
[181] *In re Johns Manville Corp.*, 60 B.R. 612, 616 (Bankr. S.D.N.Y. 1986).

being replaced. The horizontal dimension asks the question: Is the transaction an "everyday" occurrence for other businesses like the debtor's? For example, would other delicatessens sell sandwiches at lunch time? Would other delicatessens sell their kitchen equipment? Both tests are considered in determining ordinary course. If the transaction does not meet both tests, then the conservative view is that bankruptcy court approval is needed. Proceeding without court approval puts both the debtor and creditor at risk.

Section 152(5) criminalizes conduct which, absent a bankruptcy, may be perfectly legal. Consider the following situations. The debtor, a retail store, sells the company vehicles without notice to creditors or court approval, and then uses the proceeds without court approval to pay a vendor for merchandise which was ordered and received prior to bankruptcy. Both the purchaser and the vendor may be guilty of criminal conduct, if they knew that the activities were amidst a pending bankruptcy and outside the required bankruptcy procedures. If the transactions are not disclosed (*e.g.*, on the monthly operating reports required by the United States trustee), the debtor would also be committing separate crimes of concealment and false accounts.

Of course, even if the Bankruptcy Code is violated (*e.g.*, a sale outside the ordinary course of business is made without court approval), a crime is not necessarily committed. The fact that a buyer bought goods from a debtor that were sold outside the ordinary course of the debtor's business, and without court approval, will not, in itself, constitute a crime. Absent criminal intent on the part of the buyer, there is no crime. The buyer's circumvention of the bankruptcy procedures must be both knowing and fraudulent. One example would be a situation where a buyer knowingly bought assets without court approval, so as to avoid a bidding process or scrutiny by the court and creditors of a bargain price or other "sweetheart" terms. By subverting the bankruptcy sale process, which seeks to ensure that the estate receives a fair price, and the best price, for the assets, the buyer may gain an advantage at the expense of the creditors and the estate. Such a purchase can also indirectly facilitate the debtor's concealment of the proceeds of such a sale by evading notice requirements. If creditors are not notified of a sale, they will be unaware of the existence of sale proceeds, and thus it will be easy for the debtor to divert or conceal them from the creditors.

While the justification for criminalizing concealment and false statements is both intuitive and obvious, crimes under § 152(5) are far less so. Why should payment of a legitimate debt owed to a creditor be a crime? The reason rests in one of the overall policies underlying the bankruptcy law: equitable distribution to creditors. If debtors can pick and choose which creditors to pay, without regard to bankruptcy restrictions and priorities, the entire bankruptcy system becomes ineffective. None of the players would have any incentive to play by the rules. Creditors would vie for preferential, extralegal treatment.

Materiality

Section 152(5) contains an express element of materiality. Materiality is a factual question. Factors which are normally considered include the amount or value of assets involved relative to the size of the estate and the effect of the transaction on other creditors, *e.g.*, did the unauthorized payment or transfer reduce the amount which other creditors received?

Property

Section 152(5) refers to "property from a debtor" as opposed to "property of the estate," the term used in § 541 of the Bankruptcy Code, or "property belonging to the estate of a debtor," the term used in section 152(1). A literal reading of § 152(5) would suggest that to constitute a crime under this subsection, the payment or transfer of property must be made by a debtor; a literal reading of the section does not limit the property at issue to that belonging to the debtor or the estate. The courts have read broadly the terms "debtor" and "property" as used in this section. While not definitively addressed by the courts, the weight of well-reasoned authority suggests that violations can occur when property is transferred (or payments made) by an individual acting on behalf of the debtor from the property or funds within that individual's control. For instance, payments by general partners of a bankrupt partnership[182] or payments from funds in which the debtor had a claim held by an affiliate of the debtor[183] are within the purview of § 152(5). To fall within § 152(5), the property which is transferred may be outside the scope of what would be considered property under § 541 of the Bankruptcy Code in the strict sense, but it must be property that belongs to the debtor or is within the control of the debtor.

Bribery

Another potential for mischief, which § 152(6) seeks to address, is the debtor's manipulation of the plan process by bribing certain creditors to support a plan with payments made outside the plan. By bribing a few creditors, the debtor can obtain enough votes in favor of a plan, thus manipulating the requisite votes to obtain confirmation of a plan over the dissent[184] of other creditors.

---

[182] *See Lurie v. United States*, 20 F.2d 589 (6th Cir. 1927).
[183] *See United States v. Cardall*, 885 F.2d 656, 678 (10th Cir. 1989).
[184] 18 U.S.C. § 152(6).

This conduct is prohibited by § 152(6), which provides that a person commits a crime who:

> knowingly and fraudulently gives, offers, receives, or attempts to obtain any money or property, remuneration, compensation, reward, advantage, or promise thereof for acting or forbearing to act in any case under title 11[.]

This section forbids bribery, either offering or accepting a bribe, in connection with a bankruptcy case.

Section 152(6) of the Bankruptcy Criminal Code may seem puzzling. The negotiation process that necessarily ensues between creditors and the debtor in a typical chapter 11 case would appear to be precisely what this section describes. In fact, "attempting to obtain money, advantages or promises" in exchange for the creditor's "acting or forbearing to act" is exactly what a creditor must do to represent its interests in a case.

At first blush, § 152(6) would appear to prohibit virtually any negotiation between a creditor and a debtor in a chapter 11 case. How does a creditor go about protecting his rights and recovering his claims if he cannot "attempt to obtain [any] money or property" in exchange for "acting or forbearing to act" in a bankruptcy case? The difference between legitimate negotiation and criminal bribery turns upon whether the action was fraudulent.

Section 152(6) is difficult to understand without specific examples of prohibited conduct. It is not a crime for a creditor to use the ability to "act" in a bankruptcy case, by filing adversary proceedings and motions such as dischargeability actions, motions for relief from stay, objections to the debtor's plan and disclosure statement, to name a few, to leverage the best possible treatment from the debtor, as long as the creditor does not do so "fraudulently." When does negotiation become fraudulent, *i.e.*, a bribe? The line is crossed when the creditor offers or extracts from the debtor consideration that the debtor may not legally give. One example is a payment from estate property which is made outside a plan and is not approved by the court.

Stealth is one of the earmarks of this kind of fraud. If the "deal," or any part of it, is not to be disclosed to other creditors, it will likely be viewed with suspicion. Two instances in which violations of this section are prone to occur are the dismissal of an action against a debtor seeking to bar discharge under § 727 of the Bankruptcy Code, or a dismissal of the case agreed upon between the debtor and creditor. Whenever a creditor agrees to a dismissal of an action seeking to bar the debtor's discharge, or to a dismissal of the bankruptcy case in exchange for consideration that is neither disclosed to creditors nor approved by the court, there may be § 152(6) implications. The reason is that these types of settlements have implications for all creditors, and all creditors are entitled to have notice and an opportunity to object after full disclosure. The aim of § 152(6) is to prevent an overzealous creditor from leveraging his position secretly to the detriment of other creditors.

The case of *Lurie v. United States*[185], a case decided under prior law,[186] is illustrative. Lurie was a creditor of Rosenberg Bros., a bankrupt partnership. Arthur Rosenberg, one of the partners of the bankrupt partnership, conspired with Lurie to have Lurie's firm persuade certain other creditors to accept the plan, which paid 20¢ on the dollar, and in return, Lurie and those creditors would secretly receive another 15¢ on the dollar. The 15¢/dollar bribe was not paid from assets of the bankruptcy estate; nevertheless, Lurie was convicted. The court stated:

> Private and special payments to a creditor to induce him to vote for a composition are not in terms here forbidden, but it cannot be the intent that the minority of creditors may be coerced by a majority secured by bribery.[187]

The court also noted that the bankrupt partnership was required to file an affidavit that he has not directly or indirectly paid or promised any creditor any undisclosed consideration. Under present law, this requirement is encompassed in § 1129 (a)(3) of the Bankruptcy Code, which requires that the plan be proposed in good faith and not by any means forbidden by law, an element for confirmation that the debtor is required to demonstrate.

Bid bribery

Another category of conduct prohibited by § 152(6) is bribery in the bidding process for a sale of assets. Examples are: (1) a prospective buyer of assets in a bankruptcy case offers money to other potential buyers if those other potential buyers agree not to bid; or (2) a prospective buyer approaches another prospec-

---

[185] *Lurie*, 20 F.2d 589.

[186] The *Lurie* case was decided under prior § 29b(4), which was the prior version of § 152(5). The conduct which was described in the *Lurie* case would, under present law, be prohibited by §§ 152(5) and (6). Section 152(5) prohibits receipt of property, whether or not property of the estate, from a debtor with intent to defeat the provisions of title 11.

[187] *Lurie*, 20 F.2d at 590.

tive buyer and asks to be paid for not bidding. It is irrelevant whether the bribe is actually accepted, if the briber (or bribee) actually buys the assets, or if either of the parties involved even bids on the assets.[188]

Bidding bribery is viewed harshly by the courts. While good faith is always a defense to bankruptcy fraud, a defendant's "good faith" belief that his conduct was not illegal is not a defense. While it is the general rule that ignorance of the law is no excuse, nowhere is this more true than in the context of a bidding bribe. Buying assets from a bankruptcy estate is typically a commercial venture and the parties entering into the process are expected to know the rules. This principle is illustrated in the bid bribery case of *United States v. Zehrbach.*[189]

Zehrbach was a businessman who sought to buy assets of bankrupt aircraft manufacturers. He retained Drizos Investments, Inc., an investment banking firm, to obtain funding for his acquisitions. Mervis, a Drizos employee with aviation experience, was assigned to work with Zehrbach. Zehrbach became interested in buying assets from Taylorcraft Aviation Corporation, an aircraft concern in chapter 7. When the trustee for Taylorcraft began to solicit bids for the Taylorcraft assets, several interested parties submitted bids. Zehrbach instructed Mervis to negotiate a "buy-out" of the other bidders' "positions." Despite the euphemistic terminology, Zehrbach intended Mervis to bribe the other bidders not to bid. Mervis later said he did not question the instruction because Zehrbach was a bankruptcy expert "who did this all the time."[190]

The first competing bidder whom Mervis approached agreed to withdraw his bid for a payment of $40,000. An agreement was drawn up and was even reviewed by a lawyer for the competing bidder, who apparently did not question its legality.

The second competing bidder agreed to withdraw from the bidding for $30,000. Drizos' lawyer at first did not realize the transaction was illegal but by the end of the day, concluded that it was and so advised Mervis. Zehrbach told the lawyer he did not know what he was talking about. Drizos obtained a legal opinion from a second lawyer who said the transaction was legal, but the second lawyer was told that the arrangement was a joint venture between Zehrbach and another bidder, not that Zehrbach was paying another bidder not to bid.

At this point, bidders other than Zehrbach seemed to be dropping rapidly out of the process one by one. Taylorcraft's trustee became suspicious and

---

[188] *United States v. Weiss*, 168 F. Supp. 728 (W.D. Pa. 1958).
[189] *United States v. Zehrbach*, 47 F.3d 1252 (3d Cir. 1995).
[190] *Zehrbach*, 47 F.3d at 1255.

called Mervis. Mervis told the trustee that "we . . . formed a joint venture and . . . merged our bidding interest."[191]

Zehrbach was the only bidder, and the trustee accepted the bid. After the sale, the trustee contacted the FBI who commenced an investigation of the circumstances surrounding the withdrawal of the other bids. Zehrbach and Mervis were each charged with bankruptcy fraud and conspiracy.

A central theme of Zehrbach's and Mervis's defense was their argument that they had made a good faith mistake and that the lawyers involved in the transaction had likewise been mistaken as to the legality of the transaction. Zehrbach challenged the trial court's jury instruction that the government was not required to prove the defendant knew his acts were unlawful. The essence of Zehrbach's argument is that the instruction confused the jury because it is the government's burden to show the defendant had criminal intent and did not act in good faith. The lower court's instruction, which was upheld by the Third Circuit, clarified the meaning of the terms "knowingly," "fraudulently" and "good faith":

> An act is done knowingly if it is done voluntarily and intentionally and not because of a mistake or accident or other innocent reason. . . . The government is not required to prove that a defendant knew his acts were unlawful. . . . [G]ood faith is a complete defense to charges of acting with fraudulent intent because good faith is simply inconsistent with the intent to defraud. A person acts with fraudulent intent and without good faith when he acts with a purpose to deceive or to cheat, and so as to deprive another person of a right or property. While the term good faith has no precise definition, it means, among other things, an absence of an intention of taking advantage of another.[192]

Zehrbach's invocation of a good faith defense was ineffective because the facts showed that Zehrbach paid competitors not to bid, in an attempt to gain advantage in bidding for the assets and thereby deceive or cheat the estate and trustee. Such intent is inconsistent with good faith. The fact that Zehrbach and Mervis may have believed what they were doing was not illegal does not equal good faith. Although not articulated by the court, the very act of bribing a competing bidder in a bankruptcy, if done intentionally, is implicitly deceitful. If there are no competing bidders, the estate is unlikely to get the best

---

[191] *Zehrbach*, 47 F.3d at 1257.
[192] *Zehrabach*, 47 F.3d at 1258-59.

price for the assets; the sole bidder inevitably pays a lower price than a competitive bid process would bring. Thus, the purpose of a bribe is for one bidder to gain an advantage at the expense of the trustee, the estate, and the creditors.

10. Fraudulent prebankruptcy transfers: 18 U.S.C. § 152(7)

Section 152(7) of title 18, United States Code, states that a person commits a crime who:

> [I]n a personal capacity or as an agent or officer of any person or corporation, in contemplation of a case under title 11 by or against the person or any other person or corporation, or with intent to defeat the provisions of title 11, knowingly and fraudulently transfers or conceals any of his property or the property of such other person or corporation[.]

The section is aimed at prohibiting individuals, such as corporate officers, from committing fraud with respect to a corporate debtor. The defendant may be an agent or officer, or neither. If the indictment alleges the defendant acted "as an agent," the government is not required to allege or prove that the defendant had any actual authority. Some relationship, however, with the debtor is necessary. The defendant must be an officer, director, agent, or employee acting on the corporate debtor's behalf.

The term "transfer" is used but not defined in the Bankruptcy Criminal Code. The term is defined in the Bankruptcy Code as follows:

> Each mode, direct or indirect, absolute or conditional, voluntary or involuntary, of disposing of or parting with-
> (i) property;
> (ii) or with an interest in property.[193]

The word "transfer" is used extensively in the Bankruptcy Code, primarily in the context of avoiding powers. Such powers include the rights of the trustee (or debtor in possession in a chapter 11 case) to recover property that was

---

[193] 11 U.S.C. § 101(54).

conveyed voluntarily or involuntarily from the debtor prior to the bankruptcy and to bring such property into the estate. Actions encompassed in the Bankruptcy Code definition of "transfer" include payments, foreclosures, sales, grants, gifts, losses, lease or contract terminations, and license revocations or suspensions.

The usage of the word "transfer" in the Bankruptcy Criminal Code is not identical to the word's meaning under the Bankruptcy Code. While the terms are not completely coextensive, they do, however, overlap to a great extent. The Bankruptcy Code definition has been often used by the courts in interpreting § 152(7).[194]

The intent element in § 152(7) is that the conduct was (1) in contemplation of a bankruptcy case; or (2) with the intent of defeating the Bankruptcy Code. The first alternative requires a nexus between the defendant's concealment and the bankruptcy case. It is not required that the defendant actually cause the bankruptcy case to be filed. Knowledge of financial problems of the debtor, and the potential for an eventual bankruptcy, has been used by the government to establish the element of "contemplation of a bankruptcy case."[195]

An example of this view of the element of "contemplation of a case under title 11" in § 152(7) is illustrated in *United States v. Micciche.*[196] *Micciche* involved a bustout scheme in which four defendants, Ward, Slingerland, Garnigan and Micciche, were charged with and convicted of conspiracy to violate § 152(7). Slingerland, Ward, and a third participant in the scheme, Wilson, established a furniture store. The store ordered a huge inventory which was trucked to various auction houses and sold at prices below wholesale cost. One of the trucks used was titled in Ward's name to conceal it from any potential bankruptcy proceedings.

Four months after the store was opened, it was completely empty. Slingerland reported to the police that the store had been robbed. This report was made presumably to cover up the fact that the inventory was diverted and disposed of by the principals.

A week and a half later, the creditors filed an involuntary petition against the company. It was not clear when the defendants learned of the bankruptcy proceedings. However, it was abundantly clear that the defendants' scheme was aimed at defrauding creditors, and there was some evidence that at least one of the defendants contemplated hiding assets from any potential bank-

---

[194] *See United States v. Pfingst*, 477 F.2d 177, 182-83 (2d Cir. 1973)

[195] *See United States v. Micciche*, 525 F.2d 544 (8th Cir. 1975); *United States v. Martin*, 408 F.2d 949, 951 (7th Cir. 1969).

[196] *Micciche*, 525 F.2d 544.

ruptcy. The convictions of the three principals were upheld, but the convictions of two employees, Micciche and Garnigan, were reversed. There was no evidence that these two employees were parties to the agreement among the principals to defeat the bankruptcy laws, despite the fact that the employees' actions, i.e., moving furniture and participating in the auction of furniture, were part of the overall scheme.

Micciche is significant in that defendants Ward, Wilson and Slingerland did not actually file the bankruptcy case themselves. Nevertheless, their actions, the rented truck in Ward's name and the phony robbery, contemplated a potential bankruptcy. Hence, their convictions under § 152(7) were sustained.

As for offenses under the "intent to defeat the provisions of title 11" clause, this language is identical to that used in § 152(5) and therefore the same interpretation is applicable.[197] The word "conceal" in § 152(7) has been construed to have the same meaning as "conceal" in § 152(1). Section 152(7), however, differs from concealment under § 152(1) in two major respects: (1) § 152(7) does not use, and thus is not limited to, property "belonging to the estate of a debtor;" and (2) § 152(7) requires proof that the act was done with "intent to defeat the provisions of title 11" or "in contemplation of a case under title 11."

The significance of these differences is illustrated by the case of *United States v. Moody*.[198] Shearn Moody was one of three general partners in a partnership which owned several properties including a bowling alley. Moody also established an insurance company, the demise of which eventually led to a large civil judgment against Moody. Shortly after the judgment was entered, Moody established a trust to which he transferred his interest in the underlying real estate in which the bowling alley was constructed. Moody filed a bankruptcy petition in which he listed his partnership interest as an asset. He did not, however, disclose that he had transferred assets into the trust within a year of the bankruptcy petition, a required disclosure. The bowling alley was sold during Moody's bankruptcy without court approval. Further, Moody received proceeds from the sale that were not disclosed to the court, Moody's trustee, or the creditors. Moody was charged both under §§ 152(1) and 152(7). In defense of the charge under § 152(1), he argued that the sale proceeds were not property of his estate, but rather property of the trust. As to § 152(7), he argued that that section only pertains to pre-petition conduct, as the section uses the term "his property" suggesting property of the debtor, as opposed to the estate. On appeal, Moody argued that his conviction on both charges was inconsistent.

---

[197] *See* chapter 9.

[198] *United States v. Moody*, 923 F.2d 341 (5th Cir. 1991).

The Court affirmed Moody's conviction and held that § 152(7) applies to both pre-petition and post-petition conduct. The court read the term "property" as used in § 152(7) to be broader than the term "property belonging to the estate of a debtor" in § 152(1).[199] The court held that the property does not need to be an asset of the estate for § 152(7) to apply. The court noted that the use of the disjunctive "or" between the phrases "in contemplation of a case under title 11" and "with intent to defeat the provisions of title 11" indicated that the section applied both to conduct occurring before and after the bankruptcy petition.[200]

Moody has been criticized not for its result, which is sound, but for the decision's summary analysis of the application of § 152(7) to the facts of the case. The funds that Moody received from the sale of the bowling alley most likely were comprised of (1) a distribution of his share of the partnership's share of proceeds from the sale; and (2) a distribution of his share of the trust's share of proceeds from the sale. The former would be property of the estate, since it represented income from estate property, *i.e.*, his interest in the partnership. The latter may or may not have been estate property. To the extent his interest in the trust was either not estate property or exempt, such funds may have been simply, in the words of § 152(7), "his property." Stated differently, a major problem with Moody's textual argument is that the debtor's property includes property of the estate.

Because of its broad sweep, § 152(7) is a powerful tool for prosecutors. The section can be used to reach conduct occurring prior to the filing of a bankruptcy case, which, but for the filing of a bankruptcy, would not necessarily be criminal.

---

[199] *See also United States v. Goodstein*, 883 F.2d 1362 (7th Cir. 1989), discussed in chapter 5.
[200] *Moody*, 923 F.2d at 346.

11. Concealment or destruction of records: 18 U.S.C. § 152(8) and (9) and § 1519

Section 152(8) states that a person commits a crime who:

> after the filing of a case under title 11 or in contemplation thereof, knowingly and fraudulently conceals, destroys, mutilates, falsifies, or makes a false entry in any recorded information (including books, documents, records and papers) relating to the property or financial affairs of a debtor[.]

Just as the bankruptcy system depends on full and truthful disclosure of financial information, it also depends on the availability and accuracy of such information. The integrity of the debtor's books and records is essential to the trustee and creditors. Section 152(8) penalizes persons who impede the bankruptcy process by destroying financial records of a debtor, either before or after the commencement of a case.

Section 152(8) encompasses a broad range of items including virtually any form of recorded information. The term "recorded information" includes not only documents, books and records, but also magnetically or electronically stored information. The acts prohibited by § 152(8) include not only destruction but also alteration or mutilation of information. The scope of information encompassed by § 152(8) includes anything that would relate to possible sources of funds or assets of the estate or means of reorganization.[201]

One of the most dramatic examples of a § 152(8) violation was where a lawyer threw financial records of the debtor in a landfill in the midst of pending discovery by creditors.[202] Tommy Brown, an associate working on Gary and Marcee Levine's bankruptcy case, destroyed certain financial records of Gary Levine's after he told Brown he did not want to continue to pay storage costs. At the time, discovery requests were pending against Marcee Levine. Later, in

---

[201] *United States v. Roberts*, 783 F.2d 767 (9th Cir. 1985); *Metheany v. United States*, 390 F.2d 559 (9th Cir. 1968).

[202] *United States v. Brown*, 943 F.2d 1246, 1252-53 (10th Cir. 1991).

response to a request by the trustee for certain information, Brown wrote, "[m]any of [the Levines'] financial records were in the storage locker and seem to have disappeared into the hands of the numerous attorneys and banks who were interested in those documents."[203] In his criminal case, Brown argued that he had complied with all discovery demands at the time he destroyed the documents. The court, however, noted that the timing of the destruction was suspect, and no records relating to the debtors' financial transactions should have been destroyed. The court also noted that, at the time he destroyed the records, Brown was aware that one of the creditors was dissatisfied with discovery.

Brown was also charged and convicted of other charges in connection with his representation of the Levines. Standing alone, his destruction of records (records which he claimed were insignificant, a claim he obviously could not prove without the records) may not have led to criminal charges. In light of the surrounding circumstances, which gave rise to numerous other charges, his destruction of records resulted in conviction on a § 152(8) charge.

Section 152(8) makes purging of files, even in the normal course of business, a risky undertaking once a company is in poor financial straights, on the verge of bankruptcy, or in a bankruptcy proceeding. In any of these circumstances, a debtor or potential debtor should not regard any destruction of records as ordinary. Often a debtor wishes to dispose of business records because storage costs are prohibitive. In that case, debtor's counsel should urge the debtor to dispose of records only after formal notice is given to the court and creditors, parties in interest, and the United States trustee, with an opportunity for all such parties to object. Such protective procedures are obviously not an option if no bankruptcy is pending yet. Record destruction in the face of potential financial problems, and thus, a potential bankruptcy, may eventually have both civil and criminal consequences. A potential debtor should destroy documents only in the ordinary course of business, and only if absolutely necessary. If possible, no financial records should be destroyed.

Records destruction under the Sarbanes-Oxley Act

The Sarbanes-Oxley Act of 2002 created a new bankruptcy crime related to the destruction and or falsification of documents § 1519 of Title 18, United States Code:

> § 1519. Destruction, alteration, or falsification of records in Federal investigations and bankruptcy. Whoever knowingly alters, destroys, mutilates,

---

[203] *Brown*, 943 F.2d at 1250.

> conceals, covers up, falsifies, or makes a false entry in any record, document, or tangible object with the intent to impede, obstruct, or influence the investigation or proper administration of any matter within the jurisdiction of any department or agency of the United States or any case filed under title 11, or in relation to or contemplation of any such matter or case, shall be fined under this title, imprisoned not more than 20 years, or both.

The most significant difference between § 1519 and §§ 152(8) and 153 is the element of intent to impede, obstruct or influence a federal investigation or matter within the jurisdiction of a federal department or agency. Since the Office of the United States Trustee falls within the definition of a federal "department or agency,", and all bankruptcy cases are within the United States Trustee's "jurisdiction," presumably any destruction or alteration in a bankruptcy case, if done with the intent to impede, obstruct or influence the case, would be susceptible to a § 1519 charge. The alteration of a document with the intent to impede or influence the case could be charged under this section, even if the defendant had no intent to defraud the Court or the creditors. For example, the destruction of documents with the intent of merely delaying the case would fall within this section. The statutory penalty under § 1519 is potentially higher as well, as the section provides for imprisonment up to 20 years.

Withholding recorded information

Section 152(9) provides that a person commits a crime who:

> after the filing of a case under title 11, knowingly and fraudulently withholds from a custodian, trustee, marshal, or other officer of the court or a United States trustee entitled to its possession, any recorded information (including books, documents, records and papers) relating to the property or financial affairs of a debtor[.]

Section 152(9) prohibits the withholding of recorded information relating to the property or financial affairs of a debtor. Section 152(9) encompasses the same scope of recorded information as section 152(8), but unlike § 152(8), it covers withholding (as opposed to destruction or mutilation) of information and is directed at post-petition conduct only. Section 152(9) proscribes withholding recorded information from an officer of the court, including a trustee, custodian, marshal or other officer, "after the filing of a case under title 11." By contrast, § 152(8) covers conduct "after the filing of a case under title 11 or in contemplation thereof." Thus, § 152(8) explicitly covers both pre- and post-petition conduct. The reason for the difference is obvious: it is only possible to *withhold* recorded information after a case is commenced; until a case is commenced, there are no officers of the court entitled to such information. On the other hand, destruction, alteration, or mutilation of records can occur before or after a case is commenced. Further, destruction, mutilation, or alteration of records prior to a bankruptcy case has just as serious an impact on the bankruptcy process as such acts which occur after a case is commenced.

The withholding of the information must be from an officer of the court entitled to possession of such information. This includes the bankruptcy trustee, the United States trustee, chapter 11 debtor in possession, or United States marshal. While the section includes the words "custodian" and "receiver," there is little or no practical significance to the inclusion of these terms. Rarely is either a custodian or a receiver involved in a bankruptcy case.

It is not clear whether "recorded information" includes documents (or for that matter, electronically stored information) which are assets in themselves, such as certificates of deposit, promissory notes or stock certificates. While the essence of such items are obviously something other than merely recorded information, they are, in fact, a source of information. On one hand, an argument could be made that charging a defendant for violations of both § 152(1) and (9) for failing to disclose and turn over a promissory note is overcharging, as the two charges are based on the identical facts. Another argument against use of § 152(9) in such cases is that the application of § 152(9) to such conduct violates lenity: the application of the term "recorded information" to instruments is not clear from the statutory language. On the other hand, a reasonable argument can be made that withholding a promissory note or stock certificate gives rise to two separate crimes and two separate harms. This question has not been definitively addressed by the courts, although § 152(9) has been so applied in at least one reported case.[204]

---

[204] *United States v. Beery*, 678 F.2d 856 (10th Cir. 1982).

12. Embezzlement against estates: 18 U.S.C. § 153

Section 153 of title 18, United States Code, states that a person commits a crime:

> . . . who has access to property or documents belonging to an estate by virtue of the person's participation in the administration of the estate as a trustee, custodian, marshal, attorney or other officer of the court or as an agent, employee, or other person engaged by such an officer to perform a service with respect to the estate[.] . . . [and] knowingly and fraudulently appropriates to [his] own use, embezzles, spends or transfers any property or secretes or destroys any document belonging to the estate of a debtor[.][205]

A violation of § 153 is a Class D felony punishable by five years imprisonment, a fine of up to $250,000[206] or both. This section criminalizes two types of conduct: (1) use or embezzlement of property, and (2) secretion or destruction of documents of the estate. Offenses committed under § 153 may in some circumstances also constitute concealment under § 152(1).[207]

The section is aimed at officers of the court, a term defined expansively in this section. The persons whose conduct is circumscribed by this section include:

- bankruptcy trustees
- custodians of records or property, such as bailees or escrow agents
- marshals and other court employees such as clerks of the court
- debtors in possession

---

[205] 18 U.S.C. § 153.
[206] Violation of § 153 carries a fine of $250,000. 18 U.S.C. § 3571(b)(3). The fine is increased to up to $500,000 if the defendant is an organization. 18 U.S.C. § 3571(c)(3). The fine may be up to twice the pecuniary gain or loss involved in the crime under certain circumstances. 18 U.S.C. § 3571(d).
[207] *Stuhley v. Hyatt*, 667 F.2d 807 (9th Cir. 1982).

- agents of the bankruptcy trustee or debtors in possession, such as employees, brokers, accountants, appraisers and investment bankers
- attorneys for bankruptcy trustees, debtors, official creditor committees, custodians, or agents of the debtor or trustee

Any of the foregoing are within the reach of § 153 to the extent such person has access to property or documents of a bankruptcy estate by virtue of such person's participation in the administration of the estate.

Borrowing assets or funds belonging to the estate is also prohibited. Section 153 includes not only transferring, spending, and embezzling, but also using estate property. Some examples of conduct prohibited by this section are:

- the use by a lawyer of funds held in an escrow account for a client, a debtor in a bankruptcy case, to pay office expenses during firm's "cash flow crunch"
- embezzlement, by a clerk of the bankruptcy court, of filing fees that were paid in connection with bankruptcy petition
- destruction by a debtor's lawyer of documents evidencing a fraudulent transfer
- a "joy ride," by a chapter 7 trustee's young associate, in a Mercedes Benz that is property of a bankrupt estate
- withdrawal of funds by a trustee which are earmarked for payment of the trustee's fees, and which are held in an estate trust account, while the trustee awaits court approval of his fee application seeking compensation in the case

Bankruptcy trustees are closely monitored by the United States trustee. When a trustee fails to account for estate funds or other assets, the United States trustee is required to commence an inquiry immediately. If the United States trustee determines that embezzlement is likely to have occurred, the trustee will be removed and a criminal referral will generally be made forthwith.

The term "property" as used in this section is not limited to property of the estate. The literal language of § 153 criminalizes embezzlement of any property by a person who has access to the property by reason of her administrative role with respect to the bankruptcy estate. While it can reasonably be argued that the phrase "belonging to the estate of a debtor" modifies both "any property" as well "any document," the more correct reading is that the term "any property" is not limited to estate property.[208] One rationale for the broader prohibition with respect to property is that estate officers, such as trustees or court clerks, frequently come into possession of property which is not or may not be estate property. Examples are filing fees or funds placed in escrow for secured creditors or placed in the registry of the court. Embezzlement of such funds falls within the scope of § 153.

Knowing and fraudulent destruction of documents by an officer, as defined for purposes of § 153, is also proscribed. While § 152(8) also covers destruction of documents of the estate, section 153, is far narrower. The two sections differ in several respects. First, § 153 only covers post-petition conduct, whereas § 152(8) covers not only post-petition conduct but also conduct "in contemplation [of the filing of a case under title 11]." Second, § 153 applies to officers of the estate, unlike § 152(8), which applies to any "person."

Section 153 only prohibits destruction of documents, while § 152(8) also prohibits concealment, mutilation, falsification, or making a false entry. Lastly, § 152(8) uses the term "recorded information . . . relating to the property or financial affairs of a debtor," which expressly includes books, documents, records, and papers. Section 153 reaches a more narrow scope of items, as it deals only with "any document belonging to the estate of a debtor." The scope of § 152(8) is not limited to documents, although the distinction between recorded information and documents has all but evaporated. More importantly, § 153 is not limited to that which belongs to the estate of a debtor.

---

[208] *See Meagher v. United States*, 36 F.2d 156, 157-58 (9th Cir. 1929).

13. Adverse interest and conduct of officers: 18 U.S.C. § 154

Section 154 states that a custodian, trustee, marshal or other officer of the court commits a crime if he:

> (1) [K]nowingly purchases, directly or indirectly, any property of the estate of which the person is such an officer in a case under title 11;
> (2) [K]nowingly refuses to permit a reasonable opportunity for the inspection by parties in interest of the documents and accounts relating to the affairs of estates in the person's charge by parties when directed by the court to do so; or
> (3) [K]nowingly refuses to permit a reasonable opportunity for inspection by the United States Trustee of the documents and accounts relating to the affairs of an estate in the person's charge[.][209]

Section 154 prohibits an officer of the estate from self-dealing or refusing to permit inspection of documents and accounts by a party in interest under a court order, or by the United States trustee. Section 154 is an infraction; no term of imprisonment can be imposed. Violations are punishable by a fine and removal from office. A trustee, examiner, or debtor in possession may be removed by means other than prosecution under this section. A trustee or examiner may be removed for cause.[210] Likewise, a debtor in possession may be displaced by the appointment of a trustee for cause.[211]

The term "other officer of the court" is not defined in § 154. This same term is used in § 153, and should have the same meaning as in that section.[212] Other officers include bankruptcy trustees, custodians, marshals, court clerks

[209] 18 U.S.C. § 154.

[210] 11 U.S.C. § 324(a) provides:
The court, after notice and a hearing, may remove a trustee, other than the United States trustee, or an examiner, for cause.

[211] *See* 11 U.S.C. § 1104.

[212] *See* chapter 12.

and employees, debtors in possession, and agents or professionals employed by the trustee, debtor, estate, or official committees.

Section 154(1) prohibits a trustee or other officer from buying any property of the estate in a case for which he is an officer. This section prohibits such a person buying an asset in a personal capacity, directly or indirectly. Some examples of conduct which potentially fall within this section are:

- a woman bids on a rug at a bankruptcy auction of a bankrupt rug dealer, for whom her husband is the trustee
- a real estate developer forms a limited liability company, the members of which are entities which he owns indirectly, to purchase, at a court-ordered bankruptcy sale, an office building from a partnership in which he is a general partner
- a court clerk buys kitchen equipment at a bankruptcy auction of a restaurant that is the subject of a chapter 7 case pending in the court in which the clerk is employed

Since the procedures for the sale of assets of the estate in the Bankruptcy Code are designed to ensure that assets are sold in a fair and reasonable manner which maximizes the value to the estate, the need for the prohibitions in § 154 is not immediately obvious. The policy reason underlying this section is similar to that underlying § 152(5) and (6). These three provisions seek to protect the integrity of the bankruptcy procedures governing disposition of property. Section 154 prohibits trustees (and certain others)[213] from buying assets personally from the estates they administer, even in the absence of any fraud.

Section 154(1) is analogous to prohibitions on insider trading. Trustees, court clerks, debtors, committees, and retained professionals are in a unique position to capitalize on inside information. Further, there is often the opportunity for an estate officer to manipulate, or at least influence, the bidding and advertising process. If there were no prohibitions against self-dealing, there would be nothing to prevent such an officer from structuring the sale process so as to increase the likelihood that there would be no other bidders, or, at the very least, that the officer would be the successful bidder. The potential to decrease the value to the estate is apparent.

Section 154(2) prohibits an officer from refusing to permit a reasonable opportunity for inspection by parties in interest of documents and accounts relating to the affairs of the estate by parties when directed by the court. The

---

[213] 11 U.S.C. § 154.

use of the words "parties in interest" with respect to a document inspection, as contrasted with the word "parties" with respect to inspection of accounts, has not been the subject of judicial comment in reported cases. "Parties in interest" is not defined in the Bankruptcy Criminal Code. The term generally means and includes creditors, equity security holders, official committees,[214] and parties to executing contracts and unexpired leases. It is less clear whether indirect equity holders (*e.g.*, shareholders or a corporate general partner of the debtor) are parties in interest. Potential purchasers of assets are generally not considered parties in interest.

Section 154(2) and (3) use the terms "documents" and "accounts," unlike § 152(9), which uses the term "recorded information." The effects of the difference in terminology between the two sections have not been addressed. The argument could be made that "documents" is narrower in scope and includes only hard copies of information, not electronic or computer diskettes, sound recordings, magnetic tapes, video tapes, and the like. Some support for this argument is found in the Bankruptcy Code, which in some instances refers to "recorded information" as including "documents," among other things.[215] On the other hand, the extension of the word "document" in civil discovery to such items is commonplace. Virtually all requests for production of documents in civil cases, including bankruptcy cases, include such items. Objections to the inclusion of such items in the definition of "document" in a civil discovery request are rarely made, and when they are made, are generally overruled summarily. In post-modern times, "document" and "recorded information" are coextensive, and this is the better-reasoned interpretation.

Section 154(2) requires that inspection be directed by the court. There are several contexts in which such an order may be issued. Fed. R. Bankr. P. 2004 provides that the court may order the examination of any entity, on motion of any party in interest. Such examination may include the production of documentary evidence. Section 541(c) provides that the court may order turnover or disclosure of recorded information to the trustee. Several Bankruptcy Code sections require disclosure of information or turnover of property without the need for a court order, including §§ 343, 542, 543, and 1106. These provisions, in certain circumstances, may operate to compel an officer to make documents available for inspection. However, § 154(2) literally does not encompass a failure to produce documents or accounts in such situations, where no court order is in effect. Where a party moves the court for an order compel-

---

[214] *See* 11 U.S.C. § 1109(b).
[215] *See, e.g.*, 11 U.S.C. § 542(e).

ling compliance with a self-executing requirement under one of these provisions, failure to produce documents as ordered would trigger the application of § 154(2).

Section 154(3) is similar to § 154(2) except that it pertains to a refusal to permit inspection by the United States trustee, rather than a party or a party in interest. No court order is required under § 154(3). The United States trustee has an administrative oversight role with respect to bankruptcy cases. Thus, the United States trustee, in requesting documents and accounts relating to an estate, is essentially acting in a quasi-judicial role. Hence, § 154(3) contains no requirement for a court order with respect to a request by the United States trustee. The United States trustee also holds supervisory responsibility over panel trustees and thus is to have access to trustees' records without the need for a court order. It is essential that this access be maintained to ensure that all estates are being properly and honestly administered by panel trustees.

14. Fee agreements in cases under title 11 and receiverships: 18 U.S.C. § 155

Section 155 of title 18, United States Code, states:

> Whoever, being a party in interest, whether as a debtor, creditor, receiver, trustee or representative of any them, or attorney for such party in interest, in any receivership or case under title 11 in any United States court or under its supervision, knowingly and fraudulently enters into any agreement, express or implied, with another such party in interest, for the purpose of fixing the fees or other compensation to be paid to any party in interest or to any attorney for any party in interest for services rendered in connection therewith, from the assets of the estate, shall be fined under this title or imprisoned not more than one year, or both.

Section 155 prohibits fee fixing in bankruptcy cases. This section was originally enacted in 1938, and is commonly known as the Borah Act, after Senator William E. Borah of Idaho, who sponsored the legislation in 1937. Originally part of title 28 of the United States Code, it was moved to title 18 in 1948.

The prohibition against fee fixing was a response to the widespread practice of lawyers in large bankruptcy cases to agree, before the case was filed, on who the receiver would be and how much all the lawyers would be paid. The natural consequence of this process was that creditors would be shortchanged; the major beneficiaries were the lawyers and the receiver, all of whom would be paid large fees. Because such arrangements were by agreement, there would often be no opportunity for creditors to object.

As a result of changes in the Bankruptcy Code regarding allowance and payment of professional fees and compensation of officers, all such fees and compensation are now subject to notice to creditors and approval by the court.[216] A trustee or debtor in possession must obtain court approval to employ attor-

---

[216] *See* 11 U.S.C. §§ 327-331.

neys, accountants, appraisers, auctioneers, or other professional persons.[217] Such professional persons must not hold or represent any interest adverse to the estate and must be disinterested persons. A disinterested person is defined in § 101(14) as a person who is not a creditor, equity security holder, an insider; is not, nor has been for the two years before the bankruptcy filing, a director, officer, or employee of the debtor; and who does not have an interest materially adverse to the estate, or any class of creditors or equity security holder.[218]

Section 328 of the Bankruptcy Code limits the compensation of professional persons. First, court approval of the terms and conditions of the retention is required.[219] Second, the court may depart from the terms of retention after the conclusion of the employment if the terms prove to have been improvident because of factors that were not capable of being anticipated at the outset.[220] The court may also deny compensation if, at any time during the engagement, the professional is not disinterested or holds an interest adverse to the estate with respect to the matter for which the professional is employed.[221]

An attorney representing a debtor must file a statement of compensation paid or agreed to be paid if such payment or agreement was within a year of the filing of the bankruptcy, and the source of such compensation.[222] The proposed arrangement for compensation and all relationships with the creditors, the debtor or other parties must be disclosed under penalty of perjury by the professional to be employed.[223]

The standard for allowance of compensation is set forth explicitly in the Bankruptcy Code. Section 330 provides in pertinent part:

> After notice to the parties in interest and the United States Trustee and a hearing, and subject to sections 326, 328, and 329, the court may award to a trustee, ... , an examiner, ... , a professional person employed under section 327 or 1103 —
>
> (A) reasonable compensation for actual, necessary services rendered by the trustee, examiner, ... , professional person, or attorney and by any paraprofessional person employed by any such person; and
>
> (B) reimbursement for actual, necessary expenses. . . .

---

[217] 11 U.S.C. § 327(a).
[218] 11 U.S.C. § 101(14).
[219] 11 U.S.C. § 328(a).
[220] 11 U.S.C. § 328(a).
[221] 11 U.S.C. § 328(c).
[222] 11 U.S.C. § 329; Fed. R. Bankr. P. 2016.
[223] Fed. R. Bankr. P. 2014(a).

(3) In determining the amount of reasonable compensation to be awarded to an examiner, trustee under chapter 11, or a professional person, the court shall consider the nature, the extent, and the value of such services, taking into account all relevant factors, including —

(A) the time spend on such services;
(B) the rates charged for such services;
(C) whether the services were necessary to the administration of, or beneficial at the time at which the service was rendered toward the completion of a case under this title;
(D) whether the services were performed within a reasonable amount of time commensurate with the complexity, importance, and nature of the problem, issue, or task addressed;
(E) with respect to a professional person, whether the person is board certified or otherwise has demonstrated skill and experience in the bankruptcy field; and
(F) whether the compensation is reasonable, based on the customary compensation charged by comparably skilled practitioners in cases other than cases under this title.[224]

The procedures and limitations on professional compensation in the Bankruptcy Code are detailed and explicit. These provisions essentially nullify any agreement made prior to the commencement of the case among the parties regarding fees. Unless the Bankruptcy Code requirements governing professional fees are evaded, private agreements for payment of fees cannot be enforced under the present law.

A central element of the crime is an agreement, express or implied. The agreement need not be a formal or written agreement; agreements to commit a crime are rarely in writing. The agreement may be an understanding or "handshake."

For a violation of § 155 to occur, there must be an agreement between parties in interest or their attorneys for the purpose of fixing fees to any party in interest or such party's attorney. The statute does not prohibit a party from reaching an agreement with that party's own lawyer regarding fees, *i.e.*, a standard retainer agreement. Section 155 states that it is illegal to enter into an agreement with "another" party, and thus agreements between a client and lawyer are not prohibited. The section bars agreements between parties in

[224] 11 U.S.C. § 330.

interest, or between the attorneys for parties in interest, or between parties in interest and attorneys for other parties in interest.

Section 155 uses the term "parties in interest" and includes in that term, a debtor, creditor, receiver, trustee, or representative of any of them. The use of the term in the Bankruptcy Code context commonly means creditor, trustee, or equity security holder.[225] Potential buyers of assets or competitors are generally not considered parties in interest.

Does § 155 prohibit parties from agreeing on mutual fee caps? This question has not been addressed in the case law. The legislative purpose was to prevent agreements that resulted in inflating fees not those directed at reducing them. An agreement among the parties to establish fee caps would literally fall within the definition of "an agreement . . . for the purpose of fixing fees or compensation." However, such an agreement would rarely be fraudulent, an element of the crime. An agreement between parties to reduce or forego compensation that would otherwise be charged does not involve deceit, and it does not create a benefit to the parties to such an agreement at the expense of other creditors in the case.

---

[225] *See* 11 U.S.C. § 1109(b).

15. Bankruptcy petition preparer fraud: 18 U.S.C. § 156

Section 156 of title 18, United States Code, states:

(a) Definitions.--In this section--

"bankruptcy petition preparer" means a person, other than the debtor's attorney or an employee of such an attorney, who prepares for compensation a document for filing.

"document for filing" means a petition or any other document prepared for filing by a debtor in a United States bankruptcy court or a United States district court in connection with a case under title 11.[226]

(b) Offense.--If a bankruptcy case or related proceeding is dismissed because of a knowing attempt by a bankruptcy petition preparer in any manner to disregard the requirements of title 11, United States Code, or the Federal Rules of Bankruptcy Procedure, the bankruptcy petition preparer shall be fined under this title, imprisoned not more than 1 year, or both.

Violation of this section is a Class A misdemeanor, punishable by up to one year in jail and a fine of up to $100,000, which may be increased to twice the amount of the loss involved in the crime.[227]

During the last two decades, the amount of consumer debt soared. Low-income, high-risk borrowers account for millions (if not billions) of consumer debt. This phenomenon, the explosion of high cost, high risk, consumer credit, has been fueled by the relaxation of laws regulating the consumer credit industry, especially state usury laws. The availability of tax deductible home equity loans to middle income home owners, who are increasingly relying on home equity lines as a lower cost alternative to credit cards, has encouraged the credit industry to reach farther down the income ladder for customers.

---

[226] The use of the word "this" in § 156 ("a case under this title") was a technical error, as the reference is intended to mean title 11, not title 18 where § 156 is contained.

[227] 18 U.S.C. § 3571(b)(5); (d).

The record-high levels of consumer debt have brought record-high levels of consumer bankruptcy filings, most of them Chapter 7 filings by individuals. In 2005, the number of individuals who filed for personal bankruptcy was approximately 2 million. Of these, over 1.6 million were Chapter 7 cases. Many of these potential debtors are easy prey for bankruptcy mill fraud, which § 156 was enacted[228] to address.

Bankruptcy mills lure desperate home owners facing foreclosure with advertisements such as, "Stop foreclosure fast." Bankruptcy may or may not be mentioned in the ads. Sometimes mortgage refinancing is mentioned: "Can't refinance? We can help." Once the client is in the door, the mill induces the client to pay a fee, typically around $1000, in exchange for which the mill will help the client keep her house. The client may or may not realize that a bankruptcy petition is being filed on her behalf. Sometimes mills use phony addresses or Social Security numbers for clients in order to file in a different venue than the client has previously filed or for other deceptive reasons. The client may or may not be aware of fraudulent statements on her petition. In some bankruptcy mill schemes, the clients are misled into believing that the mill is arranging refinancing for them so as to permanently stave off foreclosure. The mill's modus operandi is to file a petition to stop the client's foreclosure, then allowing the case to be eventually automatically dismissed for failure to file schedules or other required papers.[229]

Section 156 seeks to regulate the conduct of a "bankruptcy petition preparer", who is defined in § 156(a) as a non-lawyer[230] who charges a fee and in turn files a bankruptcy petition.[231] Compensation is an element of the offense: A non-lawyer who prepares a petition for someone else without charge is not covered by § 156. However, the petition preparer who charges a fee but characterizes the fee as for services other than the petition preparation, such as assistance in refinancing or other services which are never provided, will be

[228] Section 156 was part of the 1994 bankruptcy amendments (the Bankruptcy Reform Act of 1994, Pub. L. No. 103-394 enacted October 22, 1994).

[229] Under Fed. R. Bankr. P. 1007, the debtor must file bankruptcy schedules and a statement of financial affairs within 15 days of the petition. Failure to do so, barring an order granting an extension of time, will inevitably result in dismissal of the case. Local rules in several jurisdictions provide for automatic dismissal if the lists and schedules required by Fed. R. Bankr. P. 1007 are not filed within the time specified.

[230] It should also be noted that the Bankruptcy Abuse Prevention and Consumer Protection Act of 2005 imposes certain obligations on lawyers that prepare bankruptcy petitions. Section 707(b)(4)(C) provides that the signature of an attorney on a petition is a certification that the attorney has performed a reasonable investigation into circumstances giving rise to the petition and that the attorney has no knowledge after an inquiry that the information in the schedules filed with such petition is incorrect. Attorneys may be subject to assessment of a civil penalty for signing a petition without conducting a reasonable inquiry into the underlying facts.

considered "compensated." The section does not require that the defendant, in order to be deemed a petition preparer, actually file or even fill out the petition. The statute defines "bankruptcy petition preparer" as a person who prepares a document for filing by a debtor. "Prepare" does not necessarily require that the preparer actually file the document, only that she had some role in its preparation. Although this section is still too new to have been interpreted widely by the courts, preparation would appear to include advising a debtor how to fill out and file the bankruptcy petition.

The crux of the crime is the abuse of the bankruptcy process by invoking the automatic stay without any intention of fully pursuing the bankruptcy case. It may seem counterintuitive that filing bankruptcy to stay foreclosure could be criminal: To many debtors and lawyers, the primary reason to file a bankruptcy is to stop a foreclosure. The abuse lies not in the use of bankruptcy to stay creditor action or to protect an asset, but in doing so without complying with the commensurate duties of disclosure of assets and subjecting such assets to a trustee's administration.

Section 156 has not been the subject of any significant reported decisions. Consequently, many questions of interpretation are still open, thus providing room for arguments by both the defense and the prosecution. Some of these questions are:

1. Does receipt by a preparer of consideration other than money constitute "compensation"?
2. Does dismissal pursuant to a requirement of a local rule or standing order trigger a violation?
3. Consider the preparer who tells the debtor that her petition will be dismissed if she does not file bankruptcy schedules. Will this exonerate the preparer because the dismissal is not "because of a knowing attempt by a bankruptcy petition preparer in any matter to disregard the requirements" but rather, because of the client/debtor's own failure to file schedules?
4. If the client or preparer voluntarily dismisses the bankruptcy case, is section 156 avoided?
5. Does ignorance of the law on the part of the preparer absolve her of criminal liability, which requires a *knowing* attempt?

The definitive answers to each of these have not yet been addressed by the courts. The arguments which will likely be advanced by each side as to each of these issues are summarized as follows:

1. The prosecution may argue that the use of the word "compensation" as opposed to "money" or "a fee" is intended to broaden the reach of the statute to any one who receives any money, property, service or any consideration of any kind. The defense may argue that criminal statutes are to be strictly construed and compensation should be limited to its dictionary definition, which is payment of money. The defense argument is the likely winner on appeal.
2. A local rule is not in "title 11, United States Code or the Federal Rules of Bankruptcy Procedure." However, local rules are enacted under the authority of the Federal Rules of Bankruptcy Procedure (Rule 9029) and must be consistent with the Bankruptcy Code and rules. Courts addressing this question are likely to split, with slightly more jurisdictions rejecting local rule violations as a basis of conviction.
3. Alleged "advice" by the preparer that failure to file the schedules will result in dismissal will probably not exonerate the preparer. This question is likely to be seen as a factual issue for a jury, not a question of law for the court.
4. The defense may argue that where the dismissal is voluntary, it is not "because of" a disregard of the bankruptcy requirements. If the prosecution can show that the reason for the voluntary dismissal was the fact that the case was about to be dismissed for failure to follow the bankruptcy requirements, this would tend to show the requisite causation. The resolution of this question is likely to rest on the specific facts of each particular case.
5. Ignorance of the law is no defense. A defendant engaging in the business of bankruptcy petition preparation is on notice of the legal restrictions in this area and her actual knowledge or lack thereof will be no defense.

Relationship to Bankruptcy Code §§ 110 and 526

The Bankruptcy Code contains civil remedies against preparers for debtors whose petitions are dismissed due to disregard of the Bankruptcy Code or Rules. The section provides for compensation to the debtors whose petitions are dismissed, and for their trustees and creditors.[232] The civil remedies available to the debtor, trustee and/or creditor under the Bankruptcy Code include the debtor's actual damages, the greater of $2,000 or twice the amount of the fee paid to preparer, and reasonable attorneys fees of the moving party.

A bankruptcy petition preparer is also a "debt relief agency" and is subject to certain restrictions set forth in 11 U.S.C. § 526. The Bankruptcy Abuse Prevention and Consumer Protection Act of 2005 contains several provisions relating to "debt relief agency" which is defined in 11 U.S.C. § 101(12A) as any person who provides any "bankruptcy assistance" to an "assisted person" in return for the payment of money or other valuable consideration, or who is a bankruptcy petition preparer, with certain exceptions. The term "bankruptcy assistance" is defined expansively and includes legal services.[233] An "assisted person" is any person whose debts consist primarily of consumer debts and whose nonexempt property is less than $150,000.[234]

Section 526 prohibits a "debt relief agency" from, among other things, assisting a person to make a statement in a document filed in a bankruptcy case that is untrue or misleading or from misrepresenting the extent of the services that such agency will provide.[235] If the debt relief agency intentionally or negligently fails to comply with these new requirements, there is potential liability in the amount of fees and charges paid, for actual damages, and for reasonable attorney's fees and costs.[236] In addition to other remedies provided under state law when there is reason to believe that a person has violated these new bankruptcy provisions, an action to enjoin such violation may be brought by a chief law enforcement officer of a state or an official or agency designated by the state.[237] If a person intentionally violates the provisions of this section or engages in a clear and consistent pattern or practice of violating the new provisions, injunctive relief and civil penalties are available.[238]

Civil proceedings brought under these sections must be carefully handled by the preparer's counsel so as not to increase or create criminal consequences. In particular, counsel must be alert to self-incrimination issues and ensure that the Fifth Amendment privilege is not waived.[239] Resolution of such actions where liability exists is often advisable and may even be effective in warding off criminal prosecution, particularly if no criminal investigation is yet underway.

---

232 11 U.S.C. § 110.
233 11 U.S.C. § 101(4A).
234 11 U.S.C. § 101(3).
235 *See* 11 U.S.C. § 526(a)(2) and (3).
236 *See* 11 U.S.C. § 526(c)(2).
237 *See* 11 U.S.C. § 526(c)(3).
238 *See* 11 U.S.C. § 526(c)(5).
239 *See* chapter 33.

16. Bankruptcy fraud: 18 U.S.C. § 157

Section 157 of title 18, United States Code, provides:

> A person who, having devised or intending to devise a scheme or artifice to defraud and for the purpose of executing or concealing such a scheme or artifice or attempting to do so –
>
> (1) files a petition under title 11 including a fraudulent involuntary bankruptcy petition under section 303 of such title; or
> (2) files a document in a proceeding under title 11 including a fraudulent involuntary bankruptcy petition under section 303 of such title; or
> (3) makes a false or fraudulent representation, claim, or promise concerning or in relation to a proceeding under title 11, including a fraudulent involuntary bankruptcy petition under section 303 of such title, at any time before or after the filing of the petition, or in relation to a proceeding falsely asserted to be pending under such title,
>
> shall be fined under this title, imprisoned not more than 5 years, or both.

Violation of § 157 is a Class D felony, and may be punished by up to five years imprisonment, a fine of up to $250,000,[240] or both.

Section 157 was enacted in 1994 and was patterned after the mail and wire fraud statutes.[241] The language and basic elements of § 157 track those statutes. Section 157 addresses the use of a bankruptcy filing or purported bankruptcy filing while devising or intending to devise a "scheme or artifice to defraud," for the purpose of "executing or concealing such a scheme or artifice, or attempting to do so," much like the wire and mail

---

[240] 18 U.S.C § 3571(b)(3). The fine may be increased to $500,000 in the case of a defendant that is an organization. 18 U.S.C. § 3571(c)(3). Further, the fine may be doubled depending on the gain or loss from the crime. 18 U.S.C. § 3571(d).

[241] 18 U.S.C. §§ 1341, 1343. *See* chapter 21.

fraud statutes prohibit the use of the mails or wire communications for such purposes.

The title of this section, bankruptcy fraud, may sound too broad at first glance. Bankruptcy fraud is commonly used to mean any violation of title 18 involving a bankruptcy, as well as any civil fraud in a bankruptcy case. However, the use of the term in § 157 is much more specific. The statute is not designed to address fraud committed during the course of the bankruptcy case, but rather, the fraudulent use of a bankruptcy case, or a fraud concerning a bankruptcy case.

Bankruptcy fraud as defined in § 157 could be viewed as bankruptcy fraud in the pure sense: the use of a bankruptcy filing, or the existence or purported existence of a bankruptcy case, to perpetrate a fraud. This type of fraud is distinguishable from frauds that are committed in anticipation of, or in the process of, a bankruptcy case.

One example of a bankruptcy fraud in the strict sense is a bustout scheme, in which the take-down phase involves a bankruptcy filing. A bustout is a fraud scheme in which a business owner develops a good credit rating so as to induce vendors to deliver inventory on credit. In the take-down phase of the scheme, the inventory is then disposed of, usually sold below cost. The proceeds are then siphoned from the business. A bankruptcy filing is sometimes planned as part of the take-down phase of the scheme.

Another fraud scheme which often has § 157 implications is equity skimming. Skimming usually occurs in the commercial real estate context and refers to the diversion of cash flow, usually rental income, to another entity controlled by the owners. At the same time, the owner does not pay mortgage payments. Often a bankruptcy filing is utilized to stay foreclosure, thus facilitating further skimming of rental income.

Newer fraud schemes utilizing bankruptcy are bankruptcy mill schemes[242] and serial filer schemes. Bankruptcy mills are schemes by unscrupulous individuals who collect fees from would- be debtors, usually home owners facing foreclosure. The mills then file defective bankruptcy petitions to stay the foreclosures. The cases usually end up dismissed for lack of compliance with filing requirements. Such schemes are prohibited by § 156 but under some circumstances § 157 violations may occur. A serial filer is a debtor who files successive bankruptcy petitions to invoke the automatic stay and prevent foreclosure. Each successive bankruptcy case is eventually dismissed, either voluntarily or invol-

---

[242] *See* chapter 15.

untarily. Despite prohibitions on refiling,[243] the serial filer continues to file petitions, frustrating his mortgage holders and other creditors.

An actual bankruptcy filing need not exist. Making a fraudulent misrepresentation, as part of a fraudulent scheme, that a bankruptcy case was filed or is pending, is also prohibited by § 157.

Intent to defraud

A specific intent to defraud is required for a conviction under § 157. The element of specific intent to defraud tracks the intent requirement of the mail and wire fraud statutes. Intent to defraud means that the defendant intended to do something unlawful, *i.e.,* that he acted with the intent to defraud or deceive.[244]

The definition of "defraud" is broad and is not limited to the traditional legal causes of action for fraud. "A scheme or artifice to defraud" has been defined as intentional deception practiced to induce another to part with property or to surrender some legal right.[245] Defrauding implies "a departure from fundamental honesty, moral uprightness, or fair play and candid business dealings in the general and business life of the community."[246]

Bankruptcy integral to fraud

In order for a violation to occur, the purpose of the conduct, *i.e.*, the filing of a bankruptcy petition or document in a bankruptcy case, or the false or fraudulent representation, claim or promise with respect to a bankruptcy case, must be an integral part of the scheme to defraud or its concealment.

There is no bright line test for what constitutes an "integral part." The legislative history provides examples which shed some light on this question. The House Report indicates that a person who submits a false financial statement and later files bankruptcy does not violate § 157 if he did not plan the bankruptcy as part of a scheme in connection with the false financial statement. Similarly, a person who makes a false statement about a bankruptcy proceeding (*i.e.*, a statement that a case was filed that in fact was not, or a statement that a discharge was entered that in fact was not), would not be liable under § 157 if the dissemination of the false information was not part of the fraudulent scheme.[247] It is less clear whether the bankruptcy filing must be a material part

---

[243] *See, e.g.*, 11 U.S.C. § 109(g).

[244] *See* chapter 5.

[245] *United States v. Frost*, 125 F.3d 346, 371 (6th Cir. 1997), *cert. denied*, 525 U.S. 810 (1998).

[246] *Frost*, 125 F.3d at 371; *United States v. Van Dyke*, 605 F.2d 220, 225 (6th Cir. 1979).

[247] H.R. Rep. No. 103-835, at 57-58 (1994).

of the fraud scheme. While the legislative history contains some discussion of materiality, there is nothing in the statute that suggests any materiality requirement, *i.e.*, that the bankruptcy filing be a material aspect of the fraud.

Culpability under § 157 is not limited to debtors. Creditors or even parties unrelated to a bankruptcy proceeding can be liable under section 157. Creditors who attempt to collect debts which have been discharged by misrepresenting the fact that a bankruptcy was filed or discharge was entered may be culpable under § 157. Section 157 has been used to prosecute creditors who attempt to collect prepetition debts by inducing debtors to sign reaffirmation agreements which must be filed with, and in some instances, approved by, the court to be valid, and then attempting to enforce these agreements despite noncompliance with these requirements.[248]

---

[248] 11 U.S.C. § 524(c).

PART 3

RELATED OFFENSES

17. Statutory overlap and multiplicity

The provisions of the Bankruptcy Criminal Code (chapter 9 of title 18, United States Code) are not the only statutory provisions utilized in the prosecution of bankruptcy crimes. Conduct that constitutes a crime under the Bankruptcy Criminal Code may also be proscribed under other provisions of the Federal Criminal Code. A defendant charged with a bankruptcy crime may be subject to an ongoing FBI investigation of suspected crimes unrelated to any bankruptcy case. Conversely, a criminal referral by a United States trustee or bankruptcy judge may lead to an investigation into other suspected crimes that are not necessarily related to a bankruptcy. If the investigation ultimately leads to charges being brought, the indictment will most likely include both bankruptcy and other counts. The offenses most frequently overlapping with chapter 9 violations include mail, wire, or bank fraud, false statements, and perjury.

Frequently indictments will allege that a defendant engaged in one or more transactions, some of which may not be directly related to a bankruptcy, which were part of an overall criminal scheme. Fed. R. Crim. P. 8 contemplates and permits joinder of offenses in the same indictment in such circumstances:

> The indictment or information may charge a defendant in separate counts with 2 or more offenses if the offenses charged—whether felonies or misdemeanors or both—are of the same or similar character, or are based on the same act or transaction, or are connected with or constitute parts of a common scheme or plan.

The same set of facts can often give rise to more than one statutory violation. As a general rule, however, a defendant cannot be charged with multiplicitous counts, *i.e.*, charged with more than one crime based on the identical conduct. Multiplicity violates the Double Jeopardy Clause,[249] which protects not only subsequent prosecutions for the same offense, but multiple punishments for the same offense.[250]

The Fifth Circuit recently addressed the question of multiplicity:

> Where the question of multiplicity arises because of overlapping statutory provisions, "[t]he test for determining whether the same act or transaction constitutes two offenses or only one is whether conviction under each statutory provision requires proof of an additional fact which the other does not." (citations omitted). Where, on the other hand, the question of multiplicity arises because of a multipart transaction, the question becomes "'whether separate and distinct prohibited acts, made punishable by law, have been committed.'" (citations omitted).[251]

One example of overcharging is a situation in which one set of actions is charged under several subsections of § 152, or where two counts of concealment are charged for concealing the same asset before and after filing bankruptcy.[252] There are, however, some significant exceptions to the general rule against overcharging in the bankruptcy context.

Consider the situation in which a debtor fails to list an asset in his bankruptcy schedules and is charged both with concealment and with making a false declaration. Despite the fact that the identical conduct is at issue, this has generally not been considered overcharging.[253] The rationale is that concealment is a continuing offense, such that the moment after the false schedules were filed, the debtor was in the process of committing a separate crime — concealment. Another difficult question is whether the omission of two assets constitutes two concealments or two false declarations. Generally the duties to disclose all information and to file complete and truthful schedules are considered "all or nothing," *e.g.*, omission of two assets will be considered one offense. However, this principle is not uniformly followed, and as a result, it is unsettled whether separate counts of concealment for each asset concealed must be dismissed as duplicative.[254]

---

[249] U.S. CONST. amend V.

[250] *United States v. Cluck*, 87 F.3d 138, 140 (5th Cir. 1996).

[251] *United States v. Cluck*, 143 F.3d 174, 179 (5th Cir. 1998), *cert. denied*, 525 U.S. 1073 (1999).

[252] *United States v. Moss*, 562 F.2d 155 (2d Cir. 1977).

[253] *Cluck*, 143 F.3d 174.

[254] *Compare Moss*, 562 F.2d 155 with *Edwards v. United States*, 265 F.2d 302, 306 (9th Cir. 1959).

The question of multiplicity is often raised where a debtor tells the same lie under oath on more than one occasion, such as a series of adjourned § 341 meetings. In *United States v. Graham,*[255] the debtor, a trust and estate lawyer, failed to list his interest in a group of apartment buildings known as Megra Properties, although he did list Megra Properties as collateral for a secured debt. At Graham's § 341 meeting, he testified under oath that he did not list an interest in Megra Properties because it had been transferred to a trust for his son before the bankruptcy filing. Subsequently, Graham filed an amended schedule, which also failed to list his interest in Megra Properties. After his chapter 11 case was converted to chapter 7, he testified at a second § 341 meeting that he did not list his interest in Megra Properties because he had transferred it to his son's trust prior to bankruptcy. At a third creditor's meeting, Graham repeated the same statement, this time testifying further that he had prepared the trust document himself before witnesses.

Graham was later charged with one count of concealment and three counts of making a false statement under section 152. Graham was found guilty on two counts of making a false statement. On appeal, the Eighth Circuit found that the district court erred in not dismissing two counts of the false statement charges as multiplicitous. The court noted that the statements made at all three creditors meetings, although made to three different individuals, the United States trustee and two creditors' attorneys, were practically identical. Quoting *United States v. Feldhacker*, the court stated:

> [S]eparate false statements may be charged in separate perjury counts if they require different factual proof of their falsehood, notwithstanding their relationship to a common nexus of fact.[256]

The same factual proof of the falseness applied to all three counts. Further, the court viewed Graham's repetition of the same false statement as "adding nothing further to harm the bankruptcy action; the harm was done from the outset."[257]

A different situation is presented, however, when two different assets or two different false statements are involved. In that case, "separate and distinct facts" are involved, and charging with separate counts is not multiplicitous.[258]

---

[255] *United States v. Graham*, 60 F.3d 463 (8th Cir. 1995).

[256] *Feldhacker*, 849 F.2d 293, 297 (8th Cir. 1988).

[257] *Graham*, 60 F.3d at 467.

[258] *United States v. Melton*, 763 F.2d 401 (11th Cir. 1985).

When the elements of the crime are not identical, the same conduct which constitutes an offense under the Bankruptcy Criminal Code may also be charged under another provision of the Federal Criminal Code, such as false statements, wire and mail fraud, or perjury. The Federal Criminal Code can also be used to charge conduct that constitutes a bankruptcy crime in the broad sense but does not meet the elements of any chapter 9 offense. Where conduct violates more than one statutory provision, one section may more accurately reflect the character of the crime. For instance, advertising by a bankruptcy mill on the internet may be considered both bankruptcy petition preparer fraud under § 156 and wire fraud under § 1343. However, it could be argued that § 156 more accurately describes the crime whereas the application of § 1343 is more remote (albeit not farfetched). On the other hand, it could be argued that wire fraud is the more appropriate charge because the use of the internet is central to the fraud.

Where the same act could be considered criminal under more than one provision of title 18, the determination by the government of which offense to charge will depend on the differences in the elements of proof needed. The level of punishment will also be factor. In the case of the Internet bankruptcy mill, for instance, wire fraud is a felony with a statutory sentence of up to five years, whereas bankruptcy petition preparer fraud is a Class A misdemeanor.

The prosecutor's choice of statutory provision will be significant to a defendant for many reasons, not the least of which is the applicability of asset forfeiture. The federal government, under § 981 of title 18, United States Code, may seize property involved in a money laundering transaction, which constitutes or is derived from proceeds traceable to certain criminal violations, including false statements to a bank, bank fraud, or wire or mail fraud involving a bank, or which represents or is traceable to the gross receipts obtained from false statements, mail fraud, or wire fraud.[259]

Asset forfeiture is not available to the government with respect to transactions in violation of, or proceeds traceable to violations of, the Bankruptcy Criminal Code. However, conduct that involves bankruptcy fraud is sometimes part of a scheme or transaction that involves money laundering, bank fraud, wire fraud, mail fraud, or false statements. In such cases, a defendant may face indictment on counts of both bankruptcy fraud and bank, wire, or mail fraud, as well as civil forfeiture.

---

[259] 18 U.S.C. § 981(a)(1).

18. Aiding and abetting:18 U.S.C. § 2; principals and accessories: 18 U.S.C. § 3; and misprision: 18 U.S.C. § 4

Aiding and abetting

Section 2 of title 18, United States Code, states:

> (a) Whoever commits an offense against the United States or aids, abets, counsels, commands, induces or procures its commission is punishable as a principal.
> (b) Whoever willfully causes an act to be done which if directly performed by him or another would be an offense against the United States, is punishable as a principal.[260]

Section 2 in itself does not define conduct that is criminal; it must be considered in conjunction with some substantive offense. The section may only be applied to assisting in conduct that itself is illegal. In order for a defendant to be convicted of aiding and abetting, the government must prove beyond a reasonable doubt that a crime was committed, although not necessarily who committed it. In order for the government to obtain a conviction of aiding and abetting a bankruptcy crime, the commission of a substantive bankruptcy crime must be proven. Paradoxically, a defendant may be convicted for aiding and abetting a crime even where the principal has been acquitted.[261]

The "aiding and abetting" provision of § 2(a) makes it a crime to assist in a crime even if the defendant only contributes to one aspect or element of the crime and could not be convicted of committing the underlying crime itself. The government must prove that the defendant knowingly and intentionally participated in the commission of the crime. The essence of aiding and abet-

[260] 18 U.S.C. § 2.
[261] *Standefer v. United States*, 447 U.S. 10, 19 (1980).

ting was described colorfully by the Supreme Court, quoting Judge Learned Hand:

> In order to aid and abet another to commit a crime it is necessary that a defendant "in some sort associate himself with the venture, that he participate in it as something that he wishes to bring about, that he seek by his action to make it succeed."[262]

Corporate officers and counsel who assist in the commission of a bankruptcy fraud are logical targets for prosecution under § 2. An example is a bankruptcy lawyer who assists his client in concealment of an asset through the use of a vague description of the asset, which obscures its value.[263] In this situation, under a § 2 analysis, the attorney is equally guilty as his client, the primary perpetrator or principal. For a successful conviction, the government need only prove that: (1) a bankruptcy crime was committed; (2) the defendant aider/abettor knowingly associated himself with the actor or entity committing the crime and knowingly participated in the commission of the crime; and (3) that the accused possessed the requisite mental state as the principal actor.[264] In the case of aiding and abetting a concealment in violation of §§ 2 and 152, the essential criminal intent is "knowingly" and "fraudulently."[265]

The required mental state for prosecutions under § 2, in tandem with the substantive bankruptcy offenses found in §§ 152 through 157, is clear: "an aider and abettor 'must share in the principal's essential criminal intent'".[266]

In *United States v. Tashjian*, an illustrative case on this point, the Second Circuit reversed, in part, a conviction premised on §§ 2 and 152 where the government failed to prove the requisite element of intent. Tashjian and Campbell were among fifteen defendants named in a twenty-four count indictment. The indictment was based on allegations of a bustout enterprise. As part of the scheme, Tashjian purchased inventory from Weiner, the principal actor in the scheme and an unindicted co-conspirator. Weiner operated a retail discount store, as a bustout. Weiner obtained merchandize on credit for Abington Discount without any intention of paying for it, and with the view of eventually putting Abington Discount through bankruptcy. Tashjian proposed an ar-

---

[262] *Nye & Nissen v. United States*, 336 U.S. 613, 619 (1949).

[263] *See* chapter 6.

[264] *See United States v. Dolt*, 27 F.3d 235, 238 (6th Cir. 1994); *Nye & Nissen*, 336 U.S. at 618.

[265] *See United States v. Weinstein*, 834 F.2d 1454, 1461-62 (9th Cir. 1988); *United States v. Webster*, 125 F.3d 1024, 1034 (7th Cir. 1997). *See* chapter 6 (Intent).

[266] *United States v. Tashjian*, 660 F.2d 829, 842 (1st Cir. 1981).

rangement to Weiner whereby Tashjian would buy the inventory at an agreed, below-cost price. Weiner also ordered inventory ostensibly in the name of "Gift Box," a fictional entity, and sold that inventory to Tashjian as well. The indictment charged Tashjian with aiding and abetting a violation of § 152 in connection with the sale of the Gift Box inventory.

The Second Circuit affirmed the convictions with respect to the defendants' below-cost purchase of goods from Abington directly, but reversed charges of aiding and abetting where Tashjian purchased goods from Weiner that were ordered in the name of Gift Box. At trial, Weiner testified that the purchases by Tashjian and Campbell for Gift Box were separate and distinct from the fraudulent scheme in contemplation of Abington Discount's bankruptcy. The court, in reversing Tashjian's conviction on a count related to the Gift Box inventory, stated:

> The appellants, on the other hand, argue that because the property referred to in the count, as interpreted by the district court, was not the property of the potential bankrupt, Count Five did not allege a violation of 18 U.S.C. § 152. We need not venture into the intricacies of property rights because we find a much simpler reason to conclude that the indiscriminate marriage of Abington Discount and Gift Box in one count requires reversal of the convictions.[267]

Therefore, the defendant could not have had the requisite criminal intent.

The second prong of § 2 prohibits the act of causing another, most often an innocent intermediary, to commit a criminal offense.[268] Causing means acting through an agent or one who procures or brings about the commission of a crime.[269] Further, under § 2(b), it is no defense that the accused may not himself be legally capable of committing the substantive offense, or that the unwitting "pawn" whom the defendant has caused to do the criminal act is, himself, guiltless of any crime.[270]

Additionally, § 2(b) adds the element of "willfulness." This is often significant in prosecutions where § 2(b) is charged in tandem with section 1001 (false statements), [271] and the underlying offense involves complex or technical regulatory statutes which carry the risk that innocent persons may be charged.

---

267 *Tashjian*, 660 F.2d at 841.

268 18 U.S.C. § 2(b).

269 *United States v. Levine*, 457 F.2d 1186, 1188 (10th Cir. 1972).

270 *United States v. Lester*, 363 F.2d 68, 73 (6th Cir. 1966).

271 *See* chapter 20.

In such cases, even though § 2(b) is a "general intent" crime, the government may be required to prove a higher level of intent to satisfy the willfulness element than is typically required for such prosecutions, *e.g.*, that the defendant knew of the illegality of his actions. [272]

In the context of a bankruptcy offense, a prosecution specifically under § 2(b) is uncommon. The government is not required to specify in an indictment which prong of § 2 is being charged. Further, many circuits have held that "all charges in an indictment carry a § 2 charge," and "an indictment charging aiding and abetting may be proven by demonstrating that the aider and abettor was in fact a principal."[273]

In *United States v. Knoll*, for example, defendant Knoll, an attorney, was charged and convicted with aiding and abetting Gleave, a friend and former client, in violation of 18 U.S.C. §§ 2 and 152. The underlying cause of action involved two bank accounts opened in the Cayman Islands which were used to fund an overseas company, Atlantis International, Ltd.

As a personal favor to Knoll, who could not establish the required credit due to a prior financial problem, Gleave established two foreign bank accounts: a personal account in Gleave's name, and a corporate account in the name of an entity yet to be formed. Defendant Gleave instructed the bank to close the personal account as soon as the entity was incorporated. In the meantime, Gleave was involved with a divorce proceeding in the United States. Shortly after Gleave opened the offshore accounts, Knoll urged Gleave, as his attorney, to file for chapter 11 bankruptcy to protect himself in the event his wife was awarded his assets, thereby precluding his ability to satisfy his creditors.

Gleave followed Knoll's advice, and signed a Statement of Financial Affairs[274] prepared by Knoll which was filed in a bankruptcy court. Unbeknownst to Gleave, one of the accounts opened in the Cayman Islands, the personal account in Gleave's name, was never closed. Instead, Knoll managed the accounts without Gleave's knowledge. Accordingly, on Gleave's Statement of Financial Affairs, neither of the two accounts in the Caymans was disclosed.

The indictment charged Knoll with aiding and abetting Gleave's false financial statement in violation of 18 U.S.C. §§ 2 and 152, a charge on which Gleave was ultimately acquitted. On appeal, Knoll argued that his conviction

---

[272] *See, e.g., United States v. Curran*, 20 F.3d 560 (3d Cir. 1994)(Section 1001 charged in tandem with § 2(b) for causing another to make a false statement to the Federal Election Commission requires government to prove that the defendant knew his conduct was unlawful); *but see United States v. Hsia*, 176 F.3d 517 (D.C. Cir. 1999).

[273] *United States v. Knoll*, 16 F.3d 1313, 1323 (2d Cir. 1994), *cert. denied* 522 U.S. 1118 (1998) (citations omitted).

[274] Official Bankruptcy Form 7. *See* App. H.

under § 2 could not stand due to Gleave's acquittal, and, as required under § 2(a), a bankruptcy crime was not committed. The Second Circuit rejected Knoll's argument and upheld Knoll's conviction under § 2(b) "[s]ince a person may be convicted as a principal for causing an innocent intermediary to violate the law."[275]

Knoll is illustrative of the exposure that bankruptcy lawyers, in particular, face under § 2. Even though the client may be acquitted of the substantive offense, the lawyer can be held as the principal. This would occur most often in situations where an innocent intermediary relies on the lawyer's advice, whether in the professional or personal capacity.[276]

Principals and accessories; misprision of felony

Section 3 of Title 18 provides:

> Whoever, knowing that an offense against the United States has been committed, receives, relieves, comforts or assists the offender in order to hinder or prevent his apprehension, trial or punishment, is an accessory after the fact.
>
> Except as otherwise expressly provided by any Act of Congress, an accessory after the fact shall be imprisoned not more than one-half the maximum term or (notwithstanding section 3571) fined not more than one-half of the maximum fine prescribed for the punishment of the principal, or both; or if the principal is punishable by life imprisonment or death, the accessory shall be imprisoned not more than 15 years.

Section 4 of title 18 provides:

> Whoever, having knowledge of the actual commission of a felony cognizable by a court of the United States, conceals and does not as soon as possible make known the same to some judge or other person in civil or military authority under the United States, shall be fined under this title or imprisoned not more than three years, or both.

At first glance, the offenses of accessory after the fact and misprision appear quite similar. Both involve the concealment of a criminal offense committed by a principal actor, and both require knowledge that the underlying offense was

---

[275] *Knoll*, 16 F.3d at 1323.

[276] *Knoll*, 16 F.3d at 1323. *But see Tashjian*, 660 F.2d at 842.

committed. In fact, it is likely that in most instances of misprision, the offender is also an accessory after the fact. The sections are distinguished by different elements of proof. Section 3 requires a purposeful relationship between the acts of the offender and the principal accessory.[277] The accessory must also commit an affirmative act; that is, to receive, relieve, comfort, or assist the principal offender in order to hinder or prevent his apprehension, trial or punishment.[278] Section 4, which criminalizes the concealment of a felony, does not require an intent to benefit the principal offender, although such benefit likely results.[279]

The crimes of misprision and accessory after the fact are not as common in the bankruptcy setting as charges of aiding and abetting. Nevertheless, §§ 3 and 4 will be utilized in certain cases where the elements of section 2 are not met. Consider the case of the debtor who files a chapter 7 bankruptcy petition and conceals one of his assets, a valuable intellectual property license, with the assistance of his bankruptcy counsel, attorney A. After the bankruptcy case is closed, the debtor later retains attorney B to set up a new entity, in which the debtor will hold an indirect interest, to acquire the license which was concealed. In the course of the transaction, the debtor discloses to attorney B that the purpose of this arrangement is to insure that creditors in his bankruptcy case do not discover his interest in the license.

By assisting in the transaction, attorney B, who had no part in the commission of the § 152 offense in the beginning, may be charged with misprision and being accessory after the fact. Attorney B's conduct also has ethical ramifications.[280] Attorney B may face felony charges regardless of whether debtor is convicted of the underlying crime.[281]

---

[277] *See United States v. Daddano*, 432 F.2d 1119, 1128-29 (7th Cir. 1970).
[278] 18 U.S.C. § 3.
[279] *Daddano*, 432 F.2d at 1129.
[280] *See* chapter 38.
[281] *See United States v. Walker*, 415 F.2d 530 (9th Cir. 1969).

19. Conspiracy: 18 U.S.C. § 371

The government may use § 371, the conspiracy statute, to charge those involved in the commission of a bankruptcy crime. Section 371 states, in relevant part:

> If two or more persons conspire either to commit any offense against the United States, or to defraud the United States, or any agency thereof in any manner or for any purpose, and one or more of such persons do any act to effect the object of the conspiracy, each shall be fined under this title or imprisoned not more than five years, or both. . . .

The conspiracy statute makes it a crime for two or more persons to agree to commit a crime. To establish a conspiracy, the government must prove that "an agreement existed between two or more people to commit an offense and that one or more of the conspirators acted to affect the object of the conspiracy."[282] Agreements to commit a crime do not resemble agreements in the usual legal sense. There is virtually never a formal written document, nor is such an agreement necessary. Conspiratorial agreements may be proven by circumstantial evidence.[283]

To be guilty of conspiracy, a conspirator does not have to be involved or even know about every aspect of the crime.[284] In fact, even minor players can be charged with conspiracy. However, the government must prove beyond a reasonable doubt that the defendant had knowledge of the essential object of the conspiracy.[285]

Section 371 is often used to reach defendants whose conduct falls technically outside of chapter 9, or where the facts will not support the intent or other elements of a substantive offense under chapter 9. The application of § 371 in

---

[282] *United States v. Dolan*, 120 F.3d 856, 868 (8th Cir. 1997).

[283] *Dolan*, 120 F.3d at 868; *Henderson v. United States*, 815 F.2d 1189, 1191-92 (8th Cir. 1987).

[284] *United States v. Brown*, 943 F.2d 1246, 1250-51 (10th Cir. 1991); *United States v. Zimmerman*, 943 F.2d 1204, 1209 (10th Cir. 1991).

[285] *See Henderson*, 815 F.2d at 1191-92.

the bankruptcy context is best illustrated by cases in which bankruptcy counsel has been charged with conspiracy to commit a bankruptcy crime because of that counsel's advice and participation in the bankruptcy fraud of a client. One of the most infamous of such cases was *United States v. Levine.*[286]

Gary and Marcee Levine orchestrated complex bankruptcy crimes over an extended period of time.[287] The story of the Levines and their lawyers is a frightening example of a bankruptcy representation gone irredeemably wrong. David Schwartz and Steven Zimmerman were two law partners in the firm of Zimmerman & Schwartz, in which Tom Brown was an associate. The Levines consulted the firm for advice regarding their financial problems in connection with the Levines' furniture business, Sofa Gallery, Inc. Schwartz handled the case apparently because Zimmerman was too busy and had an upcoming vacation planned.

As part of their strategy to deal with their financial problems, and part of their scheme to defraud their creditors, the Levines induced their secured creditors to agree to a liquidation sale, and to advance additional funding so that Sofa Gallery could buy additional inventory for the sale. Unbeknownst to the secured creditors, the Levines entered into an undisclosed kickback arrangement with the liquidator. The liquidator was to pay one third of his commission to Marcee Levine. This kickback was being paid to Marcee and not Gary to insulate the funds from Gary's imminent bankruptcy filing. These funds, as well as accounts receivable proceeds collected before the sale, were deposited into the client trust account at the Zimmerman & Schwartz law firm.

The Levines accomplished their scheme with the assistance of their lawyers and accountants. The attorneys set up the client trust account and according to Mr. Levine, suggested that the Levines "hide" and "wash" funds through the account. The Levines' attorneys also prepared transfer documents for properties which were fraudulently transferred as part of the scheme to hide assets from creditors. Two law partners, one of whom had only indirect responsibility over the Levine's representation, and an associate who handled several transactional aspects of the case, were convicted of conspiracy to commit a bankruptcy crime. The conviction of the partner who was not proven to have direct involvement was later overturned on appeal.[288]

The core of the conspiracy charges was that the trust account at Zimmerman & Schwartz was used as a vehicle to conceal the Levine's funds from the bank-

---

[286] *United States v. Levine*, 970 F.2d 681 (10th Cir. 1992).

[287] The *Levine* case is discussed further in chapter 25 and 31.

[288] The fact that the partner was both charged and convicted at trial demonstrates the risk of having even indirect responsibility for a client engaged in bankruptcy fraud.

ruptcy court and creditors in the bankruptcy proceedings. The evidence introduced at trial established that over $200,000 from the liquidation sale and from preliquidation accounts receivable were deposited into the account, with periodic payments drawn on the account and issued to Marcee Levine. The convictions of partners David Schwartz and Steven Zimmerman, and associate attorney Tom Brown, stemmed from their knowledge and involvement in the concealment scheme.

The government's case against Steven Zimmerman, the convicted partner who had only indirect knowledge of the Levine conspiracy, was tenuous at best. Testimony at trial established only minor contacts between Zimmerman and Schwartz after the initial representation of the Levines was established. In fact, the prosecution's case was premised entirely upon circumstantial evidence.

On review of Zimmerman's conviction, the Tenth Circuit concluded that although his involvement was attenuated, the evidence set forth by the government, when considered as a whole, was sufficient to convict him. The government introduced evidence of a conversation between Zimmerman and Schwartz in which Schwartz apparently sought Zimmerman's advice as to whether accounts receivable arising prior to liquidation could be placed in the firm trust account. Although Zimmerman responded that he thought this was appropriate, he instructed Schwartz, the principal in the scheme, to research the matter. Another incident, which was of particular importance to the Court, was a client billing entry for a conference call with the Levines. On that same day, two checks totaling almost $15,000 were drawn on the law firm trust account and issued to Marcee Levine.

The prosecution offered testimony concerning another contact between Zimmerman, Schwartz, and Brown which was overheard by another associate at the firm. The associate, Robert Breindel, testified that Brown confronted both Schwartz and Zimmerman in the hallway of the firm in connection with the Levines' trust account. Apparently, Brown questioned both partners concerning the failure of the firm to maintain a ledger of the Levines' trust account, and the firm's practice of placing the proceeds of accounts receivable in the account. The "smoking gun" was a conversation that occurred shortly thereafter: Breindel testified that, in connection with the accounts receivable, he overheard Zimmerman say: "We had agreed from the beginning that's how we were going to handle it."[289] Breindel's testimony was never corroborated, but the court nevertheless permitted the prosecution to draw conclusions as to the relevance of Zimmerman's statement and the context in which it must have occurred.

---

[289] *Zimmerman*, 943 F.2d at 1209.

The court recognized that the threshold of sufficient evidence presented in the government's case against Zimmerman was the bare minimum upon which a jury could convict. However, the Tenth Circuit found that "even absent direct evidence . . . regarding [Zimmerman's] role as a senior partner, sufficient circumstantial evidence was introduced for a reasonable jury to convict . . ."[290]

Tom Brown, the associate working under David Schwartz on the Levine's case who was tried concurrently with Zimmerman, was also convicted in connection with the concealment scheme.[291] Unlike Zimmerman, Brown's involvement was direct. While Zimmerman's conviction was obtained through circumstantial evidence in connection with his position as a secondary actor and senior partner of the firm, Brown's conviction stemmed from his active involvement in the Levines' case. Brown drafted a quitclaim deed for the Levines that was part of an illegal transfer, and drew up articles of incorporation for a company that illegally capitalized funds in connection with the Levines' furniture store.[292] Brown also attended a deposition with Gary Levine in which complete information was not provided to the bankruptcy trustee. The Tenth Circuit found that the prosecution established that Brown was aware of the misuse of the trust account, and, as the Levines' attorney, that he knowingly and actively participated in the conspiracy.[293]

Another example of the use of § 371 to charge bankruptcy counsel for his participation in a client's crime is the case of Gary L. Dolan.[294] Dolan represented David R. Anderson in Anderson's bankruptcy proceeding. Dolan was Anderson's counsel in business litigation matters previously but had never before handled a bankruptcy case as debtor's counsel. Anderson engaged in two illegal transactions which became the focus of the case against Dolan.

---

[290] *Zimmerman*, 943 F.2d at 1210.

[291] The broad sweep of the conspiracy statute, as evidenced by *Zimmerman* and *Brown*, is often criticized, but not vitiated, for its relative vagueness. *See, e.g., United States v. Cueto*, 151 F.3d 620, 634-35 (7th Cir. 1998), *cert. denied,* 526 U.S. 1016 (1999) (the fact that section 371 is often applied to agreements not "expressly anticipated by Congress nor specifically articulated in the statute" does not create problems of ambiguity, nor does it render the statute void for vagueness).

[292] *Brown*, 943 F.2d at 1249. *See* chapter 11.

[293] At the trial of Zimmerman and Brown, the government introduced statements of two bankruptcy judges made in the Levine's earlier bankruptcy proceedings. These statements were particularly damaging as they concerned the law firm's potential involvement in the conspiracy. On appeal, the Tenth Circuit reversed both convictions. Of great significance to the court was the introduction of the bankruptcy judges' statements, which went to the very heart of the crimes for which Zimmerman and Brown were tried. The Tenth Circuit found that the introduction of the statements against Zimmerman and Brown constituted reversible error.

[294] *Dolan*, 120 F.3d 856.

First, Anderson owned a Ferrari worth $85,000, which was collateral for a $27,000 loan. Thus, Anderson had equity of $58,000 in the vehicle. Anderson did not initially list the Ferrari as an asset in his bankruptcy schedules. Anderson attempted to persuade the secured creditor to change the title on the car to Anderson's son. When the secured creditor refused, Anderson then offered the secured creditor an arrangement whereby the creditor could repossess the car and sell it to an individual of Anderson's choosing for the balance of the loan, which was obviously for less than the value of the car. The secured creditor declined that arrangement as well. Subsequently, Anderson transferred the title to the Ferrari to his son. Evidence presented at Dolan's trial, including the testimony of the secured creditor and his lawyer, showed that Dolan knew of the Ferrari and its transfer after bankruptcy without court approval.

Second, Anderson did not list his ownership interest in a corporation, nor did he list his claims in a pending lawsuit in which he and the corporation were plaintiffs. The lawsuit was settled, Anderson received $1.9 million and Dolan received $50,000 as a bonus. Dolan apparently had misgivings about these transactions but did not disclose them, allegedly because he believed that the Code of Professional Responsibility prevented him from doing so.

A major thrust of the government's case against Dolan was the fact that he had repeatedly told creditors that Anderson was unable to pay any funds toward creditors' claims, despite Dolan's knowledge that Anderson had received $1.9 million in settlement proceeds and had access to a Ferrari in which he had approximately $58,000 in equity. Dolan inducted one creditor to settle a claim for only $5,000 by representing that that was all Anderson could afford. Based on the settlements with various creditors, Dolan obtained from the court a dismissal of Anderson's bankruptcy case. In upholding Dolan's conviction, the court's recitation of the evidence, which was sufficient to sustain the verdict, is illustrative of the unfolding of a conspiracy to commit a bankruptcy crime:

- Dolan talked to Anderson about whether to disclose certain assets in the bankruptcy case.
- Dolan knew Anderson owned the Ferrari and transferred it after bankruptcy.
- Dolan knew Anderson received $1.9 in settlement proceeds and signed an acknowledgment authorizing the payment to Anderson.
- Dolan and Anderson failed to disclose the assets throughout Anderson's bankruptcy.

- Dolan heard Anderson lie under oath by testifying that he did not receive any settlement proceeds personally.
- Dolan repeatedly told creditors that Anderson lacked funds to satisfy their claims.
- Dolan sought dismissal of Anderson's bankruptcy without providing the court and creditors essential information about Anderson's assets.

In order for a conspiracy to occur, at least one of the co-conspirators must commit an overt act. A co-conspirator is considered an agent of the other co-conspirators, and thus is it not necessary to have personally committed the overt act in order to be charged, as long as one of the co-conspirators has committed an overt act. Overt acts are acts that further the ends of the conspiracy. An overt act, in itself, does not need to be illegal. For example, in a conspiracy to commit a bankruptcy crime similar to the Levine/Zimmerman/Brown case, the overt acts could include the filing of the petition and opening bank accounts. Dolan's procurement of the dismissal of the bankruptcy case was held to be an overt act in furtherance of the conspiracy to commit concealment of assets.[295]

A defendant can be convicted of a bankruptcy crime even if no bankruptcy crime ever occurs. The core of the crime is the goal of the conspiracy, *e.g.*, the knowing and willful intention to commit an offense against the United States. Unlike § 2, it is not necessary for a principal actor to bring the crime to fruition. Indeed, one can be guilty of conspiracy simply by knowingly and willfully entering into an agreement with one other person to conceal funds from a bankruptcy trustee provided that one of the co-conspirators commit an overt act, such as drafting a check or transferring funds in furtherance of that goal.

Unlike most chapter 9 offenses, which contain the element of "knowing and fraudulent", the intent element of conspiracy is mere willfulness. The government is not required to show any intent on the part of the defendant to defraud or deceive the court or the creditors. However, the element of willfulness includes knowledge. In other words, the government is required to prove that the defendant knew that the object of the conspiracy was to evade the bankruptcy law, conceal assets from creditors, or other unlawful goal. The defendant must have knowledge that he is joining a conspiracy, and that he is involving himself in a scheme to break the law.

---

[295] Dolan's statements to various creditors that Anderson lacked funds was held to be aiding and abetting in the concealment of assets.

Although proof of knowledge that the intended act is illegal is not enough to convict under § 371, such knowledge coupled with proof that the accused acted intentionally is sufficient. It is not necessary that the defendant be aware of "all the details or all the members of the conspiracy," "provided . . . that the defendant knowingly and voluntarily became part of the conspiracy."[296] In fact, as recognized by the Tenth Circuit in *Zimmerman*, "[t]he connection of the defendant to the conspiracy need only be slight, if there is sufficient evidence to establish that connection beyond a reasonable doubt."[297]

---

[296] *Zimmerman*, 943 F.2d at 1209.
[297] *Zimmerman*, 943 F.2d at 1209.

20. False statements: 18 U.S.C. §§ 1001, 1014, and 1032

Section 1001

Section 1001 of title 18, United States Code, states:

> (a) Except as otherwise provided in this section, whoever, in any matter within the jurisdiction of the executive, legislative, or judicial branch of the Government of the United Sates, knowingly and willfully –
>
> > (1) falsifies, conceals, covers up by any trick, scheme, or device a material fact;
> > (2) makes any materially false, fictitious or fraudulent statement or representation; or
> > (3) makes or uses any false writing or document knowing the same to contain any materially false, fictitious, or fraudulent statement or entry;
>
> shall be fined under this title or imprisoned not more than 5 years, or both.
> (b) Subsection (a) does not apply to a party to a judicial proceeding, or that party's counsel, for statements, representations, writings or documents submitted by such party or counsel to a judge or magistrate in that proceeding.

Section 1001 of title 18 is one of the most broadly enforced criminal statutes and covers three general categories of offenses: (1) falsification or concealment of a material fact by any trick, scheme or device; (2) the use or making of any writing with knowledge that such document is false; and (3) knowingly making any materially fictitious, false, or fraudulent statements or representations. Section 1001 offenses most often involve the submission of false or fraudulent information to the government for the purpose of receiving a monetary or proprietary benefit or other privilege or to resist a monetary claim. In order to convict a defendant for making false statements, the government need only show that the defendant, with the intent to deceive, knowingly and willfully made a materially false statement within the jurisdiction of any department or agency of the United States.[298]

The term "statements," although not defined in § 1001 nor in the accompanying legislative history, is construed broadly and covers all statements, whether written or oral, sworn or unsworn, or voluntary or involuntary.[299] The quandary presented by the absence of a precise definition of "false statement" is demonstrated in *United States v. Worthington*, where the Second Circuit turned to Black's Law Dictionary:[300] "[A] false statement is defined as one that is 'more than merely untrue or erroneous,' rather it implies that the 'statement is designedly untrue . . . and made with [the] intention to deceive the person to whom the false statement is made or exhibited.'"[301] Although the Supreme Court has not yet defined "false statement" under § 1001, it has held that information given to federal investigators is considered a statement for § 1001 purposes.[302]

Falsity is established either by false representation or by concealment of a material fact.[303] To prove concealment, the prosecution must show willful nondisclosure of a material fact through a trick, scheme, or device.[304] It is irrelevant whether the false statement actually affects the actions of the body to which it was made.[305] Whether a false statement is "capable of influencing" is measured at the time the statement was made.[306]

Materiality is also an essential element under § 1001 and, since the Supreme Court's 1995 decision in *United States v. Gaudin*,[307] it is a question of

---

[298] *See United States v. Gaudin*, 515 U.S. 506 (1995); *United States v. Arch Trading Co.*, 987 F.2d 1087, 1095 (4th Cir. 1993)(a person is guilty of making false statements when government proves: (1) "that the defendant made a false statement to a governmental agency or concealed a fact from it or used a false document knowing it to be false; (2) the defendant acted 'knowingly and willfully'; and (3) the false statement or concealed fact was material to a matter within the jurisdiction of the agency.").

[299] *See, e.g., United States v. Beacon Brass Co.*, 344 U.S. 43, 46 (1952)(holding that there is no statutory distinction between written and oral statements).

[300] *United States v. Worthington*, 822 F.2d 315 (2d Cir. 1987).

[301] *Worthington*, 822 F.2d at 319.

[302] *United States v. Rodgers*, 466 U.S. 475, 477-79 (1984) (giving false tip to FBI violates § 1001).

[303] *United States v. Sarihifard*, 155 F.3d 301, 306 (4th Cir. 1998) (describing falsity element); *Arch Trading Co.*, 987 F.2d at 1095 (same).

[304] *See* 18 U.S.C. § 1001; *see also Sarihifard*, 155 F.3d at 306 ("'A statement is material if it has a natural tendency to influence, or is capable of influencing, the decision-making body to which it was addressed.'") (quoting *United States v. Littleton*, 76 F.3d 614, 618 (4th Cir. 1996)).

[305] *Sarihifard*, 155 F.3d at 306 (citing *Arch Trading Co.*, 987 F.2d at 1095).

[306] *Sarihifard*, 155 F.3d at 307 (citing *Arch Trading Co.*, 987 F.2d at 1095).

[307] *See Gaudin*, 515 U.S. 506.

fact that must be submitted to the jury and proven beyond a reasonable doubt.[308]

Knowing and willful intent to make a false statement is required to convict under § 1001.[309] Section 1001 requires only proof of intent to deceive and not intent to defraud,[310] and several circuits have held that actual knowledge and willfulness are unnecessary if the jury can infer such intent.[311]

Indeed, the government need only prove that the defendant acted with "reckless disregard" as to whether the statement was true.[312] Additionally, because the intent element refers to falsity as opposed to materiality or jurisdiction, a defendant may be held liable under § 1001 even if completely unaware of the statement's impact on a governmental agency.[313]

To constitute a § 1001 violation, the offense or false statement must be in relation to a matter "within the jurisdiction of the executive, legislative or judicial branch of the United States."[314] A department or agency has jurisdiction over a matter if it has authority over that matter.[315] Jurisdiction is not interpreted narrowly or technically under § 1001,[316] and the defendant need not know that the department or agency has jurisdiction over the statement.

The text of § 1001 was substantially amended after the Supreme Court's decision in *United States v. Hubbard*.[317] Prior to amendment,[318] section 1001 prohibited false statements and similar misconduct occurring "in any matter within the jurisdiction of any department or agency of the United States."[319] In *Hubbard*, the Supreme Court considered the context of § 1001 in the course of a bankruptcy proceeding. In holding that a court is neither a department or agency under § 1001, the Court expressly overruled well settled precedent as

---

308 *See Gaudin*, 515 U.S. 506; *United States v. Ismail*, 97 F.3d 50, 60 (4th Cir. 1996) (recognizing *Gaudin* and noting that pre-*Gaudin* the 4th Circuit treated materiality as a question of law).

309 *United States v. Yermian*, 468 U.S. 63, 69 (1984); *Arch Trading Co.*, 987 F.2d at 1095.

310 *Nilson Van & Storage Co. v. Marsh*, 755 F.2d 362, 367 (4th Cir. 1985).

311 *See, e.g., United States v. Burns*, 104 F.3d 529, 535 (2d Cir. 1997).

312 *See United States v. Egenberg*, 441 F.2d 441, 444 (2d Cir. 1971).

313 *See Yermian*, 468 U.S. at 69 ("knowingly and willfully" do not apply to defendant's knowledge of ultimate federal jurisdiction); *United States v. Green*, 745 F.2d 1205, 1209 (9th Cir. 1984)(no need to establish mental state with respect to federal involvement for a § 1001 violation).

314 18 U.S.C. § 1001 (1996).

315 *Rodgers*, 466 U.S. at 479-80 (holding that jurisdiction under § 1001 encompasses FBI and Secret Service investigations); *Bryson v. United States*, 396 U.S. 64 (1969) (§ 1001 case involving false affidavit filed with the National Labor Relations Board).

316 *See Rodgers*, 466 U.S. at 480.

317 *United States v. Hubbard*, 514 U.S. 695 (1995).

318 *See* note 24.

319 18 U.S.C. § 1001 (1995).

set forth in *United States v. Bramblett*, which found that department under section 1001 included Congress and the federal judiciary.[320]

John Bruce Hubbard was charged under § 1001 in connection with unsworn false statements filed in bankruptcy court. In the course of Hubbard's voluntary chapter 7 bankruptcy proceeding, the trustee filed an amended complaint and moved to compel Hubbard to disclose certain bank records. In response to the trustees' allegations, Hubbard, who opposed the relief sought by the trustee, falsely denied that a well-drilling machine and parts for the machine were stored at his house and in a nearby warehouse. Hubbard also misrepresented that all of the records sought by the trustee had been produced. Both Hubbard's responses in his answer to the trustee's amended complaint and the motion to compel were filed in the bankruptcy court. The Supreme Court held that a bankruptcy court was not a department within the meaning of § 1001, and Hubbard's conviction on three counts of false statements under § 1001 was thereby reversed.[321]

Although the Supreme Court's ruling in *Hubbard* and the subsequent amendment of § 1001 limits the scope of § 1001 in bankruptcy cases, it does not insulate a defendant from prosecution for making unsworn false statements. Other provisions of title 18 can be used, as is evident in Hubbard's case. In the same indictment, Hubbard was also charged and convicted for bankruptcy fraud and mail fraud under 18 U.S.C. §§ 152 and 1341. Moreover, agents of the executive branch, such as the United States trustee or the FBI are clearly within the scope of section 1001. A debtor who lies to government officials, such as the United States trustee, whether they are in an administrative or investigatory role, are subject to prosecution under § 1001. A debtor who lies to the bankruptcy court may be prosecuted under the perjury statute or under § 152.

---

[320] *United States v. Bramblett*, 348 U.S. 503 (1955). Note, however, the Court's opinion in *Hubbard* did not confirm whether or not a judicial or legislative entity could still be considered an "agency" within the meaning of § 1001.

[321] In 1996, Congress amended § 1001, addressing the ruling in *Hubbard. See* False Statements Accountability Act (FSAA), Pub. L. No. 104-292, H.R. 3166 (October 11, 1996). The new statute eliminated the language "department" or "agency" from § 1001 and provided that false statements made to all three branches of the federal government are covered by § 1001. Accordingly, the FSAA effectively overruled *Hubbard*, but retained "certain limitations concerning statements within the jurisdiction of the judicial and legislative branches." Department of Justice Manual, Title 9, No.902 at 9-1460 (2d Ed. 1999)(the DOJ Manual). In particular, and relevant to false statements made in the context of bankruptcy proceedings, "statements made to a judge or magistrate by parties or their counsel in a judicial proceeding will not be subject to prosecution under § 1001." DOJ Manual, No. 902 at 9-1460 (this statutory protection to § 1001 prosecutions codified a long-standing judicially crafted provision known as the "judicial function exception.").

The relationship between § 1001 violations to bankruptcy offenses is illustrated by *United States v. Palmisano.*[322] A bankruptcy attorney was charged under § 1001 for making a false statement to the United States trustee in connection with an application for allowance of attorneys fees. Joseph Palmisano represented Robert and Shirley Cassani in bankruptcy proceedings in connection with their company, Cassani Electrical Services. The Cassani's daughter, Kathryn Avery, held a mortgage on a parcel of their land. Concerned about paying Palmisano's attorneys fees, Robert Cassani convinced his daughter to assign her rights on the note to Palmisano. Thereafter, Palmisano reassigned the note to a third party for $25,000. Approximately six months later, after Palmisano's fees were allegedly paid, he filed an application seeking attorneys fees in the bankruptcy case.

The United States trustee was suspicious of the transaction and questioned Palmisano's role in the assignment. Palmisano represented falsely that he was a mere conduit for Avery's willing assignment to a third party. Palmisano challenged his indictment under *Hubbard* on the basis that the false statement was made within the jurisdiction of a judicial proceeding as opposed to a matter within the jurisdiction of any department or agency. Palmisano's motion to dismiss was denied. Palmisano's false statement to the United States trustee was within the scope of § 1001.

Prosecution under § 1001 for bankruptcy related conduct may accompany charges involving concealment under (§ 152) and false claims (§ 287) without running afoul of the rule against multiplicity or overcharging. In *United States v. Allen,*[323] the debtor, Lawrence Allen, was charged and convicted for (1) knowingly and fraudulently concealing assets; (2) making false statements in a matter within the jurisdiction of a United States probation officer; and (3) making false claims against the United States. Lawrence Allen, who filed a chapter 7 bankruptcy petition seeking the discharge of unsecured debt, was charged under § 152 for the nondisclosure of over $30,000 worth of assets. After his arrest and indictment, Allen failed to disclose the ownership of a 1986 Porsche when he applied for court-appointed counsel. The government issued a superseding indictment and charged Allen with a § 1001 false statements violation and a § 287 false claim charge based on the non-disclosure of the vehicle.

On appeal, Allen claimed that the charges and his convictions under § 152 and § 1001 were multiplicative as they were based on the same conduct:

---

[322] *United States v. Palmisano,* 185 B.R. 476 (D. Vt. 1995).

[323] *United States v. Allen,* 13 F.3d 105 (4th Cir. 1993).

failing to disclose his ownership of the Porsche to the United States probation office. The Fourth Circuit disagreed and affirmed Allen's convictions on the basis that both §§ 287 and 1001 require proof of a fact that the other does not. Section 287 requires proof that a false claim was made against the government, while § 1001 requires proof of a false statement. *Allen* demonstrates that one false representation in a bankruptcy case, in some circumstances, may give rise to more than one charge.

Sections 1014 and 1032

Section 1014 of title 18 provides in relevant part:

> Whoever knowingly makes any false statement or report, or willfully overvalues any land, property or security, for the purpose of influencing in any way the action of the [certain financial institutions, agencies, and organizations] upon any application, advance, discount, purchase, purchase agreement, repurchase agreement, commitment, or loan, or any change or extension of any of the same, by renewal, deferment of action or otherwise, or the acceptance, release, or substitution of security therefore, shall be fined not more than $1,000,000 or imprisoned not more than 30 years, or both.

Section 1032 of title 18 provides:

> Whoever—
>
> (1) knowingly conceals or endeavors to conceal an asset or property from the Federal Deposit Insurance Corporation, acting as conservator or receiver or in the Corporation's corporate capacity with respect to any asset acquired or liability assumed by the Corporation under section 11, 12, or 13, of the Federal Deposit Insurance Act, the Resolution Trust Corporation, any conservator appointed by the Comptroller of the Currency or the Director of the Office of Thrift Supervision, or the National Credit Union Administration Board, acting as conservator or liquidating agent;
>
> (2) corruptly impedes or endeavors to impede the functions of such Corporation, Board, or conservator; or
>
> (3) corruptly places or endeavors to place an asset or property beyond the reach of such Corporation, Board, or conservator,
>
> shall be fined under this title or imprisoned not more than 5 years, or both.

To prove a violation of § 1014, the government must show that the debtor knowingly made or caused a false statement to be made to a governmental agency (as enumerated in the statute) upon any application, advance, commitment or loan with the purpose of influencing in any way the action of the agency.[324] The nature of the fraud associated with violations of §§ 1014 and 1032 is sometimes seen in the context of a bankruptcy case.

A chapter 7 debtor in an intricate scheme in Texas convicted of fraud exemplifies the application of § 1014 in conjunction with a bankruptcy offense.[325] Doyle Marshall Willey, a real estate and timberland developer, was the director of Sam Houston Bank in Huntsville, Texas, which failed in 1988. Following the bank's failure, FBI investigators uncovered suspicious activity with respect to property in the bank's real estate portfolio.

The property led the investigators to Albert Hornaday; the bank's President, Willey; Willey's wife, Kimberly Bacon; and Shadylane Farms, Inc., a corporation set up by Willey and Bacon. From approximately 1986 to the beginning of the investigation in 1992, Willey was associated with numerous corporate entities. Willey received significant amounts of money from the various corporations and maintained access to or control over approximately twenty personal and corporate accounts. The accounts were held at Sam Houston Bank, none of which were in Willey's name. Rather, most of the accounts were opened as trust accounts with Willey's interest undisclosed, or in the name of Bacon. Willey funneled money belonging to him and one of his companies, MWI Land Inc., through the various corporate and personal accounts for over seven years.

In 1990, Willey, with the assistance of Bacon, Hornaday, and Shadylane Farms was able to shield his assets and the assets of his companies from creditors, and declared personal and corporate bankruptcy for himself and MWI, respectively. The chapter 7 filing resulted in the discharge of approximately $46 million in unsecured debt. Willey's intricate scheme of funneling money through the trust accounts enabled him to retain undisclosed assets that were in fact part of his bankruptcy estate, including a 61 acre tract of land known as "Richards Road Property," where Hornaday resided.

Willey, Bacon, and Hornaday were ultimately charged in a thirty-two count indictment with various title 18 offenses, including bankruptcy fraud. Among other offenses, Willey was charged with aiding and abetting the making of a false statement in a loan application in violation of § 1014. Hornaday applied

---

[324] The Supreme Court has confirmed that materiality is not an element of a § 1014 offense. *See United States v. Wells*, 519 U.S. 482, 483 (1997).

[325] *United States v. Willey*, 57 F.3d 1374 (5th Cir. 1995).

for a $250,000 loan from another bank for the purchase of the Richards Road Property and to fund various improvements to the house. On the application, Hornaday falsely represented that he was the sole person responsible for repayment of the loan, when in fact, the responsible party was Willey. Based on these facts, the court upheld Willey's conviction under § 1014.

As further illustrated by *Willey*, a bankruptcy debtor may also be prosecuted for a § 1032 violation which, in part, criminalizes the knowing concealment or attempted concealment of an asset or property from the Federal Deposit Insurance Corporation (FDIC) in connection with the same false statement made both in a bankruptcy case and to the FDIC. In 1986, when Willey was contemplating bankruptcy, he transferred approximately $400,000 to various individual and corporate nominees and "trustees." Subsequently, Willey, in a deposition in connection with the collection of a judgment against him and MWI on a loan guarantee, falsely testified that he and MWI had no assets. Willey proceeded to falsify his and MWI's bankruptcy schedules. The Tenth Circuit found that on the basis of these facts alone, the jury had sufficient evidence to convict Willey for both § 1032 and § 152 concealment violations.[326]

[326] *See also United States v. Brown*, 188 F.3d 519 (10th Cir. 1999)(indictment charging §§ 152 and 1032 violations involving a complex scheme of bankruptcy fraud and concealment orchestrated by a debtor and his wife).

21. Mail, wire or bank fraud: 18 U.S.C. § 1341-1344

Mail and wire fraud

Section 1341 of title 18, United States Code, states:

> Whoever, having devised or intending to devise any scheme or artifice to defraud, or for obtaining money or property by means of false or fraudulent pretenses, representations, or promises, or to sell, dispose of, loan, exchange, alter, give away, distribute, supply, or furnish or procure for unlawful use any counterfeit or spurious coin, obligation, security, or other article, or anything represented to be or intimated or held out to be such counterfeit or spurious article, for the purpose of executing such scheme or artifice or attempting to do so, places in any post office or authorized depository for mail matter, any matter or thing whatever to be sent or delivered by the Postal Service, or deposits or causes to be deposited any matter or thing whatever to be sent or delivered by any private or interstate carrier, or takes or receives therefrom, any such matter or thing, or knowingly causes to be delivered by mail or such carrier according to the direction thereon, or at the place at which it is directed to be delivered by the person to whom it is addressed, any such matter or thing, shall be fined under this title or imprisoned not more than 20 years, or both. If the violation affects a financial institution, such person shall be fined not more than $1,000,000 or imprisoned not more than 30 years or both.

Section 1341, known as the mail fraud statute, makes it a crime to use the mail in a scheme to defraud. Section 1343 contains a similar prohibition on the use of the wire, radio or television:

> Whoever, having devised or intending to devise any scheme or artifice to defraud, or for obtaining money or property by means of false or fraudu-

> lent pretenses, representations, or promises, transmits or causes to be transmitted by means of wire, radio, or television communication in interstate or foreign commerce, any writings, signs, signals, pictures, or sounds for the purpose of executing such scheme or artifice, shall be fined under this title or imprisoned not more than 20 years, or both. If the violation affects a financial institution, such person shall be fined not more than $1,000,000 or imprisoned not more than 30 years, or both.

It is almost inevitable that a bankruptcy fraud scheme will potentially involve mail or wire fraud. Virtually any type of bankruptcy fraud will involve sending a letter by mail, making a phone call, or sending a fax. The government must show an actual connection between the use of the mail or airwaves to the fraud.[327] For example, the government must prove that a letter was sent to creditors or a phone call was made to the trustee, which were in furtherance of the scheme.

Causing a mailing triggers the application of § 1341. It is not necessary for the government to show that the defendant specifically authorized the mailings to be sent.[328] Causation is satisfied by the knowledge either that the use of the mail will follow from the act in the ordinary course of business, or that the use of the mails can be reasonably foreseen, even though not actually intended.[329] Knowledge in the execution of the fraud that letters are likely to be mailed, and in fact they are, is sufficient.[330] Thus, causing a mailing means that the mailing is reasonably foreseeable. The mailing does not have to be intended, just foreseeable.

The mailing must be an act committed in furtherance of the scheme to defraud. The mailing does not have to itself be fraudulent. It does have to be an integral part of the fraudulent scheme and not an incidental or tangential one.[331] The government does not have to show the defendant personally mailed anything to or received mail from the victim. It is sufficient that the defendant caused the use of the mails in furtherance of the fraudulent scheme.

The phrase "any scheme or artifice to defraud" means any deliberate plan or action or course of action by which someone intends to deceive or cheat another or by which someone intends to deprive another of something of value. The Sixth Circuit has defined this element as:

---

327 *United States v. Hewes*, 729 F.2d 1302, 1320-21 (11th Cir. 1984).

328 *United States v. Sternback*, 402 F.2d 353, 355 (7th Cir. 1968).

329 *See Pereira v. United States*, 347 U.S. 1, 8-9 (1954); *United States v. Calandrella*, 605 F.2d 236, 253 (6th Cir. 1979).

330 *Sternback*, 402 F.2d at 355.

331 *United States v. Bosby*, 675 F.2d 1174, 1183 (11th Cir. 1982).

> . . . consisting in deception intentionally practiced to induce another to part with property or to surrender some legal right, and which accomplishes the end designed.[332]

This element means "a departure from fundamental honesty, moral uprightness, or fair play and candid business dealings in the general" and business life of the community.[333] There must, however, be proof of a knowing misrepresentation, false statement, or omission, together with proof that the defendant specifically intended to deceive or defraud a person of ordinary prudence or comprehension. This requirement applies with respect to mail fraud and wire fraud.

Good faith is a defense to both mail fraud and wire fraud. Good faith has been defined as:

> . . . a genuine belief at the time each alleged false statement or representation was communicated, that each such statement or representation was true . . . [g]ood faith does not include the defendant's belief or faith that the venture will eventually meet his or her expectations.[334]

Good faith has also been defined as a belief or state of mind denoting honesty of purpose, and freedom from an intention to defraud.[335]

The *mens rea* requirement is the intent to defraud. This is a question of fact for the jury. The government must establish that the defendant intended to do something unlawful, *i.e.*, that he acted with the intent to defraud or deceive.[336]

The use of the mail fraud statute in a bankruptcy fraud situation is illustrated in the case of *United States v. Hewes*.[337] The *Hewes* case involved a bustout, a bankruptcy fraud scheme in which a company obtains large amounts of merchandise for which the owners have no intention of paying, and then is stripped of assets. Hewes and the other defendants set up a series of companies as part of their bustout. The defendants in *Hewes* utilized an ingenious variation on this familiar scheme: a merger of two of their companies. Letters were

---

[332] *United States v. Frost*, 125 F.3d 346, 354 (6th Cir. 1997) (citations and quotations omitted).
[333] *See Frost*, 125 F.3d at 371; *United States v. Van Dyke*, 605 F.2d 220, 225 (6th Cir. 1979).
[334] *United States v. Stull*, 743 F.2d 439, 446 n. 6 (6th Cir. 1984).
[335] *United States v. Bane*, 583 F.2d 832, 837 n.11 (6th Cir. 1978).
[336] *Frost*, 125 F.3d 346; *United States v. Smith*, 39 F.3d 119, 121-22 (6th Cir. 1994), *superseded by regulation as stated in*, *United States v. Curly*, 167 F.3d 316 (6th Cir. 1999).
[337] *Hewes*, 729 F.2d 1302.

sent to creditors of each company stating that the two companies were merging in an effort "to overcome severe financial reverses." The name of the new, merged company was "Rekcus" — which is "sucker" spelled backwards.

The defendants were charged with numerous federal crimes, including mail fraud. On appeal of their convictions, the defendants argued that the mail fraud statute was not violated because the mailings occurred after the alleged fraud, and further, were not for the purpose of executing the fraudulent scheme. The Eleventh Circuit rejected these arguments and determined that the mailings were intended to lull creditors by implicitly assuring them that they would be paid. Further, the letters were intended to deflect suspicion away from the merger, which was intended to further the fraudulent scheme. The court distinguished the instant case from the situation in which a credit card was used fraudulently and the merchant mailed the credit card slips to the issuing bank. While the latter may be foreseeable, it was not an integral aspect of the fraud, and thus did not constitute mail fraud.

The government does not have to show that the defendant actually authorized or directed the use of the mails; it is sufficient that the defendant knows that the mail is likely to be used in the scheme, and that the mail was in fact used.[338]

A defendant may be charged with separate counts of mail fraud for each mailing.[339] The mail fraud section applies whether or not the mail traveled across state lines. The wire fraud section, on the other hand, is applicable only to interstate wire communications, and is inapplicable to intrastate communications. If a telephone call is the means of interstate wire communication used, then the call does not need to be placed by the defendant.

Bank fraud

Section 1344 states:

> Whoever knowingly executes, or attempts to execute, a scheme or artifice –
> (1) to defraud a financial institution; or
> (2) to obtain any of the moneys, funds, credits, assets, securities, or other property owned by, or under the custody or control of, a financial institution, by means of false or fraudulent pretenses, representations, or promises; shall be fined not more than $1,000,000 or imprisoned not more than 30 years, or both.[340]

---

[338] *Sternback*, 402 F.2d at 354-55.
[339] *See, e.g., United States v. Crockett*, 534 F.2d 589, 600 (5th Cir. 1976).
[340] 18 U.S.C. § 1344.

A particularly illustrative example of the use of the bank fraud statute in the context of a prosecution involving various financial crimes is *United States v. Harris.*[341] Harris was the president and chief executive officer of Arochem, which operated a petroleum and petrochemical refinery complex in Puerto Rico. To provide financing for its continued business operations, Arochem entered into a revolving credit agreement with a consortium of banks to permit the companies to borrow up to $245 million over the course of two years.

Pursuant to the terms of the financing arrangement, Arochem was bound by certain financial covenants which, in part, required that the companies periodically submit borrowing base reports which set forth the companies' assets and trading positions. In the fall of 1989, Arochem's financial status began to deteriorate. Harris, in anticipation of the companies' year-end audit reports which were incorporated into the borrowing base reports and submitted to the banks, decided to engage in a practice of "creative accounting" so that net deficits in excess of $65 million would not be discovered.

Harris continued to falsify the companies' financial statements and routinely misrepresented the companies' financial health to the banks. In December 1991, the banks discovered that the companies' deficit was over $190 million and filed a petition to place Arochem into bankruptcy. Shortly thereafter, the government filed a twenty-four count indictment against Harris for various financial crimes including money laundering and conspiracy to commit wire and bank fraud. Harris' conviction was sustained on appeal.

The bank fraud statute, similar to the mail and wire fraud statute, criminalizes each execution of a fraudulent scheme, as opposed to each act in furtherance of the scheme to defraud.[342] As demonstrated by *Harris*, an indictment will not fail for multiplicity where the defendant's criminal conduct can be charged as chronologically independent schemes to defraud.

An indictment charging separate schemes of mail, wire or bank fraud coupled with violations involving the Bankruptcy Criminal Code may compound the implications for a defendant. In *Hewes*, for example, the government charged twenty-two individuals for various offenses including RICO, interstate transportation of stolen property, and several counts of mail and wire fraud in connection with a series of bustout schemes. Hewes was convicted of four counts of wire and mail fraud, one count of violating RICO and one count of RICO conspiracy. At sentencing, Hewes received concurrent ten year sentences for each of the RICO and RICO conspiracy convictions.[343]

---

[341] *United States v. Harris*, 79 F.3d 223, 232 (2d Cir. 1996).

[342] *Harris*, 79 F.3d at 232.

[343] *See Hewes*, 729 F.2d at 1306; *see* chapter 24.

22. Obstruction of justice: 18 U.S.C. § 1503

The obstruction of justice provisions are aimed at protecting the integrity of proceedings in the federal judiciary, Congress, and federal agencies. Section 1503 states:

> (a) Whoever corruptly, or by threats or force, or by any threatening letter or communication, endeavors to influence, intimidate, or impede any grand or petit juror, or officer in or of any court of the United States, or officer who may be serving at any examination or other proceeding before any United States magistrate judge or other committing magistrate, in the discharge of his duty, or injures any such grand or petit juror in his person or property on account of any verdict or indictment assented to by him, or on account of his being or having been such juror, or injures any such officer, magistrate judge, or other committing magistrate in his person or property on account of the performance of his official duties, or corruptly or by threats or force, or by any threatening letter or communication, influences, obstructs, or impedes, or endeavors to influence, obstruct, or impede, the due administration of justice, shall be punished as provided in subsection (b). If the offense under this section occurs in connection with the trial of a criminal case, and the act in violation of this section involves the threat of physical force or physical force, the maximum term of imprisonment which may be imposed for the offense shall be the higher of that otherwise provided by law or the maximum term that could have been imposed for any offense charged in such case.
>
> (b) The punishment for an offense under this section is –
>
> (1) in the case of a killing, the punishment provided in sections 1111 and 1112;
>
> (2) in the case of an attempted killing, or a case in which the offense was committed against a petit juror and in which a class A or B felony was charged, imprisonment for not more than 20 years, a fine under this title, or both; and

(3) in any other case, imprisonment for not more than 10 years, a fine under this title, or both.

Obstruction of justice proscribes conduct that seeks to prevent the execution of the legal process. The first category of conduct proscribed is the influencing of a grand or petit juror or court officer by threats, force, letter, or communication. The second category, referred to as the omnibus clause, prohibits a broad category of conduct that interferes with the judicial process.

Section 1503 applies to both attempted and actual obstruction, and a successful conviction may be secured if the government proves that: (1) there was a pending judicial proceeding; (2) the defendant knew of the proceeding; (3) the defendant acted corruptly, with the specific intent to obstruct or interfere with the proceeding or the due administration of justice.

A pending investigation by a grand jury is a judicial proceeding proscribed by § 1503.[344] Although an investigation undertaken to secure "presently contemplated presentation of evidence before the grand jury" constitutes a proceeding under § 1503,[345] the fact that an investigation may lead to evidence that might be presented to a grand jury is "insufficient to constitute a violation . . . "[346] Failure on the part of the government to prove that the defendant had knowledge of the pending judicial proceeding or grand jury investigation will also render a conviction under § 1503 insufficient.[347]

The requisite *mens rea* for a § 1503 conviction is described in the statute as "corruptly." The Second, Fourth, Fifth, Sixth, Seventh, Ninth and D.C. Circuits have held that the term "corruptly," i.e., the state of mind requirement, connotes specific intent.[348] Accordingly, if the government can show that the defendant committed the act with the specific intent of obstructing justice,[349] or at least that obstruction of justice was a reasonably foreseeable result of the act,[350] the intent element is satisfied. It is not necessary that the act achieve the desired result; an attempted obstruction is sufficient.[351]

---

[344] *United States v. Casel*, 995 F.2d 1299, 1306 (5th Cir. 1993), *vacated sub nom. on other grounds, Reed v. United States*, 510 U.S. 1188 (1994).

[345] *United States v. Maloney*, 71 F.3d 645, 657 n.7 (7th Cir. 1995) (citation omitted).

[346] *United States v. Aguilar*, 21 F.3d 1475, 1484 (9th Cir. 1994), *rev'd on other grounds*, 515 U.S. 593 (1995).

[347] *United States v. Frankhauser*, 80 F.3d 641, 650-51 (1st Cir. 1996).

[348] DOJ Manual, Title 9 Criminal, No. 1723 at 9-2240 (2d Ed. 1999).

[349] *United States v. Littleton*, 76 F.3d 614, 619 (4th Cir. 1996); *United States v. Rasheed*, 663 F.2d 843, 852 (9th Cir. 1981).

[350] *United States v. Thomas*, 916 F.2d 647, 651 (11th Cir. 1990); *United States v. Kenny*, 973 F.2d 339, 344 (4th Cir. 1992); *United States v. Neiswender*, 590 F.2d 1269, 1273 (4th Cir. 1979).

[351] *Aguilar*, 515 U.S. at 602.

The attempt to obstruct justice is described in the statute as an "endeavor," defined as "any effort or essay to accomplish the evil purpose that the section was enacted to prevent."[352] An endeavor to obstruct justice is also defined by the nexus requirement, that is, that "the act must have a relationship in time, causation or logic with the proceedings . . . or have the 'natural and probable' effect of interfering with the due administration of justice."[353]

In the conduct of an investigation of a bankruptcy crime, the FBI will often interview the target of the investigation. Should the potential defendant choose to speak with the FBI, lying could sometimes, but not always, give rise to a charge of obstruction of justice.[354] In *United States v. Aguilar,* a case suggesting a broad reading of the omnibus clause, the Supreme Court defined the circumstances under which lying to FBI agents would constitute obstruction of justice. To obtain a conviction for obstruction, the government must prove:

1. The alleged obstruction of justice has a relationship of time, causation, or logic with the judicial proceedings. This nexus requirement requires the government to show that the defendant's endeavor to influence has the natural and probable effect of interfering with the due administration of justice;
2. The defendant must have knowledge that his actions are likely to affect the proceeding; and
3. Where false statements to FBI agents are involved, the government must prove that the FBI agents were authorized or directed by the grand jury to conduct the investigation, that the agents acted as an arm of the grand jury, or that the grand jury had summoned the agents to testify.[355]

The fact that the FBI agents may testify before a grand jury is not sufficient.

A related issue is presented when a potential defendant tries to influence a possible grand jury witness. Where it is foreseeable that the witness will be

---

352 *United States v. Buffalano,* 727 F.2d 50, 53 (2d Cir. 1989) (citation omitted) (noting that an endeavor is less than an attempt).

353 *Aguilar,* 515 U.S. at 599-600 (quotations and citations omitted).

354 If, however, a target of an FBI investigation knowingly and willfully uttered a false statement to an FBI official regarding a material matter, such conduct would likely be prosecutable under 18 U.S.C. §1001. *See* chapter 20.

355 *Aguilar,* 515 U.S. at 599-600 (A logical interpretation of *Aguilar* suggest that the Supreme Court favors a broad reading of the omnibus clause).

called before the grand jury, attempting to influence the witness to lie will violate § 1503 under certain circumstances.[356]

The scope of § 1503 also reaches conduct intended to "influence, intimidate, or impede any . . . officer in or of any court of the United States." This includes federal district judges and federal bankruptcy judges.[357] In the context of a bankruptcy proceeding, a violation of § 1503 may occur where a bankruptcy petitioner sends a threatening letter to the bankruptcy judge with the specific intent to "influence, intimidate, or impede" that judge or the outcome of the proceedings.[358] If that same defendant was under a grand jury investigation for potential charges of bankruptcy fraud under the concealment prong of § 152, and destroyed or "endeavored" to destroy documents under a grand jury subpoena, such conduct would constitute an indictable offense under the omnibus clause of § 1503.[359]

An example in the bankruptcy setting is the case of Robert Ladum. Ladum was charged and convicted with various tax, bankruptcy, money laundering, and obstruction of justice charges in connection with his operation and ownership of several second-hand stores in Portland, Oregon.[360] Ladum concealed his ownership in the stores through "conduit" or "straw" nominees who held themselves out as the true owners of the stores so that he could avoid paying federal income taxes. In an effort to thwart the IRS, Ladum instructed the nominees to be as obstructive as possible and to refuse to provide information to any investigators and/or officials. Once Ladum became aware that a grand jury was impaneled, he advised the nominees to lie in the proceedings.

The indictment against Ladum and several of the nominees charged that Ladum endeavored to influence, obstruct, and impede the due administration of justice in the appearance of a witness before a federal grand jury.[361] On appeal, Ladum argued that § 1503 does not prohibit witness tampering in light of the Victim and Witness Protection Act (s§ 1512), and, even if the

---

[356] *See, e.g., Kenny*, 973 F.2d at 342-43.

[357] *See* DOJ Manual, No. 1721 at 9-2237 (the term "officer in or of any court of the United States" in the statute includes United States Bankruptcy Judges).

[358] *Cf. United States v. Fulbright*, 69 F.3d 1468, 1470 (9th Cir. 1995), *opinion withdrawn and superseded on other grounds*, 105 F.3d 443 (9th Cir. 1997) (defendant, a Montana farmer who unsuccessfully sought bankruptcy protection, mailed a series of documents to a bankruptcy judge and was charged and convicted of obstruction of justice by "intimidating or injuring federal officers," in violation of § 1503; on appeal, defendant's conviction for obstruction of justice was reversed on the grounds that the trial judge gave an improper definition of the term "proceeding" to the jury).

[359] *See United States v. Faudman*, 640 F.2d 20, 21 (6th Cir. 1981) (altering and defacing company records where federal grand jury was investigating fraud was proscribed by § 1503).

[360] *United States v. Ladum*, 141 F.3d 1328 (9th Cir. 1998).

[361] *Ladum*, 141 F.3d at 1337.

statute implicitly barred such conduct, the government did not produce sufficient evidence to sustain a conviction.

The Ninth Circuit dismissed both arguments. According to the court, the legislative history behind § 1512, and in the 1988 amendments thereto, did not alter the omnibus clause of § 1503, and thus, explicitly retained the prohibition against witness tampering.[362] This, coupled with the fact that Ladum both "suggested" that a nominee lie to the grand jury, and "approved" the nominee's plan to alter records, both acts which were carried to fruition, was sufficient to secure a conviction. Citing the Supreme Court's decision in *Aguilar*, the Ninth Circuit held that the evidence against Ladum established an "endeavor to influence, obstruct, or impede the due administration of justice in violation of § 1503."[363]

Few defenses particular to § 1503 are successful. Indeed, constitutional challenges have generally failed, and procedural defenses such as entrapment, immunity, and double jeopardy are rarely entertained. Nevertheless, courts have subscribed to the unique defense of "fear of reprisal" where a defendant can provide proof to the court that, for example, his failure to testify was based solely upon a legitimate and reasonable fear that such testimony would result in imminent harm to other witnesses or affect the safety of his family.[364]

[362] *See also United States v. Tackett*, 113 F.3d 603, 610-11 (6th Cir. 1997), *cert. denied*, 522 U.S. 1089 (1998).

[363] *Ladum*, 141 F.3d at 1338-39.

[364] *United States v. Banks*, 942 F.2d 1576 (11th Cir. 1991), *vacated on other grounds*, 988 F.2d 1106 (11th Cir. 1993).

23. Perjury: 18 U.S.C. §§ 1621-23

Section 1621 of title 18, United States Code, states:

Whoever –

(1) having taken an oath before a competent tribunal, officer, or person, in any case in which a law of the United States authorizes an oath to be administered, that he will testify, declare, depose, or certify truly, or that any written testimony, declaration, deposition, or certificate by him subscribed, is true, willfully and contrary to such oath states or subscribes any material matter which he does not believe to be true; or

(2) in any declaration, certificate, verification, or statement made under penalty of perjury as permitted under section 1746 of title 28, United States Code, willfully subscribes as true any material matter which he does not believe to be true; is guilty of perjury and shall, except as otherwise expressly provided by law, be fined under this title or imprisoned not more than five years, or both. This section is applicable whether the statement or subscription is made within or without the United States.

Section 1622 provides:

Whoever procures another to commit any perjury is guilty of subornation of perjury, and shall be fined under this title or imprisoned not more than five years, or both.

Section 1623 provides:

(a) Whoever under oath (or in any declaration, certificate, verification, or statement under penalty of perjury as permitted under section 1746 of title 28, United States Code) in any proceeding before or ancillary to any court or grand jury of the United States knowingly makes any false material declaration or makes or uses any other information, including any book, paper, document, record, recording, or other material, knowing the same to contain any false material declaration, shall be fined under this title or imprisoned not more than five years, or both.

(b) This section is applicable whether the conduct occurred within or without the United States.

(c) An indictment or information for violation of this section alleging that, in any proceedings before or ancillary to any court or grand jury of the United States, the defendant under oath has knowingly made two or more declarations, which are inconsistent to the degree that one of them is necessarily false, need not specify which declaration is false if —

(1) each declaration was material to the point in question, and

(2) each declaration was made within the period of the statute of limitations for the offense charged under this section.

In any prosecution under this section, the falsity of a declaration set forth in the indictment or information shall be established sufficient for conviction by proof that the defendant while under oath made irreconcilably contradictory declarations material to the point in question in any proceeding before or ancillary to any court or grand jury. It shall be a defense to an indictment or information made pursuant to the first sentence of this subsection that the defendant at the time he made each declaration believed the declaration was true.

(d) Where, in the same continuous court or grand jury proceeding in which a declaration is made, the person making the declaration admits such declaration to be false, such admission shall bar prosecution under this section if, at the time the admission is made, the declaration has not substantially affected the proceeding, or it has not become manifest that such falsity has been or will be exposed.

(e) Proof beyond a reasonable doubt under this section is sufficient for conviction. It shall not be necessary that such proof be made by any particular number of witnesses or by documentary or other type of evidence.

The two statutes most commonly used to prosecute perjury violations are §§ 1621 and 1623. Section 1623, the "false swearing statute,"[365] is limited to perjuries in judicially related proceedings, while § 1621, the "general federal

---

365 *See United States v. Gellene*, 182 F.3d 578, 590 (7th Cir. 1999).

perjury statute," applies to false declarations in a broad range of federal proceedings.[366] The general federal perjury provision is applicable in federal bankruptcy proceedings.[367]

Elements

A successful conviction under either of these sections requires proof beyond a reasonable doubt of the following four elements: (1) that the defendant was under oath at the time of the alleged perjured testimony; (2) that the defendant made a false statement; (3) that the defendant made the false statement with specific intent, *i.e.*, with knowledge of its falsity; and (4) that the alleged false statement was material to the judicial proceedings.

The first element of the offense is satisfied under § 1623 if the government offers proof that the false statement was made under oath, while a successful prosecution under § 1621 requires proof that the oath was administered before a competent tribunal or person.[368] The indictment must identify the false statement alleged with proof of the factual basis of its falsity.[369] Under § 1621, specific intent is established by proof that the defendant acted "willfully," while the threshold under § 1623 only requires proof that the defendant acted with knowledge.[370] Both statutes require proof that the defendant made the false statement knowing it was false. If the defendant made the statement and believed it to be true, a conviction under §§ 1621 and 1623 cannot stand.[371]

Materiality

Materiality under §§ 1621 and 1623 is established if the false statement is material to the proceedings. A false statement is material if it has a "'natural tendency to influence, or [is] capable of influencing, the decision of the decision making body to which it was addressed.'"[372] Materiality is broadly defined, and the government need not set forth proof that the statement actually misled or influenced the impending proceeding.

Prior to the Supreme Court's decision in *United States v. Gaudin*,[373] materiality was a question of law which was to be decided by the Court.[374] In

---

[366] *Gellene* 182 F.3d at 590; *see United States v. Hvass*, 355 U.S. 570, 577 n.5 (1958) (the perjury statute covers ex parte proceedings, investigations, and ordinary adversary proceedings).

[367] *Hammer v. United States*, 271 U.S. 620 (1926).

[368] *United States v. Chaplin*, 25 F.3d 1373, 1377 (7th Cir. 1994).

[369] DOJ Manual, Title 9 Criminal, No. 1746 at 9-2268 (2d Ed. 1999).

[370] *United States v. Fornaro*, 894 F.2d 508, 512 (2d Cir. 1990).

[371] DOJ Manual, No. 1747 at 9-2269.

[372] *Kungys v. United States*, 485 U.S. 759, 770 (1988) (citation omitted).

[373] *United States v. Gaudin*, 515 U.S. 506 (1995).

[374] *See, e.g., Sinclair v. United States*, 279 U.S. 263, 299 (1929), *overruled by Gaudin*, 515 U.S. 506.

Gaudin, a unanimous Supreme Court found that materiality as it applied in the context of prosecution under § 1001 was an element for the jury to determine "beyond a reasonable doubt."[375] Accordingly, courts interpreting the element of materiality in perjury cases, such as the Fourth, Seventh, Ninth and Eleventh Circuits, have extended *Gaudin* to require the issue to be decided by the jury.[376]

Two-witness rule

Prosecutions under § 1621 require the government to meet a heightened evidentiary standard and may not rest entirely upon the uncorroborated testimony of one witness. The so-called two-witness rule[377] is derived from common law, and is based on the theory that "'the accused's oath was always in effect in evidence and thus, if but one witness was offered, there would be merely . . . an oath against an oath.'"[378] As somewhat of a misnomer, the rule requires that the falsity of the perjurious statement be established either: (1) by the testimony of two independent witnesses; or (2) by one witness coupled by independent corroborating evidence that is inconsistent with the innocence of the accused.[379] Circumstantial evidence, no matter how persuasive, cannot support a conviction for perjury.

In *United States v. Maultasch*,[380] the Second Circuit defined the scope of the two-witness rule in connection with perjurious statements in a proceeding before the Securities and Exchange Commission (SEC). The defendants were controlling officers of an investment management company that managed Galaxy, a mutual fund with over one million dollars in assets. Galaxy maintained an agreement with Salmon, an over-the-counter brokerage firm, whereby Galaxy purchased Salmon's securities offerings in exchange for Salmon's promise to underwrite a public offering of the company managing Galaxy.

The defendants then entered into a separate agreement with Bernard Cohen, the owner of a car dealership, to purchase new automobiles in exchange for Cohen's investments in Galaxy. The defendants, together with Cohen, would share "profits and losses" from the investments, and any resulting profits would

---

375 *Gaudin*, 515 U.S. at 522-23; *see also* chapter 20 (False statements).

376 Cases which have extended *Gaudin* in the perjury context include: *United States v. Waldemar*, 98 F.3d 306, 313, *rev'd*, 106 F.3d 729 (7th Cir. 1996); *United States v. Keys*, 95 F.3d 874, 880-81 (9th Cir. 1996), *vacated*, 520 U.S. 1226 (1997); *United States v. Littleton*, 76 F.3d 614 (4th Cir. 1996). *But see United States v. Kramer*, 73 F.3d 1067, 1075 (11th Cir. 1996).

377 The two-witness rule does not apply to § 1623 prosecutions. *See, e.g.*, *United States v. McAffee*, 8 F.3d 1010, 1014 (5th Cir. 1993).

378 *United States v. Chaplin*, 25 F.3d 1373, 1377 (7th Cir. 1994)(citation omitted).

379 DOJ Manual, No. 1750 at 9-2273; *Weiler v. United States*, 323 U.S. 606, 609 (1945).

380 *United States v. Maultasch*, 596 F.2d 19 (2d Cir. 1979).

ultimately pay the balance of the automobiles. A similar agreement was established with the owner of a clothing store, Bernice Seidman.

Eventually, both Salmon & Co. and Galaxy collapsed, purportedly as a result of risky investments made in new issues of securities. Upon an SEC investigation of the transactions, both defendants denied having an agreement with any person who maintained an account at the brokerage firm to share in profits and losses. Through the corroborating testimony of Bernard Cohen and Bernice Seidman, however, the government provided direct evidence to the court establishing that the defendants' testimony was false. Based on this testimony, the court held that the government satisfied the requirements of the "two witness" rule: "There is a 'primary compliance' with the rule if the 'second witness has given independent testimony of another, separate and distinct incident or transaction, which if believed, would prove that what the accused said under oath was false.'"[381]

In perjury prosecutions where the alleged false statement concerns the defendant's state of mind, applications of the two-witness rule become problematic. As illustrated by the Seventh Circuit in *United States v. Chaplin*,[382] a prosecution for perjurious statements during depositions in the course of bankruptcy proceedings, the government's failure to prove the defendant's state of mind, except by circumstantial evidence, was fatal to the application of the two-witness rule.

Chaplin, the defendant, owned a firm that maintained contracts with the state of Wisconsin for construction projects at various state parks. In early 1990, the state found that Chaplin was in default on the contracts because his work was not completed according to schedule. The state filed a claim against Chaplin's bonding company, Transamerica Premium Insurance, which hired another contractor to complete the work and then sued Chaplin. Shortly thereafter, Chaplin filed for bankruptcy, and Transamerica filed proof of claim. In the course of the bankruptcy proceedings, Transamerica deposed Chaplin and asked whether Chaplin had given $8,000 in cash to his father-in-law on October 23, 1990, to which Chaplin answered no.

The Seventh Circuit reversed Chaplin's conviction in part because the government failed to establish the falsity of his response to Transamerica's question regarding the $8,000 payment. While the father-in-law's bank records showed that an $8,000 deposit was made on October 23, 1990, the court reasoned that he *could* have obtained the funds from Chaplin before that date.[383] The

---

[381] *Maultasch*, 596 F.2d at 25 (citations omitted).

[382] *Chaplin*, 25 F.3d at 1378.

[383] If Chaplin gave his father-in-law the $8,000 on October 22, and thus denied providing the funds on October 23, his statement would be literally true, although misleading. Literal truth is a defense to perjury.

court found that the father-in-law's testimony did not corroborate anything, but only established that the transactions occurred sometime in October; a mere implication that the money was received near the date in question did not constitute direct evidence that the transaction, in fact, occurred on October 23. Because the government failed to provide *any* evidence that Chaplin made the payment in question on the specified date, the requirements under the two-witness rule could not be established.

Perjury in a bankruptcy case

The false swearing statute, in particular, § 1623 (a), also criminalizes the use of a document, while under oath, knowing that the document contains a falsehood. In the context of a bankruptcy proceeding, a violation of § 1623 may be accomplished by a debtor filing a false petition and testifying to the contents of that petition at a bankruptcy hearing, or through the affirmation of the materially inaccurate contents of a fee application, under oath, by the debtor's attorney. The latter is illustrated by the case of John Gellene, an attorney convicted under § 152(3) for making false oaths in a bankruptcy proceeding. Gellene was also found guilty of committing perjury in violation of § 1623(a).[384]

Gellene submitted a fee application in connection with his firm's representation of the Buycrus-Erie Company in its bankruptcy case. Gellene, who had failed to disclose to the bankruptcy court a conflict of interest in connection with the representation of Buycrus, referred to two sworn declarations at his fee hearing to support his testimony that he had disclosed all possible conflicts to the court before seeking an award of fees.

At trial, the government introduced sufficient evidence to prove that Gellene's declaration under Fed. R. Bankr. P. 2014 was false. Indeed, two of the firm's clients were creditors of Buycrus, and their relationship to the debtor should have been disclosed to the court. The Seventh Circuit affirmed Gellene's convictions, and found that Gellene knowingly used the false declarations in violation of § 1623, to gain approval of his firm's $2 million fee request. Gellene was sentenced to fifteen months of imprisonment on each count of bankruptcy fraud and perjury, and fined $15,000.

Two literal differences between the general perjury provisions of §§ 1621 and 1623, and the bankruptcy false oath and declaration provisions of §§ 152(2) and (3), are as follows: (1) materiality is a statutory element of the general perjury statute, while it is a judicially engrafted element of § 152; and (2) the intent element of the general perjury statute is willful, whereas the intent element of § 152 is knowing and fraudulent.

---

[384] *Gellene*, 182 F.3d at 590. *See* chapters 7 (Materiality) and 38 (Conflicts of interest).

These statutory differences rarely have any practical impact. Materiality for purposes of § 152 has been very broadly defined. A false statement is material for purposes of §§ 152(2) and 152(3) if it (1) bears a relationship to the debtor's business or financial issues, assets, or the history of the debtor's financial transactions; (2) potentially impacts the estate, estate administration or the creditors; or (3) is aimed at securing a particular adjudication by the bankruptcy court.[385] There may be room to argue that materiality for purposes of the general perjury statute has a narrower meaning.

Recantation

Recantation is a defense to perjury under § 1623(d). In order to successfully invoke this defense, the statute requires that (1) the false declaration has not substantially affected the proceeding; and[386] (2) it has not become manifest that the falsity has been or will be exposed.

For the defense to be successful, the recantation must be explicit. This is illustrated in *United States v. Tobias.*[387] In a criminal trial in which he was called as a defense witness, Tobias was asked if he knew a man named Conrad, and he answered, under oath, that he did not. After being confronted on cross-examination with a tape of a conversation between Tobias and Conrad, Tobias said his prior answer was truthful because

> The way I'm interpreting "knowing" is knowing someone that you have conversation with every day, that you have dinner with, that you spend time with. Knowing. If that guy walked into this room today, I wouldn't be able to identify him.[388]

In the subsequent prosecution against Tobias for perjury, Tobias moved to dismiss the indictment on the grounds of recantation under § 1623(d). The Ninth Circuit noted the requirement in other circuits, including the First and the Second Circuits, that the recantation be explicit, and held that a defendant must unequivocally repudiate his prior testimony to satisfy § 1623(d). Rejecting Tobias' motion, the court stated:

---

[385] *See* chapter 7.

[386] The statute uses the disjunctive "or," but this has been read as "and." *United States v. Moore*, 613 F.2d 1029, 1040 (D.C. Cir. 1980).

[387] *United States v. Tobias*, 863 F.2d 685 (9th Cir. 1988).

[388] *Tobias*, 863 F.2d at 686-687.

> . . . Tobias merely attempted to explain his inconsistent statements by using a contorted definition of the word "knowing." Despite repeated questioning, he never admitted that he knew [Conrad].[389]

The court distinguished Tobias' case from the situation in which a defendant's answer was literally true — a defense to perjury. Tobias' answer was not literally true; he lied when he testified he did not know Conrad.

Literal truth

Literal truth was held to be a complete defense to a charge of perjury by the Supreme Court in *Bronston v. United States*.[390] Bronston, a chapter 11 debtor, entered into an arrangement with creditors on behalf of his company, Samuel Bronston Productions, Inc. Bronston Productions, Inc. produced motion pictures in various European countries and, to finance these enterprises, established bank accounts in a number of foreign countries. As president of Bronston Productions, Inc., Samuel Bronston supervised transactions involving the overseas accounts. At Bronston Production, Inc.'s bankruptcy hearing[391] , Samuel Bronston was asked various questions regarding whether he personally maintained any accounts at Swiss banks. To these questions, Bronston answered "No Sir," or indicated that the company maintained accounts there at one time.

Based on his testimony, Bronston was charged and convicted of perjury under § 1621. A unanimous Supreme Court reversed Bronston's conviction. The Court recognized the significance of truthful testimony in bankruptcy hearings, "since the proceeding is a 'searching inquiry into the condition of the estate of the bankrupt, to assist in discovering and collecting the assets,'"[392] yet refused to apply § 1621 to Bronston's unequivocal responses as "the statute does not make it a criminal act for a witness to willfully state any material matter which he does not believe to be true."[393]

Indeed, the Court found that, even if a witness gives misleading testimony, it is the lawyer's responsibility to conduct effective cross-examination and bring the witness back to the mark. Interrogation may create an atmosphere where a witness, whether nervous or embarrassed, may provide answers that are not entirely responsive or are otherwise misleading. Nevertheless, the defense of

---

[389] *Tobias*, 863 F.2d at 689.

[390] *Bronston v. United States*, 409 U.S. 352 (1973).

[391] The hearing in question was the equivalent under the former Bankruptcy Act of the § 341 meeting.

[392] *Bronston*, 409 U.S. at 357 (citation omitted).

[393] *Bronston*, 409 U.S. at 357 (citation omitted).

literal truth cannot stand if a witness provides testimony he knows to be false. Perjurious testimony is treated merely as a misleading statement of fact only where the witness believes the statement to be true, albeit shrewdly attempts to evade the question.

24. Racketeer Influenced and Corrupt Organizations Act: 18 U.S.C. § 1962

Section 1962 of title 18, United States Code, states that:

(a) It shall be unlawful for any person who has received any income derived, directly or indirectly, from a pattern of racketeering activity or through collection of an unlawful debt in which such person has participated as a principal within the meaning of section 2, title 18, United States Code, to use or invest, directly or indirectly, any part of such income, or the proceeds of such income, in acquisition of any interest in, or the establishment or operation of, any enterprise which is engaged in, or the activities of which affect, interstate or foreign commerce. A purchase of securities on the open market for purposes of investment, and without the intention of controlling or participating in the control of the issuer, or of assisting another to do so, shall not be unlawful under this subsection if the securities of the issuer held by the purchaser, the members of his immediate family, and his or their accomplices in any pattern or racketeering activity or the collection of an unlawful debt after such purchase do not amount in the aggregate to one percent of the outstanding securities of any one class, and do not confer, either in law or in fact, the power to elect one or more directors of the issuer.

(b) It shall be unlawful for any person through a pattern of racketeering activity or through collection of an unlawful debt to acquire or maintain, directly or indirectly, any interest in or control of any enterprise which is engaged in, or the activities of which affect, interstate or foreign commerce.

(c) It shall be unlawful for any person employed by or associated with any enterprise engaged in, or the activities of which affect, interstate or foreign commerce, to conduct or participate, directly or indirectly, in the conduct of such enterprise's affairs through a pattern of racketeering activity or collection of unlawful debt.

(d) It shall be unlawful for any person to conspire to violate any of the provisions of subsection (a), (b), or (c) of this section.

The Racketeer Influenced and Corrupt Organizations Act (RICO) became law as part of the Organized Crime Control Act of 1970.[394] The purpose of the RICO statute is "the elimination of the infiltration of organized crime and racketeering into legitimate organizations operating in interstate commerce."[395] This statute, however, is sufficiently broad to include illegal acts relating to any enterprise affecting interstate or foreign commerce.[396] The statute provides for both criminal and civil causes of action for a violation of its provisions. Accordingly, DOJ may seek a criminal indictment or file a civil complaint alleging RICO violations.[397] The penalties for a criminal conviction include mandatory forfeiture, in addition to possible imprisonment and fines.[398]

Elements Required for a RICO Prosecution

For a successful prosecution under § 1962, the government must prove first, that the subject charged engaged in: (1) a pattern of, (2) racketeering activity, only insofar as (3) an enterprise is involved, as defined in § 1961 of title 18.[399] Section 1961(1) defines "racketeering activity" as any one of specifically listed criminal acts. These acts are commonly referred to as "predicate acts."[400]

Crimes within the scope of predicate acts include "any offense involving fraud connected with a case under title 11 . . ." (the Bankruptcy Code).[401] Racketeering activity involving property in bankruptcy cases includes: fraudulent transfer or concealment of property;[402] improper offer and receipt of property;[403] concealment, destruction, or alteration of information relating to the property;[404] and misappropriation of property by the trustee or other officer of the court who has access to the property.[405]

---

394 18 U.S.C. §§ 1961-1968.

395 S. Rep. No. 91-317 (1969).

396 DOJ Manual, Chapter 9 Criminal, No. 9-110.100 at 9-423 (2d Ed. 1999).

397 *See* DOJ Manual, No. 9-110.100 *et seq.*

398 18 U.S.C. § 1963(a).

399 *See, e.g., Bennett v. Berg*, 685 F.2d 1053, 1060 (8th Cir. 1981).

400 *See Sedima v. Imrex Co., Inc.*, 473 U.S. 479, 495 (1985)(concluding that "'racketeering activity' consists of no more and no less than commission of a predicate act, § 1961(1)"); *United States v. Turkette*, 452 U.S. 576, 583 (1981)(holding that in order to secure a conviction under the RICO statute, the government must prove "the existence of an 'enterprise' and the connected 'pattern of racketeering activity'").

401 18 U.S.C. § 1961(1)(D).

402 *See* 18 U.S.C. § 152(1). *See* chapter 6.

403 *See* 18 U.S.C. § 152(6) *See* chapter 9.

404 *See* 18 U.S.C. § 152(8), (9). *See* chapter 11.

405 *See* 18 U.S.C. § 153. *See* chapter 12.

Other crimes that constitute predicate acts related to a bankruptcy case include: making a false oath or account in or in relation to such a case;[406] making a false declaration or statement;[407] or presenting or using any false claim for proof against the estate of a debtor.[408] Racketeering activity, however, does not include the crime of bankruptcy fraud under § 157.[409]

A pattern of racketeering activity is defined by the statute as a commission of at least two predicate acts within a ten year period, the first having to be committed after the effective date of the statute.[410] The acts must be separate, and no pattern is found when a single act constitutes more than one criminal violation.[411] The federal courts have generally found that any two separate predicate acts, such as two separate mailings, which are directly or indirectly related may constitute a pattern of such racketeering activity.[412] If there are similarities between the acts with respect to the victim, methodology, goal, etc., and there is evidence of a threat of a continuation of such activity, those acts may constitute a pattern even though they may be simultaneous.[413]

Finally, the pattern of racketeering activity must be conducted by or related to an "enterprise."[414] The term "enterprise" is defined by the statute to include "any individual, partnership, corporation, association, or other legal entity, and any union or group of individuals associated in fact although not a legal entity."[415] The enterprise must also affect interstate or foreign commerce;[416] however, this requirement is minimal and easily met.[417]

The concept of enterprise focuses on a group of people.[418] Therefore, to prove the existence of an enterprise, the government must first establish that there exists an entity or a group of persons "associated together for a common purpose of engaging in a course of conduct."[419] This includes illegitimate as well as legitimate businesses.[420] Second, the government must show that the

---

[406] *See* 18 U.S.C. § 152 (2). *See* chapter 7.
[407] *See* 18 U.S.C. § 152(3). *See* chapter 7.
[408] *See* 18 U.S.C. § 152(4). *See* chapter 8.
[409] *See* 18 U.S.C. § 1961(1)(D). *See* chapter 16.
[410] *See* 18 U.S.C. § 1961(5).
[411] *See United States v. Walgren*, 885 F.2d 1417, 1426 (9th Cir. 1989). *See also* chapter 21 discussing mail, wire, and bank fraud.
[412] *See United States v. Indelicato*, 865 F.2d 1370, 1380-81 (2d Cir. 1989).
[413] *Indelicato*, 865 F.2d at 1383.
[414] *See Bennett v. Berg*, 685 F.2d 1053, 1060 (8th Cir. 1981).
[415] *See* 18 U.S.C. § 1961(4).
[416] *See* 18 U.S.C. §§ 1962 (a)-(c).
[417] *See, e.g., United States v. Robinson*, 763 F.2d 778, 781 (6th Cir. 1985).
[418] *Indelicato*, 865 F.2d at 1384.
[419] *Turkette*, 452 U.S. at 583.
[420] *Turkette*, 452 U.S. at 586-87.

various associates "function as a continuing unit."[421] Next, there must be a clear relationship between the pattern of racketeering activity and the enterprise, generally requiring that the facilities and services of the enterprise were used to coordinate the pattern of racketeering activity. The evidence for proving the existence of the enterprise and the pattern of racketeering activity often overlap, and does not diminish the existence of either.[422]

Prohibited conduct

Section 1962 of title 18 spells out the four types of conduct that constitute a criminal RICO violation. Section 1962(a) makes it unlawful to use or invest any income derived from a pattern of racketeering activity in an enterprise.[423] Section 1962(b) makes it unlawful for any person to acquire or maintain any interest or control of any enterprise through a pattern of racketeering activity.[424]

The most common prosecutions of RICO claims fall under § 1962(c), which makes it unlawful for any person who is employed by or associated with an enterprise to conduct or participate in the conduct of the affairs of such enterprise through a pattern of racketeering activity. The final provision of § 1962 makes it a criminal offense to conspire to violate any of the provisions of subsections (a), (b) or (c). The usual elements of conspiracy must be proven to prevail on a § 1962(d) action.[425]

An example of a RICO violation in connection with a criminal bankruptcy charge can be found in *United States v. Robinson*.[426] Robinson was the president of Renoja, a corporation that operated restaurants from which money was skimmed from the cash registers. Renoja filed a petition for reorganization under chapter 11. During the bankruptcy proceedings, Renoja was required to report accurately its income and expenses, and to preserve its assets for the benefit of creditors.

---

421 *Turkette*, 452 U.S. at 583. *See also United States v. Mazzei*, 700 F.2d 85, 91 (2d Cir. 1983)(concluding that an indictment sufficiently alleged an enterprise by stating that a group of individuals shared the common purpose of influencing college basketball games to secure a profit).

422 *See Mazzei*, 700 F.2d at 89. *See also In re: Sattler's, Inc.*, 73 B.R. 780, 785 (S.D.N.Y. 1987)(discussing what constitutes an "enterprise" under RICO).

423 *See, e.g., United States v. Zang*, 703 F.2d 1186 (10th Cir. 1982)(holding that a building purchased with tainted funds was subject to forfeiture under RICO).

424 *See, e.g., United States v. Local 560*, 780 F.2d 267 (3d Cir. 1985)(holding that the acquisition of a union through instances of murder and extortion constituted a RICO violation).

425 *See* 18 U.S.C. § 371.

426 *United States v. Robinson*, 8 F.3d 398 (7th Cir. 1993).

Robinson utilized his skimming techniques during the pendency of the bankruptcy proceedings complete with a separate set of books. However, he failed to report these receipts to bankruptcy court, thereby making those funds unavailable to the corporation's creditors, in direct violation of 18 U.S.C. § 152. In December of 1988, federal agents seized physical evidence of the skimming activities including bags of cash and documents showing how the activities were conducted.

Count one of a 54 count indictment alleged bankruptcy fraud, mail fraud, and wire fraud, as the predicate acts in violation of the RICO statute. Robinson was tried, convicted, and sentenced to 72 months imprisonment and ordered to forfeit over $600,000 under 18 U.S.C. §§ 1962(c) and 1963. Robinson then appealed both the convictions and the forfeiture.

On appeal, Robinson argued that the indictment failed to properly allege a RICO violation, namely, the existence of an enterprise, thereby requiring an overturn of his conviction. He argued that the indictment was faulty because the enterprise charged, Renoja, was not a distinct and separate entity from Robinson as its sole shareholder.[427]

Robinson further argued that the alleged enterprise was indistinguishable from the alleged pattern of racketeering. This argument was based tangentially on the Supreme Court's decision in *Turkette* in which the court held that a pattern of activity does not, in and of itself, create an enterprise.[428] Robinson argued that the enterprise charged, Renoja, was nothing more than the name for the offenses the defendants agreed to commit, and the government thereby collapsed the statutory elements of pattern of activity and enterprise into one.[429]

The Court of Appeals upheld the RICO convictions, rejecting both of these arguments. First, it found that although Robinson was the sole shareholder of Renoja, the corporation employed a large number of people, and filed its own tax returns, thereby distinguishing itself from Robinson as a separate entity. Second, the court found that Renoja was a legally incorporated business that performed legitimate functions, and was used by Robinson and the other defendants to perpetrate the cash skimming scheme. Thus, the purpose of the enterprise included actions other than carrying out the racketeering activity.

---

[427] The Seventh Circuit in *United States v. DiCaro*, 772 F.2d 1314 (7th Cir. 1985) and other cases have held that a RICO enterprise could not solely consist of the individual who supposedly conducted his own affairs through a pattern of racketeering activity. *See Robinson*, 8 F.3d at 406-7.

[428] *See United States v. Turkette*, 452 U.S. 576, 583 (1981).

[429] *See Robinson*, 8 F.3d at 407.

25. Money laundering: 18 U.S.C. § 1956

18 U.S.C. § 1956 states, in pertinent part:

(a)(1) Whoever, knowing that the property involved in a financial transaction represents the proceeds of some form of unlawful activity, conducts or attempts to conduct such a financial transaction which in fact involves the proceeds of specified unlawful activity —

(A) (i) with the intent to promote the carrying on of specified unlawful activity; or. . . .

(ii) with intent to engage in conduct constituting a violation of section 7201 or 7206 of the Internal Revenue Code of 1986; or

(B) knowing that the transaction is designed in whole or in part—

(i) to conceal or disguise the nature, the location, the source, the ownership, or the control of the proceeds of specified unlawful activity; or

(ii) to avoid a transaction reporting requirement under State or Federal law,

shall be sentenced to a fine, not more than $500,000 or twice the value of the property involved in the transaction, whichever is greater, or imprisonment for not more than twenty years or both.

(2) Whoever transports, transmits, or transfers, or attempts to transport, transmit or transfer a monetary instrument or funds from a place in the United States to or through a place outside the United States or to a place in the United States from or through a place outside the United States —

(A) with the intent to promote the carrying on of a specified unlawful activity; or

(B) knowing that the monetary instrument or funds involved in the transportation represent the proceeds of some form of un-

> lawful activity and knowing that such transportation, transmission or transfer is designed in whole or in part —
> (i) to conceal or disguise the nature, location, the source, the ownership, or the control of the proceeds of specified unlawful activity; or
> (ii) to avoid a transaction reporting requirement under State or Federal law,
> shall be sentenced to a fine of not more than $500,000 or twice the value of the monetary instrument or funds involved in the transportation, transmission, or transfer, whichever is greater or imprisonment not more than twenty years or both.[430]

Section 1956(a)(1)(A) prohibits the act of money laundering which promotes the carrying on of unlawful activity. Section 1956(a)(1)(B) is aimed at money laundering designed to conceal the attributes of the proceeds of unlawful activity. Part (a)(2)(A) and (2)(B) of § 1956, often referred to as "transportation" money laundering, criminalizes the transportation, transfer, or transmission of a monetary instrument or funds with the intent to promote the specified unlawful activity, or to conceal the attributes of the proceeds.[431] Transportation money laundering is similar to § 1956(a)(1), except that the proceeds must be transported to or from the United States, as opposed to the use of a financial transaction.[432]

A *prime facie* violation of *any* subsection under § 1956(a)(1) requires the government to initially prove (1) a financial transaction; and (2) that the funds which were used in the financial transaction were in fact the proceeds of one of

---

[430] 18 U.S.C. § 1956. Section 1956(b) provides a civil penalty for the violation of subsections (a)(1), (a)(2) and (a)(3). Such civil penalty is imposed in addition to any fine imposed for the criminal offense. Section 1956(h) criminalizes the act of conspiring to commit any offense set forth in the statute.

[431] The requisite *mens rea* necessary for a § 1956(a)(1)(A) or (a)(2)(A) conviction requires proof that the defendant "intended" to promote the carrying on of a specified unlawful activity. The Ninth and Tenth Circuits have concluded that circumstantial evidence of "intent to promote" a fraudulent scheme exists if the transfer lends an "aura of legitimacy" to the scheme. *See United States v. Johnson*, 971 F.2d 562, 566 (10th Cir. 1992); *United States v. Savage*, 67 F.3d 1435, 1440 (9th Cir. 1995). The Sixth Circuit has held that "promotion" of an ongoing fraudulent scheme may be shown by wiring funds to pay for narcotics, *United States v. King*, 169 F.3d 1035, 1039 (6th Cir. 1999), and that the payment of office expenses and salespersons' commissions is sufficient to constitute a "promotion" in connection with a fraudulent investment scheme. *See United States v. Westine*, No. 92-3664, 1994 WL 88831, at *8 (6th Cir. March 17, 1994).

[432] Financial transaction is defined in 18 U.S.C. § 1956(c)(4).

[433] 18 U.S.C. § 1956(a)(1). The unlawful acts are enumerated in 18 U.S.C. § 1956(c)(7).

the specified unlawful acts enumerated in the statute.[433] The government is further required to establish that the defendant knew "that the property involved in [the] financial transaction represents the proceeds of some form of unlawful activity."[434]

Each subsection of § 1956(a)(1) requires an additional element of proof. Accordingly, a charge under § 1956(a)(1)(A)(i) requires proof that the defendant conducted or attempted to conduct a financial transaction with the intent to promote the carrying on of a specified unlawful activity; under § 1956 (a)(1)(B)(i), the government must prove that the defendant's actions were designed, in whole or in part, to conceal or disguise the nature, location, source, ownership or control of the proceeds from such unlawful activity.[435]

Unlike §§ 1956(a)(1)(A) and (B), under § 1956(a)(2)(A), there is no requirement that the funds or monetary instrument be the proceeds of an unlawful activity, nor is there any scienter requirement.[436] Instead, a successful prosecution under § 1956(a)(2)(A) requires proof that the defendant knowingly transported, transmitted or transferred, or attempted to transport, transmit or transfer, the monetary instrument or funds (from a place in the United States to or through a place outside the United States, or to a place in the United States from or through a place outside the United States) with the intent to promote the carrying on of a specified unlawful activity.[437]

Subsection (a)(2)(B) requires additional elements of proof. A *prime facie* violation of § (a)(2)(B) is established with proof: (1) that the defendant knowingly transported, transmitted or transferred, or attempted to transport, transmit or transfer, the monetary instrument or funds (from a place in the United States to or through a place outside the United States, or to a place in the United States from or through a place outside the United States); (2) that the defendant had knowledge that the funds or monetary instrument involved represent the proceeds of some form of an unlawful activity; and (3) that the trans-

---

[434] 18 U.S.C. § 1956(a)(1).

[435] 18 U.S.C. § 1956(a)(1)(B).

[436] 18 U.S.C. § 1956(a)(2)(A). A *prima facie* case of a § 1956 (a)(2)(A) violation, unlike its predecessor 1956 (a)(1)(A), does not require (1) that the monetary instrument or funds be the product of unlawful activity; or (2) that the defendant had "knowledge" that the property involved represented proceeds of the unlawful activity. *See United States v. Piervinazi*, 23 F.3d 670, 679 (2d Cir. 1994); *United States v. Hamilton*, 931 F.2d 1046, 1051-52 (5th Cir. 1991).

[437] DOJ Manual, Title 9 Criminal, No. 2131 at 9-2663 (2d Ed. 1999).

[438] *See* DOJ Manual, Nos. 2132-2133 at 9-2664-2665. Violations of § 1956 have a "maximum potential twenty year prison sentence and a $500,000 fine, or twice the amount involved in the transaction, whichever is greater." DOJ Manual, No. 2101 at 9-2631.

action was designed in whole or in part to "conceal" the proceeds of the specified unlawful activity.[438]

Bankruptcy fraud is one of the "unlawful acts" enumerated in § 1956,[439] and charges of bankruptcy offenses often accompany money laundering violations where the core of the underlying indictment is premised upon concealment under §§ 152(1) or 152(7).[440] The case of *United States v. Levine* is illustrative of this point.[441]

Mr. and Mrs. Levine owned and operated a furniture store in Colorado which was experiencing financial difficulty. The business was in jeopardy because the Levines had overstated the store's inventory by over $1.1 million dollars. The secured lenders, who believed that far more collateral existed than actually did, finally demanded that the Levines provide them with a physical inventory. Once the shortage was discovered, the Levines were forced to liquidate the business. To recoup their losses, several of the creditors loaned the Levines additional funds to purchase additional inventory to facilitate the liquidation sale. Five months later, it became evident that there was no money for the creditors.

The Levines, within six months of each other, filed for chapter 7 bankruptcy, and their debts were discharged the following year. The events that lead to their indictments on several felony charges, however, involved conduct that was much more egregious than the initial overstatement of inventory. The Levines, with the assistance of their attorney, their accountant, and others, transferred and hid assets from their creditors, and embezzled pension and profit-sharing plan assets from their employees. To accomplish their crimes, the Levines engaged in kickback schemes with the bankruptcy liquidator, and hid funds, including monies received as tax refunds, in accounts established by the Levines' attorney and accountant.

The Levines were charged and convicted with violation of 18 U.S.C. § 152 and 18 U.S.C. § 1956(a)(1)(B)(i). On appeal, the Levines challenged certain of the money laundering counts on the grounds that the funds involved in the counts were proceeds from their tax returns, rather than the proceeds of illegal activity as enumerated in the statute. The Tenth Circuit disagreed, concluding that the hidden assets were funds "diverted and concealed from the bankruptcy estate"[442] within the scope of § 1956.

---

[439] 18 U.S.C. § 1956 (c)(7)(D).

[440] *See United States v. Levine*, 970 F.2d 681, 686 (10th Cir. 1992); *United States v. McIntosh*, 124 F.3d 1330 (10th Cir. 1997); *see also* chapters 6 and 10.

[441] *Levine*, 970 F.2d at 681.

[442] *Levine*, 970 F.2d at 686.

In another and more recent opinion by the Tenth Circuit, however, the definition of "proceeds from an unlawful activity" was not so broadly construed. In *United States v. McIntosh*,[443] McIntosh, an attorney, was charged and convicted with money laundering under § 1956(a)(1)(A)(i) and § 1956(a)(1)(B)(i), and with violation of § 152(7) and section 152(3). The underlying conduct that led to McIntosh's indictment involved the concealment of a contingency fee received during his bankruptcy proceedings but subsequent to the filing of his chapter 11 bankruptcy petition.

Pursuant to the contingency fee arrangement, McIntosh received approximately $125,000 which was divided into two checks: one was payable to his law firm and the other payable to him individually. In the monthly operating report submitted to the bankruptcy trustee, McIntosh only reported receipt of the fee made payable to his law firm, and did not disclose the remainder of the funds. On appeal, the Tenth Circuit reversed all nine of McIntosh's money laundering convictions on the grounds that the funds were not "proceeds" of an unlawful activity; *i.e.,* the funds involved in the transaction were not the proceeds of bankruptcy fraud.

A violation of § 1956(a)(2) may also occur in the bankruptcy setting. Indeed, a bankruptcy offense in violation of § 152 may accompany a charge of money laundering in violation of § 1956(a)(2)(A) where the defendant not only conceals the proceeds of the bankruptcy offense, but also wires the funds overseas for added protection. In this case, the prosecutor's task is much less cumbersome, since it is not necessary to prove that the monetary instrument or funds are the proceeds of an unlawful activity, that is, bankruptcy fraud. Consider Gary and Marcee Levine, the furniture store owners who were convicted of bankruptcy fraud and six counts of money laundering in violation of § 1956(a)(1)(B).[444] Had the Levines, in an effort to conceal their assets from the bankruptcy trustee, wired the funds from their secret trusts to an overseas account, they may have been charged under § 1956(a)(2)(A). The prosecution would have to prove that the defendants wired the funds overseas with the intent to commit bankruptcy fraud.

Likewise, had McIntosh wired the funds overseas prior to filing his chapter 11 petition in an effort to conceal those assets from the bankruptcy trustee, the Tenth Circuit may have reached a different conclusion. For conviction under § 1956(a)(1)(A), the prosecution would have had to prove that the defendant knew that the funds he transferred were proceeds of unlawful activity (bankruptcy fraud), and that he intentionally designed the transfer to conceal the

---

[443] *McIntosh*, 124 F.3d 1330.

[444] The Levines' case is discussed at length in chapters 6, 10, 19, and 31.

assets from the bankruptcy trustee. Under this scenario, a § 1956(a)(2)(A) charge would also lie.

Consider the hypothetical case of a lawyer who, in addition to a failing law practice, owns and operates several second-hand stores. The lawyer conceals his ownership interests in these stores for the sole purpose of avoiding the payment of taxes on their income through the use of "conduit" nominees who held themselves out as owners of the stores.[445] Upon filing for bankruptcy, the lawyer, consistent with his scheme against the IRS, conceals the income and profits earned by the stores (property of his bankruptcy estate) from the trustee. To facilitate the concealment, the lawyer arranges for the funds to be wired from the stores to accounts in the names of fictitious entities. At this point, the lawyer has violated §§ 1956(a)(1)(A) and (a)(1)(B). If the government can provide evidence that the funds were wired to overseas accounts, the prosecution may also seek a conviction under §§ 1956(a)(2)(A) and (a)(2)(B).

Charges of money laundering may also accompany violations of the Racketeer Influenced Corrupt Organizations Act (RICO), and 18 U.S.C. § 1001 and § 1603.

---

[445] A similar scheme recently occurred in the Ninth Circuit in *United States v. Ladum*, 141 F.3d 1328 (9th Cir. 1998), discussed at chapter 22.

26. Other related provisions

Several other statutory offenses are occasionally applicable to bankruptcy frauds, but their use is not as common as the statutory provisions previously discussed.

18 U.S.C. § 201 prohibits bribery of public officials and witnesses. The term "public officials" includes employees of the federal government. The section prohibits giving anything of value to a public official in order to influence any official act or commit a fraud against the United States. Receipt of a bribe is also prohibited. For example, bribing a court clerk to falsify a court filing would be punishable under § 201.

18 U.S.C. § 645 prohibits a United States marshal, clerk, referee, receiver, or other court official or deputy, assistant, or employee of such officer, from embezzlement of money coming into his hands in his official capacity. This section overlaps with § 153, but the penalty under § 645 is more severe. Violations are punishable by up to ten years if the amount embezzled exceeds $1,000.

18 U.S.C. § 664 prohibits theft or embezzlement from an employee benefit plan. This section could be utilized in a situation where a debtor siphons funds from an employee benefit plan covered by the Employee Retirement Income Security Act of 1974 (ERISA). Violations of this section are sometimes seen in cases of financial distress in which a principal has both the incentive and opportunity to use employees' pension funds.

Other provisions that are occasionally applicable but only rarely utilized include: 18 U.S.C. § 1911 (receiver mismanaging property); § 2314 (transportation of stolen goods, securities, moneys, fraudulent state tax stamps, or articles used in counterfeiting); and § 2315 (sale or receipt of stolen goods, securities, moneys, or fraudulent state tax stamps).

PART 4

PROSECUTION AND DEFENSE

27. Investigation

The Attorney General has the original authority to prosecute bankruptcy crimes. This responsibility is typically delegated to the United States attorneys for each district.[446] Since the launching of Operation Total Disclosure, enforcement of bankruptcy crimes has become a multi-agency effort spearheaded by the Department of Justice. The United States attorneys in several districts have bankruptcy fraud or economic crime task forces, which focus directly on this category of crime. The United States trustee also plays a significant role in enforcement of the criminal bankruptcy laws. In July 2003, the United States Trustee Program established a Criminal Enforcement Unit. The mission of this unit is to assist in the investigation and prosecution of bankruptcy crimes.

Statutory predicates

The Federal Criminal Code imposes an obligation on certain officials to report suspected bankruptcy crimes to the United States attorney for investigation. Section 3057 of title 18, United States Code, provides:

> (a) Any judge, receiver, or trustee having reasonable grounds for believing that any violation under chapter 9 of this title or other laws of the United States relating to insolvent debtors, receiverships or reorganization plans has been committed, or that an investigation should be had in connection therewith, shall report to the appropriate United States attorney all the facts and circumstances of the case, the names of the witnesses and the offense or offenses believed to have been com-

---

[446] 28 U.S.C. § 515, 516.

mitted. Where one of such officers has made the report, the others need not do so.

(b) The United States attorney thereupon shall inquire into the facts and report thereon to the judge, and if it appears probable that any such offense has been committed, shall without delay, present the matter to the grand jury, unless upon inquiry and examination he decides that the ends of public justice do not require investigation or prosecution, in which case he shall report the facts to the Attorney General for his direction.

This statute requires (1) a bankruptcy judge, receiver or trustee who has a reasonable basis to believe a bankruptcy crime has been committed to report it to the United States attorney; and (b) the United States attorney to investigate and either present the matter to the grand jury if it is probable that an offense has been committed, or report the matter to the Attorney General. The statute is mandatory: the judge or trustee must report suspected crimes to the United States attorney. "Reasonable basis" is a low threshold standard and is less than probable cause, the level needed to sustain a criminal information.

The United States trustee is also required by law to report suspected bankruptcy crimes. Section 586 of title 28 provides, in pertinent part:

> Each United States trustee, within the region for which such United States trustee is appointed, shall —
>
> (3) supervise the administration of cases and trustees in cases under chapter 7, 11, 12, or 13 of title 11 by, whenever the United States trustee considers it to be appropriate —
>
> (F) notifying the appropriate United States attorney of matters which relate to the occurrence of any action which may constitute a crime under the laws of the United States and, on the request of the United States attorney, assisting the United States attorney in carrying out prosecutions based on such action[.][447]

Reports of suspected bankruptcy crimes are most often brought to the attention of the United States attorney by the United States trustee or the United States bankruptcy judge, but not all referrals come from judges or trustees.

---

[447] 28 U.S.C. § 586(a)(3)(f).

Investigations are also initiated upon tips from creditors or other parties in a bankruptcy case. Further, the procedures outlined in §§ 3057(a) and (b) of title 18 and § 586 of title 28 are not a prerequisite for prosecution.[448] Creditors are often the first to suspect that the debtor has committed bankruptcy fraud. In fact, some creditors may suspect fraud on the part of any debtor who fails to meet his obligations. Some creditors, such as federal banks, are even obligated by law to report suspected federal crimes.[449]

In chapter 11 cases, creditors' committees are frequently appointed as a matter of course under § 1102 of the Bankruptcy Code. These committees have the right to conduct extensive discovery of the debtor's financial transactions. These official committees are sometimes in a position to retain their own accountants, particularly if there are insider transactions or other suspicious financial activity before or during the case.[450] Thus, committees and their attorneys and accountants are also in a position to uncover bankruptcy fraud.[451]

Unique role of the United States Trustees and bankruptcy trustee

Suspected fraud is frequently reported to the United States trustee or the bankruptcy trustee, rather than the United States attorney. The bankruptcy trustee and the United States trustee are uniquely situated to receive information from creditors and investigate such reports. The bankruptcy trustee has dual obligations: he is a fiduciary who serves the interests of the creditors collectively, and he is an officer of the court charged with the duty to report suspected criminal conduct. Unlike creditors, the United States trustee and the bankruptcy trustee can be objective in assessing such reports, as they have no vested interest in finding that fraud has been committed. Discovery of bankruptcy fraud can sometimes lead the trustee to undisclosed assets, but such information does not always bear fruit in the form of an economic recovery. It may be argued that a bankruptcy trustee has an economic incentive to uncover fraud because he will receive a commission on concealed assets that are discovered and liquidated, but this is not truly the case. A trustee's compensation is dependent only on whether the asset is liquidated, not whether fraud was committed.

The bankruptcy trustee sometimes witnesses the actual crime — for instance, when the debtor lies under oath at a § 341 meeting, giving rise to a violation of § 152(2), or withholds books and records from a trustee, giving rise

---

[448] *See United States v. Filiberti*, 353 F. Supp. 252 (D. Conn. 1973).

[449] 12 C.F.R. § 21.11.

[450] *See* 11 U.S.C. § 1103.

[451] A creditor may recover the actual necessary expenses incurred in connection with the prosecution of a criminal offense relating to the bankruptcy case or the business or property of the debtor. 11 U.S.C. § 503(b)(3)(C).

to a violation under § 152(9). The bankruptcy trustee also has access to information that may reveal a bankruptcy crime. For example, the trustee has the right to assert or waive the debtor's attorney-client privilege.[452] Under guidelines promulgated by the United States trustee program, bankruptcy trustees are to report suspected crimes to the United States attorney.[453] Sometimes this referral is made through the United States trustee. The referrals generally include: the bankruptcy case information (name, case number, name of presiding judge), details including dates, facts, and the names of persons involved in the suspected crime, names of potential witnesses, any relevant documents, and an estimate of the amount of loss involved.[454]

The Criminal Enforcement Unit was established in 2003 within the United States trustee program to strengthen the role of the United States trustees in criminal enforcement, from referrals through investigation and prosecution. A particular focus of the unit is emerging bankruptcy crimes, such as bankruptcy fraud schemes, bankruptcy mills, and credit card bust out schemes. One key feature of the United States Trustee's criminal enforcement capabilities is the Criminal Enforcement Tracking System which tracks pre-referral allegations, actual referrals, and types of crimes referred. From time to time attorneys in the United States Trustee program also assist directly in the prosecution of bankruptcy crimes by serving as expert witnesses or Special Assistant United States Attorneys.[455]

Rights and immunities accorded to trustee

Bankruptcy trustees have unique rights in bankruptcy crime investigations involving the debtors for whose estates they serve as trustees. At least one court has held that a bankruptcy trustee has absolute immunity when he reports a suspected bankruptcy crime.[456] The theory behind conferring such immunity on the trustee is the view that:

> [T]he trustee's obligation to report perceived violations of federal law to the United States attorney and to cooperate with any ensuing investigation and prosecution is one of those 'tasks so integral or intertwined with the

[452] The attorney-client privilege in bankruptcy cases and the trustee's rights with respect to the privilege are discussed in chapter 32.

[453] The Office of the U.S. Trustee made 744 criminal referrals in the year 2005.

[454] U.S. Dep't. of Justice, *United States Trustee Manual*, Vol. 5, § 5-3.3.4.

[455] *Testimony of Lawrence A. Friedman before Subcommittee on Commercial and Administrative Law of the Committee on the Judiciary, United States House of Representatives, March 9, 2004.*

[456] *In re Heinsohn*, 231 B.R. 48 (Bankr. E.D. Tenn. 1999).

judicial process' so that the trustee should be 'considered an arm of the judicial officer who is immune.'[457]

The bankruptcy trustee is also part of the law enforcement agency — the DOJ, of which the FBI is a part — in the broad sense, since she is required by statute to report bankruptcy related crimes.[458] Bankruptcy trustees are entitled to seek compensation from the bankruptcy estate of the debtor/defendant for making a criminal referral and cooperating with the United States attorney in a bankruptcy crime prosecution.[459] The Bankruptcy Code expressly provides that a creditor is entitled to reimbursement of expenses, but not professional fees, in connection with a criminal prosecution of the debtor.[460] The Bankruptcy Code does not contain either an express limitation or express authorization for the trustee's expenses in this regard, but support for such compensation is found in practice.

Communications to and from the bankruptcy judge, United States trustee, or bankruptcy trustee[461] who makes such a referral, are protected by the law enforcement privilege accorded under common law to the federal government.[462] This privilege covers the investigation and reporting of suspected bankruptcy crimes and is intended to protect the government from being forced to disclose the identity of informants.[463]

While there is scant case law on this issue, the authoritative view is that the privilege extends to the bankruptcy judge, the bankruptcy trustee, the trustee's attorney and the United States trustee. The law enforcement privilege is not absolute and may be lifted by the court where necessary to protect the rights of the accused.[464]

Post-referral actions

Once the referral is made to the United States attorney, further investigation is handled by the FBI, which is responsible for the investigation of federal crimes including bankruptcy crimes. In many districts, the criminal referral from the United States trustee is sent to the FBI as a matter of course. The FBI may

---

457 *In re Heinsohn*, 231 B.R. at 62 (citation omitted).

458 *In re Heinsohn*, 231 B.R. at 61-62; *see* 18 U.S.C. § 3057(a).

459 *In re Holder*, 207 B.R. 574 (Bankr. M.D. Tenn. 1997).

460 11 U.S.C. § 503(b)(3)(C).

461 *See* chapter 5 (The trustee).

462 *Kittay v. Fowler* (*In re Stockbridge Funding Corp.*), 153 B.R. 654 (Bankr. S.D.N.Y. 1993); *In re Heinsohn*, 231 B.R. at 62.

463 *Roviaro v. United States*, 353 U.S. 53 (1957).

464 *Roviaro*, 353 U.S. 53.

interview persons who may have knowledge of the suspected crime, such as the debtor's employees, creditors, relatives, or neighbors. The government can also obtain authority under a warrant to intercept telephone communications, commonly known as a "wire tap."[465] The United States attorney will often convene a grand jury for the purpose of issuing a grand jury subpoena to obtain documents in connection with the suspected crime being investigated. Search warrants may also be used where necessary. In addition to the FBI, the United States trustee is usually involved in the investigation of a suspected bankruptcy crime.

Once the investigation has advanced to the point where the United States attorney believes a crime has occurred, he will decide whether the case should be prosecuted. Criminal investigations and prosecutions are not stayed by the pendency of a bankruptcy case.[466] If he decides to prosecute, the United States attorney will generally seek a grand jury indictment, except in certain limited circumstances where information is permitted.[467]

Other agencies sometimes involved in the investigation of a bankruptcy crime are the Internal Revenue Service, the United States Postal Inspection Service, and the Social Security Administration. The Financial Crimes Enforcement Network may occasionally be involved as well, where information is needed concerning monetary transactions over $10,000.

---

[465] 18 U.S.C. § 2516(1).

[466] 11 U.S.C. § 362(b)(1).

[467] *See* chapter 28.

28. Indictment

The prosecution of a bankruptcy crime is generally commenced by the filing of an indictment or information in federal district court. The procedures governing the prosecution of bankruptcy crimes are set forth in the Federal Rules of Criminal Procedure. Fed. R. Crim. P. 7 provides in pertinent part:

> (a) When Used
> (1) Felony. An offense (other than criminal contempt) must be prosecuted by an indictment if it is punishable:
> (A) by death; or
> (B) by imprisonment for more than one year.
> (2) Misdemeanor. An offense punishable by imprisonment for one year or less may be prosecuted in accordance with Rule 58(b)(1).[468]

In turn, Fed. R. Crim. P. 58 provides in relevant part that the prosecution of "a misdemeanor may proceed on an indictment, information, or complaint...."

The indictment or information comprises the formal written charge of an alleged offense that is issued against a defendant. Both the information and indictment are analogous to a complaint in a civil case in that each constitute the pleading filed with the United States District Court to commence the case. An information can be filed by the United States attorney on her own initiative, without leave of court. An indictment, on the other hand, requires a grand jury, which must be convened to hear evidence and to determine whether to return an indictment. The Fifth Amendment of the United States Constitution states that:

> No person can be held to answer for a capital, or otherwise infamous crime, unless on a presentment or indictment of a Grand Jury[.][469]

---

[468] Fed. R. Crim. P. 7(a).
[469] U.S. CONST. amend. V.

The Fifth Amendment is the source of a felony defendant's right to have every element of the offense presented to the grand jury for determination of whether probable cause exists for an indictment. The procedures for convening the grand jury are provided in Fed. R. Crim. P. 6.

The grand jury will usually return the indictment as presented to it by the United States attorney. There is a popular saying that a grand jury would indict a ham sandwich. This is obviously an exaggeration; however, since the grand jury essentially hears only the prosecution's case, the overwhelming likelihood is that the requested indictment will be returned.

An information, on the other hand, is filed by the United States attorney without submission to a grand jury. The defendant has a right, before the case can be tried, to a preliminary hearing to determine if there is probable cause.[470] Cases are rarely dismissed at the "probable cause" hearing, but the hearing does give the defendant (and defense counsel) the opportunity to find out the essence of the government's case.

Most bankruptcy crimes are felonies punishable by imprisonment for a term exceeding a year, except for offenses under §§ 154, 155, and 156. Section 152 violations are the most commonly charged, and these must be prosecuted by indictment absent a waiver. For these reasons, unless the defendant waives indictment,[471] indictment will be required for the majority of bankruptcy crimes.

While it is rare for a defendant to successfully challenge an indictment on technical grounds, such challenges are occasionally raised. The technical requirements for an indictment are set forth in Fed. R. Crim. P. 7(c)(1), which requires that an indictment contain:

- a plain, concise and definite written statement of the essential facts constituting the offense charged
- signature of the attorney for the government
- the statute, rule, regulation, or other provision of law which the defendant is alleged to have violated

Like civil complaints, each count must stand on its own, but allegations in a count or counts may be incorporated by reference into other count or counts.[472]

---

[470] Fed. R. Crim. P. 5.1.

[471] A felony defendant may waive the requirement of indictment and thus may be prosecuted by information. Fed. R. Crim. P. 7(b). Since such a waiver is a waiver of the constitutional right to be indicted by a grand jury, such a waiver must be made knowingly, voluntarily, and understandingly. *Bartlett v. United States*, 354 F.2d 745 (8th Cir. 1966).

[472] Fed. R. Crim. P. 7(c)(1).

In order for an indictment to be sufficient, all elements of the offense must be alleged with respect to each count. The indictment must also meet the requirement of specificity. Historically, courts have taken a minimalistic approach to the requirements of specificity and sufficiency in an indictment for bankruptcy fraud.[473] The modern approach is that an indictment does not need to list every detail of the alleged crime, but it must set forth the elements of the offense charged with ample detail to assure against double jeopardy and to apprise the defendant of what he will have to be prepared to defend.[474]

Concealment

As concealment is perhaps the most frequently charged bankruptcy crime, the majority of reported decisions addressing sufficiency of an indictment for bankruptcy fraud address concealment charges. An indictment for concealment must allege the time and place of the concealment, describe the property concealed, and state the person from whom the property was concealed, and must allege that the property was property of the bankruptcy estate, and that the concealment was knowing and fraudulent.[475] A concealment count must also indicate the manner in which the concealment was accomplished.[476] The indictment does not need to allege specific facts demonstrating that the assets or property belong to the bankruptcy estate.[477] There is some support for the proposition that the indictment does not necessarily need to state the value of the property that was concealed,[478] but it must describe the property with sufficient particularity to enable a defendant to prepare a defense.

Venue

Venue, the district where the indictment is filed, lies in the district where the offense is alleged to have been committed.[479] Venue may lie in the district

---

[473] *See, e.g., United States v. Cohan*, 46 F.2d 310 (M.D. Pa. 1931) (place of concealment does not need to be alleged); *Kanner v. United States*, 21 F.2d 285 (2d Cir. 1927) (value of property concealed does not need to be alleged); *United States v. Vanderburg*, 358 F.2d 6 (7th Cir. 1966) (facts showing the manner of concealment does not need to be alleged).

[474] *United States v. Falcone*, 544 F.2d 607, 611 (2d Cir. 1976).

[475] *United States v. Arge*, 418 F.2d 721 (10th Cir. 1969).

[476] *United States v. Mathies*, 203 F. Supp. 797, 799-800 (W.D. Pa. 1962).

[477] *Pallett v. United States*, 228 F.2d 671 (5th Cir. 1956).

[478] *Kanner*, 21 F.2d 285. *But see United States v. Lynch*, 11 F.2d 298 (W.D. La. 1926).

[479] Fed. R. Crim. P. 18 provides:

Unless a statute or these rules permit otherwise, the government must prosecute an offense in a district where the offense was committed.

where the trustee is located[480] or where the bankruptcy case is pending.[481] As a result, a defendant can be prosecuted in a district in which the concealed assets were never located, or even a district in which he has never set foot.

The application of the venue rule is illustrated in *United States v. Schireson*.[482] Schireson filed a bankruptcy petition in the Eastern District of Pennsylvania. Seven years prior to his bankruptcy filing, while he and his wife were living in Chicago, Schireson transferred $130,000 in securities to her. She eventually placed them in a safety deposit box in a bank in Merchantville, New Jersey. Schireson argued that his prosecution in the Eastern District of Pennsylvania was improper because the assets that were allegedly concealed were originally located in Illinois, were transferred in Illinois, and were subsequently moved to New Jersey. The court articulated the issue as follows:

> The question is squarely raised whether a man can be guilty of the offense of concealing in the Eastern District of Pennsylvania when the physical things alleged to have been concealed are elsewhere.[483]

Rejecting Schireson's argument, the court explained that the crime in fact had been committed in Philadelphia:

> It must be borne in mind that concealment is no crime until bankruptcy comes about. There can be no concealment from a trustee prior to the appointment of a trustee (citation omitted). . . . Certainly it was no indictable concealment to have valuable objects in a bank vault in New Jersey before bankruptcy. The wrongdoing came only after bankruptcy had supervened. . . . [T]he acts which the defendant did thereafter were done in Pennsylvania.[484]

Venue for conspiracy to commit a bankruptcy crime lies in the district where any overt act occurred.[485]

---

[480] *United States v. Gordon*, 379 F.2d 788, 791 (2d Cir. 1967).

[481] *See, e.g., United States v. Martin*, 408 F.2d 949, 952-53 (7th Cir. 1969); *United States v. Schireson*, 116 F.2d 881 (3d Cir. 1940).

[482] *Schireson*, 116 F.2d 881.

[483] *Schireson*, 116 F.2d at 883.

[484] *Schireson*, 116 F.2d 883, 884.

[485] *Gretsch v. United States*, 242 F. 897, 899 (3d Cir. 1917).

29. Overview of defenses

Most defenses raised to bankruptcy charges fall into one of the following categories: (1) defenses that attack the validity of the prosecution or the indictment; (2) defenses that negate elements of the offense. There is no bright line separating these categories; in practice, various defense arguments will overlap.

Two defenses are discussed in the two chapters following this overview: the statute of limitations (chapter 30) and advice of counsel (chapter 31). Defenses uniquely germane to certain bankruptcy crimes are also discussed in the chapters relating to the specific offense.[486]

Affirmative defenses

Certain affirmative defenses, or defects in the indictment or in the institution of prosecution, will warrant dismissal of the indictment. Such defenses may be raised prior to trial by a motion to dismiss under Fed. R. Crim. P. 12(b). Failure to raise certain defenses in a pretrial motion will constitute a waiver of such defenses. All defenses based on defects in the indictment or the institution of the prosecution, other than lack of jurisdiction and failure to charge an offense, must be raised by a motion to dismiss before trial. These include grand jury irregularities.[487] Defenses which may be raised by motion but are not waived for failure to raise before trial include: double jeopardy; immunity; lack of jurisdiction; failure to charge an offense; the statute of limitations,[488] overcharging,[489] and constitutional infractions.

Numerous constitutional rights come into play in a criminal prosecution, including the right to a grand jury finding of probable cause;[490] the right against unreasonable search and seizure;[491] the right to a speedy trial;[492] the right to a

[486] Among the principal defenses discussed in other chapters are overcharging (chapter 17); materiality (chapters 6 and 7); literal truth (chapters 7 and 23); and recantation (chapter 23).

[487] Fed. R. Crim. P. 12, Advisory Committee Notes, 1944 Adoption.

[488] *See* chapter 30.

[489] *See* chapter 17.

[490] U.S. CONST., amend. V. *See* chapter 28.

[491] U.S. CONST., amend. IV.

[492] U.S. CONST., amend. VI. This right is also guaranteed in federal cases by statute. 18 U.S.C. § 3161.

trial by a jury;[493] the right to counsel;[494] the right to confront witnesses;[495] and the right against double jeopardy.[496] Violation of certain constitutional rights will act as a bar to prosecution. Other affirmative defenses that may be raised by motion to dismiss include selective prosecution, vindictive prosecution, or government misconduct in the investigation.

Lack of *mens rea*

Intent is frequently the pivotal issue in the prosecution of a bankruptcy crime and is sometimes the only issue open to doubt. For that reason, a great number of reported decisions in the bankruptcy fraud area discuss the element of intent.

Defenses that seek to negate the element of intent include good faith, advice of counsel,[497] literal truth,[498] consciousness of innocence, insanity, and diminished capacity. Certain other closely related defenses, such as curative acts and legal compliance, can also be viewed as "intent" defenses.

The argument that the law was uncertain and therefore the defendant's violation of the law could not have been willful, is another approach used to negate intent. This argument is based upon due process principles and the requirement of fair notice.[499] If the law is ambiguous, then a law-abiding citizen could not have fair warning of the conduct that is proscribed. In order for conduct to be criminal, there must be an intentional violation of a knowable duty. If the obligation was not knowable because the law is ambiguous, no crime can exist. In fact, the defendant's actual intent is irrelevant under this approach.

Another intent argument is good faith. The argument that the defendant had a good faith belief that his conduct was lawful seeks to negate the elements of "knowing" and "fraudulent." This defense is viable in a situation in which the defendant made a good faith mistake or the alleged crime was accidental. The defense will be unsuccessful in situations in which the conduct was deceitful, dishonest, or sought to take advantage of another person or the bankruptcy process. An example is a bidder at a bankruptcy sale bribing other bidders not

---

[493] U.S. CONST., amend. VI.

[494] U.S. CONST., amend. VI.

[495] U.S. CONST., amend. VI.

[496] U.S. CONST., amend. V. Multiplicity, *i.e.*, charging more than one offense for the same crime, is barred by the double jeopardy principle. *See* chapter 17.

[497] *See* chapter 31.

[498] *See* chapters 7 and 20.

[499] *See* chapter 4.

to bid. Courts have viewed such behavior as inherently deceitful, even where the bidder in question believed his actions were not illegal.[500]

Insufficient bankruptcy nexus

A defendant may occasionally be in a position to assert that the relationship of his alleged conduct to bankruptcy is too tangential to constitute a bankruptcy crime. Such defenses seek to negate one or more of the statutory elements of a chapter 9 offense. Some examples of such arguments include

- the invalidity or dismissal of the bankruptcy case
- the property allegedly concealed, transferred, destroyed, or the like, was not property of the estate as the term is defined in the Bankruptcy Code
- the status of the property as estate property was unclear or undetermined

The most frequent argument of this nature is the assertion that the property was not property of the estate, or that the defendant did not believe the property was property of the estate, an argument also directed at negating criminal intent. Uncertainty as to whether the property was estate property can arise in the case of assets owned indirectly by an individual debtor, *e.g.*, the assets are owned by a business entity such as a corporation, limited liability company, or partnership in which the debtor has an controlling interest.

From a purely civil standpoint, such assets would not be considered property of the estate under 11 U.S.C. § 541. An individual debtor would not be required to list the assets (as opposed to his interest in the entity with title to the assets) on his bankruptcy schedules. The sale or transfer of such assets would not require bankruptcy court approval. Nevertheless, indirectly held assets have been the subject of numerous criminal prosecutions. The courts in such cases will look beyond the technical to determine if the failure to disclose the assets, or the transfer of the assets, was fraudulent.[501]

Curative acts

Acts that negate the alleged conduct, whether prior or subsequent to the alleged offense, may also constitute defenses. These include recantation, prior or subsequent disclosure, disgorgement, turnover, ratification, and prior or retroactive bankruptcy court approval.

---

[500] *See* chapter 9 (Bribery).

[501] *See* chapter 5 (Property of the estate); chapter 6 (Property).

Defenses based on curative acts vary in their effectiveness, depending on the specific offense and the nature of the curative act. Recantation can exculpate a defendant under the general perjury statute. The effect of recantation with respect to the bankruptcy false oath and declaration statute will in most instances be the same. Not every recantation, however, will eliminate the defendant's culpability.[502]

Disclosure is logically raised as a defense to offenses under § 152. This defense is most effective when the disclosure is made prior to the alleged offense and least effective when made afterward. Disclosure is almost always ineffective as a defense when the disclosure is made after discovery of the alleged conduct by the trustee, creditors, or court.[503]

Approval by the bankruptcy court is a type of curative act. Illustrations of the use of this defense are: the argument that the bankruptcy court approved the sale of assets outside the ordinary course of business and thus a buyer did not violate § 152(5) by receiving a conveyance of property from the debtor; or the court authorized abandonment of books and records, and therefore the debtor's destruction of those books and records did not violate § 152(8). Retroactive bankruptcy court approval of an illegal transaction usually will not exonerate a defendant.[504] This is especially true in cases where the bankruptcy court was not fully apprised of the nature and details of the transaction. Prior court approval in cases where all material facts were disclosed to the court should prove to be a solid defense in most cases.

Civil compliance

Technical compliance with civil bankruptcy law should always be explored as a defense. Civil compliance, however, is not a safe harbor where the substance of the transaction is fraudulent in the broad sense. This is illustrated in the case of *United States v. Goodstein.*

Goodstein, a bankruptcy lawyer, transferred his stock in a bankrupt company to a company that was not in bankruptcy. Goodstein then moved the assets of the debtor to the location of the acquiring company's location. Since the creditors holding security interests in the assets did not have financing statements on file in the jurisdiction in which the acquiring company was located, the perfection of their interests was jeopardized. Goodstein later sought retroactive court approval for the transaction.

---

[502] *See* chapter 23 (Recantation).

[503] *See, e.g., United States v. Gellene,* 182 F.3d 578 (7th Cir. 1999).

[504] The rejection of retroactive court approval as a defense is illustrated by the case of *United States v. Goodstein,* 883 F.2d 1362 (7th Cir. 1989).

In defense to charges of transferring and concealment of property with the intent to defeat the bankruptcy laws, Goodstein argued unsuccessfully that the court had retroactively approved the transaction. He also argued civil compliance: under the Bankruptcy Code he was permitted to transfer his individually held stock in the debtor without court approval, and a change in location was an ordinary course transaction for which no court approval was required. The court rejected each of these arguments, deeming the transaction an indirect transfer of property with fraudulent intent. This case illustrates the principle that technical compliance with the civil provisions of the Bankruptcy Code will not insulate an individual from criminal liability or provide a "safe harbor" defense.

Materiality

Lack of materiality is not always germane as a defense. There are some offenses in which materiality is irrelevant, at least from a technical standpoint. Materiality is not an element of concealment under § 152(1). Nevertheless, there is some support for a materiality argument in limited circumstances. Failure to disclose an asset of *de minimus* value may arguably not constitute an offense, because the property was nil.[505] In the case of certain other offenses, lack of materiality will be a valid, albeit difficult, defense.

Materiality is a judicially engrafted element of crimes under §§ 152(2) and 152(3) (false oaths, accounts, and declarations) and an explicit statutory element of crimes under § 152(5); however, materiality is broadly construed.[506] A misstatement concerning ownership of a ream of paper in a multi-million dollar bankruptcy is probably not material.[507] However, for purposes of §§ 152(2) and (3), virtually all matters concerning the extent, nature, or history of the debtor's financial transactions, and all statements designed to secure adjudication by the court, are material.[508] The materiality of a false oath account or declaration is a question of law for the court, not a question of fact for the jury. On the other hand, materiality as an element of a false statement charge under § 1014 is a question of fact for the jury.

Materiality should always be considered as a possible defense where the facts warrant, whether or not materiality is an express element of the offense.

---

[505] *See* chapter 6, note 36.

[506] *United States v. Yagow,* 953 F.2d 427 (8th Cir. 1992).

[507] *United States v. Key,* 859 F.2d 1257, 1261 (7th Cir. 1988).

[508] *See* chapter 7 (Materiality).

30. Statute of limitations

The statute of limitations for federal crimes is generally five years unless otherwise specified. Section 3282 provides:

> Except as otherwise expressly provided by law, no person shall be prosecuted, tried, or punished for any offense, not capital, unless the indictment is found or the information is instituted within five years next after such offense shall have been committed.[509]

The purpose of the criminal statute of limitations is to limit exposure to a certain fixed period of time. This is to protect individuals from having to defend themselves against charges as to which the facts have been obscured by the passage of time.[510] The statute of limitations is intended to ensure that the defendant receives notice, within the prescribed time, of the charges so he can assemble evidence relevant to his defense before it is lost by the passage of time.[511] Statutes of limitations in criminal cases are to be liberally interpreted in favor of repose.[512] The statute of limitations is a bar to prosecution which should be raised prior to trial by a motion to dismiss the indictment.[513]

The five-year statute of limitations applies to all bankruptcy crimes, with one exception. Section 3284 provides:

> The concealment of assets of a debtor in a case under title 11 shall be deemed to be a continuing offense until the debtor shall have been finally discharged or a discharge denied, and the period of limitations shall not begin to run until such final discharge or denial of discharge.[514]

---

[509] 18 U.S.C. § 3282.

[510] *Toussie v. United States*, 397 U.S. 112 (1970); *United States v. DiSantillo*, 615 F.2d 128 (3d Cir. 1980).

[511] *United States v. O'Neill*, 463 F. Supp. 1205, 1208 (E.D. Pa. 1979).

[512] *See, e.g., United States v. Dolan*, 120 F.3d 856 (8th Cir. 1997).

[513] *See* Fed. R. Crim. P. 12(b).

[514] 18 U.S.C. § 3284.

The limitations period runs from the granting or denial of the debtor's discharge, whether or not the defendant is the debtor.[515] This rule also applies to cases in which the defendant is charged with aiding or abetting a concealment.[516]

In some bankruptcy cases, the bankruptcy court may not have the opportunity to either grant or deny a discharge before the case is closed or dismissed. In such a case, the statute will begin to run from the date on which a discharge became impossible.[517] In a case where there is neither a denial nor a granting of a discharge, the date on which the statute begins to run is the date on which a discharge is irrevocably barred as a matter of law, such as the entry of an order finding that the discharge was waived.[518] If there is no such triggering event or order, then the date of dismissal will trigger the running of the statute.[519]

Concealments for which the statute of limitations are governed by § 3284 include both charges brought under § 152(2) and § 152(7). The special statute of limitations, which does not begin to run until virtually the end of the bankruptcy case, reflects the view that concealment is a continuing crime.[520] Concealment is considered one offense for the entire concealment period.[521]

If the debtor concealed an asset by not disclosing it on his bankruptcy schedules, and thereby made a false declaration, the extended statute of limitations under § 3284 governs the concealment but does not extend the running of the statute of limitations for the false declaration, which is five years from the commission of the offense.[522] This rule is demonstrated by the cases involving Ted Gleave and his lawyer, David Knoll, who were both convicted of bankruptcy fraud. Gleave's and Knoll's cases became the subject of two widely cited decisions concerning the statute of limitations for bankruptcy crimes. Among other things, Gleave opened a bank account in the Cayman Islands. Later, when Gleave filed chapter 11 (presumably to protect his assets from his wife in a divorce), Knoll prepared, and Gleave signed, bankruptcy schedules and a statement of financial affairs which failed to disclose the account. Gleave was charged with concealment and with making a false declaration. Knoll was charged with aiding and abetting a false declaration. Knoll's and Gleave's convictions on the false declaration charges were reversed by the Second Circuit:

[515] *United States v. Guglielmini*, 425 F.2d 439 (2d Cir. 1970).

[516] *United States v. Gleave*, 786 F. Supp. 258, 266 (W.D.N.Y. 1992), *remanded on other grounds sub nom., United States v. Knoll*, 16 F.3d 1313 (2d Cir. 1994), *cert. denied*, 522 U.S. 1118 (1998).

[517] *Dolan*, 120 F.3d 856; *Guglielmini*, 425 F.2d at 439.

[518] *Guglielmini*, 425 F.2d at 443.

[519] *See Dolan*, 120 F.3d 856.

[520] *See Sultan v. United States*, 249 F.2d 385 (5th Cir. 1957).

[521] *Somberg v. United States*, 71 F.2d 637 (7th Cir. 1934).

[522] *United States v. Knoll*, 16 F.3d 1313, 1318 (2d Cir. 1994), *cert. denied*, 522 U.S. 1118 (1998).

> Despite the fact that the purpose of making the false statement in Gleave's case may well have been to conceal assets, the substance [of the count] charged only the making of a false statement in connection with bankruptcy proceedings. It did not charge either appellant with the offense of concealment of assets. Hence, the extension of the limitations period provided for in § 3284 has no application[.][523]

A corporation is not entitled to, and thus does not receive, a discharge in a chapter 7 case. Consider the case of an individual who is charged with concealing the assets of the corporation in connection with the corporation's chapter 7 case. If the statute of limitations begins to run from the granting of a discharge, an event which will never occur in such a case, when does the statute of limitations begin to run? There is little case law on this question, but the weight of existing authority suggests that the commencement of a corporate chapter 7 case (either by initial filing or conversion) will trigger the running of the five year statute.[524] The theory underlying these decisions is consistent with the rule that the time begins to run when a discharge is waived or irrevocably barred. In a chapter 7 case of a corporation, the discharge is never available and thus is barred from the outset; hence, the statute begins to run upon the filing of, or the conversion to, the case under chapter 7.

The statute of limitations for all bankruptcy crimes, other than concealment, is five years from the commission of the offense. The offense is deemed to be committed when all acts required to commit the offense are completed.[525] The case of a continuing crime, such as concealment, is an exception to this rule.

The indictment or information must be served within the limitations period; an arrest does not toll the statute.[526] Flight from the jurisdiction tolls the statute.[527] Once an indictment has been filed, a superseding indictment may be filed and will relate back to the date of the initial indictment for statute of limitations purposes, provided that the superseding indictment does not materially broaden or substantially amend the initial charges.[528]

---

523 *Knoll*, 16 F.3d at 1318.

524 *United States v. Gilbert*, 136 F.3d 1451 (11th Cir. 1998); *see Rudin v. United States*, 254 F.2d 45 (6th Cir. 1958); *but see United States v. Zisblatt*, 78 F. Supp. 9 (S.D.N.Y. 1948) (statute of limitations began to run upon commission of offense in case where corporation did not apply for discharge; decided under prior law).

525 *DiSantillo*, 615 F.2d 128.

526 *See Powell v. United States*, 352 F.2d 705, 707 (D.C. Cir. 1965).

527 *United States v. Singleton*, 702 F.2d 1159, 1169 (D.C. Cir. 1983).

528 *United States v. Friedman*, 649 F.2d 199, 202-03 (3d Cir. 1981); *United States v. Grady*, 544 F.2d 598, 601-602 (2d Cir. 1976).

In a prosecution for conspiracy to commit a bankruptcy crime, the government must allege and prove that at least one overt act in furtherance of the conspiracy by one of the conspirators was committed within the limitations period.[529] At trial, the government may satisfy this requirement by proving the occurrence of an overt act not listed in the indictment.[530]

United States v. Dolan[531] involved a conspiracy to commit bankruptcy fraud by a bankruptcy lawyer who allegedly conspired with his client to conceal the client's assets in the client's bankruptcy case. The only overt act alleged in the indictment that occurred within the period of the statute of limitations was the bankruptcy court's dismissal of the bankruptcy case. Dolan argued that the innocent act of a third party, here, the bankruptcy court, could not satisfy the statute of limitations. The government argued that a conversation in which the defendant lied to a creditor of the debtor's occurred within the limitations period, though this conversation was not alleged in the indictment. The court stated:

> The government, to prevent the indictment from being found defective on its face, "must allege and prove the commission of at least one overt act by one of the conspirators within [the five-year] period in furtherance of the conspiratorial agreement."[532]

The indictment stated that defendant "committed and caused to be committed" the dismissal. The court found that the defendant's participation in the hearing on dismissal of the bankruptcy case was the overt act alleged in the indictment. The court in *Dolan* did not directly reach the question whether the act of a third party nonconspirator may satisfy the statute of limitations, but the decision, as well as the weight of other well reasoned authority, suggests it does not. The court also held that an overt act not listed in the indictment by a conspirator can satisfy the statute. [533]

---

[529] *Dolan*, 120 F.3d at 864.
[530] *Dolan*, 120 F.3d at 866.
[531] *Dolan* is discussed further in chapter 19.
[532] *Dolan*, 120 F.3d at 864 (citing *United States v. Davis*, 533 F.2d 921, 926 (5th Cir. 1976)).
[533] *Dolan*, 120 F.3d at 866.

31. Advice of counsel

The criminal defendant in a bankruptcy crime prosecution will sometimes argue that the conduct for which he is charged was undertaken on the advice of counsel. This argument seeks to negate the presence of criminal intent, an element of the crime. All bankruptcy crimes have a *mens rea* requirement. Virtually all bankruptcy crimes are predicated on fraudulent intent and/or knowing willfulness. Sections 152, 153 and 155 require that the conduct be "knowing and fraudulent." Section 154 requires that the conduct be knowing, and § 157, that the conduct be fraudulent. Thus, the "advice of counsel" defense is not an affirmative defense raised by a pretrial motion to dismiss, but rather, is a factual defense raised at trial, which seeks to disprove the element of intent.

There are several pitfalls to invoking "advice of counsel." Courts tend to evaluate this defense by a subjective test (did the defendant, in fact, rely on the advice of counsel), an objective test (would a reasonable defendant have relied on the alleged advice), or both. These standards are usually not distinguished, and the line between the two is often blurred. If no reasonable defendant would have relied on the advice, then the defendant in question probably did not either.

The defense is only effective if the advice given by the attorney is, in fact, linked to the defendant's state of mind. If the advice did not influence the defendant's intention because the defendant did not seek the legal advice in good faith to start with, then the defense will fail. One example is the situation where the defendant did not fully and in good faith tell his lawyer the complete facts.[534]

Consider the case of the insider who, purportedly on the advice of counsel, asserts a claim in a bankruptcy against a debtor corporation based on an alleged loan by the insider to the company. If the insider failed to tell his counsel that the funds were actually payment for stock in the debtor, which the insider purchased, and not a true loan, then the defense will be unhelpful. Seeking legal advice without disclosing the facts honestly to one's lawyer is viewed as

---

[534] *Levinson v. United States*, 263 F. 257 (3d Cir. 1920).

consulting a lawyer merely as a subterfuge. The consultation is not truly for the purpose of obtaining legal advice.[535]

If the attorney actually assisted the defendant in committing the crime, or the defendant was otherwise on notice that his attorney's advice or conduct was wrong, the defense will fail. The case of *United States v. Levine*,[536] illustrates the pitfalls of this defense. The Levines operated a furniture business that overstated its inventory by $1.1 million. When the secured creditors discovered the shortage, they insisted on a liquidation sale, and were induced to make additional loans to facilitate the process. All sale proceeds were to be deposited into the bank, which was the major secured creditor. Several months later, the bank learned that there was no money. Thereafter, Mr. and Mrs. Levine filed bankruptcy petitions. Prior to bankruptcy, the Levines concealed funds in trust accounts that their attorneys established.[537] Mr. Levine testified that his lawyers suggested "'hiding' and 'washing' funds in the attorneys' secret trust account".[538] The court noted that Mr. Levine's terminology itself suggested that he did not think the advice was legal. The court also viewed the bankruptcy judge's remarks at a hearing in the Levines' case — at which the bankruptcy judge stated that the evidence suggested that the law firm was either acting unethically or was conspiring with the debtor to conceal funds — as bearing on the Levines' alleged belief that their attorneys' conduct was correct.[539]

Levine illustrates a mixed subjective/objective approach to the "advice of counsel" defense. The objective aspect is the fact that the advice was so incredible, the defendant should have known it was incorrect. An example of such objectively incredible advice is the lawyers' suggestion that the defendants launder money through the lawyers' account, and that doing so would permit the defendants to have full use of the money while denying any ownership of it.[540] Clients are presumed to have common sense. In the case of bankruptcy representation, this means knowing that bankruptcy is not a license to lie, cheat, and steal. The subjective aspect is the fact that the clients were on notice, based on statements by the bankruptcy judge, that their lawyers' advice was unethical.

Another circumstance where reliance on advice of counsel is an ineffective defense is a debtor's failure to disclose assets on the bankruptcy schedules where it is evident that the asset must be disclosed. Such cases are often viewed under

---

[535] *Levinson*, 263 F. at 259-260.

[536] *United States v. Levine*, 970 F.2d 681, 685 (10th Cir. 1992).

[537] The Levines were ultimately convicted of bankruptcy fraud for concealing assets.

[538] *Levine*, 970 F.2d at 685.

[539] *Levine*, 970 F.2d at 689.

[540] *Levine*, 970 F. 2d at 685.

the "objective test," *i.e.*, no reasonable debtor would rely on the advice of a lawyer who tells him to lie under oath.

If the defendant failed to follow his lawyer's advice, the fact that he sought legal advice is irrelevant. The fact that legal advice was sought but not followed fails to negate, and may even prove, criminal intent.

Use of this defense will inevitably lead to a waiver of the attorney-client privilege. Waiver of the privilege in turn may result in incriminating disclosures by the client or the lawyer. Unless the defense is supported by testimony of the attorney whose advice was allegedly given and followed, the defense is unlikely to succeed.

The successful use of this defense will usually require the testimony of the lawyer upon whose advice the defendant relied. Under the rules of professional conduct in most states, a lawyer who is a necessary witness in a trial generally cannot act as an advocate at that trial, but that lawyer's firm is not precluded from acting as trial counsel for the client in the case.[541]

---

[541] *See* Rule 3.7 of the ABA Model Rules of Professional Conduct.

32. Attorney-client privilege

Confidential communications between a client and attorney are generally considered privileged and thus protected at common law from disclosure against the will of the client. The Supreme Court has stated:

> The attorney-client privilege is the oldest of the privileges for confidential communications known to the common law. 8 J. Wigmore, Evidence § 2290 (McNaughton rev. 1961). Its purpose is to encourage full and frank communications between attorneys and their clients and thereby promote broader public interests in the observance of the law and administration of justice. The privilege recognizes that sound legal advice or advocacy serves public ends and such advocacy depends on the lawyer's being fully informed by the client.[542]

The attorney-client privilege is made applicable in bankruptcy cases by Rule 501 of the Federal Rules of Evidence:

> Except as otherwise required by the Constitution of the United States or provided by Act of Congress, or in rules prescribed by the Supreme Court pursuant to statutory authority, the privilege of a witness, person, government, State, or political subdivision thereof shall be governed by the principles of the common law as they may be interpreted by the courts of the United States in light of reason and experience.[543]

This rule provides that the Federal Rules of Evidence are applicable in bankruptcy cases and federal bankruptcy criminal prosecutions. Federal common law, rather than state law, governs the attorney-client privilege in such cases.[544] The privilege is recognized under federal common law. Therefore,

---

[542] *Upjohn Co. v. United States*, 449 U.S. 383, 389 (1981).
[543] Fed. R. Evid. 501.
[544] *United States v. Zolin*, 491 U.S. 554 (1989).

disclosure of confidential attorney-client communications generally cannot be compelled in a bankruptcy criminal prosecution.

Under federal common law, the attorney-client privilege applies if (1) the asserted holder of the privilege is, or sought to become, a client; (2) the person to whom the communication is made is a member of the bar, or her subordinate, who is acting as a lawyer in connection with the communication; (3) the communication relates to a fact of which the attorney was informed by her client, not in the presence of strangers, for the purpose of obtaining a legal opinion, legal services, or assistance in a legal proceeding and not for the purpose of committing a crime or tort; and (4) the privilege is claimed and not waived by the client.[545]

Another frequently cited statement of the privilege is:

> . . . where legal advice of any kind is sought from a professional legal advisor in his capacity as such, the communications relevant to that purpose, made in confidence by the client, are at his insistence permanently protected from disclosure by himself or by the legal advisor[.][546]

The attorney-client privilege may be extended under the joint defense or common interest privilege. Normally, the presence of third parties during an attorney-client communication will destroy the privilege. The joint defense (or common interest) privilege is an exception to this rule. The common interest exception applies to communications with parties having a common interest or their lawyer. To have a common interest, the parties do not necessarily have to be actually involved in litigation, as long as litigation is contemplated or foreseeable. In order to invoke the joint defense privilege, the communication in question must be made in the course of, and in furtherance of, a joint defense effort.[547] The fact that the parties may have adverse (as well as common) interests does not vitiate the privilege, as long as the communication in question related to their common interest.[548]

Communications between lawyers and their clients in the course of a bankruptcy case are fraught with a number of complications in which the privilege does not attach, is deemed waived, or is inapplicable. In the course of a bankruptcy case, who is the client for purposes of holding the privilege may be

---

[545] *Diversified Indus., Inc. v. Meredith*, 572 F.2d 596 (8th Cir. 1977).

[546] *Diversified Indus.*, 572 F.2d at 602 (citing *Wonneman v. Stratford Securities Co.*, 23 F.R.D. 281, 285 (S.D.N.Y. 1959)).

[547] *In re Bevill, Bresler & Schulman Asset Management Corp.*, 805 F.2d 120, 126 (3d Cir. 1986).

[548] *Eisenberg v. Gagnon*, 766 F.2d 770, 787-88 (3d Cir. 1985).

different from who would be the client in a situation that was similar but was outside the bankruptcy context. Further, who holds the privilege may change over the course of the case.

Corporate privilege

One of the most problematic areas in which privilege questions arise is when the client is a corporation. When a corporate debtor's principal retains an attorney to represent the corporate debtor, the privilege is held by the corporation, not the principal, although it is the principals who engage counsel and typically engage in communications with counsel on the corporation's behalf. Since corporations act through individuals, questions often arise as to whether communications by or to certain categories of corporate agents or employees are privileged.

Historically, two standards have been used to determine whether an employee is a client for purposes of the privilege. One was enunciated in *Harper Row Publishers, Inc. v. Decker*,[549] which held that an employee of the corporation is sufficiently identified with the corporation so that his communication with the corporation's lawyer is privileged where: (1) the employee made the communication at the direction of his superiors, and (2) the subject matter about which the lawyer's advice was sought by the corporation and dealt with in the communication was within the performance by the employee of the duties of his employment.

The other approach, the "control" test, holds that the attorney-client privilege is limited to the control group of a corporation.[550] The "control" approach has been widely criticized in that it ignores the practicalities involved in corporate representation by protecting only a limited range of top level management. Frequently an attorney must interview and obtain sensitive information from employees who are merely middle management or not in management at all. In a bankruptcy context information regarding financial and operational matters is often assembled by non-management employees.

The "control" test was criticized and rejected, although not expressly overruled, by the Supreme Court in *Upjohn*.[551] In *Upjohn*, the corporation's in-house counsel sent questionnaires requesting information from non-control group employees regarding potentially illegal payments. The IRS later sought the

---

[549] *Harper Row Publishers, Inc. v. Decker*, 423 F.2d 487, 491-92 (7th Cir. 1970), *aff'd.*, 400 U.S. 348 (1971).

[550] *City of Philadelphia v. Westinghouse Electric Corp.*, 210 F. Supp. 483 (E.D. Pa.), *mandamus and prohibition denied sub nom., General Electric Co. v. Kilpatrick*, 312 F.2d 742 (3d Cir. 1962).

[551] *Upjohn Co.*, 449 U.S. 383.

production of the completed questionnaires. In upholding the corporation's claim that these materials were privileged, the Supreme Court stated:

> In the case of the individual client the provider of the information and the person who acts on the lawyer's advice are one and the same. In the corporate context, however, it will frequently be employees beyond the control group . . . who will possess the information needed by the corporation's lawyers. Middle-level — and indeed lower level — employees can, by actions within the scope of their employment, embroil the corporation in serious legal difficulties, and . . . these employees would have the relevant information needed by corporate counsel if he is to adequately advise the client . . . .[552]

The power to waive the privilege is held by the corporation's top management, *i.e.*, its officers and directors, who have a fiduciary duty to act in the best interests of the corporation.[553] When control of the corporation passes to new management, the authority to assert and waive the privilege passes as well.[554]

Exceptions to the privilege

In a bankruptcy fraud prosecution against a corporation's president for embezzlement of assets from a corporation, communications between the president and the corporation's attorney are not protected from disclosure once a bankruptcy trustee is appointed for the corporation. The trustee then holds and may waive the attorney-client privilege.[555] While the Bankruptcy Code does not explicitly grant the trustee the power to assert or waive the privilege, the trustee acquires such power because control of the corporation, including the privilege, passes to the corporation's trustee.[556] In the case of an individual debtor, however, it is unresolved whether the trustee holds the privilege.[557] The attorney-client privilege held by an officer or director, as to his communication with his individual counsel, is unaffected by the rights of the corporation's trustee.[558]

When information is required to be disclosed, the information is not considered confidential. This is frequently the case when the subject of the com-

---

552 *Upjohn Co.*, 449 U.S. at 391.

553 *Commodity Futures Trading Comm'n. v. Weintraub*, 471 U.S. 343 (1986).

554 *Weintraub*, 471 U.S. 343.

555 *Weintraub*, 471 U.S. 343.

556 *Weintraub*, 471 U.S. 343; *see also Citibank, N.A. v. Andros*, 666 F.2d 1192 (8th Cir. 1981).

557 *Weintraub*, 471 U.S. at 356.

558 *Weintraub*, 471 U.S. 343.

munication is financial information which the debtor is required to disclose under bankruptcy law. Information transmitted to counsel with the intent that the information be disclosed to a third party is not confidential and thus is not privileged. The United States Court for the Seventh Circuit has stated:

> When information is disclosed for the purpose of assembly into a bankruptcy petition and supporting schedules, there is no intent for the information to be held in confidence because the information is to be disclosed in documents publicly filed with the bankruptcy court.[559]

This exception to the privilege may also encompass information transmitted to bankruptcy counsel in connection with a myriad of other required disclosures, such as monthly operating reports and the disclosure statement.

Crime/fraud exception

Another important exception to the privilege is the "crime/fraud" exception. The privilege is inapplicable to "communications 'made for the purpose of getting advice for the commission of a fraud' or crime."[560] The Fifth Circuit stated:

> Privileges are recognized because law makers and courts consider protecting confidential relationships more important to society than ferreting out what was said within the relationship. The privilege for communications between client and attorney ceases when the purpose of the privilege is abused, when the lawyer becomes either the accomplice or the unwitting tool in a continuing or planned wrongful act.[561]

Even if the lawyer is not complicit in the fraud, the communication is excepted from the privilege under the crime-fraud exception. This principle is illustrated in *United States v. Ballard*.[562] The *Ballard* case involved a situation that is all too familiar to many bankruptcy lawyers: The would-be debtor "shops" for bankruptcy counsel until he gets the advice he wants, or at least until he educates himself on what information to withhold from his lawyer. Before consulting a lawyer, Ballard transferred property to his father-in-law and placed the cash proceeds in his wife's safety deposit box. When Ballard con-

---

[559] *United States v. White*, 950 F.2d 426 (7th Cir. 1991); *see also United States v. Cote*, 456 F.2d 142 (8th Cir. 1972).

[560] *Zolin*, 491 U.S. at 563 (citation omitted).

[561] *United States v. Ballard*, 779 F.2d 287, 292 (5th Cir. 1986).

[562] *Ballard*, 779 F.2d 287.

sulted an attorney about a possible bankruptcy, Ballard was advised that asset transfers occurring within a year before bankruptcy needed to be disclosed, and thus, he should wait a year before filing a bankruptcy petition. He then consulted a second bankruptcy lawyer, who filed his bankruptcy case without disclosing the assets. The court noted that the first lawyer's advice concerning the illegality of the plan was presumably the reason Ballard hired other counsel. Holding that the crime/fraud exception to the privilege applied, the court upheld the admissibility of the evidence.[563]

The crime/fraud exception only pertains to communications intended to further commission of a crime. Conversations about past criminal conduct are privileged.[564]

Where the claim of privilege is challenged under this exception, the court may conduct an *in camera* review to determine the merits of the claim.[565] Such *in camera* review does not terminate the privilege.[566] Before an *in camera* review is conducted, the party opposing the privilege must show "a factual basis adequate to support a good faith belief by a reasonable person" that the crime/fraud exception applies.[567] Once such a showing is made, the decision to conduct an *in camera* review rests within the sound discretion of the court.[568] The government does not need to show that a crime was actually committed to overcome the privilege. It needs only to show that probable cause exists that the communications were made in furtherance of a crime.[569]

---

[563] *Ballard*, 779 F.2d 287.
[564] *Zolin*, 491 U.S. 554.
[565] *Zolin*, 491 U.S. 554.
[566] *Zolin*, 491 U.S. 554.
[567] *Zolin*, 491 U.S. 554.
[568] *Zolin*, 491 U.S. 554.
[569] *United States v. Gleave*, 786 F. Supp. 258, 293 (W.D.N.Y. 1992), *remanded on other grounds sub nom.*, *United States v. Knoll*, 16 F.3d 1313 (2d Cir. 1994), *cert. denied*, 522 U.S. 1118 (1998).

33. The Fifth Amendment privilege

The Fifth Amendment provides:

> No person shall be . . . compelled in any criminal case to be a witness against himself . . .[570]

The purpose of the privilege against self-incrimination is to "avoid confronting the witness with the 'cruel trilemma' of self-accusation, perjury or contempt."[571] The Fifth Amendment privilege protects an individual from being compelled to give testimony (oral or written) which would provide a link in the chain of evidence needed for criminal prosecution.[572] Only an individual has a privilege against self-incrimination. A corporation has no such privilege.

Bankruptcy cases pose a unique dilemma when the right to remain silent is concerned. The debtor in a bankruptcy case is under a duty to answer questions, under oath or penalty of perjury, as to his assets, liabilities, and financial transactions, and some of these answers may tend to incriminate him.

In some instances, the information on the bankruptcy petition itself could be incriminating, as could the bankruptcy schedules and statement of financial affairs filed at the outset of the case.[573] The debtor must testify under oath at the meeting convened pursuant to § 341 of the Bankruptcy Code. If requested by the trustee, a creditor, or a party in interest and ordered by the court, the debtor must submit to an oral examination under oath.[574] The debtor's testimony in these situations may also present the potential for self-incrimination.

Occasions for self-incrimination may also arise in the course of contested matters and adversary proceedings in the bankruptcy case. Consider the case of a bank creditor which files an adversary proceeding against the debtor, seeking

---

[570] U.S. CONST. amend. V.

[571] *Martin-Trigona v. Belford* (*In re Martin-Trigona*), 732 F.2d 170, 174 (2d Cir. 1984) (quoting *Murphy v. Waterfront Comm'n*, 378 U.S. 52, 55 (1964)).

[572] *Braswell v. United States*, 487 U.S. 99, 104 (1988).

[573] *See* Official Bankruptcy Form 1, 6, 7; Fed. R. Bankr. P. 1007; chapter 5.

[574] *See* Fed. R. Bankr. P. 2004; chapter 5.

a determination that the claim (based on a loan to the debtor) is nondischargeable because it was made based on a false financial statement. In the course of the adversary proceeding, the bank deposes the debtor and asks questions directed at establishing that the financial statement submitted by the debtor to the bank was false.

Similarly, litigation in the bankruptcy court over a contested plan of confirmation, a creditor's or trustee's motion to dismiss the case, and motions to convert a chapter 11 to a case under chapter 7 or to appoint a trustee, all pose the prospect of potential self-incrimination by a debtor. The potential for self-incrimination may arise in the context of discovery, objections, and evidentiary hearings in connection with such matters. This issue is faced not only by a debtor. Occasionally bankruptcy proceedings will have self-incrimination implications for a trustee, creditor, or equity security holder.

The privilege against self-incrimination may be asserted if three elements are present: (1) compelled disclosure which is (2) testimonial and (3) incriminatory.[575] Compelled disclosure means that there is moral or physical compulsion on the individual to testify.[576] The § 341 meeting, Fed. R. Bankr. P. 2004 examinations, and depositions in bankruptcy proceedings are all instances of compulsion as the word is used in this context. Compulsion is deemed to be present in these three instances because the debtor is required by statute (in the case of the § 341 meeting), by the court (in the case of the Fed. R. Bankr. P. 2004 examination) or by threat of civil sanctions (in the case of depositions).

Testimonial means a communication which reflects the contents of an individual's mind.[577] Incriminatory means that the witness has a reasonable apprehension[578] that the disclosure would tend to incriminate him, whether or not he would actually be prosecuted.

In some instances, acts may be regarded as testimonial. An act may be testimonial when it probes the state of mind, memory, perception, or cognition of the witness.[579] An example is producing documents, which may often reflect the state of mind of the producer.

Document production

Some of the most problematic Fifth Amendment issues arising in the bankruptcy context involve production of documents. Documents may tend to

---

[575] *Fisher v. United States*, 425 U.S. 391, 408-09 (1976).
[576] *Holt v. United States*, 218 U.S. 245 (1910).
[577] *Doe v. United States*, 487 U.S. 201, 210 n.9 (1988).
[578] *Hoffman v. United States*, 341 U.S. 479, 486 (1951).
[579] *Braswell*, 487 U.S. at 126.

incriminate an individual either because they establish guilt by their nature and/or content, or because producing the documents is in itself incriminating. Producing documents may be testimonial in any of three ways: (1) producing the documents is a statement that the documents exist; (2) producing the documents is a statement that person who is producing them has the documents; (3) producing the documents is a statement that the person who is producing them believes they are responsive to the request.[580]

As a general rule, the contents of documents are not subject to a Fifth Amendment privilege. There are limited exceptions to this general proposition, but the exceptions rarely have any applicability in a bankruptcy case. The debtor's books and records may not be withheld under any claim of Fifth Amendment privilege. A debtor is required to turn over all books, records, and other documents relating to his financial transactions and estate. Bankruptcy law prohibits a debtor from withholding such documents. In a chapter 7 case, the trustee has the right to obtain the books and records,[581] and failure by the debtor to turn over the books and records is a crime.[582]

The books and records of a bankruptcy estate also arguably fall within the "public records" doctrine. Public records and official documents made or kept in the administration of public office may not be withheld under a claim of Fifth Amendment privilege.[583] This principle has been applied against a chapter 7 trustee with respect to documents pertaining to the administration of an estate for which his removal was being sought.[584] The chapter 7 trustee is an officer of the court and is required by the Bankruptcy Code to maintain records. Thus, estate records are public records subject to compelled disclosure notwithstanding the Fifth Amendment.[585] The role of a chapter 11 debtor parallels that of a trustee, and therefore the same principle applies with respect to a chapter 11 debtor.

An alternative basis for the compelled production of documents of a bankruptcy estate is the principle that the documents are not privileged if they are required to be produced as part of a noncriminal, governmental regulatory process.[586] It is not clear that this rationale is correctly applied to the bankruptcy process, although some courts have suggested its applicability.[587] The Bank-

---

[580] *United States v. Doe*, 465 U.S. 605, 613 n.11 (1984).

[581] *In re Harris*, 221 U.S. 274 (1911).

[582] 18 U.S.C. § 152(9); *see* chapter 11 (Withholding recorded information).

[583] *Wilson v. United States*, 221 U.S. 361, 380 (1911).

[584] *In re Grand Jury Proceedings*, 119 B.R. 945 (E.D. Mich. 1990).

[585] *In re Grand Jury Proceedings*, 119 B.R. at 950.

[586] *In re Ross*, 156 B.R. 272 (Bankr. D. Idaho 1993); *Baltimore City Department of Social Services v. Bouknight*, 493 U.S. 549 (1990).

[587] *United States v. Falcone*, 544 F.2d 607, 611 (2d Cir. 1976).

ruptcy Code and Bankruptcy Criminal Code are part of a comprehensive statutory scheme that is both civil and criminal in nature. The bankruptcy process is not truly noncriminal, nor is it regulatory.

An officer of a corporation in a representative capacity or a records custodian has no right to assert a Fifth Amendment privilege in response to a request for production of documents issued to a corporation, even if producing the records would tend to incriminate the individual in question.[588] The individual nevertheless has Fifth Amendment rights in his or her personal capacity. As a result of this incongruity, a corporation may be required to appoint an agent to respond to a document request who can do so without risk of self-incrimination. A former officer who has corporate records but does not hold them as a representative of the corporation may, however, be entitled to claim a Fifth Amendment privilege with respect to documents and thereby withhold the documents.[589]

Immunity

If a debtor invokes the Fifth Amendment at a § 341 meeting, the meeting will likely be adjourned while an order compelling his testimony is sought. Section 344 provides:

> Immunity for persons required to submit to examination, to testify, or to provide information in a case under this title may be granted under part V of title 18.[590]

Under title 18, United States Code, § 6003, the United States attorney may petition the United States district court to issue an order granting immunity and compelling testimony. The United States attorney must show that (1) the testimony or information sought may be in the public interest; and (2) the witness has refused or is likely to refuse to provide the testimony or information on the basis of the privilege against self-incrimination.[591] If the debtor is then ordered to testify, he receives derivative use immunity (also called use immunity).[592] This type of immunity prohibits only the use, in a later criminal prosecution of the witness, of information derived from the witness's testimony.

---

[588] *Braswell*, 487 U.S. 99.

[589] *In re Grand Jury Subpoena Duces Tecum*, 722 F.2d 981, 986-87 (2d Cir. 1983).

[590] 11 U.S.C. § 344.

[591] 18 U.S.C. § 6003(b).

[592] If the debtor refuses to testify notwithstanding such a grant of use immunity, he may suffer civil consequences, such as denial of his discharge.

Use immunity is consistent with the Fifth Amendment privilege in that it prevents the government from using compelled testimony, either directly or indirectly.[593] This is a more limited form of immunity than transactional immunity, which affords an individual full immunity from prosecution for the conduct which the testimony concerns. The Supreme Court has held that a grant of use immunity is sufficient to compel testimony consistent with Fifth Amendment rights, stating that immunity is not synonymous with amnesty.[594] If the debtor refuses to testify notwithstanding such a grant of use immunity, he will be subject to various punishments, including civil and criminal contempt.[595]

Civil consequences

An individual cannot be punished for invoking the Fifth Amendment privilege.[596] An individual is not shielded, however, from all negative consequences in civil proceedings which result, directly or indirectly, from invoking the privilege. He may suffer civil consequences, such as dismissal of his bankruptcy case,[597] denial of discharge, or other adverse rulings on various matters, based on negative inferences drawn from his refusal to testify.

A debtor may be confronted with the prospect of litigating a civil bankruptcy matter in the bankruptcy court and at the same time defending a criminal prosecution in a state or federal court.[598] A debtor facing a criminal investigation or indictment for a bankruptcy crime during the pendency of civil bankruptcy proceedings faces a strategic dilemma. Such simultaneous bankruptcy and criminal actions inevitably have overlapping issues.

Consider the case of a secretarial "temp" agency, which places personnel at law firms on an hourly basis. The agency contracts with each "temp" secretary as an independent contractor, collects payment for the "temp's" services from the law firm, and then pays the "temp" the amount paid by the law firm, less a hefty fee. When the agency develops financial problems (because of skyrocketing overhead), the agency falls behind in paying the "temps." Shortly after the agency files for chapter 11, several of the "temps" — now creditors in the chapter 11 case — approach the local district attorney to file fraud and embezzle-

---

[593] *Kastigar v. United States*, 406 U.S. 441 (1972).

[594] *Kastigar*, 406 U.S. 441.

[595] 18 U.S.C. § 401(3).

[596] *See, e.g., Lefkowitz v. Cunningham*, 431 U.S. 801, 805 (1977).

[597] *In re Connelly*, 59 B.R. 421, 448 (Bankr. N.D. Ill. 1986).

[598] The filing of a bankruptcy petition constitutes an order for relief, which creates an automatic stay of virtually all creditor collection actions. Criminal investigations and prosecutions are expressly excepted from the automatic stay. 11 U.S.C. § 362(b)(1).

ment charges against the owner of the agency. The basis of the criminal complaint is the failure of the owner to pay moneys which the "temps" claim rightfully belonged to them and which were paid to the debtor as their agent. The adjudication of the civil claims of the "temps," as well as the financial transactions at issue in the criminal investigation, are central issues in the agency's chapter 11 case. These matters will foreseeably be the subject of Fed. R. Bankr. P. 2004 examinations and other discovery conducted in the chapter 11 case, and inquiry by the trustee and the creditors at the Section 341 meeting. Further, the debtor will be required to address these issues in its disclosure statement and chapter 11 plan. The owner of the agency will be confronted with the risk of asserting the Fifth Amendment privilege in the bankruptcy, with the possible consequence of negative inferences being drawn in the plan confirmation process, or waiving the privilege and having his statements used against him by the prosecutor.

Preserving and not waiving the privilege in a bankruptcy case requires great care. At the same, asserting the privilege may jeopardize or at least compromise the debtor's position in his bankruptcy case. Where the debtor is faced with a Hobson's choice of either (1) invoking the privilege and compromising the outcome of his bankruptcy case; or (2) testifying in his bankruptcy case and risking waiver of his Fifth Amendment privilege, the debtor may be well advised to seek a stay of his bankruptcy case. In some cases, the prosecution wishes to seek a stay to prevent the defendant from utilizing the bankruptcy case to obtain discovery for use in the criminal case.

The bankruptcy court has the inherent power to stay a bankruptcy case.[599] The factors which are considered by the bankruptcy court in determining whether to stay a bankruptcy case are essentially the same factors as apply to the issuance of injunctive relief generally. In this context, the factors have been articulated as follows: (1) the interest of the plaintiff and the potential prejudice to the plaintiff due to a stay; (2) the potential burden on the defendant, absent a stay; (3) judicial economy and convenience; (4) the interest of nonparties; (5) the public interest.[600]

Of course, sometimes the bankruptcy process presents an opportunity to resolve issues such as these in a way that facilitates a favorable outcome in the criminal proceedings. For instance, the prosecutor may be persuaded not to bring charges in light of the bankruptcy court's confirmation of a plan which pays creditors in full, or the bankruptcy court's finding that no fraud was committed. On the other hand, in some cases, the prospect of a favorable disposi-

---

[599] 11 U.S.C. § 105; *In re Ahead By A Length*, 78 B.R. 708, 710 (Bankr. S.D.N.Y. 1987).
[600] *In re Ahead By A Length*, 78 B.R. at 713.

tion in the bankruptcy court may be too uncertain or unlikely to risk the possibility of an adverse ruling. The risk to the defendant/debtor is compounded by the possibility of a waiver of the Fifth Amendment privilege by his testifying in the bankruptcy case as to the transactions at issue in the criminal case.

PART 5

PENALTIES

34. Federal Sentencing Guidelines

In 1984, Congress enacted the Sentencing Reform Act of 1984[601] (Title II of the Comprehensive Crime Control Act of 1984[602]) (the "SRA"), which abolished parole in the federal criminal justice system and delegated broad authority to the United States Sentencing Commission to develop guidelines for federal criminal sentencing.

The Commission is an independent agency within the judicial branch and is composed of seven voting and two non-voting members. The Commission completed its initial task and submitted its recommendations to Congress on April 13, 1987. The Federal Sentencing Guidelines took effect on November 1, 1987 and apply to all offenses committed after that date. The Guidelines were amended in 1988, 1989, 1990, 1991, 1992, 1993, 1994, 1995, 1998, 2000, 2001, 2002, 2003 and 2004. From inception until January 2005, the FSG were mandatory, but became advisory under the Supreme Court's ruling in *United States v. Booker.*[603]

Policy objectives

The stated policy objectives of the Guidelines are to make sentencing uniform, fair and honest. Honesty in this context requires predictability. Before the enactment of the Act and the promulgation of the Guidelines, district court judges had broad discretion in sentencing; thus, the sentence imposed on two similarly situated defendants convicted of the same crime could vary greatly. The sentence that the judge imposed bore no resemblance to the sentence actu-

---

[601] 18 U.S.C. § 3551-3742.

[602] Pub. L. No. 98-473, Title II (1984), reprinted in 1984 U.S.C.C.A.N. 3220.

[603] *United States v. Booker*, 543 U.S. 220 (2005).

ally served. The actual length of the sentence was ultimately in the hands of the parole commission, and defendants typically served only a third of their sentence.

The Guidelines sought to bring about proportionality, while at the same time ensuring uniformity. The effort to reconcile these competing goals led to an involved set of guidelines prescribing the range of punishment according to a sophisticated formula.

The Commission, in its effort to decide what factors are relevant in sentencing, confronted the fundamental philosophical question: What is the purpose of a criminal sentence? There are, of course, several different purposes, goals, and theories underlying the penal system. One goal that virtually everyone can agree upon is crime control. The objective is to prevent crime, either by keeping the criminal behind bars where he cannot commit other crimes, or making him disinclined to commit more crimes upon release, and to deter others from committing crimes through fear of punishment. Another concept of punishment is the so called "just desserts" principle, punishing the criminal as an objective in itself, either to vindicate the victim or society.

The Commission avoided the philosophical questions in favor of an empirical approach. In short, the Commission attempted to do what works, or at least what has worked in the past.

The fundamental approach of the Guidelines is that punishment is driven by the defendant's conduct, not by the subjectivity of courts or the charges brought by prosecutors. This is referred to as "real offense" sentencing as opposed to "charge offense" sentencing. As a result, a bankruptcy crime may be covered by one of several guidelines, depending on whether the conduct involved is tantamount to fraud, theft, bribery, or perjury.

Constitutionality

Section 3742(e) of the SRA made the FSG mandatory, but this provision was struck down by the Supreme Court in *United States v. Booker.*[604] This result was foreshadowed in June 2004, when the Supreme Court in *Blakely v. Washington,* held that the Washington State sentencing guidelines violated the defendant's Sixth Amendment right to a trial by jury because certain factors which were used to impose the defendant's sentence were found only by a judge, not proven to a jury beyond a reasonable doubt.[605] While Justice Scalia noted in a footnote in the *Blakely* decision that "[t]he federal guidelines are not before us, and we express no opinion on them," the constitutionality of the

[604] *United States v. Booker*, 543 U.S. 220 (2005).

[605] *Blakely v. Washington*, 542 U.S. 296 (2004).

FSG was shortly thereafter addressed by the Supreme Court.[606] On January 12, 2005, the Supreme Court held that the mandatory nature of the FSG is unconstitutional since it is incompatible with a defendant's Sixth Amendment right to a jury trial as to every fact on which a sentence is mandated. The court invalidated the provisions of the Sentencing Reform Act of 1984 that have the effect of making the FSG mandatory, and severed those provisions, thus rendering the FSG advisory.

Sentencing of Bankruptcy Crimes

Many different activities can give rise to the same bankruptcy crime with varying degrees of culpability. The sentence imposed for a bankruptcy crime will vary not only according to the nature of the offense involved, but also on the application of a number of factors relating to the defendant's conduct, including the circumstances of the crime and the defendant's criminal history. The sentence will be determined by the total number of points calculated according to a formula that takes into account a number of factors. Points are added or subtracted accordingly (the "offense level") and the criminal history category is determined by a formula. A grid-type numerical table dictates the range of incarceration for each offense level and criminal history category.

Applicability of Guidelines and Amendments

As discussed above, the Federal Sentencing Guidelines were amended in 1988, 1989, 1990, 1991, 1992, 1993, 1994, 1995, 1998, 2000, 2001, 2002, 2003 and 2004. The frequent amendment to these Guidelines creates numerous sentencing difficulties. These difficulties arise where the Guidelines are amended between the date of the commission of the crime and the date of sentencing. USSG § 1B1.11(a) of the Guidelines instructs courts to use only the Guidelines in effect on the date that the defendant is sentenced.[607] If one or more of the amendments works in favor of the defendant, then no issue is presented. It is when one of the amendments to the Guidelines makes a sentence more severe that problems arise because under those circumstances the Ex Post Facto Clause of the United States Constitution is implicated. Under those circumstances, USSG § 1B1.11(b)(1) will be applied. This section provides:

> [I]f a court determines that use of the Guidelines Manual in effect on the date that the defendant is sentenced would violate the ex post facto clause

---

[606] 542 U.S. at 305 at n. 9.

[607] USSG § 1B1.11(a).

of the United States Constitution, the court shall use the Guidelines Manual in effect on the date that the offense of conviction was committed.[608]

At first glance, what appears to remedy the problem in actuality creates more difficulties. This is because an amendment to one Guideline may benefit the defendant while an amendment to another may be detrimental. In such circumstances, the Guidelines employ the "one book rule" which states that a court should use the Guidelines in effect on the date of sentencing unless this would violate the Ex Post Facto Clause, in which case the "guidelines Manual in effect on a particular date shall be applied in its entirety."[609] In other words, the sentence range is determined by applying only one version of the Guidelines, *i.e.* the version that overall is most beneficial to the defendant among all possible alternatives.

Where a "defendant is convicted of two offenses, the first committed before, and the second committed after, a revised edition of the Guidelines became effective, the revised edition of the Guidelines is to be applied to both offenses" even if the revised edition results in an increased penalty for the first offense.[610] For example, if a defendant is sentenced in January 2005 for a bank robbery committed in October 1999 and one committed in November 2003, the November 2003 Guidelines should be used to determine a combined guideline range for both counts.[611]

Finally, for ongoing offenses such as conspiracy or fraud, where the conduct occurs partially before and partially after an amendment to the Guidelines, the revised amendment may be applied to all conduct that occurred during the entire offense. However, it would violate the Ex Post Facto Clause to apply the revised amendment where the offense terminates before any amendment to the Guidelines.

---

[608] USSG § 1B1.11(b)(1) (emphasis in the original).

[609] USSG § 1B1.11(b)(2).

[610] USSG § 1B1.11(b)(3). It should be noted that the Circuits are divided over whether this violates the Ex Post Facto Clause. The Third and Ninth Circuits hold that this subsection violates the Ex Post Facto Clause and require the court to apply the pre-amendment guideline to pre-amendment convictions. *See U.S. v. Bertoli,* 40 F.3d 1384, 1388 (3d Cir. 1994); *U.S. v. Ortland,* 109 F.3d 539, 546-47 (9th Cir. 1997). The First, Fourth, Fifth, Tenth, and Eleventh Circuits find no ex post facto violation where all of the counts would be considered relevant conduct under the guidelines. *See U.S. v. Regan,* 989 F.2d 44, 47-48 (1st Cir. 1993); *U.S. v. Lewis,* 235 F. 3d 215, 219 (4th Cir. 2000); *U.S. Kimler,* 167 F.3d 889, 893-95 (5th Cir. 1999); *U.S. Sullivan,* 255 F.3d 1256 (10th Cir. 2001); *U.S. Bailey,* 123 F.3d 1381, 1402-07 (11th Cir. 1997). The Seventh Circuit finds no ex post facto violaton. *See U.S. v. Vivit,* 214 F.3d 908, 917-19 (7th Cir. 2000).

[611] USSG § 1B1.11(b) comment 2.

Base offense level

The starting point in the analysis is the base offense level. The Guidelines establish base offense levels, which are the number of points assigned to a given category of offense, each of which covers numerous statutory crimes. There are three Guidelines applicable to bankruptcy crimes:[612] Embezzlement and fraud (USSG § 2B1.1)[613]; commercial bribery (USSG § 2B4.1); and perjury (USSG § 2J1.3). The base offense level for embezzlement and fraud is 6; for perjury or subornation of perjury, 14; and for bribery, 8.

Most bankruptcy crimes fall under USSG § 2B1.1 (embezzlement and fraud). Offenses under 18 U.S.C. § 152(1), (4), (5), (7), (8) and (9), and §§ 155, 156 and 157 usually are treated under this Guideline. USSG § 2B1.1 will most likely be applied to offenses under section 153. USSG § 2J1.3 (perjury) is usually applied to violations of §§ 152(2) and (3). USSG § 2B4.1 (bribery) is usually applied in instances of violations of § 152(6). These are not hard and fast rules, as the specific Guideline to be applied will depend on the conduct involved in the particular case.

The calculation of a sentence for an offense falling under USSG § 2B1.1 (embezzlement and fraud) begins with the base offense level of 6. The base level is then increased for specific offense characteristics. The first is the amount of the loss, with adjustments on a scale ranging from zero if a loss of less than $5,000 is involved, up to an increase of 30 for a loss of over $400 million (USSG § 2B1.1(b)(1)). If a person has defrauded more than ten victims, as will be the case in a bankruptcy case with more than 10 creditors, the multiple victim enhancement will apply and will result in a two-level increase.

Further, the base level is also increased by two levels or to level 10 if the offense involves a misrepresentation or other fraudulent action during the course of a bankruptcy proceeding.[614] If there was a misrepresentation that a charitable, religious, educational or religious institution was involved, or a government agency, or a violation of any judicial or administrative order not addressed elsewhere in the Guidelines, then the offense level is increased by 2 or to 10, whichever results in a higher offense level.[615] If reckless risk of serious bodily injury or possession of a dangerous weapon was involved, then the offense level

---

[612] The Guidelines do not apply to Class B or C misdemeanors or infractions. Therefore, the Guidelines will not apply to violations of section 154, which is an infraction. Sections 155 and 156 are Class A misdemeanors.

[613] USSG § 2F1.1 (fraud and deceit) was deleted by consolidation with USSG § 2B1.1 (embezzlement) effective November 1, 2001.

[614] USSG § 2B1.1(b)(8).

[615] USSG § 2B1.1(b)(8).

is increased by 2 or to 14, whichever results in a higher offense level.[616] If the offense involved the use of foreign bank accounts or transactions to conceal the true nature or extent of the fraudulent activity, then the offense level is increased by 2 or to 14.[617] Finally, if the offense substantially jeopardized the safety of a financial institution, the offense level is increased by 4 or to 24, whichever results in a higher offense level.[618]

Loss amount

The loss amount determination is particularly troublesome in bankruptcy cases. The most obvious and typical measure of loss in such cases is the value of the concealed asset. The amount of the loss for purposes of USSG § 2B1.1 (embezzlement and fraud) is the value of the money, property, or services unlawfully taken, but does not include interest the victim could have earned on the funds.[619]

The measure of value is fair market value. The amount of the intended loss is applied if it is greater than the actual loss.[620] The loss does not need to be determined precisely; the court need only make a reasonable estimate.[621] The gain by the defendant will be an alternative measure of loss only if there is a loss but it reasonably cannot be determined.[622] Even if the defendant never received the fruits of his attempted fraud, his offense level will be enhanced based on the amount he intended to claim or conceal through his fraudulent conduct.[623]

In *United States v. Hernandez*, the FBI seized the debtor's vehicles on his brother's business premises, where the vehicles were for sale, but not yet sold.[624] The vehicles were later sold by the debtor's trustee, and thus the proceeds were not in fact received by the debtor, but rather, by his trustee. The court rejected Hernandez' argument that the value of the vehicles should not have been included in the amount of loss for sentencing purposes. The court held that under the Guidelines, the amount of intended loss was controlling. In this case, Hernandez intended concealment of the vehicles. The fact that his scheme was not successful and the injury to creditors was averted by the FBI, does not

---

616 USSG § 2B1.1(b)(12).
617 USSG § 2B1.1(b)(9).
618 USSG § 2B1.1(b)(13).
619 USSG § 2B1.1, comment (n.3).
620 USSG § 2B1.1, comment (n.3).
621 USSG § 2B1.1, comment (n.3).
622 USSG § 2B1.1, comment.(n.3).
623 *United States v. Hernandez,* 160 F.3d 661, 667 (11th Cir. 1998)
624 *Hernandez,* 160 F.3d 661.

reduce the amount of loss for sentencing purposes. In a similar vein, the fact that the concealed assets would have been exempt if they had been disclosed, does not eliminate the value of the concealed assets from the loss calculation.[625]

The loss amount for Guideline purposes may have little relationship to the actual impact on the debtor's crime on the creditors in his case. When a debtor conceals an asset in his bankruptcy case, this does not always affect the amount of recovery his creditors receive. Conversely, the debtor may not necessarily derive the value of the concealed asset. For instance, the debtor may have sold the asset for less than its value or the proceeds may not have been received by the debtor at all. As a practical matter, the actual injury to creditors or benefit to the debtor may have no relationship to the value of the concealed asset. Even so, the value of the concealed asset will still determine the loss.[626]

Fraudulent action in a bankruptcy proceeding or violation of judicial process

Two offense characteristics applied in bankruptcy crimes are the two-level enhancement for fraudulent action in a bankruptcy proceeding or violation of a court order or process. USSG § 2B1.1(b)(8) provides:

> [If the offense involved] (B) a misrepresentation or other fraudulent action during the course of a bankruptcy proceeding; (C) violation of any judicial or administrative order, injunction, decree, or process not addressed elsewhere in the guidelines ... increase by **2** levels. If the resulting offense level is less than level **10**, increase to level **10** (emphasis added).

Of the few cases imposing a sentence enhancement under subsection (B),[627] courts found conduct triggering this enhancement includes the concealment of the fraudulently obtained wire transfer funds from the bankruptcy trustee during a Chapter 7 bankruptcy proceeding[628] and testimony by a co-conspiritor during his bankruptcy proceeding that he and the defendant agreed to conceal information from the bankruptcy court.[629]

The more oft imposed sentence enhancement in a bankruptcy proceeding is subsection (C). Prior to the enactment of subsection (B), subsection (C) was applied by the majority of courts to fraud committed during bankruptcy pro-

---

[625] *United States v. Shadduck*, 112 F.3d 523 (1st Cir. 1997).

[626] *Hernandez*, 160 F.3d 661.

[627] Subsection (B) was originally enacted in USSG § 2F1.1(b)(4) but deleted by consolidation with USSG § 2B1.1 in November 2001.

[628] *U.S. v. Eddy*, 102 Fed.Appx. 643, 646 (10th Cir. 2004)

[629] *U.S. v. Coyle*, 154 Fed.Appx. 173, 176 (11th Cir. 2005)

ceedings.[630] Conduct triggering this enhancement includes filing fraudulent petitions,[631] failure to declare truthfully all assets and liabilities,[632] concealing assets from the trustee,[633] and violating court-approved cash collateral agreements.[634]

This enhancement is particularly relevant in the bankruptcy fraud context because bankruptcy fraud almost invariably involves violation of the judicial process.[635] A bankruptcy case is a judicial process which involves "the kind of formalities that undergird orders, injunctions and decrees."[636] Bankruptcy fraud involves a higher level of culpability than other offenses to which USSG 2B1.1 – formerly USSG 2F1.1 — applies, because it is deception of the court and therefore the offense warrants a greater punishment.[637]

In the case of an offense falling under the perjury Guideline (USSG § 2J1.3), the base level of 14 will be increased by 3 levels if there was a substantial interference with the administration of justice. In the case of an offense falling under the bribery Guideline (USSG § 2B4.1), the base level of 8 will be increased depending on the amount of the bribe. In the case of an offense falling under the embezzlement Guideline (USSG § 2B1.1), the base level of 6 will be increased for the amount of the loss.

Adjustments

Once the base offense level is calculated after consideration of all offense characteristics, adjustments may be made for victim-related (USSG § 3A1.1), role in the offense (USSG § 3B1.1) and obstruction of justice factors (USSG § 3C1.1). Many such adjustments, such as international terrorism or hate crime motivation, are rarely applicable in bankruptcy cases.

Certain adjustments are relatively common in bankruptcy cases. For instance, the base level for any of these categories of offenses — fraud, bribery, perjury or embezzlement — may be enhanced by two levels if any of the following are present: An abuse of trust or a special skill that significantly facilitated the commission or concealment of the offense (USSG § 3B1.3); if the defen-

---

[630] *Guthrie*, 144 F.3d at 1009-10 (applying § 2F1.1(b)); *United States v. Kubrick*, 205 F.3d 1117 (9th Cir. 1999) (same); *United States v. Welch*, 103 F.3d 906 (9th Cir. 1996) (same); *United States v. Messner*, 107 F.3d 1448, 1457 (10th Cir. 1997) (same); *Michalek*, 54 F.3d at 330-31 (same); *United States v. Lloyd*, 947 F.2d 339 (8th Cir. 1991) (same). *Contra*, *Shadduck*, 112 F.3d 523 (same).

[631] *Welch*, 103 F.3d 906.

[632] *Michalek*, 54 F.3d 325.

[633] *United States v. Mohammad*, 53 F.3d 1426,1437-3 (7th Cir. 1995); *Guthrie*, 144 F.3d at 1009-10.

[634] *United States v. Gunderson*, 55 F.3d 1332 (7th Cir. 1995).

[635] *Messner*, 107 F.3d at 1457.

[636] *Welch*, 103 F.3d at 908 (citing *United States v. Linville*, 10 F.3d 630, 633 (9th Cir. 1993), and *Michalek*, 54 F.3d at 333).

dant had an aggravating role in the defense (USSG § 3B1.1); or if the defendant obstructed or impeded the administration of justice during the investigation, prosecution, or sentencing of the instant offense (USSG § 3C1.1). Section 3C1.1 (obstruction of justice enhancement) does not apply to conduct that is a part of the crime itself.[638] Accordingly, the conduct of concealing assets and testifying falsely under oath during a bankruptcy proceeding will not in itself give rise to this enhancement where such conduct is itself the basis of the bankruptcy fraud charges.[639]

The "special skill" enhancement (2 level increase for abuse of trust or a special skill) is often applied to lawyers convicted of bankruptcy crimes.[640] The Guideline notes state:

> 'Special skill' refers to a skill not possessed by members of the general public and usually requiring substantial education, training or licensing. Examples would include pilots, lawyers, doctors, accountants, chemists, and demolition experts.[641]

For instance, where a bankruptcy crime involved a scheme to transfer an interest in property to a family trust, the defendant's skill as a trusts and estates lawyer facilitated the commission of the crime, warranting the enhancement.[642] This enhancement was applied to a lawyer who was convicted of bankruptcy fraud for making a false declaration that failed to disclose his firm's conflicts and that was the predicate for the court's approval of his firm's retention and compensation as bankruptcy counsel.[643]

Certain factors can decrease the offense level as well. The offense level may be decreased by 2-3 levels for acceptance of responsibility. Acceptance of responsibility means that the defendant has pled guilty and admitted the conduct comprising the offense. Other factors include voluntary restitution, surrender, cooperation with the authorities and rehabilitation efforts.[644]

The downward adjustment for acceptance of responsibility is within the district court's discretion.[645] The court may decline to make the adjustment

---

[637] *Guthrie*, 144 F.3d at 1010; *Mohammad*, 53 F.3d at 1437-38.

[638] *Lloyd*, 947 F.2d 339.

[639] *Lloyd*, 947 F.2d 339.

[640] *United States v. Graham*, 60 F.3d 463, 468-69 (8th Cir. 1995).

[641] USSG § 3B1.3, comment.(n.3).

[642] *Graham*, 60 F.3d at 468-69.

[643] *United States v. Gellene*, 182 F.3d 578 (7th Cir. 1999).

[644] USSG § 3E1.1, comment. (n.1).

[645] *Hernandez*, 160 F.3d at 667.

where the defendant denies the undeniable or refuses to answer questions about his conduct, and in so doing, acts in a manner inconsistent with acceptance of responsibility.[646] An example is where the defendant still denies irrefutable facts pertaining to his fraudulent conduct or refuses to answer questions posed by the probation officer in connection with his presentencing report. If the defendant had a mitigating role in the offense, the offense level will be decreased by 4 levels if the defendant was a minimal participant and by 2 levels if he was a minor participant.[647]

Multiple counts

In many cases, a defendant will be indicted, and ultimately will enter a plea of guilty or be convicted, on more than one count. The Guidelines prescribe in detail the process for determining sentences involving multiple counts. The most serious offense will be used as a base, and will be increased according to complex rules set out in USSG, Part D of Chapter 3. Generally speaking, separate bankruptcy counts will be considered to be a group of closely related counts, and the highest offense level of the counts will be considered the offense level applicable to the group.[648]

Criminal history

Once the offense level is determined, a defendant's criminal history points are determined. Points are added for prior sentences and offenses.[649] The criminal history factors were developed by the Commission based on empirical research on recidivism and patterns of criminal behavior. The Guidelines provide for a departure from the applicable Guideline range where the criminal history category does not adequately reflect the seriousness of the defendant's past criminal conduct or likelihood of recidivism.[650]

One of the most relevant departure factors in the bankruptcy fraud context is prior similar misconduct established by a civil adjudication or a failure to comply with an administrative order.[651] For instance, in a prior bankruptcy case, a bankruptcy court's finding that a debtor's concealment of assets barred his discharge could be considered a departure factor under USSG § 4A1.3. However, a civil adjudication in the same bankruptcy case or arising from the

---

[646] *Hernandez,* 160 F.3d at 668.
[647] USSG § 3B1.2.
[648] *See* USSG § 3D1.2, 3D1.3.
[649] USSG § 4A1.1.
[650] USSG § 4A1.3.
[651] USSG § 4A1.3(a)(2)(C).

same fraudulent conduct would not be grounds for departure under this Guideline.

While certain offender characteristics — the defendant's role in the offense, criminal history, and criminal livelihood — are specifically considered in determining the sentencing range, offender characteristics that are not conduct related are not.[652] The Guidelines specify which offender characteristics are not normally relevant to the term of imprisonment, although the Guidelines acknowledge that some of these characteristics may be considered in the court's determination of a sentence within the prescribed range or the conditions of probation or supervised release.[653] The factors that should not be considered in the length of a sentence include age,[654] education and vocational skills,[655] mental and emotional conditions,[656] physical appearance or condition including drug or alcohol dependence or abuse,[657] employment record,[658] family ties and responsibilities and community ties,[659] race, sex, national origin, creed, religion, socio-economic status,[660] military, civic, charitable or public service, employment-related contributions, record of prior good works,[661] and lack of guidance as a youth.[662]

Once the offense level and the criminal history are calculated, the sentencing range is set forth in a sentencing table.[663] The Guideline sentencing table contains "zones": Zone A encompasses sentences of 0-6 months; Zone B, 4-12 months; Zone C, 8-16 months; Zone D, 12 months - life. The zone will determine what terms the judge may impose, *e.g.*, what alternatives to incarceration, such as probation, home detention or intermittent incarceration.

Sentencing

As a general proposition, once the offense level and criminal history category are determined, the range of sentence (as specified in the sentencing table) is mandatory and the judge has no discretion to impose a longer or shorter sentence. Certain factors, called "departures," can, however, justify the imposition of a

---

[652] USSG § 5H1.1-12.
[653] USSG, Ch.5, Pt.H, intro. comment.
[654] USSG § 5H1.1.
[655] USSG § 5H1.2.
[656] USSG § 5H1.3.
[657] USSG § 5H1.4.
[658] USSG § 5H1.5.
[659] USSG § 5H1.6.
[660] USSG § 5H1.10.
[661] USSG § 5H1.11.
[662] USSG § 5H1.12.
[663] 58 USSG, Ch.5, Pt.A, Sentencing Table.

sentence below the statutorily required minimum. The sentencing court may depart from the mandated sentence only if "an aggravating or mitigating circumstance exists that was not adequately taken into consideration by the Sentencing Commission in formulating the guidelines and that should result in a sentence different from that described."[664] Departures are for the odd case that does not fit the norm. One of the most common departure factors is substantial assistance to authorities.[665] This factor applies when the defendant has provided significant information useful to the government's investigation and prosecution of other crimes, in a timely manner.

The Guidelines preclude the court from providing a sentence of probation as opposed to incarceration, except in certain instances. Probation is only available for a Guideline range of Zone A or Zone B but then only in conjunction with intermittent confinement, community confinement, or home detention. Probation is not authorized in the case of a Class A or Class B felony, or for an offense which expressly precludes probation as a sentence.[666]

A sentence of probation carries with it several conditions. These conditions will be included in every sentencing order. First, the defendant shall not commit another crime under federal, state, or local law. Restitution, a fine, and/or community service will be required unless extraordinary circumstances exist, in which case the court will impose other conditions.[667] There are numerous other standard conditions of probation, including: the defendant is not permitted to leave the area without the permission of his probation officer; he must report periodically to his probation officer; he must answer his probation officer's questions truthfully and follow his instructions; he must meet his family obligations including support of dependants; he must work, or, with his probation officer's permission, go to school; he must tell his probation officer if he moves or changes jobs; he must not drink excessively or use illegal drugs; he must not associate with criminals or frequent places where illegal drugs are used or sold; he must allow his probation officer to conduct home visits and confiscate contraband in plain view; and he must tell his probation officer if he is arrested.[668]

Intermittent confinement, which is custody for intervals of times, may be imposed as a condition of probation, as appropriate, on a case-by-case basis.[669]

---

664 18 U.S.C. § 3553(b).
665 USSG § 5K1.1.
666 USSG § 5B1.1(b).
667 USSG § 5B1.3(b); 18 U.S.C. § 3563(a)(2), (b).
668 USSG § 5B1.3(c).
669 USSG § 5B1.3(e)(6).

Other optional conditions of probation include community confinement,[670] home detention,[671] and community service.[672]

Where a prison sentence is imposed, it is often followed by a term of supervised release. A term of supervised release is mandatory where a prison sentence of more than a year is imposed.[673]

Organizations

Organizations[674] are sentenced differently from persons under the sentencing Guidelines. Like individuals, organizations may be required to pay restitution to any identifiable victim.[675] Organizations may also be required to perform community service or some other condition of probation to remedy the harm of their conduct.[676] Organizations can also be required to pay a fine based on the determined loss or the offense level,[677] which is then adjusted by a "multiplier" determined by the organization's "culpability score."[678] Departures from sentencing calculations may also be appropriate for organizations.[679] Finally, organizations may be subject to unique probation and special assessments, forfeitures, and costs.[680]

---

[670] USSG § 5F1.1.
[671] USSG § 5F1.2.
[672] USSG § 5F1.3.
[673] USSG § 5D1.1.
[674] An organization is "a person other than an individual," and includes corporations, partnerships, associations, governments, and trust funds. USSG § 8A1.1, comment. (n.1).
[675] USSG § 8B1.1.
[676] USSG § 8B1.2 and 1.3.
[677] Offense levels for organizations are calculated in the identical manner as individuals. USSG § 8C2.3.
[678] A culpability score is based upon the organization's involvement or toleration of criminal behavior, prior history, past violations of orders, or self-reporting and acceptance of responsibility. USSG § 8C2.5. The multiplier to be applied to the fine, which can range from .20 to 4.00, is then determined based on the culpability score. USSG § 8C2.6.
[679] USSG §§ 8C4.1-8C4.11.
[680] USSG § 8D and § 8E.

35. Restitution, fines and forfeitures

Federal crimes are punishable not only by terms of imprisonment but also by economic penalties — restitution, fines, and forfeitures. The sentence imposed for a bankruptcy crime will, as a general rule, include a fine and restitution.[681]

Restitution

Except in limited circumstances that are usually inapplicable in bankruptcy cases, restitution is mandatory under the Guidelines.[682] The amount of restitution is based on the actual loss caused by the defendant's offense.[683] The government has the burden of demonstrating the amount of the loss.[684]

The approach to calculating the loss for restitution purposes differs from that used in determining the offense level for sentencing purposes; in the latter case, the intended loss, not the actual loss, is used. Thus, in the case of concealment of an asset, if the asset was eventually liquidated by the trustee and thus no actual loss was sustained by creditors, the court may not include the asset value in its restitution order.[685] Losses caused to the bankruptcy trustee and creditors are considered.[686] The court will not impose restitution with respect to a loss for which the victim has already received compensation.[687]

Indigence is not a defense to restitution. The court is to look at the defendant's ability to pay in the future, not just at his immediate situation.[688]

The fixing of restitution is a judicial act. The court may not abdicate its responsibility by authorizing a probation officer to determine the manner of restitution, although the probation officer may administer and enforce the court's order.[689]

---

681 USSG § 5E1.1; 5E1.2.

682 USSG § 5E1.1.

683 *United States v. Messner*, 107 F.3d 1448, 1455 (10th Cir. 1997).

684 *Messner*, 107 F.3d at 1455.

685 *Messner*, 107 F.3d at 1455.

686 *United States v. Cluck*, 143 F.3d 174, 180 (5th Cir. 1998), *cert. denied*, 525 U.S. 1073 (1999).

687 *United States v. Lindholm*, 24 F.3d 1078, 1085 (9th Cir. 1994); 18 U.S.C. § 3663(e)(1).

688 *United States v. Blanchard*, 9 F.3d 22, 25 (6th Cir. 1993).

689 *United States v. Mohammad*, 53 F.3d 1426, 1438 (7th Cir. 1995).

Fines

In addition to restitution, the Guidelines also require the court to:

> [I]mpose a fine in all cases, except where the defendant establishes that he is unable to pay and is not likely to become able to pay any fine.[690]

The Guidelines list the following factors which the court should consider in determining the amount of the fine:[691]

1. the need for the combined sentence to reflect the seriousness of the offense, to promote respect for the law, to provide just punishment, and to afford adequate deterrence;
2. the defendant's ability to pay, including over a period of time, in light of his earning capability and financial resources;
3. the burden that the fine places on the defendant and his dependants;
4. any restitution or reparation that the defendant has made or is obligated to make;
5. any collateral consequences of conviction, including civil obligations arising from the defendant's conduct;
6. any previous fines for similar offenses;
7. the expected costs to the government of any term of probation, or term of imprisonment and term supervised release imposed; and
8. other pertinent equitable considerations.

The defendant has the burden of proof in demonstrating that he is unable to pay a fine.[692]

The amount of the fine is determined by reference to the offense level in accordance with a fine table in the Guidelines.[693] Individuals and organizations are treated separately with respect to the determination of the fine.[694]

Where necessary, the defendant may be allowed to pay the fine in installments. If the fine is the sole sentence (*e.g.*, where the Guidelines do not require imprisonment), the Guidelines recommend that the court impose probation conditioned upon payment of the fine.[695] In other words, the defendant must

---

690 USSG § 5E1.2(a).

691 USSG § 5E1.2(d).

692 *Blanchard,* 9 F.3d at 26; *United States v. Nazifpour,* 944 F.2d 472, 475 (9th Cir. 1991).

693 USSG § 5E1.2(c)(3).

694 USSG § 5E1.2.

695 USSG § 5E1.2, comment. (n.1).

pay the fine or the court may revoke probation and impose a jail sentence. Under the Guidelines, a sentence of probation is not a "suspended" sentence, but a sentence in and of itself. When the conditions of probation are violated, the court will determine whether to revoke, modify, or continue probation.[696]

A fine or order of restitution constitutes a lien in favor of the United States on all property of the defendant, to the same extent as a tax lien.[697] The government must file a notice of lien, as is required to perfect a tax lien.[698] Fines are not discharged by a bankruptcy proceeding.[699]

The Guidelines also require the imposition of the costs of the prosecution on the defendant where provided by statute; however, chapter 9 of title 18 does not contain any such requirement.[700]

Forfeiture

Forfeiture is not available with respect to violations of the Bankruptcy Criminal Code standing alone.[701] However, defendants charged with a bankruptcy crime are sometimes also charged with other offenses in the same indictment, for which forfeiture is applicable, such as money laundering or RICO. The Guidelines impose forfeiture upon a convicted defendant where provided by statute.[702]

Forfeiture is a statutory remedy[703] whereby the federal government may seize and acquire property which facilitates illegal activities or the proceeds of illegal activities. Forfeiture is an extremely far reaching power of the federal government. The government has the power to seize property[704] without prior opportunity to be heard by the owner or other parties claiming an interest in the property.

There are two forms of forfeiture, civil and criminal. Civil forfeiture is an *in rem* proceeding that may be invoked whether or not the owner of the property at issue is innocent or guilty. Criminal forfeiture is an *in personem* proceeding invoked against a criminal defendant.

---

[696] USSG, Ch.7, Pt.A, intro. Comment. 2(a). Under certain circumstances, revocation is mandatory. *See* USSG § 7B1.1, *et seq.*

[697] 18 U.S.C. § 3613(c).

[698] 18 U.S.C. § 3613(d).

[699] 18 U.S.C. § 3613(e). *See also* 11 U.S.C. § 523(a)(7).

[700] *Cf.* USSG § 5E1.5.

[701] *See* chapter 17.

[702] USSG § 5E1.4.

[703] Forfeiture is expressly provided in several statutes, including 21 U.S.C. § 881.

[704] Personal property may be seized without a prior hearing. *See, e.g., Colero-Toledo v. Pearson Yacht Leasing Co.*, 416 U.S. 663 (1974) ; *United States v. Neuman*, 474 U.S. 242, 257 (1986). The seizure of real property requires opportunity for a prior hearing. *United States v. James Daniel Goode Real Property*, 510 U.S. 43 (1993).

The conflict between the rights of the federal government to seize assets under its forfeiture powers, and the rights of a bankruptcy trustee to compel turnover of estate property, is currently unsettled. In *United States v. Whiting Pools*,[705] property of the debtor had been seized prior to bankruptcy by the IRS, but title had not yet passed to the IRS and thus remained with the debtor. The Supreme Court held that in such an instance, the property in question remains property of the bankruptcy estate. Under certain conditions, a debtor in possession or trustee can compel turnover, and can use, sell or lease property of the bankruptcy estate.[706]

Where the federal government seizes property in a forfeiture action, title generally does not vest in the government until a court adjudicates the condemnation of the property, *i.e.*, an order of forfeiture is entered. Once the court has made such adjudication, the transfer of title to the government relates back to time of the illegal act which gave rise to the forfeiture.[707] Therefore, if assets are seized prior to the filing of the bankruptcy petition, but an order of forfeiture vesting title in the government has not yet been entered, the assets become property of the bankruptcy estate and will, at least hypothetically, be subject to turnover to the trustee or debtor in possession.

There are significant obstacles, however, to a trustee's or debtor-in-possession's ability to actually compel turnover of assets seized in a forfeiture. First, criminal forfeitures are not stayed, as they come within the exception to the automatic stay.[708] The question of whether civil forfeitures are stayed is not completely settled, but the weight of well reasoned authority suggests that civil forfeiture are stayed under 11 U.S.C. § 362(a).[709] Further, the bankruptcy court may lack jurisdiction over forfeited property, given that forfeiture divests the debtor's interest as of the commission of the criminal act.[710] If the court has no jurisdiction, then it cannot compel turnover. Even if the court has jurisdiction, if the forfeiture is expressly excepted from the automatic stay and thus permitted to proceed under the Bankruptcy Code, the turnover provision, § 542, would be inapplicable. The property would not qualify as property subject to turnover under § 542, since it would not be property which the trustee could use, sell or lease. In any event, the application of § 542 to forfeited property would contravene the statutory exception to the stay.

---

[705] *United States v. Whiting Pools*, 462 U.S. 198 (1983).

[706] *See* 11 U.S.C. § 363; § 542(a) and (b).

[707] *See, e.g.*, 21 U.S.C. § 881(h).

[708] *See* 11 U.S.C. § 362(b)(1).

[709] *See, e.g.,Geoff v. Oklahoma* (*In re Geoff*), 159 B.R. 33 (Bankr. N.D. Okla. 1993); *Sachs v. Ryan* (*In re Ryan*), 15 B.R. 514 (Bankr. D. MD 1981).

Similarly, the trustee's avoidance powers under § 544 may provide a means of setting aside a pre-petition forfeiture, but avoidance would ultimately be futile to the extent the forfeiture action is not subject to the automatic stay, because the government could simply recommence the forfeiture. Section 544 allows a trustee to set aside a pre-petition transfer that would be invalid as to a bona fide purchaser. To the extent that a hypothetical bona fide purchaser of the property would be able to challenge a forfeiture of that property, § 544 could potentially allow the trustee to recover the property notwithstanding the seizure. Section 544 may provide the trustee a means of setting aside a pre-petition, civil forfeiture seizure. It is not clear, however, whether § 544 could be utilized after an order of forfeiture is entered.

Section 549 may also provide a means of setting aside a forfeiture that occurs post-petition, but only to the extent the court deems the forfeiture to have occurred in violation of the stay. Section 549 permits a trustee to avoid transfers not authorized by the Bankruptcy Code. To the extent a forfeiture occurrs in violation of the automatic stay, § 549 could be used to set aside the forfeiture. As the trend in the law is the view that criminal forfeitures are excepted from the automatic stay but that civil forfeitures are not, §§ 544 and 549 have utility only with respect to a civil forfeiture. Given that a criminal forfeiture action is not stayed, the trustee's avoidance powers under § 549 would be inapplicable, since the forfeiture would not be "unauthorized" by the Bankruptcy Code. Indeed, it would be expressly authorized by the applicable stay exception. In any event, if criminal forfeitures are excepted from the stay, then the use of avoidance powers to invalidate the effects of a forfeiture, would essentially defeat the legislative purpose underlying the stay exception.

The key question in determining who ultimately has greater rights to property subject to forfeiture — the government or the trustee — turns on a critical question: does the bankruptcy court have jurisdiction over assets which are the subject of a forfeiture proceeding? A closely related question is whether civil forfeiture actions are excepted from the automatic stay. While the prevailing authority suggests they are not, this question is far from settled. Until both of these questions are resolved definitively, there can be no certainty of outcome in cases where forfeiture law and bankruptcy collides.

36. Plea agreements

Bankruptcy criminal charges are often, if not usually, adjudicated by a plea agreement rather than a trial. Plea agreements operate essentially as negotiated dispositions of criminal charges. A plea is a defendant's answer to the indictment or information: a defendant may plead guilty, not guilty, or with the court's consent, *nolo contendere*.[711] A defendant may negotiate with the prosecutor for the government's disposition or recommended disposition of the case in exchange for the defendant's guilty plea. This is commonly known as a plea agreement.

Fed. R. Crim. P. 11 governs plea agreements. Typically, a plea agreement will provide that the defendant pleads guilty, but this is not always the case. Occasionally, pleas of *nolo contendere* are accepted. A plea agreement will provide for obligations on both the part of the defendant and the prosecutor. For example, the defendant will sometimes be required to cooperate in another prosecution; the prosecution will usually agree to drop or not to bring some additional charge and to recommend, or at least not oppose, a particular sentence. Plea agreements are subject to acceptance or rejection by the court. The court is not required to accept a plea agreement.

Before the court may accept a plea agreement, several requirements must be met. The court may not accept a plea of guilty without first determining that the plea is voluntary and not the result of force, threats, or promises other than those contained in the plea agreement.[712] Before accepting a guilty plea or *nolo contendere* plea, the court must ask the defendant directly in open court if he or she understands the following:

1. the government's right, in a prosecution for perjury or false statement, to use against the defendant any statement that the defendant gives under oath;
2. the right to plead not guilty, or having already so pleaded, to persist in that plea;

---

[710] *See* 11 U.S.C. § 541(a)(1).

[711] Fed. R. Crim. P. 11(a)(1).

[712] Fed. R. Crim. P. 11(b)(2).

3. the right to a jury trial;
4. the right to be represented by counsel—and if necessary have the court appoint counsel—at trial and at every other stage of the proceeding;
5. the right at trial to confront and cross-examine adverse witnesses, to be protected from compelled self-incrimination, to testify and present evidence, and to compel the attendance of witnesses;
6. the defendant's waiver of these trial rights if the court accepts a plea of guilty or nolo contendere;
7. the nature of each charge to which the defendant is pleading;
8. any maximum possible penalty, including imprisonment, fine, and term of supervised release;
9. any mandatory minimum penalty;
10. any applicable forfeiture;
11. the court's authority to order restitution;
12. the court's obligation to impose a special assessment;
13. the court's obligation to apply the Sentencing Guidelines, and the court's discretion to depart from those guidelines under some circumstances; and
14. the terms of any plea-agreement provision waiving the right to appeal or to collaterally attack the sentence.[713]

The United States attorneys generally use a model form of agreement developed by federal prosecutors. Such "standard" plea agreements typically incorporate a number of provisions that have consequences to a defendant at sentencing as well as in collateral civil proceedings. One such typical provision is the waiver of the defendant's right to appeal the sentence. Waivers of the right to appeal sentencing issues are enforceable so long as the waiver was knowing and voluntary.[714]

Plea agreements may be accompanied by a written stipulation of facts relevant to the sentencing.[715] Such stipulations will be binding and will impact the sentencing process in a number of ways. The facts relating to the defendant's conduct will form the basis for the calculation of the offense level under the Guidelines. The stipulations will often quantify the loss amount for purposes not only of offense characteristics[716] but also for purposes of setting restitution and fines.[717]

---

[713] Fed. R. Crim. P. 11(b)(1).

[714] *See, e.g., United States v. Bushert*, 997 F.2d 1343, 1350 (11th Cir. 1992).

[715] USSG § 6B1.4 (a).

[716] *See* chapter 34.

[717] *See* chapter 35.

PART 6

CIVIL AND COLLATERAL ISSUES

37. Relationship between civil and criminal proceedings

Numerous questions arise over the relationship between criminal proceedings involving a bankruptcy case, and the civil bankruptcy case with respect to which the alleged criminal offense arises. Among the most frequent questions are the following:

- What effect does a conviction or acquittal in a criminal case have on the civil bankruptcy case?
- Will conviction of a bankruptcy crime bar a debtor's discharge?
- Are findings of fact or conclusions of law by the bankruptcy court *res judicata* or collateral estoppel in a criminal case?

Section 727, which is applicable to cases under chapter 7 of the Bankruptcy Code,[718] provides that the bankruptcy court shall grant a debtor a discharge, except under certain circumstances. Section 727(c) provides that a creditor in the United States may object to the granting of a discharge. The grounds for objection to discharge include:

> (2) the debtor, with intent to hinder, delay, or defraud a creditor or an officer of the estate charged with custody of property under this title, has transferred, removed, destroyed, mutilated, or concealed, or has permitted to be transferred, removed, destroyed, mutilated, or concealed -
>
> (A) property of the debtor, within one year before the date of the filing of the petition; or

---

[718] 11 U.S.C. § 103(b).

(B) property of the estate, after the date of the filing of the petition;

(3) the debtor has concealed, destroyed, mutilated, falsified, or failed to keep or preserve any recorded information, including books, documents, records, and papers, from which the debtor's financial condition or business transactions might be ascertained, unless such act or failure to act was justified under all of the circumstances of the case;
(4) the debtor knowingly and fraudulently, in or in connection with the case -

(A) made a false oath or account;
(B) presented or used a false claim;
(C) gave, offered, received, or attempted to obtain money, property, or advantage, or a promise of money, property, or advantage, for acting or forbearing to act; or
(D) withheld from an officer of the estate entitled to possession under this title, any recorded information, including books, documents, records, and papers, relating to the debtor's property or financial affairs;

(5) the debtor has failed to explain satisfactorily, before determination of denial of discharge under this paragraph, any loss of assets or deficiency of assets to meet the debtor's liabilities;
(6) the debtor has refused, in the case -

(A) to obey any lawful order of the court, other than an order to respond to a material question or to testify;
(B) on the ground of privilege against self-incrimination, to respond to a material question approved by the court or to testify, after the debtor has been granted immunity with respect to the matter concerning which such privilege was invoked; or
(C) on a ground other than the properly invoked privilege against self-incrimination, to respond to a material question approved by the court or to testify;

(7) the debtor has committed any act specified in paragraph (2), (3), (4), (5), or (6) of this subsection, on or within one year before the date of the filing of the petition, or during the case, in connection

> with another case, under this title or under the Bankruptcy Act, concerning an insider[.][719]

There is an obvious overlap between the grounds for objection to chapter 7 discharge and the Bankruptcy Criminal Code. For instance, § 727(a)(2) would generally encompass violations of § 152(1) and (7); § 727(a)(3) would generally encompass violations of § 152(8), § 727(a)(4) would generally encompass violations of § 152(2), (3), (4), (6), and (9).

A debtor's conviction or guilty plea will constitute collateral estoppel on factual issues in common between § 727 and the bankruptcy criminal statute.[720] Collateral estoppel precludes a party from litigating an issue if the identical issue has been actually litigated in a prior suit that could not have been decided without resolving the issue. The Eleventh Circuit in *Raiford* noted that there is a growing trend toward the view that a criminal conviction precludes relitigation of the same issue in a civil suit.[721] Although a criminal action and civil bankruptcy case involve different parties, collateral estoppel will apply where the factual issues in connection with denial of a discharge are the same as those in the criminal proceeding.[722] Mutuality of parties is not required for use of collateral estoppel.[723] A possible exception of this principle is when the debtor did not have the incentive to litigate the issue fully in the first proceeding. This would rarely be the case in a felony prosecution.[724]

On the other hand, civil rulings are not binding on either the prosecution or defense in a criminal proceeding. A defendant is not barred from relitigating issues that were determined against him in a bankruptcy proceeding. The primary reason for this view is the difference in the standard of proof in a civil case. The civil ruling is usually based on preponderance of the evidence or some other standard which is lower than the standard in a criminal case, which is beyond a reasonable doubt.[725]

---

719 11 U.S.C. § 727(a).
720 *Raiford v. Abney (In re Raiford)*, 695 F.2d 521 (11th Cir. 1983).
721 *Raiford*, 695 F.2d at 523.
722 *United States v. Lloyd*, 142 B.R. 866 (Bankr. E.D. Ark. 1992); *see also In re Chaplin*, 179 B.R. 123 (Bankr. E.D. Wis. 1995).
723 *Parklane Hosiery Co. v. Shore*, 439 U.S. 322 (1979).
724 *See Raiford*, 695 F.2d at 524.
725 *United States v. Robbins*, 997 F.2d 390 (8th Cir. 1993).

38. Ethics and professional responsibility

Book editors often say that the most important chapters in a book are the first and the last. It is for that reason that this last chapter deals with ethics and professional responsibility. For a practicing lawyer, ethical and professional considerations should be paramount.

Bankruptcy fraud cases present novel and difficult ethical and professional issues. The analytical and decision- making process for resolving an ethical question differs from the usual type of legal analysis lawyers perform every day. The focal point of the inquiry is the lawyer, not the client. It is the lawyer's rights, duties, choices, and actions that must be evaluated rather than the client's.

In examining such questions, the lawyer is confronted with a clash of rules and principles. The rules governing a lawyer's conduct derive principally from four distinct sources: (1) the rules governing professional conduct enacted in the jurisdiction in which the lawyer practices;[726] (2) federal and state civil and criminal statutes; (3) federal, state, and local court rules, some of which encompass rules of professional conduct; (3) common law principles, such as the attorney-client privilege and the duty to exercise reasonable care; and (4) the lawyer's own mind and will. In a given instance, these various rules and principles cannot always be reconciled.

The last category — the lawyer's own mind and will — refers to the standard of conduct dictated by the lawyer's conscience, internal moral compass, religious beliefs, and spiritual values. What a lawyer believes is the "right" thing to do may be prohibited by the applicable rules of professional conduct or by civil or criminal law. A lawyer who is faced with an ethical dilemma will sometimes, wisely or not, let his own sense of right and wrong override the

---

[726] The ABA has promulgated Model Rules of Professional Conduct (the "Model Rules"), which are the ABA's recommended ethical rules. The Model Rules have been adopted, with modifications in some instances, in many states. In a number of states that have not adopted the Model Rules, codes of professional responsibility govern ethical questions. In several states, such codes have been replaced by the Model Rules. Thus, the rules governing professional conduct vary from state to state, and a full discussion of the rules in each jurisdiction is beyond the scope of this work. Since there is a growing trend toward adoption of the Model Rules, the Model Rules will be used as a standard reference point in this chapter. The Model Rules quoted in this chapter are set forth in full in Appendix J.

dictates of the bar and the law. What the lawyer thinks or feels is right, however, may have no bearing on how the lawyer's conduct is viewed by a bar disciplinary committee, a judge, or a jury.

Two recurring ethical questions that arise in the bankruptcy context are: (1) What are counsel's responsibilities when he or she discovers that a client has committed, is in the process of committing, or is about to commit, a bankruptcy crime? (2) When can counsel's own conduct become bankruptcy fraud? These questions are best examined in the context of the specific circumstances lawyers commonly encounter. The starting point for determining the permissibility of the lawyer's actions are the rules of professional conduct, which prohibit a lawyer from assisting the client from committing a crime or a fraud.[727]

Asset planning

One common situation encountered by bankruptcy lawyers is the client or potential client who asks for assistance in what is euphemistically called "asset planning" or "bankruptcy planning." Asset planning or bankruptcy planning are often buzzwords for hiding assets from creditors. In fact, there are some individuals who believe that the primary function of a bankruptcy lawyer is to put assets beyond the reach of creditors.

Some common devices used to shelter assets from creditors include:

- converting a non-exempt asset to an exempt asset, such as transferring funds to annuities and retirement plans
- creating a spendthrift or other protective trust for a spouse or children
- transferring properties into family limited partnerships, rendering equity interests difficult to attach
- transferring real estate to tenancy by the entirety
- placing assets in foreign accounts and trusts
- embarking on a prebankruptcy "spending spree"

Planning ranges from the innocuous to the sinister. Most plans, naturally, fall somewhere in between. Consider the case of a corporate president who is in jeopardy of being named as a defendant in a shareholder derivative suit. He consults a lawyer to make sure his assets are secure — that is, unreachable by the judgment creditors he fears he eventually will have. Upon reviewing his financial statement, the lawyer notes several individual assets. The president has just married his second wife, and is not much more trusting of her than of

---

[727] *See* Model Rule 1.2(d).

his shareholders. Thus, he has not put the title to their new house in joint names. The standard legal advice which most bankruptcy lawyers give in this situation, if the client lives in a jurisdiction that recognizes tenancy by the entirety, is to immediately put the title of the residence in the names of "husband and wife." Another standard tip is to use funds stockpiled in an individually held bank account to pay down the principal on the mortgage on the residence, once it is safely held as tenants by the entirety. While not entirely free from challenge, such steps will generally not be deemed fraudulent.[728]

Setting up trusts and family limited partnerships may have some justifiable tax or estate planning objectives. Usually, however, when they are undertaken in the face of impending financial problems and with no apparent reason other than to hinder creditors, such measures will be subject to challenge under state fraudulent conveyance law or federal bankruptcy law.

Asset planning poses an extreme dilemma to bankruptcy lawyers. Lawyers have an ethical obligation to represent their clients with reasonable diligence and promptness,[729] a more precise and arguably higher standard than the "zealous" representation required by codes of professional responsibility. Further, lawyers have a duty to provide competent representation to a client[730] and to meet the standard of reasonable care. The standard of care requires that a lawyer use the same skill, prudence, and diligence as other lawyers commonly exercise in the practice area. A lawyer who fails to meet this standard risks civil liability to the client.

The standard of care, however, does not charge a lawyer with a duty to make a perfect decision or an right decision with respect to an unsettled question of law. Asset planning presents numerous unsettled issues of law, and therefore it would be difficult for a client to prevail in a claim against a lawyer who fails to advise his client of every conceivably legitimate asset planning strategy. However, a claim could arise when a lawyer fails to give advice that other competent bankruptcy lawyers in the community would give as to asset protection measures that are completely free from challenge. There are virtually no measures that are completely certain of success and free from potential challenge. Thus, a client's claim against a lawyer who did not provide him with the means to shelter his assets from creditors would probably be frivolous.

---

[728] The weight of authority indicates that conversion of nonexempt property to exempt property is not fraudulent *per se*. *See, e.g., In re Moreno*, 892 F.2d 417, 419 (5th Cir. 1990); *Norwest Bank Neb., N.A. v. Tveten*, 848 F.2d 871, 874 (8th Cir. 1988)

[729] *See* Model Rule 1.3.

[730] *See* Model Rule 1.1.

In the case of a lawyer who undertakes asset planning for the client and does so improperly, malpractice liability can result. Some examples of negligent asset planning include the failure to effectuate transfers, or effectuating a transfer that leads to adverse consequences. Some asset planning strategies can result in disastrous civil and criminal consequences to the client. A lawyer's recommendation or implementation of an asset planning strategy that ultimately leads to the client's denial of a discharge and/or to his criminal conviction would also be a breach of the duty of reasonable care.

Asset transfers undertaken solely to hide assets from creditors may be tantamount to fraud or concealment. When a bankruptcy later ensues, the creditors and trustee, if one is appointed, scrutinize transfers that were undertaken prior to bankruptcy. Certain types of asset planning may be considered prebankruptcy concealment in violation of section 152(7).

Advising a client on asset planning is fraught with potential civil, as well as criminal, liability for the lawyer. The lawyer who assists in concealment may be charged with aiding and abetting the commission of a felony, conspiracy to commit a bankruptcy crime, being an accessory after the fact, or misprision of a felony[731] . Legal advice can constitute aiding and abetting.[732] Further, the debtor who is convicted of concealment may be subject to denial of discharge. On occasion, lawyers have been found liable for malpractice in such instances.

The line between ethical but aggressive representation and criminal conspiratorial conduct is sometimes blurry. Some conduct, however, is clearly over the line. It is easier to identify what the lawyer cannot do than what the lawyer can do. Among the activities clearly proscribed are: allowing a client to use the attorney's client trust account to keep assets out of the reach of creditors; or drafting and/or recording a deed conveying property to a third party in the absence of any bona fide consideration, strictly for the purpose of keeping the property from the reach of creditors. Unfortunately, asset planning questions are usually not so cut and dried.

Confidentiality

Another common ethical quandary is the question when a lawyer can, may, or must divulge a client confidence. The lawyer's duty to keep a client's confidence presents a unique dilemma when the lawyer is confronted with a suspected or known fraud of a client. The questions of when a lawyer cannot speak, when a lawyer may speak, and when a lawyer is required to speak, may

---

[731] *See* chapter 18.

[732] *See United States v. Knoll*, 16 F.3d 1313 (2d Cir. 1994), *cert. denied*, 522 U.S. 1118 (1998), discussed in chapter 18.

have more than one answer. The lawyer must arrive at the right answer, the answer that correctly reconciles conflicting authority. The consequences of a wrong answer, and the wrong decision that inevitably follows it, can be serious, ranging from a reprimand from a bar counsel to a criminal conviction.[733]

The lawyer's duty to keep information confidential must be distinguished from the attorney-client privilege. The attorney-client privilege is an evidentiary privilege, which is primarily invoked in court proceedings. On the other hand, the duty to keep confidences is a broad, overarching principle, which prohibits disclosures of information obtained in a representation permanently, regardless of whether court proceedings are in prospect. These two principles are separate in their origin and significance, although there is obviously some overlap as a practical matter.

The attorney-client privilege is a common law right of a client which protects from disclosure certain communications between the lawyer and client.[734] The privilege belongs to, and may be waived by, the client. This privilege protects such communications from compelled discovery in a civil or criminal proceeding. A lawyer who discloses information that is subject to the attorney-client privilege may face civil liability if the disclosure was negligent.

Confidentiality, on the other hand, is an ethical rule imposed on lawyers. While the rule is not uniform in all jurisdictions, the majority of states have promulgated rules that are similar in principle to Model Rule 1.6.

The information that would be considered confidential under this rule would include, but would not be limited to, information subject to the attorney-client privilege. The duty to keep client confidences is broader in several respects. Most importantly, it encompasses information that was obtained from sources other than the client.

In some circumstances, the law and the rules governing professional responsibility require the lawyer to divulge a confidence.[735] Model Rule 3.3 requires that a bankruptcy lawyer who discovers that a client is about to commit perjury or make a false declaration, or who has already done so, must "take reasonable remedial measures." The requirement that a lawyer take reasonable remedial measures is not blanket permission for the lawyer to disclose confidences; the lawyer is permitted to do so, however, if there is no other alternative to remedy the perjury.

A lawyer could conceivably argue that not all statements made in the bankruptcy schedules or at the § 341 meeting are "evidence" or "material evidence."

---

[733] *See* chapter 18.

[734] *See* chapter 32.

[735] *See* Model Rule 3.3.

This argument is refuted, however, by the weight of authority which holds that virtually all statements made in a bankruptcy case under oath or declaration are material.[736] By analogy, these cases would tend to support the view that such false statements are precisely the kind to which Model Rule 3.3 refers.

The situations in which a bankruptcy lawyer may be confronted with the confidentiality and disclosure questions can be summarized as follows:

Scenario 1: Counsel discovers that client has committed a bankruptcy crime. Counsel's duties will depend on whether the bankruptcy crime involves a fraud against the court, or if the crime is continuing or not. Some bankruptcy crimes (in particular, concealment) are continuing offenses. If the crime is not a continuing one, and does not involve offering false evidence to the bankruptcy court, then the lawyer may not reveal the crime[737]. If the crime is a fraud upon the court,[738] such as a concealment of assets, the lawyer must take reasonable remedial measures.

Scenario 2: Counsel discovers that client is in the process of committing a bankruptcy crime. Counsel must try to convince the client not to commit the crime. If counsel is unsuccessful, counsel may reveal the crime only if the lawyer believes that the crime is likely to result in imminent death or substantial bodily harm. This exception rarely if ever applies in a bankruptcy case. Further, if the crime that is in progress involves offering false evidence to the bankruptcy court, the lawyer must take reasonable remedial measures.

Scenario 3: Counsel discovers that client is about to commit a bankruptcy crime. *Counsel must try to convince the client not to commit the crime. Counsel may not advise the client to commit the crime or assist the client in any way in the commission of the crime.*

The inherent difficulty in reconciling the rules and principles governing the lawyer's conduct when the client has committed or is committing fraud is illustrated by the following situation. The case involves a lawyer, "L," his corporate client, "C," and its president, "P." L is retained to file a chapter 11 case on behalf of C, in which P is the president and a 50% shareholder. Several months into the case, on the eve of a secured creditor's Fed. R. Bankr. P. 2004 examination of P, P asks L if the creditor is allowed to ask about transfers of assets which occurred prior to bankruptcy, and if so, for what prepetition period are such questions permitted. After L presses P to explain why he is asking this question, P tells L that shortly before bankruptcy, P transferred a signifi-

---

[736] *See* chapter 7.

[737] This is the case under the Model Rules and in many, but not all, jurisdictions.

[738] Arguably, all bankruptcy crimes involve fraud upon the court.

cant asset to a new corporation ("NC") which P established, in which P is the sole shareholder. The transfer was without consideration and was not disclosed on the bankruptcy schedules or statement of financial affairs. P tells L that if asked if any assets were transferred without consideration prior to bankruptcy, P intends to answer "no." Further, P declines L's request that amended schedules be filed to disclose the asset.

Counsel L's response to the situation is complicated by the fact that P's failure to schedule the asset and/or its apparently fraudulent transfer, is both a false statement to the tribunal and a continuing concealment. Thus the problem falls into the category of discovery of a crime in prospect, not merely a crime which has already been committed. Further, because the nature of the crime falls into the Model Rule 3.3 category — giving false evidence — remedial measures must be taken.

A standard response for many lawyers when placed in an ethical quandary is to withdraw from the case. Withdrawal, however, even if the court allows it, does not solve counsel's problem. In the case outlined above, L is required to take reasonable remedial steps. If P persists in withholding information about the asset, the harm to the bankruptcy estate and creditors will not be remedied. How can L remedy his client's nondisclosure without divulging the client's confidence?

L's quandary is exacerbated by the fact that his client is C, a corporation, not P, its president. P, however, acts on behalf of C, and as the corporation's management, P directs L's actions as counsel. The fact that C's economic interest lies in disclosure and recovery of the asset for C's estate, is obscured by the fact that P's interests are adverse to C in this respect.

This situation is precisely the quandary that Model Rule 1.13 seeks to address. Rule 1.13 delineates the duties of corporate counsel where the actions of an officer, employee or other person associated with the organization violates that person's legal duty to the organization or may result in legal liability or substantial injury to the organization. The rule states that

> "[u]nless the lawyer reasonably believes that it is not necessary in the best interest of the organization to do so, the lawyer shall refer the matter to higher authority in the organization, including, if warranted by the circumstances to the highest authority that can act on behalf of the organization as determined by applicable law." [739]

---

[739] Model Rule 1.13.

If, after the lawyer refers the matter to the highest corporate authority, that authority insists on the course of action which will result in a violation or the law and is likely to result in substantial injury to the organization, then the lawyer may reveal information relating to the representation whether or not such disclosure is permitted by Rule 1.6.

Most lawyers, however, are extremely reluctant to divulge a confidence, even where they are permitted or even required to do so by law. Disclosure of client confidences, even where permitted or required by law and the rules of professional conduct, does not easily square with a lawyer's own internal "code." Lawyers by nature are intensely loyal to the individuals they represent. Violating a client's confidence, even where the client is dishonest, criminal or outright evil, is anathema to many lawyers.

Sometimes the opposite situation is presented: When disclosure of the fraud is not permitted because it is past or because the crime will not involve imminent bodily harm, but a grave injustice or harm will result from the lawyer's silence. Lawyers feel the same internal conflict in the case of the confidence they are forced to keep, as they do in the case of the confidence they are forced to break. At these times, a lawyer would be well-advised to seek legal counsel of his own.

Conflict of interest

Another ethical problem with bankruptcy fraud implications is the issue of conflict of interest. Until a few years ago, this topic would not be seen as having any place in a book about bankruptcy crime. In recent years, however, conflicts of interest have led to significant civil, and occasionally criminal, consequences for lawyers. In one such recent case, a conflict of interest, which was not disclosed until well into the bankruptcy case, eventually led to conviction and imprisonment of debtor's counsel.[740]

Unlike the problems of asset planning or client confidentiality in the face of past, current or future fraud, the problem of conflict of interest usually originates with the lawyer or the law firm, not with the client. The problem starts with a lack of awareness of the conflict of interest principles. The problem is exacerbated by the intense competition in the market for legal services and skyrocketing overhead costs. Such economic pressures have blinded many lawyers and law firms to conflicts, as recognition of conflicts may necessitate turning away business. The growing conflict problems for legal professionals are largely the result of ignorance, fear, or greed.

---

[740] *United States v. Gellene*, 182 F.3d 578 (7th Cir. 1999).

The vast majority of cases involving conflicts of interest of counsel in bankruptcy cases involve large law firms. Small firms are less likely to have conflicts, and conflicts are easier for a small firm to spot. An additional reason is that the economics of partnership in a large firm require significantly higher levels of business generation than in a small practice setting. Large firms have large overhead and large expectations. When faced with the prospect of a large fee, there is a strong temptation to look the other way to avoid seeing a conflict.

Conflicts are not always easy to identify. Failure to identify conflicts in a bankruptcy case, however, has more severe consequences than in nonbankruptcy cases, because counsel must file a declaration under Fed. R. Bankr. P. 2014 under penalty of perjury as to the firm's disinterestedness and connections with the debtor, creditors, and parties in interest. A willful and knowing failure to disclose a conflict will violate § 152 of the Bankruptcy Criminal Code.

In *United States v. Gellene*,[741] the New York City firm of Milbank, Tweed, Hadley and McCloy was employed as counsel to the debtor in a large chapter 11 case in Milwaukee. On behalf of the firm, John Gellene filed a declaration under Fed. R. Bankr. P. 2014, which did not disclose the firm's simultaneous representation of the principals of the management of a major creditor. This failure was later compounded by an amended declaration and Gellene's testimony at a fee application, both of which failed to disclose the conflict. Gellene was ultimately convicted of a bankruptcy crime and sentenced to a jail term.

The circumstances in the *Gellene* case sound all too familiar to most bankruptcy lawyers. Conflicts are either not fully appreciated or else they are consciously ignored. There is an expression heard frequently in large firms about partners who are insensitive to conflicts: "He never saw a conflict he didn't like." There is a widespread belief that all ills can be cured by disclosure, but in fact most conflicts are not cured merely by disclosure.[742] Disclosure is a bankruptcy requirement designed to facilitate the court's determination of counsel's disinterestedness and lack of any material adverse interest to the estate. The rules governing conflicts provide a minimum standard for determining what connections must be disclosed in a bankruptcy case. They are not exhaustive, however; certain relationships in a bankruptcy case will trigger a disclosure requirement even though they would not create a conflict in a nonbankruptcy context.

A few of the most common sources of potential conflicts in a bankruptcy case can be summarized as follows: (1) simultaneous representation of a debtor

---

[741] *Gellene*, 182 F.3d 578 (7th Cir. 1999).

[742] If a conflict is presented by a multiple representation, an informed waiver by both clients is required. Model Rule 1.7; 1.9. Some conflicts cannot be waived.

corporation (or partnership) and its shareholders, officers, or directors (or partners); (2) simultaneous representation of a debtor and a creditor; (3) successive representation of more than one party in the same case; (4) representation of two debtors, one of which is a creditor of the other; and (5) representation of affiliated entities where intercompany transfers or loans have occurred.

Multiple representation is not the only source of potential conflicts, nor is it the only source of potential criminal liability for improper disclosure. Accepting compensation from parties other than the debtor in payment for legal fees rendered to the estate can be a source of serious problems for bankruptcy counsel, both civil and criminal. All proposed compensation arrangements must be disclosed by counsel under penalty of perjury (Fed. R. Bankr. P. 2014) and all compensation actually received, and its source, must be disclosed in any fee application filed seeking compensation from the estate.[743]

In addition to the restrictions set forth in state rules of professional conduct, many bankruptcy courts have held that such payments create an inherent conflict of interest, particularly when the payment comes from insiders or creditors. These restrictions are not just annoying technicalities. They are intended to prevent the problems of divided loyalty and to protect the integrity of the bankruptcy system.

In addition to the potential ethical breaches, evasion of these restrictions by acceptance of undisclosed payments may also give rise to a number of bankruptcy offenses. Agreements for or acceptance of such payments may give rise to violations of §§ 152(5), 152(6), or 155 of the Bankruptcy Criminal Code.

Ethical questions are perhaps the hardest questions that any lawyer must answer. As with other difficult questions, it is useful to have a framework for resolving such questions. The following steps are time-honored ways of finding the right answers to the hardest questions:

1. Think of the lawyer you most respect: A judge, a law school professor, or a senior lawyer in your practice area. Put yourself in that lawyer's place and visualize what he or she would do if personally confronted with the same problem.
2. If step #1 is unavailing, call that lawyer whom you most respect and ask for advice on a confidential basis. Better still, make an appointment and seek advice face-to-face.
3. If you have no mentor or respected advisor you can consult, ask a colleague to recommend a senior lawyer in your area of practice, per-

---

[743] Fed. R. Bankr. P. 2016.

haps even someone retired from active practice. Older, seasoned lawyers are most likely to have actually confronted a similar problem in their careers.

4. If your firm, corporation, or agency has a lawyer who is assigned to address ethical issues, such as a conflicts or ethics officer, consult him or her.
5. Once a possible course is identified, assess it from several different perspectives. Do you have qualms about the proposed action? Is the action consistent with your own mind and will? Once you take this action, will you be ashamed once others know what you have done? Would the action set a good example or precedent in your organization and among lawyers as a whole?

If you are uncomfortable about what you are about to do, chances are it is the wrong decision.

APPENDIX A

EXCERPTS FROM TITLE 11, UNITED STATES CODE (THE FEDERAL BANKRUPTCY CODE)

§101. Definitions

In this title the following definitions shall apply:

(1) The term "accountant" means accountant authorized under applicable law to practice public accounting, and includes professional accounting association, corporation, or partnership, if so authorized.

(2) The term "affiliate" means—

(A) entity that directly or indirectly owns, controls, or holds with power to vote, 20 percent or more of the outstanding voting securities of the debtor, other than an entity that holds such securities—

(i) in a fiduciary or agency capacity without sole discretionary power to vote such securities; or

(ii) solely to secure a debt, if such entity has not in fact exercised such power to vote;

(B) corporation 20 percent or more of whose outstanding voting securities are directly or indirectly owned, controlled, or held with power to vote, by the debtor, or by an entity that directly or indirectly owns, controls, or holds with power to vote, 20 percent or more of the outstanding voting securities of the debtor, other than an entity that holds such securities—

(i) in a fiduciary or agency capacity without sole discretionary power to vote such securities; or

(ii) solely to secure a debt, if such entity has not in fact exercised such power to vote;

(C) person whose business is operated under a lease or operating agreement by a debtor, or person substantially all of whose property is operated under an operating agreement with the debtor; or

(D) entity that operates the business or substantially all of the property of the debtor under a lease or operating agreement.

~~(3) [Redesignated]~~

(3) The term "assisted person" means any person whose debts consist primarily of consumer debts and the value of whose nonexempt property is less than $150,000.

(4) The term "attorney" means attorney, professional law association, corporation, or partnership, authorized under applicable law to practice law.

(4A) The term "bankruptcy assistance" means any goods or services sold or otherwise provided to an assisted person with the express or implied purpose of providing information, advice, counsel, document preparation, or filing, or attendance at a creditors' meeting or appearing in a case or proceeding on behalf of another or providing legal representation with respect to a case or proceeding under this title.

(5) The term "claim" means—

(A) right to payment, whether or not such right is reduced to judgment, liquidated, unliquidated, fixed, contingent, matured, unmatured, disputed, undisputed, legal, equitable, secured, or unsecured; or

(B) right to an equitable remedy for breach of performance if such breach gives rise to a right to payment, whether or not such right to an equitable remedy is reduced to judgment, fixed, contingent, matured, unmatured, disputed, undisputed, secured, or unsecured.

(6) The term "commodity broker" means futures commission merchant, foreign futures commission merchant, clearing organization, leverage transaction merchant, or commodity options dealer, as defined in section 761 of this title, with respect to which there is a customer, as defined in section 761 of this title.

(7) The term "community claim" means claim that arose before the commencement of the case concerning the debtor for which property of the kind specified in section 541(a)(2) of this title is liable, whether or not there is any such property at the time of the commencement of the case.

(7A) The term "commercial fishing operation" means—

(A) the catching or harvesting of fish, shrimp, lobsters, urchins, seaweed, shellfish, or other aquatic species or products of such species; or

(B) for purposes of section 109 and chapter 12, aquaculture activities consisting of raising for market any species or product described in subparagraph (A).

(7B) The term "commercial fishing vessel" means a vessel used by a family fisherman to carry out a commercial fishing operation.

(8) The term "consumer debt" means debt incurred by an individual primarily for a personal, family, or household purpose.

(9) The term "corporation"—

(A) includes—

(i) association having a power or privilege that a private corporation, but not an individual or a partnership, possesses;

(ii) partnership association organized under a law that makes only the capital subscribed responsible for the debts of such association;

(iii) joint-stock company;

(iv) unincorporated company or association; or

(v) business trust; but

(B) does not include limited partnership.

(10) The term "creditor" means—

(A) entity that has a claim against the debtor that arose at the time of or before the order for relief concerning the debtor;

(B) entity that has a claim against the estate of a kind specified in section 348(d), 502(f), 502(g), 502(h) or 502(i) of this title; or

(C) entity that has a community claim.

(10A) The term "current monthly income" –

(A) means the average monthly income from all sources that the debtor receives (or in a joint case the debtor and the debtor's spouse receive) without regard to whether such income is taxable income, derived during the 6-month period ending on –

(i) the last day of the calendar month immediately preceding the date of the commencement of the case if the debtor files the schedule of current income required by section 521(a)(1)(B)(ii); or

(ii) the date on which current income is determined by the court for purposes of this title if the debtor does not file the schedule of current income required by section 521(a)(1)(B)(ii); and

(B) includes any amount paid by any entity other than the debtor (or in a joint case the debtor and the debtor's spouse), on a regular basis for the household expenses of the debtor or the debtor's dependents (and in a joint case the debtor's spouse if not otherwise a dependent), but excludes benefits received under the Social Security Act, payments to victims of war crimes or crimes against humanity on account of their status as victims of such crimes, and payments to victims of international terrorism (as defined in section 2331 of title 18) or domestic terrorism (as defined in section 2331 of title 18) on account of their status as victims of such terrorism.

(11) The term "custodian" means—

(A) receiver or trustee of any of the property of the debtor, appointed in a case or proceeding not under this title;

(B) assignee under a general assignment for the benefit of the debtor's creditors; or

(C) trustee, receiver, or agent under applicable law, or under a contract, that is appointed or authorized to take charge of property of the debtor for the purpose of enforcing a lien against such property, or for the purpose of general administration of such property for the benefit of the debtor's creditors.

(12) The term "debt" means liability on a claim.

(12A) The term "debt relief agency" means any person who provides any bankruptcy assistance to an assisted person in return for the payment of money or other valuable consideration, or who is a bankruptcy petition preparer under section 110, but does not include—

(A) any person who is an officer, director, employee, or agent of a person who provides such assistance or of the bankruptcy petition preparer;

(B) a nonprofit organization that is exempt from taxation under section 501(c)(3)of the Internal Revenue Code of 1986;

(C) a creditor of such assisted person, to the extent that the creditor is assisting such assisted person to restructure any debt owed by such assisted person to the creditor;

(D) a depository institution (as defined in section 3 of the Federal Deposit Insurance Act) or any Federal credit union or State credit union (as those terms are defined in section 101 of the Federal Credit Union Act), or any affiliate or subsidiary of such depository institution or credit union; or

(E) an author, publisher, distributor, or seller of works subject to copyright protection under title 17, when acting in such capacity.

(13) The term "debtor" means person or municipality concerning which a case under this title has been commenced.

(13A) The term "debtor's principal residence" –

(A) means a residential structure, including incidental property, without regard to whether that structure is attached to real property; and

(B) includes an individual condominium, or cooperative unit, a mobile or manufactured home, or trailer.

(14) The term "disinterested person" means person that—

(A) is not a creditor, an equity security holder, or an insider;

(B) is not and was not, within 2 years before the date of the filing of the petition, a director, officer, or employee of the debtor; and

(C) does not have an interest materially adverse to the interest of the estate or of any class of creditors or equity security holders, by reason of any direct or indirect relationship to, connection with, or interest in, the debtor, or for any other reason.

(14A) The term "domestic support obligation" means a debt that accrues before, on, or after the date of the order for relief in a case under this title, including interest that accrues on that debt as provided under applicable nonbankrtupcy law notwithstanding any other provision of this title, that is—

(A) owed to or recoverable by—

(i) a spouse, former spouse, or child of the debtor or such child's parent, legal guardian, or responsible relative; or

(ii) governmental unit;

(B) in the nature of alimony, maintenance, or support (including assistance provided by a governmental unit) of such spouse, former spouse, or child of the debtor or such child's parent, without regard to whether such debt is expressly so designated;

(C) established or subject to establishment before, on, or after that date of the order for relief in a case under this title, by reason of applicable provisions of—

(i) a separation agreement, divorce decree, or property settlement agreement;

(ii) an order of a court of record; or

(iii) a determination made in accordance with applicable nonbankruptcy law by a governmental unit; and

(D) not assigned to a nongovernmental entity, unless that obligation is assigned voluntarily by the spouse, former spouse, child of the debtor, or such child's parent, legal guardian, or responsible relative for the purpose of collecting the debt.

(15) The term "entity" includes person, estate, trust, governmental unit, and United States trustee.

(16) The term "equity security" means—

(A) share in a corporation, whether or not transferable or denominated "stock", or similar security;

(B) interest of a limited partner in a limited partnership; or

(C) warrant or right, other than a right to convert, to purchase, sell, or subscribe to a share, security, or interest of a kind specified in subparagraph (A) or (B) of this paragraph.

(17) The term "equity security holder" means holder of an equity security of the debtor.

(18) The term "family farmer" means—

(A) individual or individual and spouse engaged in a farming operation whose aggregate debts do not exceed $3,237,000 and not less than 50 percent of whose aggregate noncontingent, liquidated debts (excluding a debt for the principal residence of such individual or such individual and spouse unless such debt arises out of a farming operation), on the date the case is filed, arise out of a farming operation owned or operated by such individual or such individual and spouse, and such individual or such individual and spouse receive from such farming operation more than 50 percent of such individual's or such individual and spouse's gross income for—

(i) the taxable year preceding; or

(ii) each of the 2d and 3d taxable years preceding;

the taxable year in which the case concerning such individual or such individual and spouse was filed; or

(B) corporation or partnership in which more than 50 percent of the outstanding stock or equity is held by one family, or by one family and the relatives of the members of such family, and such family or such relatives conduct the farming operation, and

(i) more than 80 percent of the value of its assets consists of assets related to the farming operation;

(ii) its aggregate debts do not exceed $3,237,000 and not less than 50 percent of its aggregate noncontingent, liquidated debts (excluding a debt for one dwelling which is owned by such corporation or partnership and which a shareholder or partner maintains as a principal residence, unless such debt arises out of a farming operation), on the date the case is filed, arise out of the farming operation owned or operated by such corporation or such partnership; and

(iii) if such corporation issues stock, such stock is not publicly traded.

(19) The term "family farmer with regular annual income" means family farmer whose annual income is sufficiently stable and regular to enable such family farmer to make payments under a plan under chapter 12 of this title.

(19A) The term "family fisherman" means—

(A) an individual or individual and spouse engaged in a commercial fished operation—

(i) whose aggregate debts do not exceed $1,500,000 and not less than 80 percent of whose aggregate noncontingent, liquidated debts (excluding a debt for the principal residence of such individual or such individual and spouse, unless such debt arises out of a commercial fishing operation), on the date the case is filed, arise out of a commercial fishing operation owned or operated by such individual or such individual and spouse; and

(ii) who receive from such commercial fishing operation more than 50 percent of such individual's or such individual's and spouse's gross income for the taxable year preceding the taxable year in which the case concerning such individual or such individual and spouse was filed; or

(B) a corporation or partnership—

(i) in which more than 50 percent of the outstanding stock or equity is held by—

(I) 1 family that conducts the commercial fishing operation; or

(II) 1 family and the relatives of the members of such family, and such family or such relatives conduct the commercial fishing operation; and

(ii) (I) more than 80 percent of the value of its assets consists of assets related to the commercial fishing operation;

(II) its aggregate debts do not exceed $1,500,000 and not less than 80 percent of its aggregate noncontingent, liquidated debts (excluding a debt for 1 dwelling which is owned by such corporation or partnership and which a shareholder or partner maintains as a principal residence, unless such debt arises out of a commercial fishing operation), on the date the case is filed, arise out of a commercial fishing operation owned or operated by such corporation or such partnership; and

(III) if such corporation issues stock, such stock is not publicly traded.

(19B) The term "family fisherman with regular annual income" means a family fisherman whose annual income is sufficiently stable and regular to enable such family fisherman to make payments under a plan under chapter 12 of this title.

(20) The term "farmer" means (except when such term appears in the term "family farmer"') person that received more than 80 percent of such person's gross income during the taxable year of such person immediately preceding the taxable year of such person during which the case under this title concerning such person was commenced from a farming operation owned or operated by such person.

(21) The term "farming operation" includes farming, tillage of the soil, dairy farming, ranching, production or raising of crops, poultry, or livestock, and production of poultry or livestock products in an unmanufactured state.

(21A) The term "farmout agreement" means a written agreement in which—

(A) the owner of a right to drill, produce, or operate liquid or gaseous hydrocarbons on property agrees or has agreed to transfer or assign all or a part of such right to another entity; and

(B) such other entity (either directly or through its agents or its assigns), as consideration, agrees to perform drilling, reworking, recompleting, testing, or similar or related operations, to develop or produce liquid or gaseous hydrocarbons on the property.

(21B) The term "Federal depository institutions regulatory agency" means—

(A) with respect to an insured depository institution (as defined in section 3(c)(2) of the Federal Deposit Insurance Act) for which no conservator or receiver has been appointed, the appropriate Federal banking agency (as defined in section 3(q) of such Act);

(B) with respect to an insured credit union (including an insured credit union for which the National Credit Union Administration has been appointed conservator or liquidating agent), the National Credit Union Administration;

(C) with respect to any insured depository institution for which the Resolution Trust Corporation has been appointed conservator or receiver, the Resolution Trust Corporation; and

(D) with respect to any insured depository institution for which the Federal Deposit Insurance Corporation has been appointed conservator or receiver, the Federal Deposit Insurance Corporation.

(22) The term "financial institution" means—

(A) a Federal reserve bank, or an entity (domestic or foreign) that is a commercial or savings bank, industrial savings bank, savings and loan association, trust company, federally-insured credit union, or receiver, liquidating agent, or conservator for such entity and, when any such Federal reserve bank, receiver, liquidating agent, conservator or entity is acting as agent or custodian for a customer in connection with a securities contract (as defined in section 741) such customer; or

(B) in connection with a securities contract (as defined in section 741) an investment company registered under the Investment Company Act of 1940.

(22A)The term "financial participant" means—

(A) an entity that, at the time it enters into a securities contract, commodity contract, swap agreement, repurchase agreement, or forward contract, or at the time of the date of the filing of the petition, has one or more agreements or transactions described in paragraph (1), (2), (3), (4),

(5), or (6) of section 561(a) with the debtor or any other entity (other than an affiliate) of a total gross dollar value of not less than $1,000,000,000 in notional or actual principal amount outstanding on any day during the previous 15-month period, or has gross mark-to-market positions of not less than $100,000,000 (aggregated across counterparties) in one or more such agreements or transactions with the debtor or any other entity (other than an affiliate) on any day during the previous 15-month period; or

(B) a clearing organization (as defied in section 402 of the Federal Deposit Insurance Corporation Improvement Act of 1991).

(23) The term "foreign proceeding" means a collective judicial or administrative proceeding in a foreign country, including an interim proceeding, under a law relating to insolvency or adjustment of debt in which proceeding the assets and affairs of the debtor are subject to control or supervision by a foreign court, for the purpose of reorganization or liquidation.

(24) The term "foreign representative" means a person or body, including a person or body appointed on an interim basis, authorized in a foreign proceeding to administer the reorganization or the liquidation of the debtor's assets or affairs or to act as a representative of such foreign proceeding.

(25) The term "forward contract" means—

(A) a contract (other than a commodity contract) for the purchase, sale, or transfer of a commodity, as defined in section 761(8) of this title, or any similar good, article, service, right, or interest which is presently or in the future becomes the subject of dealing in the forward contract trade, or product or byproduct thereof, with a maturity date more than two days after the date the contract is entered into, including, but not limited to, a repurchase transaction, reverse repurchase transaction, consignment, lease, swap, hedge transaction, deposit, loan, option, allocated transaction, unallocated transaction, or any other similar agreement;

(B) any combination of agreements or transactions referred to in subparagraph (A) or (C);

(C) any option to enter into an agreement or transaction referred to in subparagraph (A) or (B);

(D) a master agreement that provides for an agreement or transaction referred to in subparagraph (A), (B), or (C), together with all supplements to any such master agreement, without regard to whether such master agreement provides for an agreement or transaction that is not a forward contract under this paragraph, except that such master agreement shall be considered to be a forward contract under this paragraph only with respect to each agreement or transaction under such master agreement that is referred to in subparagraph (A), (B), or (C); or

(E) any security agreement or arrangement, or other credit enhancement related to any agreement or transaction referred to in subparagraph (A), (B), (C), or (D), including any guarantee or reimbursement obligation by or to a forward contract merchant or financial participant in connection with any agreement or transaction referred to in any such subparagraph, but not to exceed the damages in connection with any such agreement or transaction, measured in accordance with section 562.

(26) The term "forward contract merchant" means a Federal reserve bank, or an entity the business of which consists in whole or in part of entering into forward contracts as or with merchants in a commodity (as defined in section 761) or any similar good, article, service, right, or interest which is presently or in the future becomes the subject of dealing in the forward contract trade.

(27) The term "governmental unit" means United States; State; Commonwealth; District; Territory; municipality; foreign state; department, agency, or instrumentality of the United States (but not a United States trustee while serving as a trustee in a case under this title), a State, a Commonwealth, a District, a Territory, a municipality, or a foreign state; or other foreign or domestic government.

(27A) The term "health care business" —

(A) means any public or private entity (without regard to whether that entity is organized for profit or not for profit) that is primarily engaged in offering to the general public facilities and services for —

(i) the diagnosis or treatment of injury, deformity, or disease; and

(ii) surgical, drug treatment, psychiatric, or obstetric care; and

(B) includes —

(i) any —

(I) general or specialized hospital;

(II) ancillary ambulatory, emergency, or surgical treatment facility;

(III) hospice;

(IV) home health agency; and

(V) other health care institution that is similar to an entity referred to in subclause (I), (II), (III), or (IV); and

(ii) any long-term care facility, including any —

(I) skilled nursing facility;

(II) intermediate care facility;

(III) assisted living facility;

(IV) home for the aged;

(V) domiciliary care facility; and

(VI) health care institution that is related to a facility referred to in subclause (I), (II), (III), (IV), or (V), if that institution is primarily engaged in offering room, board, laundry, or personal assistance with activities of daily living and incidentals to activities of daily living.

(27B) The term "incidental property" means, with respect to a debtor's principal residence —

(A) property commonly conveyed with a principal residence in the area where the real property is located;

(B) all easements, rights, appurtenances, fixtures, rents, royalties, mineral rights, oil or gas rights or profits, water rights, escrow funds, or insurance proceeds; and

(C) all replacements or additions.

(28) The term "indenture" means mortgage, deed of trust, or indenture, under which there is outstanding a security, other than a voting-trust certificate, constituting a claim against the debtor, a claim secured by a lien on any of the debtor's property, or an equity security of the debtor.

(29) The term "indenture trustee" means trustee under an indenture.

(30) The term "individual with regular income" means individual whose income is sufficiently stable and regular to enable such individual to make payments under a plan under chapter 13 of this title, other than a stockbroker or a commodity broker.

(31) The term "insider" includes—

(A) if the debtor is an individual—

(i) relative of the debtor or of a general partner of the debtor;

(ii) partnership in which the debtor is a general partner;

(iii) general partner of the debtor; or

(iv) corporation of which the debtor is a director, officer, or person in control;

(B) if the debtor is a corporation—

(i) director of the debtor;

(ii) officer of the debtor;

(iii) person in control of the debtor;

(iv) partnership in which the debtor is a general partner;

(v) general partner of the debtor; or

(vi) relative of a general partner, director, officer, or person in control of the debtor;

(C) if the debtor is a partnership—

(i) general partner in the debtor;

(ii) relative of a general partner in, general partner of, or person in control of the debtor;

(iii) partnership in which the debtor is a general partner;

(iv) general partner of the debtor; or

(v) person in control of the debtor;

(D) if the debtor is a municipality, elected official of the debtor or relative of an elected official of the debtor;

(E) affiliate, or insider of an affiliate as if such affiliate were the debtor; and

(F) managing agent of the debtor.

(32) The term "insolvent" means—

(A) with reference to an entity other than a partnership and a municipality, financial condition such that the sum of such entity's debts is greater than all of such entity's property, at a fair valuation, exclusive of—

(i) property transferred, concealed, or removed with intent to hinder, delay, or defraud such entity's creditors; and

(ii) property that may be exempted from property of the estate under section 522 of this title;

(B) with reference to a partnership, financial condition such that the sum of such partnership's debts is greater than the aggregate of, at a fair valuation—

(i) all of such partnership's property, exclusive of property of the kind specified in subparagraph (A)(i) of this paragraph; and

(ii) the sum of the excess of the value of each general partner's nonpartnership property, exclusive of property of the kind specified in subparagraph (A) of this paragraph, over such partner's nonpartnership debts; and

(C) with reference to a municipality, financial condition such that the municipality is—

(i) generally not paying its debts as they become due unless such debts are the subject of a bona fide dispute; or

(ii) unable to pay its debts as they become due.

(33) The term "institution-affiliated party"—

(A) with respect to an insured depository institution (as defined in section 3(c)(2) of the Federal Deposit Insurance Act), has the meaning given it in section 3(u) of the Federal Deposit Insurance Act; and

(B) with respect to an insured credit union, has the meaning given it in section 206(r) of the Federal Credit Union Act.

(34) The term "insured credit union" has the meaning given it in section 101(7) of the Federal Credit Union Act.

(35) The term "insured depository institution"—

(A) has the meaning given it in section 3(c)(2) of the Federal Deposit Insurance Act; and

(B) includes an insured credit union (except in the case of paragraphs (23) and (35) of this subsection).

(35A) The term "intellectual property" means—

(A) trade secret;

(B) invention, process, design, or plant protected under title 35;

(C) patent application;

(D) plant variety;

(E) work of authorship protected under title 17; or

(F) mask work protected under chapter 9 of title 17;

to the extent protected by applicable nonbankruptcy law.

(36) The term "judicial lien" means lien obtained by judgment, levy, sequestration, or other legal or equitable process or proceeding.

(37) The term "lien" means charge against or interest in property to secure payment of a debt or performance of an obligation.

(38) The term "margin payment" means, for purposes of the forward contract provisions of this title, payment or deposit of cash, a security or other property, that is commonly known in the forward contract trade as original margin, initial margin, maintenance margin, or variation margin, including mark-to-market payments, or variation payments.

(38A) The term "master netting agreement" —

(A) means an agreement providing for the exercise of rights, including rights of netting, setoff, liquidation, termination, acceleration, or close out, under or in connection with one or more contracts that are described in any one or more of paragraphs (1) through (5) of section 561(a), or any security agreement or arrangement or other credit enhancement related to one or more of the foregoing, including any guarantee or reimbursement obligation related to 1 or more of the foregoing; and

(B) if the agreement contains provisions relating to agreements or transactions that are not contracts described in paragraphs (1) though (5) of section 561(a), shall be deemed to be a master netting agreement only with respect to those agreements or transactions that are described in any one or more of paragraphs (1) through (5) of section 561(a).

(38B) The term "master netting agreement participant" means an entity that, at any time before the date of the filing of the petition, is a party to an outstanding master netting agreement with the debtor.

(39) The term "mask work" has the meaning given it in section 901(a)(2) of title 17.

(39A) The term "median family income" means for any year —

(A) the median family income both calculated and reported by the Bureau of the Census in the then most recent year; and

(B) if not so calculated and reported in the then current year, adjusted annually after such most recent year until the next year in which median family income is both calculated and reported by the Bureau of the Census, to reflect the percentage change in the Consumer Price Index for All Urban Consumers during the period of years occurring after such most recent year and before such current year.

(40) The term "municipality" means political subdivision or public agency or instrumentality of a State.

(40A) The term "patient" means any individual who obtains or receives services from a health care business.

(40B) The term "patient records" means any written document relating to a patient or record recorded in a magnetic, optical, or other form of electronic medium.

(41) The term "person" includes individual, partnership, and corporation, but does not include governmental unit, except that a governmental unit that—

(A) acquires an asset from a person—

(i) as a result of the operation of a loan guarantee agreement; or

(ii) as receiver or liquidating agent of a person;

(B) is a guarantor of a pension benefit payable by or on behalf of the debtor or an affiliate of the debtor; or

(C) is the legal or beneficial owner of an asset of—

(i) an employee pension benefit plan that is a governmental plan, as defined in section 414(d) of the Internal Revenue Code of 1986; or

(ii) an eligible deferred compensation plan, as defined in section 457(b) of the Internal Revenue Code of 1986;

shall be considered, for purposes of section 1102 of this title, to be a person with respect to such asset or such benefit.

(41A) The term "personally identifiable information" means —

(A) if provided by an individual to the debtor in connection with obtaining a product or a service from the debtor primarily for a personal, family, or household purposes—

(i) the first name (or initial) and last name of such individual, whether given at birth or time of adoption, or resulting from a lawful change of name;

(ii) the geographical address of a physical place of residence of such individual;

(iii) an electronic address (including an e-mail address) of such individual;

(iv) a telephone number dedicated to contacting such individual at such physical place of residence;

(v) a social security account number issues to such individual; or

(vi) the account number of a credit card issued to such individual; or

(B) if identified in connection with 1 or more of the items of information specified in subparagraph (A) —

(i) a birth date, the number of a certificate of birth or adoption, or a place of birth; or

(ii) any other information concerning an identified individual that, if disclosed, will result in contacting or identifying such individual physically or electronically.

(42) The term "petition" means petition filed under section 301, 302, 303, or 304 of this title, as the case may be, commencing a case under this title.

(42A) The term "production payment" means a term overriding royalty satisfiable in cash or in kind—

(A) contingent on the production of a liquid or gaseous hydrocarbon from particular real property; and

(B) from a specified volume, or a specified value, from the liquid or gaseous hydrocarbon produced from such property, and determined without regard to production costs.

(43) The term "purchaser" means transferee of a voluntary transfer, and includes immediate or mediate transferee of such a transferee.

(44) The term "railroad" means common carrier by railroad engaged in the transportation of individuals or property or owner of trackage facilities leased by such a common carrier.

(45) The term "relative" means individual related by affinity or consanguinity within the third degree as determined by the common law, or individual in a step or adoptive relationship within such third degree.

(46) The term "repo participant" means an entity that, at any time before the filing of the petition, has an outstanding repurchase agreement with the debtor.

(47) The term "repurchase agreement" (which definition also applies to a reverse repurchase agreement)—

(A) means—

(i) an agreement, including related terms, which provides for the transfer of one or more certificate of deposit, mortgage related securities (as defined in section 3 of the Securities Exchange Act of 1934), mortgage loans, interests in mortgage related securities or mortgage loans, eligible bankers' acceptances, qualified foreign government securities (defined as a security that is a direct obligation of, or that is fully guaranteed by, the central government of a member of the Organization for Economic Cooperation and Development), or securities that are direct obligations of, or that are fully guaranteed by, the United States or any agency of the United States against the transfer of funds by the transferee of such certificates of deposit, eligible bankers' acceptances, securities, mortgage loans, or interests, with a simultaneous agreement by such transferee to transfer to the transferor thereof certificates of deposit, eligible bankers' acceptance, securities, mortgage loans, or interests of the kind described in this clause, at a date certain not later than 1 year after such transfer or on demand, against the transfer of finds;

(ii) any combination of agreements or transactions referred to in clauses (i) and (iii);

(iii) an option to enter into an agreement or transaction referred to in clause (i) or (ii);

(iv) a master agreement that provides for an agreement or transaction referred to in clause (i), (ii), or (iii), together with all supplements to any such master agreement, without regard to whether such master agreement provides for an agreement or transaction that is not a repurchase agreement under this paragraph, except that such master agreement shall be considered to be a repurchase agreement under this paragraph only with respect to each agreement or transaction under the master agreement that is referred to in clause (i), (ii), or (iii); or

(v) any security agreement or arrangement or other credit enhancement related to any agreement or transaction referred to in clause (i), (ii), (iii), or (iv), including any guarantee or reimbursement obligation by or to a repo participant or financial participant in connection with any agreement or transaction referred to in any such clause, but not to exceed the damages in connection with any such agreement or transaction, measured in accordance with section 562 of this title; and

(B) does not include a repurchase obligation under a participation in a commercial mortgage loan.

(48) The term "securities clearing agency" means person that is registered as a clearing agency under section 17A of the Securities Exchange Act of 1934, or exempt from such registration under such section pursuant to an order of the Securities and Exchange Commission, or whose business is confined to the performance of functions of a clearing agency with respect to exempted securities, as defined in section 3(a)(12) of such Act for the purposes of such section 17A.

(48A) The term "securities self regulatory organization" means either a securities association registered with the Securities and Exchange Commission under section 15A of the Securities Exchange Act of 1934 or a national securities exchange registered with the Securities and Exchange Commission under section 6 of the Securities Exchange Act of 1934.

(49) The term "security"—

(A) includes—

(i) note;

(ii) stock;

(iii) treasury stock;

(iv) bond;

(v) debenture;

(vi) collateral trust certificate;

(vii) pre-organization certificate or subscription;

(viii) transferable share;

(ix) voting-trust certificate;

(x) certificate of deposit;

(xi) certificate of deposit for security;

(xii) investment contract or certificate of interest or participation in a profit-sharing agreement or in an oil, gas, or mineral royalty or lease, if such contract or interest is required to be the subject of a registration statement filed with the Securities and Exchange Commission under the provisions of the Securities Act of 1933, or is exempt under section 3(b) of such Act from the requirement to file such a statement;

(xiii) interest of a limited partner in a limited partnership;
(xiv) other claim or interest commonly known as "security"; and
(xv) certificate of interest or participation in, temporary or interim certificate for, receipt for, or warrant or right to subscribe to or purchase or sell, a security; but

(B) does not include—
(i) currency, check, draft, bill of exchange, or bank letter of credit;
(ii) leverage transaction, as defined in section 761 of this title;
(iii) commodity futures contract or forward contract;
(iv) option, warrant, or right to subscribe to or purchase or sell a commodity futures contract;
(v) option to purchase or sell a commodity;
(vi) contract or certificate of a kind specified in subparagraph (A)(xii) of this paragraph that is not required to be the subject of a registration statement filed with the Securities and Exchange Commission and is not exempt under section 3(b) of the Securities Act of 1933 from the requirement to file such a statement; or
(vii) debt or evidence of indebtedness for goods sold and delivered or services rendered.

(50) The term "security agreement" means agreement that creates or provides for a security interest.

(51) The term "security interest" means lien created by an agreement.

(51A) The term "settlement payment" means, for purposes of the forward contract provisions of this title, a preliminary settlement payment, a partial settlement payment, an interim settlement payment, a settlement payment on account, a final settlement payment, a net settlement payment, or any other similar payment commonly used in the forward contract trade.

(51B) The term "single asset real estate" means real property constituting a single property or project, other than residential real property with fewer than 4 residential units, which generates substantially all of the gross income of a debtor and on which no substantial business is being conducted by a debtor other than the business of operating the real property and activities incidental thereto.

(51C) The term "small business case" means a case filed under chapter 11 of this title in which the debtor is a small business debtor.

(51D) The term "small business debtor" —

(A) subject to subparagraph (B), means a person engaged in commercial or business activities (including any affiliate of such person that is also a debtor under this title and excluding a person whose primary activity is the business of owning or operating real property or activities incidental thereto) that has aggregate noncontingent liquidated secured and unsecured debts as of the date of the petition or the date of the order for relief in an amount not more than $2,000,000 (excluding debts owed to 1 or more affiliates or insiders) for a case in which the United States trustee has not appointed under section 1102(a)(1) a committee of unsecured creditors or where the court has determined that the committee of unsecured creditors is not sufficiently active and representative to provide effective oversight of the debtor; and

(B) does not include any member of a group of affiliated debtors that has aggregate noncontingent liquidated secured and unsecured debts in an amount greater than $2,000,000 (excluding debt owed to 1 or more affiliates or insiders).

(52) The term "State" includes the District of Columbia and Puerto Rico, except for the purpose of defining who may be a debtor under chapter 9 of this title.

(53) The term "statutory lien" means lien arising solely by force of a statute on specified circumstances or conditions, or lien of distress for rent, whether or not statutory, but does not include security interest or judicial lien, whether or not such interest or lien is provided by or is dependent on a statute and whether or not such interest or lien is made fully effective by statute.

(53A) The term "stockbroker" means person—

(A) with respect to which there is a customer, as defined in section 741 of this title; and

(B) that is engaged in the business of effecting transactions in securities—

(i) for the account of others; or

(ii) with members of the general public, from or for such person's own account;

(53B) The term "swap agreement" —

(A) means —

(i) any agreement, (including the terms and conditions incorporated by reference in such agreement, which is —

(I) an interest rate swap, option, future, or forward agreement, including a rate floor, rate cap, rate collar, cross- currency rate swap, and basis swap;

(II) a spot, same day-tomorrow, tomorrow-next, forward, or other foreign exchange or precious metals agreement;

(III) a currency swap, option, future, or forward agreement;
(IV) an equity index or equity swap, option, future or forward agreement;
(V) a debt index or debt swap, option, future, or forward agreement;
(VI) a total return, credit spread or credit swap, option, future, or forward agreement;
(VII) a commodity index or a commodity swap, option, future, or forward agreement; or
(VIII) a weather swap, weather derivative, or weather option;

(ii) any agreement or transaction that is similar to any other agreement or transaction referred to in this paragraph and that —
(I) is of a type that has been, is presently, or in the future becomes, the subject of recurrent dealings in the swap markets (including terms and conditions incorporated by reference therein); and
(II) is a forward, swap, future, or option on one or more rates, currencies, commodities, equity securities, or other equity instruments, debt securities or other debt instruments, quantitative measures associated with an occurrence, extent of an occurrence, or contingency associated with a financial, commercial, or economic consequence, or economic or financial indices or measures of economic or financial risk or value;

(iii) any combination of agreements or transactions referred to in this subparagraph;

(iv) any option to enter into an agreement or transaction referred to in this subparagraph;

(v) a master agreement that provides for an agreement or transaction referred to in clause (i), (ii), (iii), or (iv), together with all supplements to any such master agreement, and without regard to whether the master agreement contains an agreement or transaction that is not a swap agreement under this paragraph, except that the master agreement shall be considered to be a swap agreement under this paragraph only with respect to each agreement or transaction under the master agreement that is referred to in clause (i), (ii), (iii), or (iv); or

(vi) any security agreement or arrangement or other credit enhancement related to any agreements or transactions referred to in clause

(i) though (v), including any guarantee or reimbursement obligation by or to a swap participant or financial participant in connection with any agreement or transaction referred to in any such clause, but not to exceed the damages in connection with any such agreement or transaction, measured in accordance with section 562; and

(B) is applicable for purposes of this title only, and shall not be construed or applied so as to challenge or affect the characterization, definition, or treatment of any swap agreement under any other statute, regulation, or rule, including the Securities Act of 1933, the Securities Exchange Act of 1934, the Public Utility Holding Company Act of 1935, the Trust Indenture Act of 1939, the Investment Company Act of 1940, the Investment Advisers Act of 1940, the Securities Investor Protection Act of 1970, the Commodity Exchange Act, the Gramm-Leach-Bliley Act, and the Legal Certainty for Bank Products Act of 2000.

(53C) The term "swap participant" means an entity that, at any time before the filing of the petition, has an outstanding swap agreement with the debtor.

(56A)[53D] The term "term overriding royalty" means an interest in liquid or gaseous hydrocarbons in place or to be produced from particular real property that entitles the owner thereof to a share of production, or the value thereof, for a term limited by time, quantity, or value realized.

(53D)[53E] The term "timeshare plan" means and shall include that interest purchased in any arrangement, plan, scheme, or similar device, but not including exchange programs, whether by membership, agreement, tenancy in common, sale, lease, deed, rental agreement, license, right to use agreement, or by any other means, whereby a purchaser, in exchange for consideration, receives a right to use accommodations, facilities, or recreational sites, whether improved or unimproved, for a specific period of time less than a full year during any given year, but not necessarily for consecutive years, and which extends for a period of more than three years. A ``timeshare interest" is that interest purchased in a timeshare plan which grants the purchaser the right to use and occupy accommodations, facilities, or recreational sites, whether improved or unimproved, pursuant to a timeshare plan.

(54) The term "transfer" means —

(A) the creation of a lien;

(B) the retention of title as a security interest;

(C) the foreclosure of a debtor's equity of redemption; or

(D) each mode, direct or indirect, absolute or conditional, voluntary or involuntary, of disposing of or parting with —

(i) property; or

(ii) an interest in property.

(54A) The term "uninsured State member bank" means a State member bank (as defined in section 3 of the Federal Deposit Insurance Act) the deposits of which are not insured by the Federal Deposit Insurance Corporation.

(55) The term "United States", when used in a geographical sense, includes all locations where the judicial jurisdiction of the United States extends, including territories and possessions of the United States.

§ 109. Who may be a debtor

(a) Notwithstanding any other provision of this section, only a person that resides or has a domicile, a place of business, or property in the United States, or a municipality, may be a debtor under this

title.

(b) A person may be a debtor under chapter 7 of this title only if such person is not—

(1) a railroad;

(2) a domestic insurance company, bank, savings bank, cooperative bank, savings and loan association, building and loan association, homestead association, a New Markets Venture Capital company as defined in section 351 of the Small Business Investment Act of 1958, a small business investment company licensed by the Small Business Administration under section 301 of the Small Business Investment Act of 1958, credit union, or industrial bank or similar institution which is an insured bank as defined in section 3(h) of the Federal Deposit Insurance Act, except that an uninsured State member bank, or a corporation organized under section 25A of the Federal Reserve Act, which operates, or operates as, a multilateral clearing organization pursuant to section 409 of the Federal Deposit Insurance Corporation Improvement Act of 1991 may be a debtor if a petition is filed at the direction of the Board of Governors of the Federal Reserve System; or

(3) (A) a foreign insurance company, engaged in such business in the United States; or

(B) a foreign bank, savings bank, cooperative bank, savings and loan association, building and loan association or credit union, that has a branch or agency (as defined in section 1(b) of the International Banking Act of 1978) in the United States.

(c) An entity may be a debtor under chapter 9 of this title if and only if such entity—

(1) is a municipality;

(2) is specifically authorized, in its capacity as a municipality or by name, to be a debtor under such chapter by State law, or by a governmental officer or organization empowered by State law to authorize such entity to be a debtor under such chapter;

(3) is insolvent;

(4) desires to effect a plan to adjust such debts; and

(5) (A) has obtained the agreement of creditors holding at least a majority in amount of the claims of each class that such entity intends to impair under a plan in a case under such chapter;

(B) has negotiated in good faith with creditors and has failed to obtain the agreement of creditors holding at least a majority in amount of the claims of each class that such entity intends to impair under a plan in a case under such chapter;

(C) is unable to negotiate with creditors because such negotiation is impracticable; or

(D) reasonably believes that a creditor may attempt to obtain a transfer that is avoidable under section 547 of this title.

(d) Only a railroad, a person that may be a debtor under chapter 7 of this title (except a stockbroker or a commodity broker), and an uninsured State member bank, or a corporation organized under section 25A of the Federal Reserve Act, which operates, or operates as, a multilateral clearing organization pursuant to section 409 of the Federal Deposit Insurance Corporation Improvement Act of 1991 may be a debtor under chapter 11 of this title.

(e) Only an individual with regular income that owes, on the date of the filing of the petition, noncontingent, liquidated, unsecured debts of less than $307,675 and noncontingent, liquidated, secured debts of less than $922,975, or an individual with regular income and such individual's spouse, except a stockbroker or a commodity broker, that owe, on the date of the filing of the petition, noncontingent, liquidated, unsecured debts that aggregate less than $307,675 and noncontingent, liquidated, secured debts of less than $922,975 may be a debtor under chapter 13 of this title.

(f) Only a family farmer or family fisherman with regular annual income may be a debtor under chapter 12 of this title.

(g) Notwithstanding any other provision of this section, no individual or family farmer may be a debtor under this title who has been a debtor in a case pending under this title at any time in the preceding 180 days if—

(1) the case was dismissed by the court for willful failure of the debtor to abide by orders of the court, or to appear before the court in proper prosecution of the case; or

(2) the debtor requested and obtained the voluntary dismissal of the case following the filing of a request for relief from the automatic stay provided by section 362 of this title.

(h) (1) Subject to paragraphs (2) and (3), and notwithstanding any other provision of this section, an individual may not be a debtor under this title unless such individual has, during the 180-day period preceding the date of filing of the petition by such individual, received from an approved nonprofit budget and credit counseling agency described in section 111(a) an individual or group briefing (including a briefing conducted by telephone or on the Internet) that outlined the opportunities for available credit counseling and assisted such individual in performing a related budget analysis.

(2) (A) Paragraph (1) shall not apply with respect to a debtor who resides in a district for which the United States trustee (or the bankruptcy administrator, if any) determines that the approved nonprofit budget and credit counseling agencies for such district are not reasonably able to provide adequate services to the additional individuals who would otherwise seek credit counseling from such agencies by reason of the requirements of paragraph (1).

(B) The United States trustee (or the bankruptcy administrator, if any) who makes a determination described in subparagraph (A) shall review such determination not later than 1 year after the date of such determination, and not less frequently than annually thereafter. Notwithstanding the preceding sentence, a nonprofit budget and credit counseling agency may be disapproved by the United States trustee (or the bankruptcy administrator, if any) at any time.

(3) (A) subject to subparagraph (B), the requirements of paragraph (1) shall not apply with respect to a debtor who submits to the court a certification that—

(i) describes exigent circumstances that merit a waiver of the requirements of paragraph (1);

(ii) states that the debtor requested credit counseling services from an approved nonprofit budget and credit counseling agency, but was unable to obtain the services referred to in paragraph (1) during the 5-day period beginning on the date on which the debtor made that request; and

(iii) is satisfactory to the court.

(B) With respect to a debtor, an exemption under subparagraph (A) shall cease to apply to that debtor on the date on which the debtor meets the requirements of paragraph (1), but in no case may the exemption apply to that debtor after the date that is 30 days after the debtor files a petition, except that the court, for cause, may order an additional 15 days.

(4) The requirements of paragraph (1) shall not apply with respect to a debtor whom the court determines, after notice and hearing, is unable to complete those requirements because of incapability, disability, or active military duty in a military combat zone. For the purposes of this paragraph, "incapacity" means that the debtor is impaired by reason of mental illness or mental deficiency so that he is incapable of realizing and making rational decisions with respect to his financial responsibilities; and "disability" means that the debtor is so physically impaired as to be unable, after reasonable effort, to participate in an in person, telephone, or Internet briefing required under paragraph (1).

§ 341. Meetings of creditors and equity security holders

(a) Within a reasonable time after the order for relief in a case under this title, the United States trustee shall convene and preside at a meeting of creditors.

(b) The United States trustee may convene a meeting of any equity security holders.

(c) The court may not preside at, and may not attend, any meeting under this section including any final meeting of creditors. Notwithstanding any local court rule, provision of a State constitution, any otherwise applicable nonbankruptcy law, or any other requirement that representation at the meeting of creditors under section (a) be by an attorney, a creditor holding a consumer debt or any representative of the creditor (which may include an entity or an employee of an entity and may be a representative for more than 1 creditor) shall be permitted to appear at and participate in the meeting of creditors in a case under chapter 7 or 13, either alone or in conjunction with an attorney for the creditor. Nothing in this subsection shall be construed to require any creditor to be represented by an attorney at any meeting of creditors.

(d) Prior to the conclusion of the meeting of creditors or equity security holders, the trustee shall orally examine the debtor to ensure that the debtor in a case under chapter 7 of this title is aware of—

(1) the potential consequences of seeking a discharge in bankruptcy, including the effects on credit history;

(2) the debtor's ability to file a petition under a different chapter of this title;

(3) the effect of receiving a discharge of debts under this title; and

(4) the effect of reaffirming a debt, including the debtor's knowledge of the provisions of section 524(d) of this title.

(e) Notwithstanding subsections (a) and (b), the court, on the request of a party in interest and after notice and a hearing, for cause may order that the United States trustee not convene a meeting of creditors or equity security holders if the debtor has filed a plan as to which the debtor solicited acceptances prior to the commencement of the case.

§ 344. Self-incrimination; immunity

Immunity for persons required to submit to examination, to testify, or to provide information in a case under this title may be granted under part V of title 18.

§ 363. Use, sale, or lease of property

(a) In this section, "cash collateral" means cash, negotiable instruments, documents of title, securities, deposit accounts, or other cash equivalents whenever acquired in which the estate and an entity other than the estate have an interest and includes the proceeds, products, offspring, rents, or profits of property and the fees, charges, accounts or other payments for the use or occupancy of rooms and other public facilities in hotels, motels, or other lodging properties subject to a security interest as provided in section 552(b) of this title, whether existing before or after the commencement of a case under this title.

(b)(1) The trustee, after notice and a hearing, may use, sell, or lease, other than in the ordinary course of business, property of the estate; except that if the debtor in connection with offering a product or a service discloses to an individual a policy prohibiting the transfer of personally identifiable information about individuals to persons that are not affiliated with the debtor and if such policy is in effect on the date of the commencement of the case, then the trustee may not sell or lease personally identifiable information to any person unless—

(A) such sale or such lease is consistent with such policy; or

(B) after appointment of a consumer privacy ombudsman in accordance with section 332, and after notice and a hearing, the court approves such sale or such lease—

(i) giving due consideration to the facts, circumstances, and conditions of such sale or such lease; and

(ii) finding that no showing was made that such sale or such lease would violate applicable nonbankruptcy law.

(2) If notification is required under subsection (a) of section 7A of the Clayton Act in the case of a transaction under this subsection, then—

(A) notwithstanding subsection (a) of such section, the notification required by such subsection to be given by the debtor shall be given by the trustee; and

(B) notwithstanding subsection (b) of such section, the required waiting period shall end on the 15th day after the date of the receipt, by the Federal Trade Commission and the Assistant Attorney General in charge of the Antitrust Division of the Department of Justice, of the notification required under such subsection (a), unless such waiting period is extended—

(i) pursuant to subsection (e)(2) of such section, in the same manner as such subsection (e)(2) applies to a cash tender offer;

(ii) pursuant to subsection (g)(2) of such section; or

(iii) by the court after notice and a hearing.

(c)(1) If the business of the debtor is authorized to be operated under section 721, 1108, 1203, 1204, or 1304 of this title and unless the court orders otherwise, the trustee may enter into transactions, including the sale or lease of property of the estate, in the ordinary course of business, without notice or a hearing, and may use property of the estate in the ordinary course of business without notice or a hearing.

(2) The trustee may not use, sell, or lease cash collateral under paragraph (1) of this subsection unless—

(A) each entity that has an interest in such cash collateral consents; or

(B) the court, after notice and a hearing, authorizes such use, sale, or lease in accordance with the provisions of this section.

(3) Any hearing under paragraph (2)(B) of this subsection may be a preliminary hearing or may be consolidated with a hearing under subsection (e) of this section, but shall be scheduled in accordance with the needs of the debtor. If the hearing under paragraph (2)(B) of this subsection is a preliminary hearing, the court may authorize such use, sale, or lease only if there is a reasonable likelihood that the trustee will prevail at the final hearing under subsection (e) of this section. The court shall act promptly on any request for authorization under paragraph (2)(B) of this subsection.

(4) Except as provided in paragraph (2) of this subsection, the trustee shall segregate and account for any cash collateral in the trustee's possession, custody, or control.

(d) The trustee may use, sell, or lease property under subsection (b) or (c) of this section only—

(1) in accordance with applicable nonbankruptcy law that governs the transfer of property by a corporation or trust that is not a moneyed, business, or commercial corporation or trust; and

(2) to the extent not inconsistent with any relief granted under subsection (c),(d), (e) or (f) of section 362.

(e) Notwithstanding any other provision of this section, at any time, on request of an entity that has an interest in property used, sold, or leased, or proposed to be used, sold, or leased, by the trustee, the court, with or without a hearing, shall prohibit or condition such use, sale, or lease as is necessary to provide adequate protection of such interest. This subsection also applies to property that is subject to any unexpired lease of personal property (to the exclusion of such property being subject to an order to grant relief from the stay under section 362).

(f) The trustee may sell property under subsection (b) or (c) of this section free and clear of any interest in such property of an entity other than the estate, only if—

(1) applicable nonbankruptcy law permits sale of such property free and clear of such interest;

(2) such entity consents;

(3) such interest is a lien and the price at which such property is to be sold is greater than the aggregate value of all liens on such property;

(4) such interest is in bona fide dispute; or

(5) such entity could be compelled, in a legal or equitable proceeding, to accept a money satisfaction of such interest.

(g) Notwithstanding subsection (f) of this section, the trustee may sell property under subsection (b) or (c) of this section free and clear of any vested or contingent right in the nature of dower or curtesy.

(h) Notwithstanding subsection (f) of this section, the trustee may sell both the estate's interest, under subsection (b) or (c) of this section, and the interest of any co-owner in property in which the debtor had, at the time of the commencement of the case, an undivided interest as a tenant in common, joint tenant, or tenant by the entirety, only if—

(1) partition in kind of such property among the estate and such co-owners is impracticable;

(2) sale of the estate's undivided interest in such property would realize significantly less for the estate than sale of such property free of the interests of such co-owners;

(3) the benefit to the estate of a sale of such property free of the interests of co-owners outweighs the detriment, if any, to such co-owners; and

(4) such property is not used in the production, transmission, or distribution, for sale, of electric energy or of natural or synthetic gas for heat, light, or power.

(i) Before the consummation of a sale of property to which subsection (g) or (h) of this section applies, or of property of the estate that was community property of the debtor and the debtor's spouse immediately before the commencement of the case, the debtor's spouse, or a co-owner of such property, as the case may be, may purchase such property at the price at which such sale is to be consummated.

(j) After a sale of property to which subsection (g) or (h) of this section applies, the trustee shall distribute to the debtor's spouse or the co-owners of such property, as the case may be, and to the estate, the proceeds of such sale, less the costs and expenses, not including any compensation of the trustee, of such sale, according to the interests of such spouse or co-owners, and of the estate.

(k) At a sale under subsection (b) of this section of property that is subject to a lien that secures an allowed claim, unless the court for cause orders otherwise the holder of such claim may bid at such sale, and, if the holder of such claim purchases such property, such holder may offset such claim against the purchase price of such property.

(l) Subject to the provisions of section 365, trustee may use, sell, or lease property under subsection (b) or (c) of this section, or a plan under chapter 11, 12, or 13 of this title may provide for the use, sale, or lease of property, notwithstanding any provision in a contract, a lease, or applicable law that is conditioned on the insolvency or financial condition of the debtor, on the commencement of a case under this title concerning the debtor, or on the appointment of or the taking possession by a trustee in a case under this title or a custodian, and that effects, or gives an option to effect, a forfeiture, modification, or termination of the debtor's interest in such property.

(m) The reversal or modification on appeal of an authorization under subsection (b) or (c) of this section of a sale or lease of property does not affect the validity of a sale or lease under such authorization to an entity that purchased or leased such property in good faith, whether or not such entity knew of the pendency of the appeal, unless such authorization and such sale or lease were stayed pending appeal.

(n) The trustee may avoid a sale under this section if the sale price was controlled by an agreement among potential bidders at such sale, or may recover from a party to such agreement any amount by which the value of the property sold exceeds the price at which such sale was consummated, and may recover any costs, attorneys' fees, or expenses incurred in avoiding such sale or recovering such amount. In addition to any recovery under the preceding sentence, the court may grant judgment for punitive damages in favor of the estate and against any such party that entered into such an agreement in willful disregard of this subsection.

(o) Notwithstanding subsection (f), if a person purchases any interest in a consumer credit transaction that is subject to the Truth in Lending Act or any interest in a consumer credit contract (as defined in section 433.1 of title 16 of the Code of Federal Regulations (January 1, 2004), as amended from time to time), and if such interest is purchased through a sale under this section, then such person shall remain subject to all claims and defenses that are related to such consumer credit transaction or such consumer credit contract, to the same extent as such person would be subject to such claims and defenses of the consumer had such interest been purchased at a sale not under this section.

(p) In any hearing under this section—

(1) the trustee has the burden of proof on the issue of adequate protection; and

(2) the entity asserting an interest in property has the burden of proof on the issue of the validity, priority, or extent of such interest.

§ 521. Debtor's duties

(a) The debtor shall—

(1) file—

(A) a list of creditors; and

(B) unless the court orders otherwise—

(i) a schedule of assets and liabilities;

(ii) a schedule of current income and current expenditures; and

(iii) a statement of the debtor's financial affairs, and, if section 342(b) applies, a certificate—

(I) of an attorney whose name is indicated on the petition as the attorney for the debtor, or a bankruptcy petition preparer signing the petition under section 110(b)(1), indicating that such attorney or the bankruptcy petition preparer delivered to the debtor the notice required by section 342(b); or

(II) if no attorney is so indicated, and no bankruptcy petition preparer signed the petition, of the debtor that such notice was received and read by the debtor;

(iv) copies of all payment advices or other evidence of payment received within 60 days before the date of the filing of the petition, by the debtor from any employer of the debtor;

(v) a statement of the amount of monthly net income, itemized to show how the amount is calculated; and

(vi) a statement disclosing any reasonably anticipated increase in income or expenditures over the 12-month period following the date of the filing of the petition;

(2) if an individual debtor's schedule of assets and liabilities includes debts which are secured by property of the estate—

(A) within thirty days after the date of the filing of a petition under chapter 7 of this title or on or before the date of the meeting of creditors, whichever is earlier, or within such additional time as the court, for cause, within such period fixes, the debtor shall file with the clerk a statement of his intention with respect to the retention or surrender of such property and, if applicable, specifying that such property is claimed as exempt, that the debtor intends to redeem such property, or that the debtor intends to reaffirm debts secured by such property;

(B) within 30 days after the first date set for the meeting of creditors under section 341(a) or within such additional time as the court, for cause, within such 30-day period fixes, the debtor shall perform his intention with respect to such property, as specified by subparagraph (A) of this paragraph; and

(C) nothing in subparagraphs (A) and (B) of this paragraph shall alter the debtor's or the trustee's rights with regard to such property under this title, except as provided in section 362(h);

(3) if a trustee is serving in the case or an auditor serving under section 586(f) of title 28, cooperate with the trustee as necessary to enable the trustee to perform the trustee's duties under this title;

(4) if a trustee is serving in the case or an auditor serving under section 586(f) of title 28, surrender to the trustee all property of the estate and any recorded information, including books, documents, records, and papers, relating to property of the estate, whether or not immunity is granted under section 344 of this title,

(5) appear at the hearing required under section 524(d) of this title;

(6) in a case under chapter 7 of this title in which the debtor is an individual, not retain possession of personal property as to which a creditor has an allowed claim for the purchase price secured in whole or in part by an interest in such personal property unless the debtor, not later than 45 days after the first meeting of creditors under section 341(a), either—

(A) enters into an agreement with the creditor pursuant to section 524(c) with respect to the claim secured by such property; or

(B) redeems such property from the security interest pursuant to section 722.

If the debtor fails to so act within the 45-day period referred to in paragraph (6), the stay under section 362(a) is terminated with respect to the personal property of the estate or of the debtor which is affected, such property shall no longer be property of the estate, and the creditor may take whatever action as to such property as is permitted by applicable nonbankruptcy law, unless the court determines on the motion of the trustee filed before the expiration of such 45-day period, and after notice and a hearing, that such property is of consequential value or benefit to the estate, orders appropriate adequate protection of the creditor's interest, and orders the debtor to deliver any collateral in the debtor's possession to the trustee; and

(7) unless a trustee is serving in the case, continue to perform the obligations required of the administrator (as defined in section 3 of the Employee Retirement Income Security Act of 1974) of an employee benefit plan if at the time of the commencement of the case the debtor (or any entity designated by the debtor) served as such administrator.

(b) In addition to the requirements under subsection (a), a debtor who is an individual shall file with the court—

(1) a certificate from the approved nonprofit budget and credit counseling agency that provided the debtor services under section 109(h) describing the services provided to the debtor; and

(2) a copy of the debt repayment plan, if any, developed under section 109(h) through the approved nonprofit budget and credit counseling agency referred to in paragraph (1).

(c) In addition to meeting the requirements under subsection (a), a debtor shall file with the court a record of any interest that a debtor has in an education individual retirement account (as defined in section 530(b)(1) of the Internal Revenue Code of 1986) or under a qualified State tuition program (as defined in section 529(b)(1) of such Code).

(d) If the debtor fails timely to take the action specified in subsection (a)(6) of this section, or in paragraphs (1) and (2) of section 362(h), with respect to property which a lessor or bailor owns and has leased, rented, or bailed to the debtor or as to which a creditor holds a security interest not otherwise voidable under section 522(f), 544, 545, 547, 548, or 549, nothing in this title shall prevent or limit the operation of a provision in the underlying lease or agreement that has the effect of placing the debtor in default under such lease or agreement by reason of the occurrence, pendency, or existence of a proceeding under this title or the insolvency of the debtor. Nothing in this subsection shall be deemed to justify limiting such a provision in any other circumstance.

(e) (1) If the debtor in a case under chapter 7 or 13 is an individual and if a creditor files with the court at any time a request to receive a copy of the petition, schedules, and statement of financial affairs filed by the debtor, then the court shall make such petition, such schedules, and such statement available to such creditor.

(2)(A) The debtor shall provide—

(i) not later than 7 days before the date first set for the first meeting of creditors, to the trustee a copy of the Federal income tax return required under applicable law (or at the election of the debtor, a transcript of such return) for the most recent tax year ending immediately before the commencement of the case and for which a Federal income tax return was filed; and

(ii) at the same time the debtor complies with clause (i), a copy of such return (or if elected under clause (i), such transcript) to any creditor that timely requests such copy.

(B) If the debtor fails to comply with clause (i) or (ii) of subparagraph (A), the court shall dismiss the case unless the debtor demonstrates that the failure to so comply is due to circumstances beyond the control of the debtor.

(C) If a creditor requests a copy of such tax return or such transcript and if the debtor fails to provide a copy of such tax return or such transcript to such creditor at the time the debtor provides such tax return or such transcript to the trustee, then the court shall dismiss the case unless the debtor demonstrates that the failure to provide a copy of such tax return or such transcript is due to circumstances beyond the control of the debtor.

(3) If a creditor in a case under chapter 13 files with the court at any time a request to receive a copy of the plan filed by the debtor, then the court shall make available to such creditor a copy of the plan—

(A) at a reasonable cost; and

(B) not later than 5 days after such request is filed.

(f) At the request of the court, the United States trustee, or any party in interest in a case under chapter 7, 11, or 13, a debtor who is an individual shall file with the court—

(1) at the same time filed with the taxing authority, a copy of each Federal income tax return required under applicable law (or at the election of the debtor, a transcript of such tax return) with respect to each tax year of the debtor ending while the case is pending under such chapter;

(2) at the same time filed with the taxing authority, each Federal income tax return required under applicable law (or at the election of the debtor, a transcript of such tax return) that had not been filed with such authority as of the date of the commencement of the case and that was subsequently filed for any tax year of the debtor ending in the 3-year period ending on the date of the commencement of the case;

(3) a copy of each amendment to any Federal income tax return or transcript filed with the court under paragraph (1) or (2); and

(4) in a case under chapter 13—

(A) on the date that is either 90 days after the end of such tax year or 1 year after the date of the commencement of the case, whichever is later, if a plan is not confirmed before such later date; and

(B) annually after the plan is confirmed and until the case is closed, not later than the date that is 45 days before the anniversary of the confirmation of the plan;

a statement, under penalty of perjury, of the income and expenditures of the debtor during the tax year of the debtor most recently concluded before such statement is filed under this paragraph, and of the monthly income of the debtor, that shows how income, expenditures, and monthly income are calculated.

(g) (1) A statement referred to in subsection (f)(4) shall disclose—

(A) the amount and sources of the income of the debtor;

(B) the identity of any person responsible with the debtor for the support of any dependent of the debtor; and

(C) the identity of any person who contributed, and the amount contributed, to the household in which the debtor resides.

(2) The tax returns, amendments, and statement of income and expenditures described in subsections (e)(2)(A) and (f) shall be available to the United States trustee (or the bankruptcy administrator, if any), the trustee, and any party in interest for inspection and copying, subject to

the requirements of section 315(c) of the Bankruptcy Abuse Prevention and Consumer Protection Act of 2005.

(h) If requested by the United States trustee or by the trustee, the debtor shall provide—

(1) a document that establishes the identity of the debtor, including a driver's license, passport, or other document that contains a photograph of the debtor; or

(2) such other personal identifying information relating to the debtor that establishes the identity of the debtor.

(i) (1) Subject to paragraphs (2) and (4) and notwithstanding section 707(a), if an individual debtor in a voluntary case under chapter 7 or 13 fails to file all of the information required under subsection (a)(1) within 45 days after the date of the filing of the petition, the case shall be automatically dismissed effective on the 46th day after the date of the filing of the petition.

(2) Subject to paragraph (4) and with respect to a case described in paragraph (1), any party in interest may request the court to enter an order dismissing the case. If requested, the court shall enter an order of dismissal not later than 5 days after such request.

(3) Subject to paragraph (4) and upon request of the debtor made within 45 days after the date of the filing of the petition described in paragraph (1), the court may allow the debtor an additional period of not to exceed 45 days to file the information required under subsection (a)(1) if the court finds justification for extending the period for the filing.

(4) Notwithstanding any other provision of this subsection, on the motion of the trustee filed before the expiration of the applicable period of time specified in paragraph (1), (2), or (3), and after notice and a hearing, the court may decline to dismiss the case if the court finds that the debtor attempted in good faith to file all the information required by subsection (a)(1)(B)(iv) and that the best interests of creditors would be served by administration of the case.

(j) (1) Notwithstanding any other provision of this title, if the debtor fails to file a tax return that becomes due after the commencement of the case or to properly obtain an extension of the due date for filing such return, the taxing authority may request that the court enter an order converting or dismissing the case.

(2) If the debtor does not file the required return or obtain the extension referred to in paragraph (1) within 90 days after a request is filed by the taxing authority under that paragraph, the court shall convert or dismiss the case, whichever is in the best interests of creditors and the estate.

§ 1125. Postpetition disclosure and solicitation

(a) In this section—

(1) "adequate information" means information of a kind, and in sufficient detail, as far as is reasonably practicable in light of the nature and history of the debtor and the condition of the debtor's books and records, including a discussion of the potential material Federal tax consequences of the plan to the debtor, any successor to the debtor, and a hypothetical investor typical of the holders of claims or interests in the case, that would enable such a hypothetical investor of the relevant class to make an informed judgment about the plan, but adequate information need not include such information about any other possible or proposed plan and in determining whether a disclosure statement provides adequate information, the court shall consider the complexity of the case, the benefit of additional information to creditors and other parties in interest, and the cost of providing additional information; and

(2) "investor typical of holders of claims or interests of the relevant class" means investor having—

(A) a claim or interest of the relevant class;

(B) such a relationship with the debtor as the holders of other claims or interests of such class generally have; and

(C) such ability to obtain such information from sources other than the disclosure required by this section as holders of claims or interests in such class generally have.

(b) An acceptance or rejection of a plan may not be solicited after the commencement of the case under this title from a holder of a claim or interest with respect to such claim or interest, unless, at the time of or before such solicitation, there is transmitted to such holder the plan or a summary of the plan, and a written disclosure statement approved, after notice and a hearing, by the court as containing adequate information. The court may approve a disclosure statement without a valuation of the debtor or an appraisal of the debtor's assets.

(c) The same disclosure statement shall be transmitted to each holder of a claim or interest of a particular class, but there may be transmitted different disclosure statements, differing in amount, detail, or kind of information, as between classes.

(d) Whether a disclosure statement required under subsection (b) of this section contains adequate information is not governed by any otherwise applicable non-bankruptcy law, rule, or regulation, but an agency or official whose duty is to administer or enforce such a law, rule, or regulation may be heard on the issue of whether a disclosure statement contains adequate information. Such an agency or official may not appeal from, or otherwise seek review of, an order approving a disclosure statement.

(e) A person that solicits acceptance or rejection of a plan, in good faith and in compliance with the applicable provisions of this title, or that participates, in good faith and in compliance with the applicable provisions of this title, in the offer, issuance, sale, or purchase of a security, offered or sold under the plan, of the debtor, of an affiliate participating in a joint plan with the debtor, or of a newly organized successor to the debtor under the plan, is not liable, on account of such solicitation or participation, for violation of any applicable law, rule, or regulation governing solicitation of acceptance or rejection of a plan or the offer, issuance, sale, or purchase of securities.

(f) Notwithstanding subsection (b), in a small business case—

(1) the court may determine that the plan itself provides adequate information and that a separate disclosure statement is not necessary;

(2) the court may approve a disclosure statement submitted on standard forms approved by the court or adopted under section 2075 of title 28; and

(3) (A) the court may conditionally approve a disclosure statement subject to final approval after notice and a hearing;

(B) acceptances and rejections of a plan may be solicited based on a conditionally approved disclosure statement if the debtor provides adequate information to each holder of a claim or interest that is solicited, but a conditionally approved disclosure statement shall be mailed not later than 25 days before the date of the hearing on confirmation of the plan; and

(C) the hearing on the disclosure statement may be combined with the hearing on confirmation of a plan.

(g) Notwithstanding subsection (b), an acceptance or rejection of the plan may be solicited from a holder of a claim or interest if such solicitation complies with applicable nonbankruptcy law and if such holder was solicited before the commencement of the case in a manner complying with applicable nonbankruptcy law.

§ 1129. Confirmation of plan

(a) The court shall confirm a plan only if all of the following requirements are met:

(1) The plan complies with the applicable provisions of this title.

(2) The proponent of the plan complies with the applicable provisions of this title.

(3) The plan has been proposed in good faith and not by any means forbidden by law.

(4) Any payment made or to be made by the proponent, by the debtor, or by a person issuing securities or acquiring property under the plan, for services or for costs and expenses in or in connection with the case, or in connection with the plan and incident to the case, has been approved by, or is subject to the approval of, the court as reasonable.

(5) (A) (i) The proponent of the plan has disclosed the identity and affiliations of any individual proposed to serve, after confirmation of the plan, as a director, officer, or voting trustee of the debtor, an affiliate of the debtor participating in a joint plan with the debtor, or a successor to the debtor under the plan; and

(ii) the appointment to, or continuance in, such office of such individual, is consistent with the interests of creditors and equity security holders and with public policy; and

(B) the proponent of the plan has disclosed the identity of any insider that will be employed or retained by the reorganized debtor, and the nature of any compensation for such insider.

(6) Any governmental regulatory commission with jurisdiction, after confirmation of the plan, over the rates of the debtor has approved any rate change provided for in the plan, or such rate change is expressly conditioned on such approval.

(7) With respect to each impaired class of claims or interests—

(A) each holder of a claim or interest of such class—

(i) has accepted the plan; or

(ii) will receive or retain under the plan on account of such claim or interest property of a value, as of the effective date of the plan, that is not less than the amount that such holder would so receive or retain if the debtor were liquidated under chapter 7 of this title on such date; or

(B) if section 1111(b)(2) of this title applies to the claims of such class, each holder of a claim of such class will receive or retain under the plan on account of such claim property of a value, as of the effective date of the plan, that is not less than the value of such holder's interest in the estate's interest in the property that secures such claims.

(8) With respect to each class of claims or interests—

(A) such class has accepted the plan; or

(B) such class is not impaired under the plan.

(9) Except to the extent that the holder of a particular claim has agreed to a different treatment of such claim, the plan provides that—

(A) with respect to a claim of a kind specified in section 507(a)(2) or 507(a)(3) of this title, on the effective date of the plan, the holder of such claim will receive on account of such claim cash equal to the allowed amount of such claim;

(B) with respect to a class of claims of a kind specified in section 507(a)(1), 507(a)(3), 507(a)(5), 507(a)(6), or 507(a)(7) of this title, each holder of a claim of such class will receive—

(i) if such class has accepted the plan, deferred cash payments of a value, as of the effective date of the plan, equal to the allowed amount of such claim; or

(ii) if such class has not accepted the plan, cash on the effective date of the plan equal to the allowed amount of such claim;

(C) with respect to a claim of a kind specified in section 507(a)(8) of this title, the holder of such claim will receive on account of such claim regular installment payments in cash—

(i) of a total value, as of the effective date of the plan, equal to the allowed amount of such claim;

(ii) over a period ending not later than 5 years after the date of the order for relief under section 301, 302, or 303; and

(iii) in a manner not less favorable than the most favored nonpriority unsecured claim provided for by the plan (other than cash payments made to a class of creditors under section 1122(b)); and

(D) with respect to a secured claim which would otherwise meet the description of an unsecured claim of governmental unit under section 507(a)(8), but for a secured status of that claim, the holder of that claim will receive on account of that claim, cash payments, in the same manner and over the same period, as prescribed in subparagraph (C).

(10) If a class of claims is impaired under the plan, at least one class of claims that is impaired under the plan has accepted the plan, determined without including any acceptance of the plan by any insider.

(11) Confirmation of the plan is not likely to be followed by the liquidation, or the need for further financial reorganization, of the debtor or any successor to the debtor under the plan, unless such liquidation or reorganization is proposed in the plan.

(12) All fees payable under section 1930 of title 28, as determined by the court at the hearing on confirmation of the plan, have been paid or the plan provides for the payment of all such fees on the effective date of the plan.

(13) The plan provides for the continuation after its effective date of payment of all retiree benefits, as that term is defined in section 1114 of this title, at the level established pursuant to subsection (e)(1)(B) or (g) of section 1114 of this title, at any time prior to confirmation of the plan, for the duration of the period the debtor has obligated itself to provide such benefits.

(14) If the debtor is required by a judicial or administrative order, or by statute, to pay a domestic support obligation, the debtor has paid all amounts payable under such order or such statute for such obligation that first become payable after the date of the filing of the petition.

(15) In a case in which the debtor is an individual and in which the holder of an allowed unsecured claim objects to the confirmation of the plan—

(A) the value, as of the effective date of the plan, of the property to be distributed under the plan on account of such claim is not less than the amount of such claim; or

(B) the value of property to be distributed under the plan is not less than the projected disposable income of the debtor as defined in section 1325(b)(2)) to be received during the 5-year period beginning on the date that the first payment is due under the plan, or during the period for which the plan provides payments, whichever is longer.

(16) All transfers of property of the plan shall be made in accordance with any applicable provisions of nonbankruptcy law that govern the transfer of property by a corporation or trust that is not a moneyed, business, or commercial corporation or trust.

(b)(1) Notwithstanding section 510(a) of this title, if all of the applicable requirements of subsection (a) of this section other than paragraph (8) are met with respect to a plan, the court, on request of the proponent of the plan, shall confirm the plan notwithstanding the requirements of such paragraph if the plan does not discriminate unfairly, and is fair and equitable, with respect to each class of claims or interests that is impaired under, and has not accepted, the plan.

(2) For the purpose of this subsection, the condition that a plan be fair and equitable with respect to a class includes the following requirements:

(A) With respect to a class of secured claims, the plan provides—

(i) (I) that the holders of such claims retain the liens securing such claims, whether the property subject to such liens is retained by the debtor or transferred to another entity, to the extent of the allowed amount of such claims; and

(II) that each holder of a claim of such class receive on account of such claim deferred cash payments totaling at least the allowed amount of such claim, of a value, as of the effective date of the plan, of at least the value of such holder's interest in the estate's interest in such property;

(ii) for the sale, subject to section 363(k) of this title, of any property that is subject to the liens securing such claims, free and clear of such liens, with such liens to attach to the proceeds of such sale, and the treatment of such liens on proceeds under clause (i) or (iii) of this subparagraph; or

(iii) for the realization by such holders of the indubitable equivalent of such claims.

(B) With respect to a class of unsecured claims—

(i) the plan provides that each holder of a claim of such class receive or retain on account of such claim property of a value, as of the effective date of the plan, equal to the allowed amount of such claim; or

(ii) the holder of any claim or interest that is junior to the claims of such class will not receive or retain under the plan on account of such junior claim or interest any property, except that in a case in which the debtor is an individual, the debtor may retain property included in the estate under section 1115, subject to the requirements of subsection (a)(14) of this section.

(C) With respect to a class of interests—

(i) the plan provides that each holder of an interest of such class receive or retain on account of such interest property of a value, as of the effective date of the plan, equal to the greatest of the allowed amount of any fixed liquidation preference to which such holder is entitled, any fixed redemption price to which such holder is entitled, or the value of such interest; or

(ii) the holder of any interest that is junior to the interests of such class will not receive or retain under the plan on account of such junior interest any property.

(c) Notwithstanding subsections (a) and (b) of this section and except as provided in section 1127(b) of this title, the court may confirm only one plan, unless the order of confirmation in the case has been revoked under section 1144 of this title. If the requirements of subsections (a) and (b) of this section are met with respect to more than one plan, the court shall consider the preferences of creditors and equity security holders in determining which plan to confirm.

(d) Notwithstanding any other provision of this section, on request of a party in interest that is a governmental unit, the court may not confirm a plan if the principal purpose of the plan is the avoidance of taxes or the avoidance of the application of section 5 of the Securities Act of 1933. In any hearing under this subsection, the governmental unit has the burden of proof on the issue of avoidance.

(e) In a small business case, the court shall confirm a plan that complies with the applicable provisions of this title and that is filed in accordance with section 1121(e) not later than 45 days after the plan is filed unless the time for confirmation is extended in accordance with section 1121(e)(3).

APPENDIX B

EXCERPTS FROM TITLE 18, UNITED STATES CODE (CRIMES AND CRIMINAL PROCEDURE)

§ 2. Principals

(a) Whoever commits an offense against the United States or aids, abets, counsels, commands, induces or procures its commission, is punishable as a principal.

(b) Whoever willfully causes an act to be done which if directly performed by him or another would be an offense against the United States, is punishable as a principal.

§ 3. Accessory after the fact

Whoever, knowing that an offense against the United States has been committed, receives, relieves, comforts or assists the offender in order to hinder or prevent his apprehension, trial or punishment, is an accessory after the fact.

Except as otherwise expressly provided by any Act of Congress, an accessory after the fact shall be imprisoned not more than one-half the maximum term of imprisonment or (notwithstanding section 3571) fined not more than one-half the maximum fine prescribed for the punishment of the principal, or both; or if the principal is punishable by life imprisonment or death, the accessory shall be imprisoned not more than 15 years.

§ 4. Misprision of felony

Whoever, having knowledge of the actual commission of a felony cognizable by a court of the United States, conceals and does not as soon as possible make known the same to some judge or other person in civil or military authority under the United States, shall be fined under this title or imprisoned not more than three years, or both.

§ 151. Definition

As used in this chapter, the term "debtor" means a debtor concerning whom a petition has been filed under title 11.

§ 152. Concealment of assets; false oaths and claims; bribery

A person who—

(1) knowingly and fraudulently conceals from a custodian, trustee, marshal, or other officer of the court charged with the control or custody of property, or, in connection with a case under title 11, from creditors or the United States Trustee, any property belonging to the estate of a debtor;

(2) knowingly and fraudulently makes a false oath or account in or in relation to any case under title 11;

(3) knowingly and fraudulently makes a false declaration, certificate, verification, or statement under penalty of perjury as permitted under section 1746 of title 28, in or in relation to any case under title 11;

(4) knowingly and fraudulently presents any false claim for proof against the estate of a debtor, or uses any such claim in any case under title 11, in a personal capacity or as or through an agent, proxy, or attorney;

(5) knowingly and fraudulently receives any material amount of property from a debtor after the filing of a case under title 11, with intent to defeat the provisions of title 11;

(6) knowingly and fraudulently gives, offers, receives, or attempts to obtain any money or property, remuneration, compensation, reward, advantage, or promise thereof for acting or forbearing to act in any case under title 11;

(7) in a personal capacity or as an agent or officer of any person or corporation, in contemplation of a case under title 11 by or against the person or any other person or corporation, or with intent to defeat the provisions of title 11, knowingly and fraudulently transfers or conceals any of his property or the property of such other person or corporation;

(8) after the filing of a case under title 11 or in contemplation thereof, knowingly and fraudulently conceals, destroys, mutilates, falsifies, or makes a false entry in any recorded information (including books, documents, records, and papers) relating to the property or financial affairs of a debtor; or

(9) after the filing of a case under title 11, knowingly and fraudulently withholds from a custodian, trustee, marshal, or other officer of the court or a United States Trustee entitled to its possession, any recorded information (including books, documents, records, and papers) relating to the property or financial affairs of a debtor,

shall be fined under this title, imprisoned not more than 5 years, or both.

§ 153. Embezzlement against estate

(a) Offense.—A person described in subsection (b) who knowingly and fraudulently appropriates to the person's own use, embezzles, spends, or transfers any property or secretes or destroys any document belonging to the estate of a debtor shall be fined under this title, imprisoned not more than 5 years, or both.

(b) Person to Whom Section Applies.—A person described in this subsection is one who has access to property or documents belonging to an estate by virtue of the person's participation in the administration of the estate as a trustee, custodian, marshal, attorney, or other officer of the court or as an agent, employee, or other person engaged by such an officer to perform a service with respect to the estate.

§ 154.

Adverse interest and conduct of officers

A person who, being a custodian, trustee, marshal, or other officer of the court—

(1) knowingly purchases, directly or indirectly, any property of the estate of which the person is such an officer in a case under title 11;

(2) knowingly refuses to permit a reasonable opportunity for the inspection by parties in interest of the documents and accounts relating to the affairs of estates in the person's charge by parties when directed by the court to do so; or

(3) knowingly refuses to permit a reasonable opportunity for the inspection by the United States Trustee of the documents and accounts relating to the affairs of an estate in the person's charge, shall be fined under this title and shall forfeit the person's office, which shall thereupon become vacant.

§ 155. Fee agreements in cases under title 11 and receiverships

Whoever, being a party in interest, whether as a debtor, creditor, receiver, trustee or representative of any of them, or attorney for any such party in interest, in any receivership or case under title 11 in any United States court or under its supervision, knowingly and fraudulently enters into any agreement, express or implied, with another such party in interest or attorney for another such party in interest, for the purpose of fixing the fees or other compensation to be paid to any party in interest or to any attorney for any party in interest for services rendered in connection therewith, from the assets of the estate, shall be fined under this title or imprisoned not more than one year, or both.

§ 156. Knowing disregard of bankruptcy law or rule

(a) Definitions.—In this section—

"bankruptcy petition preparer" means a person, other than the debtor's attorney or an employee of such an attorney, who prepares for compensation a document for filing.

"document for filing" means a petition or any other document prepared for filing by a debtor in a United States bankruptcy court or a United States district court in connection with a case under this title.

(b) Offense.—If a bankruptcy case or related proceeding is dismissed because of a knowing attempt by a bankruptcy petition preparer in any manner to disregard the requirements of title 11, United States Code, or the Federal Rules of Bankruptcy Procedure, the bankruptcy petition preparer shall be fined under this title, imprisoned not more than 1 year, or both.

§ 157. Bankruptcy fraud

A person who, having devised or intending to devise a scheme or artifice to defraud and for the purpose of executing or concealing such a scheme or artifice or attempting to do so—

(1) files a petition under title 11;

(2) files a document in a proceeding under title 11; or

(3) makes a false or fraudulent representation, claim, or promise concerning or in relation to a proceeding under title 11, at any time before or after the filing of the petition, or in relation to a proceeding falsely asserted to be pending under such title,

shall be fined under this title, imprisoned not more than 5 years, or both.

§ 371. Conspiracy to commit offense or to defraud United States

If two or more persons conspire either to commit any offense against the United States, or to defraud the United States, or any agency thereof in any manner or for any purpose, and one or more of such persons do any act to effect the object of the conspiracy, each shall be fined under this title or imprisoned not more than five years, or both.

If, however, the offense, the commission of which is the object of the conspiracy, is a misdemeanor only, the punishment for such conspiracy shall not exceed the maximum punishment provided for such misdemeanor.

§ 1001. Statements or entries generally

(a) Except as otherwise provided in this section, whoever, in any matter within the jurisdiction of the executive, legislative, or judicial branch of the Government of the United States, knowingly and willfully-

(1) falsifies, conceals, or covers up by any trick, scheme, or device a material fact;

(2) makes any materially false, fictitious, or fraudulent statement or representation; or

(3) makes or uses any false writing or document knowing the same to contain any materially false, fictitious, or fraudulent statement or entry;

shall be fined under this title or imprisoned not more than 5 years, or, if the offense involves international or domestic terrorism (as defined in section 2331), imprisoned not more than 8 years, or both.

(b) Subsection (a) does not apply to a party to a judicial proceeding, or that party's counsel, for statements, representations, writings or documents submitted by such party or counsel to a judge or magistrate in that proceeding.

(c) With respect to any matter within the jurisdiction of the legislative branch, subsection (a) shall apply only to—

(1) administrative matters, including a claim for payment, a matter related to the procurement of property or services, personnel or employment practices, or support services, or a document required by law, rule, or regulation to be submitted to the Congress or any office or officer within the legislative branch; or

(2) any investigation or review, conducted pursuant to the authority of any committee, subcommittee, commission or office of the Congress, consistent with applicable rules of the House or Senate.

§ 1014. Loan and credit applications generally; renewals and discounts; crop insurance

Whoever knowingly makes any false statement or report, or willfully overvalues any land, property or security, for the purpose of influencing in any way the action of the Farm Credit Administration, Federal Crop Insurance Corporation or a company the Corporation reinsures, the Secretary of Agriculture acting through the Farmers Home Administration, the Rural Development Administration or successor agency, any Farm Credit Bank, production credit association, agricultural credit association, bank for cooperatives, or any division, officer, or employee thereof, or of any regional agricultural credit corporation established pursuant to law, or a Federal land bank, a Federal land bank association, a Federal Reserve bank, a small business investment company, as defined in section 103 of the Small Business Investment Act of 1958 (15 U.S.C. 662), or the Small Business Administration in connection with any provision of that Act, a Federal credit union, an insured State-chartered credit union, any institution the accounts of which are insured by the Federal Deposit Insurance Corporation, the Office of Thrift Supervision, any Federal home loan bank, the Federal Housing Finance Board, the Federal Deposit Insurance Corporation, the Resolution Trust Corporation, the Farm Credit System Insurance Corporation, or the National Credit Union Administration Board, a branch or agency of a foreign bank (as such terms are defined in paragraphs (1) and (3) of section 1(b) of the International Banking Act of 1978), or an organization operating under section 25 or section 25(a) of the Federal Reserve Act, upon any application, advance, discount, purchase, purchase agreement, repurchase agreement, commitment, or loan, or any change or extension of any of the same, by renewal, deferment of action or otherwise, or the acceptance, release, or substitution of security therefor, shall be fined not more than $1,000,000 or imprisoned not more than 30 years, or both. The term "State-chartered credit union" includes a credit union chartered under the laws of a State of the United States, the District of Columbia, or any commonwealth, territory, or possession of the United States.

§ 1032. Concealment of assets from conservator, receiver, or liquidating agent of financial institution

Whoever—

(1) knowingly conceals or endeavors to conceal an asset or property from the Federal Deposit Insurance Corporation, acting as conservator or receiver or in the Corporation's corporate capacity with respect to any asset acquired or liability assumed by the Corporation under section 11, 12, or 13, of the Federal Deposit Insurance Act, the Resolution Trust Corporation, any conservator appointed by the Comptroller of the Currency or the Director of the Office of Thrift Supervision, or the National Credit Union Administration Board, acting as conservator or liquidating agent;

(2) corruptly impedes or endeavors to impede the functions of such Corporation, Board, or conservator; or

(3) corruptly places or endeavors to place an asset or property beyond the reach of such Corporation, Board, or conservator,

shall be fined under this title or imprisoned not more than 5 years, or both.

§ 1341. Frauds and swindles

Whoever, having devised or intending to devise any scheme or artifice to defraud, or for obtaining money or property by means of false or fraudulent pretenses, representations, or promises, or to sell, dispose of, loan, exchange, alter, give away, distribute, supply, or furnish or procure for unlawful use any counterfeit or spurious coin, obligation, security, or other article, or anything represented to be or intimated or held out to be such counterfeit or spurious article, for the purpose of executing such scheme or artifice or attempting so to do, places in any post office or authorized depository for mail matter, any matter or thing whatever to be sent or delivered by the Postal Service, or deposits or causes to be deposited any matter or thing whatever to be sent or delivered by any private or commercial interstate carrier, or takes or receives therefrom, any such matter or thing, or knowingly causes to be delivered by mail or such carrier according to the direction thereon, or at the place at which it is directed to be delivered by the person to whom it is addressed, any such matter or thing, shall be fined under this title or imprisoned not more than 20 years, or both. If the violation affects a financial institution, such person shall be fined not more than $1,000,000 or imprisoned not more than 30 years, or both.

§ 1342. Fictitious name or address

Whoever, for the purpose of conducting, promoting, or carrying on by means of the Postal Service, any scheme or device mentioned in section 1341 of this title or any other unlawful business, uses or assumes, or requests to be addressed by, any fictitious, false, or assumed title, name, or address or name other than his own proper name, or takes or receives from any post office or authorized depository of mail matter, any letter, postal card, package, or other mail matter addressed to any such fictitious, false, or assumed title, name, or address, or name other than his own proper name, shall be fined under this title or imprisoned not more than five years, or both.

§ 1343. Fraud by wire, radio, or television

Whoever, having devised or intending to devise any scheme or artifice to defraud, or for obtaining money or property by means of false or fraudulent pretenses, representations, or promises, transmits or causes to be transmitted by means of wire, radio, or television communication in interstate or foreign commerce, any writings, signs, signals, pictures, or sounds for the purpose of executing such scheme or artifice, shall be fined under this title or imprisoned not more than 20 years, or both. If the violation affects a financial institution, such person shall be fined not more than $1,000,000 or imprisoned not more than 30 years, or both.

§ 1344. Bank fraud

Whoever knowingly executes, or attempts to execute, a scheme or artifice—

(1) to defraud a financial institution; or

(2) to obtain any of the moneys, funds, credits, assets, securities, or other property owned by, or under the custody or control of, a financial institution, by means of false or fraudulent pretenses, representations, or promises;

shall be fined not more than $1,000,000 or imprisoned not more than 30 years, or both.

§ 1503. Influencing or injuring officer or juror generally

(a) Whoever corruptly, or by threats or force, or by any threatening letter or communication, endeavors to influence, intimidate, or impede any grand or petit juror, or officer in or of any court of the United States, or officer who may be serving at any examination or other proceeding before any United States magistrate judge or other committing magistrate, in the discharge of his duty, or injures any such grand or petit juror in his person or property on account of any verdict or indictment assented to by him, or on account of his being or having been such juror, or injures any such officer, magistrate judge, or other committing magistrate in his person or property on account of the performance of his official duties, or corruptly or by threats or force, or by any threatening letter or communication, influences, obstructs, or impedes, or endeavors to influence, obstruct, or impede, the due administration of justice, shall be punished as provided in subsection (b). If the offense under this section occurs in connection with a trial of a criminal case, and the act in violation of this section involves the threat of physical force or physical force, the maximum term of imprisonment which may be imposed for the offense shall be the higher of that otherwise provided by law or the maximum term that could have been imposed for any offense charged in such case.

(b) The punishment for an offense under this section is—

(1) in the case of a killing, the punishment provided in sections 1111 and 1112;

(2) in the case of an attempted killing, or a case in which the offense was committed against a petit juror and in which a class A or B felony was

charged, imprisonment for not more than 20 years, a fine under this title, or both; and

(3) in any other case, imprisonment for not more than 10 years, a fine under this title, or both.

§ 1519. Destruction, alteration, or falsification of records in Federal investigations and bankruptcy

Whoever knowingly alters, destroys, mutilates, conceals, covers up, falsifies, or makes a false entry in any record, document, or tangible object with the intent to impede, obstruct, or influence the investigation or proper administration of any matter within the jurisdiction of any department or agency of the United States or any case filed under title 11, or in relation to or contemplation of any such matter or case, shall be fined under this title, imprisoned not more than 20 years, or both.

§ 1956. Laundering of monetary instruments

(a)(1) Whoever, knowing that the property involved in a financial transaction represents the proceeds of some form of unlawful activity, conducts or attempts to conduct such a financial transaction which in fact involves the proceeds of specified unlawful activity—

(A) (i) with the intent to promote the carrying on of specified unlawful activity; or

(ii) with intent to engage in conduct constituting a violation of section 7201 or 7206 of the Internal Revenue Code of 1986; or

(B) knowing that the transaction is designed in whole or in part—

(i) to conceal or disguise the nature, the location, the source, the ownership, or the control of the proceeds of specified unlawful activity; or

(ii) to avoid a transaction reporting requirement under State or Federal law,

shall be sentenced to a fine of not more than $500,000 or twice the value of the property involved in the transaction, whichever is greater, or imprisonment for not more than twenty years, or both.

(2) Whoever transports, transmits, or transfers, or attempts to transport, transmit, or transfer a monetary instrument or funds from a place in the United States to or through a place outside the United States or to a place in the United States from or through a place outside the United States—

(A) with the intent to promote the carrying on of specified unlawful activity; or

(B) knowing that the monetary instrument or funds involved in the transportation, transmission, or transfer represent the proceeds of some form of unlawful activity and knowing that such transportation, transmission, or transfer is designed in whole or in part—

(i) to conceal or disguise the nature, the location, the source, the ownership, or the control of the proceeds of specified unlawful activity; or

(ii) to avoid a transaction reporting requirement under State or Federal law,

shall be sentenced to a fine of not more than $500,000 or twice the value of the monetary instrument or funds involved in the transportation, transmission, or transfer, whichever is greater, or imprisonment for not more than twenty years, or both. For the purpose of the offense described in subparagraph (B), the defendant's knowledge may be established by proof that a law enforcement officer represented the matter specified in subparagraph (B) as true, and the defendant's subsequent statements or actions indicate that the defendant believed such representations to be true.

(3) Whoever, with the intent—

(A) to promote the carrying on of specified unlawful activity;

(B) to conceal or disguise the nature, location, source, ownership, or control of property believed to be the proceeds of specified unlawful activity; or

(C) to avoid a transaction reporting requirement under State or Federal law,

conducts or attempts to conduct a financial transaction involving property represented to be the proceeds of specified unlawful activity, or property used to conduct or facilitate specified unlawful activity, shall be fined under this title or imprisoned for not more than 20 years, or both. For purposes of this paragraph and paragraph (2), the term "represented" means any representation made by a law enforcement officer or by another person at the direction of, or with the approval of, a Federal official authorized to investigate or prosecute violations of this section.

(b) Penalties.—

(1) In general.— Whoever conducts or attempts to conduct a transaction described in subsection (a)(1) or (a)(3), or section 1957, or a transportation, transmission, or transfer described in subsection (a)(2), is liable to the United Stats for a civil penalty of not more than the greater of –

(A) the value of the property, funds, or monetary instrument involved in the transaction; or

(B) $10,000.

(2) Jurisdiction over foreign persons.— For purposes of adjudicating an action filed or enforcing a penalty ordered under this section, the district courts shall have jurisdiction over any foreign person, including any financial institution authorized under the laws of a foreign county, against whom the action is brought, if service of process upon the foreign person is made under the Federal Rules of Civil Procedure or the laws of the country in which the foreign person is found, and—

(A) the foreign person commits an offense under subsection (a) involving a financial transaction that occurs in whole or in party in the United State;

(B) the foreign person converts, to his or her own use, property in which the United States has an ownership interest by virtue of the entry of an order of forfeiture by a court of the Untied States; or

(C) the foreign person is a financial institution that maintains a bank account at a financial institution in the United States.

(3) Court authority over assets.— A court described in paragraph (2) may issue a pretrial restraining order or take any other action necessary to ensure that any bank account or other property held by the defendant in the United States is available to satisfy a judgment under this section.

(4) Federal receiver.—

(A) In general.— A court described in paragraph (2) may appoint a Federal Receiver, in accordance with subparagraph (B) of this paragraph, to collect, marshal, and take custody, control, and possession of all assets of the defendant, wherever located, to satisfy a civil judgment under this subsection, a forfeiture judgment under section 981 or 982, or a criminal sentence under section 1957 or subsection (a) of this section, including an order of restitution to any victim of a specified unlawful activity.

(B) Appointment and authority.— A Federal Receiver described in subparagraph (A) —

(i) may be appointed upon application of a Federal prosecutor or a Federal or State regulator, by the court having jurisdiction over the defendant in the case;

(ii) shall be an officer of the court, and the powers of the Federal Receiver shall include the powers set out in the section 754 of title 28, United States Code; and

(iii) shall have standing equivalent to that of a Federal prosecutor for the purpose of submitting requests to obtain information regarding the assets of the defendant —

(I) from the Financial Crimes Enforcement Network of the Department of the Treasury; or

(II) from a foreign county pursuant to a mutual legal assistance treaty, multilateral agreement, or other arrangement for international law enforcement assistance, provided that such requests are in accordance with the policies and procedures of the Attorney General.

(c) As used in this section—

(1) the term "knowing that the property involved in a financial transaction represents the proceeds of some form of unlawful activity" means that the person knew the property involved in the transaction represented proceeds from some form, though not necessarily which form, of activity that constitutes a felony under State, Federal, or foreign law, regardless of whether or not such activity is specified in paragraph (7);

(2) the term "conducts" includes initiating, concluding, or participating in initiating, or concluding a transaction;

(3) the term "transaction" includes a purchase, sale, loan, pledge, gift, transfer, delivery, or other disposition, and with respect to a financial institution includes a deposit, withdrawal, transfer between accounts, exchange of currency, loan, extension of credit, purchase or sale of any stock, bond, certificate of deposit, or other monetary instrument, use of a safe deposit box, or any other payment, transfer, or delivery by, through, or to a financial institution, by whatever means effected;

(4) the term "financial transaction" means

(A) a transaction which in any way or degree affects interstate or foreign commerce

(i) involving the movement of funds by wire or other means or

(ii) involving one or more monetary instruments, or

(iii) involving the transfer of title to any real property, vehicle, vessel, or aircraft, or

(B) a transaction involving the use of a financial institution which is engaged in, or the activities of which affect, interstate or foreign commerce in any way or degree;

(5) the term "monetary instruments" means (i) coin or currency of the United States or of any other country, travelers' checks, personal checks, bank checks, and money orders, or (ii) investment securities or negotiable instruments, in bearer form or otherwise in such form that title thereto passes upon delivery;

(6) the term "financial institution" includes—

(A) any financial institution, as defined in section 5312(a)(2) of title 31, United States Code, or the regulations promulgated thereunder; and

(B) any foreign bank, as defined in section 1 of the International Banking Act of 1978 (12 U.S.C. 3101);

(7) the term "specified unlawful activity" means—

(A) any act or activity constituting an offense listed in section 1961(1) of this title except an act which is indictable under subchapter II of chapter 53 of title 31;

(B) with respect to a financial transaction occurring in whole or in part in the United States, an offense against a foreign nation involving—

(i) the manufacture, importation, sale, or distribution of a controlled substance (as such term is defined for the purposes of the Controlled Substances Act);

(ii) murder, kidnapping, robbery, extortion, destruction of property by means of explosive or fire, or a crime of violence (as defined in section 16);

(iii) fraud, or any scheme or attempt to defraud, by or against a foreign bank (as defined in paragraph 7 of section 1(b) of the International Banking Act of 1978);

(iv) bribery of a public official, or the misappropriation, theft, or embezzlement of public funds by or for the benefit of a public official;

(v) smuggling or export control violations involving—

(I) an item controlled on the United States Munitions List established under section 38 of the Arms Export Control Act (22 U.S.C. 2778); or

(II) an item controlled under regulations under the Export Administration Regulations (15 C.F.R. Parts 730-774); or

(vi) an offense with respect to which the United States would be obligated by a multilateral treaty, either to extradite the alleged offender or to submit the case for prosecution, if the offender were found within the territory of the United States;

(C) any act or acts constituting a continuing criminal enterprise, as that term is defined in section 408 of the Controlled Substances Act (21 U.S.C. 848);

(D) an offense under section 32 (relating to the destruction of aircraft), section 37 (relating to violence at international airports), section 115 (relating to influencing, impeding, or retaliating against a Federal official by threatening or injuring a family member), section 152 (relating to concealment of assets; false oaths and claims; bribery), section 175c (relating to the variola virus) section 215 (relating to commissions or gifts for procuring loans), section 351 (relating to congressional or Cabinet officer assassination), any of sections 500 through 503 (relating to certain counterfeiting offenses), section 513 (relating to securities of States and private entities), section 541 (relating to goods falsely classified) section 542 (relating to entry of goods by means of false statements), section 545 (relating to smuggling goods into the United States), section 549 (relating to removing goods from Customs custody), section 641 (relating to public money, property, or records), section 656 (relating to theft, embezzlement, or misapplication by bank officer or employee), section 657 (relating to lending, credit, and insurance institutions), section 658 (relating to property mortgaged or pledged to farm credit agencies), section 666 (relating to theft or bribery concerning programs receiving Federal funds), section 793, 794, or 798 (relating to espionage), section 831 (relating to prohibited transactions involving nuclear materials), section 844(f) or (i) (relating to destruction by explosives or fire of Government property or property affecting interstate or foreign commerce), section 875 (relating to interstate communications), section 922(l) (relating to the unlawful importation of firearms), section 924(n) (relating to firearms trafficking) section 956 (relating to conspiracy to kill, kidnap, maim, or injure certain property in a foreign country), section 1005 (relating to fraudulent bank entries), 1006 (relating to fraudulent Federal credit institution entries), 1007 (relating to Federal Deposit Insurance transactions), 1014 (relating to fraudulent loan or credit applications), section 1030 (relating to computer fraud and abuse), 1032 (relating to concealment of assets from conservator, receiver, or liquidating agent of financial institution), section 1111 (relating to murder), section 1114 (relating to murder of United States law enforcement officials), section 1116 (relating to murder of foreign officials, official guests, or internationally protected persons), section 1201 (relating to kidnapping), section 1203 (relating to hostage taking), section 1361 (relating to willful injury of Government property), section 1363 (relating to destruction of property within the special maritime and territorial jurisdiction), section 1708 (theft from the mail), section 1751 (relating to Presidential assassination), section 2113 or 2114 (relating to bank and postal robbery and theft), section 2280 (relating to violence against maritime navigation), section 2281 (relating to violence against maritime fixed platforms), section 2319 (relating to copyright infringement), section 2320 (relating to trafficking in counterfeit goods and services), section 2332 (relating to terrorist acts abroad against United States nationals), section 2332a (relating to use of weapons of mass destruction), section 2332b (relating to international terrorist acts transcending national boundaries), section 2332g (relating to missile systems designed to destroy aircraft), section 2332h (relating to radiological dispersal devices) or section 2339A or 2339B (relating to providing material support to terrorists) of this title, section 46502 of title 49, United States Code, a felony violation of the Chemical Diversion and Trafficking Act of 1988 (relating to precursor and essential chemicals), section 590 of the Tariff Act of 1930 (19 U.S.C. 1590) (relating to aviation smuggling), section 422 of the Controlled Substances Act (relating to transportation of drug paraphernalia), section 38(c) (relating to criminal violations) of the Arms Export Control Act, section 11 (relating to violations) of the Export Administration Act of 1979, section 206 (relating to penalties) of the International Emergency Economic Powers Act, section 16 (relating to offenses and punishment) of the Trading with the Enemy Act, any felony violation of section 15 of the Food Stamp Act of 1977 (relating to food stamp fraud) involving a quantity of coupons having a value of not less than $5,000, any violation of section 543(a)(1) of the Housing Act of 1949 (relating to equity skimming), any felony violation of the Foreign Agents Registration Act of 1938, any felony violation of the Foreign Corrupt Practices Act, or section 92 of the Atomic Energy Act of 1954 (42 U.S.C. 2122) (relating to prohibitions governing atomic weapons); or environmental crimes

(E) a felony violation of the Federal Water Pollution Control Act (33 U.S.C. 1251 et seq.), the Ocean Dumping Act (33 U.S.C. 1401 et seq.), the Act to Prevent Pollution from Ships (33 U.S.C. 1901 et seq.), the Safe Drinking Water Act (42 U.S.C. 300f et seq.), or the Resources Conservation and Recovery Act (42 U.S.C. 6901 et seq.).

(F) Any act or activity constituting an offense involving a Federal health care offense;

(8) the term "State" includes a State of the United States, the District of Columbia, and any commonwealth, territory, or possession of the United States.

(d) Nothing in this section shall supersede any provision of Federal, State, or other law imposing criminal penalties or affording civil remedies in addition to those provided for in this section.

(e) Violations of this section may be investigated by such components of the Department of Justice as the Attorney General may direct, and by such components of the Department of the Treasury as the Secretary of the Treasury may direct, as appropriate and, with respect to offenses over which the United States Postal Service has jurisdiction, by the Postal Service. Such authority of the Secretary of the Treasury and the Postal Service shall be exercised in accordance with an agreement which shall be entered into by the Secretary of the Treasury, the Postal Service, and the Attorney General. Violations of this section involving offenses described in paragraph (c)(7)(E) may be investigated by such components of the Department of Justice as the Attorney General may direct, and the National Enforcement Investigations Center of the Environmental Protection Agency.

(f) There is extraterritorial jurisdiction over the conduct prohibited by this section if—

(1) the conduct is by a United States citizen or, in the case of a non-United States citizen, the conduct occurs in part in the United States; and

(2) the transaction or series of related transactions involves funds or monetary instruments of a value exceeding $10,000.

(g) Notice of Conviction of Financial Institutions.—If any financial institution or any officer, director, or employee of any financial institution has been found guilty of an offense under this section, section 1957 or 1960 of this title, or section 5322 or 5324 of title 31, the Attorney General shall provide written notice of such fact to the appropriate regulatory agency for the financial institution.

(h) Any person who conspires to commit any offense defined in this section or section 1957 shall be subject to the same penalties as those prescribed for the offense the commission of which was the object of the conspiracy.

(i) Venue.—

(1) Except as provided in paragraph (2), a prosecution for an offense under this section or section 1957 may be brought in —

(A) any district in which the financial or monetary transaction is conducted; or

(B) any district where a prosecution for the underlying specified unlawful activity could be brought, if the defendant participated in the transfer of the proceeds of the specified unlawful activity from that district to the district where the financial or monetary transaction is conducted.

(2) A prosecution for an attempt or conspiracy offense under this section or section 1957 may be brought in the district where venue would lie for the completed offense under paragraph (1), or in any other district where an act in furtherance of the attempt or conspiracy took place.

(3) For purposes of this section a transfer of funds from 1 place to another, by wire or any other means, shall constitute a single, continuing transaction. Any person who conducts (as that term is defined in subsection (c)(2)) any portion of the transaction may be charged in any district in which the transaction takes place.

§ 1961. Definitions

As used in this chapter—

(1) "racketeering activity" means

(A) any act or threat involving murder, kidnapping, gambling, arson, robbery, bribery, extortion, dealing in obscene matter, or dealing in a controlled substance or listed chemical (as defined in section 102 of the Controlled Substances Act), which is chargeable under State law and punishable by imprisonment for more than one year;

(B) any act which is indictable under any of the following provisions of title 18, United States Code: Section 201 (relating to bribery), section 224 (relating to sports bribery), sections 471, 472, and 473 (relating to counterfeiting), section 659 (relating to theft from interstate shipment) if the act indictable under section 659 is felonious, section 664 (relating to embezzlement from pension and welfare funds), sections 891-894 (relating to extortionate credit transactions), section 1028 (relating to fraud and related activity in connection with identification documents), section 1029 (relating to fraud and related activity in connection with access devices), section 1084 (relating to the transmission of gambling information), section 1341 (relating to mail fraud), section 1343 (relating to wire fraud), section 1344 (relating to financial institution fraud), section 1425 (relating to the procurement of citizenship or nationalization unlawfully), section 1426 (relating to the reproduction of naturalization or citizenship papers), section 1427 (relating to the sale of naturalization or citizenship papers), sections 1461-1465 (relating to obscene matter), section 1503 (relating to obstruction of justice), section 1510 (relating to obstruction of criminal investigations), section 1511 (relating to the obstruction of State or local law enforcement), section 1512 (relating to tampering with a witness, victim, or an informant), section 1513 (relating to retaliating against a witness, victim, or an informant), section 1542 (relating to false statement in application and use of passport), section 1543 (relating to forgery or false use of passport), section 1544 (relating to misuse of passport), section 1546 (relating to fraud and misuse of visas, permits, and other documents), sections 1581-1588 (relating to peonage, slavery, and trafficking in persons), section 1951 (relating to interference with commerce, robbery, or extortion), section 1952 (relating to racketeering), section 1953 (relating to interstate transportation of wagering paraphernalia), section 1954 (relating to unlawful welfare fund payments), section 1955 (relating to the prohibition of illegal gambling businesses), section 1956 (relating to the laundering of monetary instruments), section 1957 (relating to engaging in monetary transactions in property derived from specified unlawful activity), section 1958 (relating to use of interstate commerce facilities in the commission of murder-for-hire), sections 2251, 2251A, 2252, and 2260 (relating to sexual exploitation of children), sections 2312 and 2313 (relating to interstate transportation of stolen motor vehicles), sections 2314 and 2315 (relating to interstate transportation of stolen property), section 2318 (relating to trafficking in counterfeit labels for phonorecords, computer programs or computer program documentation or packaging and copies of motion pictures or other audiovisual works), section 2319 (relating to criminal infringement of a copyright), section 2319A (relating to unauthorized fixation of and trafficking in sound recordings and music videos of live musical performances), section 2320 (relating to trafficking in goods or services bearing counterfeit marks), section 2321 (relating to trafficking in certain motor vehicles or motor vehicle parts), sections 2341-2346 (relating to trafficking in contraband cigarettes), sections 2421-24 (relating to white slave traffic), sections 175-178 (relating to biological weapons), sections 229-229F (relating to chemical weapons), section 831 (relating to nuclear materials),

(C) any act which is indictable under title 29, United States Code, section 186 (dealing with restrictions on payments and loans to labor organizations) or section 501(c) (relating to embezzlement from union funds),

(D) any offense involving fraud connected with a case under title 11 (except a case under section 157 of this title), fraud in the sale of securities, or the felonious manufacture, importation, receiving, concealment, buying, selling, or otherwise dealing in a controlled substance or listed chemical (as defined in section 102 of the Controlled Substances Act), punishable under any law of the United States,

(E) any act which is indictable under the Currency and Foreign Transactions Reporting Act,

(F) any act which is indictable under the Immigration and Nationality Act, section 274 (relating to bringing in and harboring certain aliens), section 277 (relating to aiding or assisting certain aliens to enter the United States), or section 278 (relating to importation of alien for immoral purpose) if the act indictable under such section of such Act was committed for the purpose of financial gain, or

(G) any act that is indictable under any provision listed in section 2332b(g)(5)(B);

(2) "State" means any State of the United States, the District of Columbia, the Commonwealth of Puerto Rico, any territory or possession of the United States, any political subdivision, or any department, agency, or instrumentality thereof;

(3) "person" includes any individual or entity capable of holding a legal or beneficial interest in property;

(4) "enterprise" includes any individual, partnership, corporation, association, or other legal entity, and any union or group of individuals associated in fact although not a legal entity;

(5) "pattern of racketeering activity" requires at least two acts of racketeering activity, one of which occurred after the effective date of this chapter and the last of which occurred within ten years (excluding any period of imprisonment) after the commission of a prior act of racketeering activity;

(6) "unlawful debt" means a debt (A) incurred or contracted in gambling activity which was in violation of the law of the United States, a State or political subdivision thereof, or which is unenforceable under State or Federal law in whole or in part as to principal or interest because of the laws relating to usury, and (B) which was incurred in connection with the business of gambling in violation of the law of the United States, a State or political subdivision thereof, or the business of lending money or a thing

of value at a rate usurious under State or Federal law, where the usurious rate is at least twice the enforceable rate;

(7) "racketeering investigator" means any attorney or investigator so designated by the Attorney General and charged with the duty of enforcing or carrying into effect this chapter;

(8) "racketeering investigation" means any inquiry conducted by any racketeering investigator for the purpose of ascertaining whether any person has been involved in any violation of this chapter or of any final order, judgment, or decree of any court of the United States, duly entered in any case or proceeding arising under this chapter;

(9) "documentary material" includes any book, paper, document, record, recording, or other material; and

(10) "Attorney General" includes the Attorney General of the United States, the Deputy Attorney General of the United States, the Associate Attorney General of the United States, any Assistant Attorney General of the United States, or any employee of the Department of Justice or any employee of any department or agency of the United States so designated by the Attorney General to carry out the powers conferred on the Attorney General by this chapter. Any department or agency so designated may use in investigations authorized by this chapter either the investigative provisions of this chapter or the investigative power of such department or agency otherwise conferred by law.

§ 3057. Bankruptcy investigations

(a) Any judge, receiver, or trustee having reasonable grounds for believing that any violation under chapter 9 of this title or other laws of the United States relating to insolvent debtors, receiverships or reorganization plans has been committed, or that an investigation should be had in connection therewith, shall report to the appropriate United States attorney all the facts and circumstances of the case, the names of the witnesses and the offense or offenses believed to have been committed. Where one of such officers has made such report, the others need not do so.

(b) The United States attorney thereupon shall inquire into the facts and report thereon to the judge, and if it appears probable that any such offense has been committed, shall without delay, present the matter to the grand jury, unless upon inquiry and examination he decides that the ends of public justice do not require investigation or prosecution, in which case he shall report the facts to the Attorney General for his direction.

§ 3553. Imposition of a sentence

(a) Factors To Be Considered in Imposing a Sentence.—The court shall impose a sentence sufficient, but not greater than necessary, to comply with the purposes set forth in paragraph (2) of this subsection. The court, in determining the particular sentence to be imposed, shall consider—

(1) the nature and circumstances of the offense and the history and characteristics of the defendant;

(2) the need for the sentence imposed—

(A) to reflect the seriousness of the offense, to promote respect for the law, and to provide just punishment for the offense;

(B) to afford adequate deterrence to criminal conduct;

(C) to protect the public from further crimes of the defendant; and

(D) to provide the defendant with needed educational or vocational training, medical care, or other correctional treatment in the most effective manner;

(3) the kinds of sentences available;

(4) the kinds of sentence and the sentencing range established for—

(A) the applicable category of offense committed by the applicable category of defendant as set forth in the guidelines—

(i) issued by the Sentencing Commission pursuant to section 994(a)(1) of title 28, United States Code, subject to any amendments made to such guidelines by act of Congress (regardless of whether such amendments have yet to be incorporated by the Sentencing Commission into amendments issued under section 994(p) of title 28); and

(ii) that, except as provided in section 3742(g), are in effect on the date the defendant is sentenced; or

(B) in the case of a violation of probation or supervised release, the applicable guidelines or policy statements issued by the Sentencing Commission pursuant to section 994(a)(3) of title 28, United States Code, taking into account any amendments made to such guidelines or policy statements by act of Congress (regardless of whether such amendments have yet to be incorporated by the Sentencing Commission into amendments issued under section 994(p) of title 28);

(5) any pertinent policy statement

(A) issued by the Sentencing Commission pursuant to 28 U.S.C. 994(a)(2) of title 28, United States Code, subject to any amendments made to such policy statement by act of Congress (regardless of whether such amendments have yet to be incorporated by the Sentencing Commission into amendments issued under section 994(p) of title 28);

(B) that, except as provided in section 3742(g), is in effect on the date the defendant is sentenced;

(6) the need to avoid unwarranted sentence disparities among defendants with similar records who have been found guilty of similar conduct; and

(7) the need to provide restitution to any victims of the offense.

(b) Application of Guidelines in Imposing a Sentence.—

(1) In general

Except as provided in paragraph (2), the court shall impose a sentence of the kind, and within the range, referred to in subsection (a)(4) unless the court finds that there exists an aggravating or mitigating circumstance of a kind, or to a degree, not adequately taken into consideration by the Sentencing Commission in formulating the guidelines that should result in a sentence different from that described. In determining whether a circumstance was adequately taken into consideration, the court shall consider only the sentencing guidelines, policy statements, and official commentary of the Sentencing Commission. In the absence of an applicable sentencing guideline, the court shall impose an appropriate sentence, having due regard for the purposes set forth in subsection (a)(2). In the absence of an applicable sentencing guideline in the case of an offense other than a petty offense, the court shall also have due regard for the relationship of the sentence imposed to sentences prescribed by guidelines applicable to similar offenses and offenders, and to the applicable policy statements of the Sentencing Commission.

(2) Child crimes and sexual offenses

(A) 2 Sentencing

In sentencing a defendant convicted of an offense under section 1201 involving a minor victim, an offense under section 1591, or an offense under chapter 71, 109A, 110, or 117, the court shall impose a sentence of the kind, and within the range, referred to in subsection (a)(4) unless—

(i) the court finds that there exists an aggravating circumstance of a kind, or to a degree, not adequately taken into consideration by the Sentencing Commission in formulating the guidelines that should result in a sentence greater than that described;

(ii) the court finds that there exists a mitigating circumstance of a kind or to a degree, that—

(I) has been affirmatively and specifically identified as a permissible ground of downward departure in the sentencing guidelines or policy statements issued under section 994(a) of title 28, taking account of any amendments to such sentencing guidelines or policy statements by Congress;

(II) has not been taken into consideration by the Sentencing Commission in formulating the guidelines; and

(III) should result in a sentence different from that described; or

(iii) the court finds, on motion of the Government, that the defendant has provided substantial assistance in the investigation or prosecution of another person who has committed an offense and that this assistance established a mitigating circumstance of a kind, or to a degree, not adequately taken into consideration by the Sentencing Commission in formulating the guidelines that should result in a sentence lower than that described.

In determining whether a circumstance was adequately taken into consideration, the court shall consider only the sentencing guidelines, policy statements, and official commentary of the Sentencing Commission, together with any amendments thereto by act of Congress. In the absence of an applicable sentencing guideline, the court shall impose an appropriate sentence, having due regard for the purposes set forth in subsection (a)(2). In the absence of an applicable sentencing guideline in the case of an offense other than a petty offense, the court shall also have due regard for the relationship of the sentence imposed to sentences prescribed by guidelines applicable to similar offenses and offenders, and to the applicable policy statements of the Sentencing Commission, together with any amendments to such guidelines or policy statements by act of Congress.

(c) Statement of Reasons for Imposing a Sentence.—The court, at the time of sentencing, shall state in open court the reasons for its imposition of the particular sentence, and, if the sentence—

(1) is of the kind, and within the range, described in subsection (a)(4), and that range exceeds 24 months, the reason for imposing a sentence at a particular point within the range; or

(2) is not of the kind, or is outside the range, described in subsection (a)(4), the specific reason for the imposition of a sentence different from that described, which reasons must also be stated with specificity in the

written order of judgment and commitment, except to the extent that the court relies upon statements received in camera in accordance with Federal Rule of Criminal Procedure 32. In the event that the court relies upon statements received in camera in accordance with Federal Rule of Criminal Procedure 32 the court shall state that such statements were so received and that it relied upon the content of such statements.

If the court does not order restitution, or orders only partial restitution, the court shall include in the statement the reason therefor. The court shall provide a transcription or other appropriate public record of the court's statement of reasons, together with the order of judgment and commitment, to the Probation System and to the Sentencing Commission, and, if the sentence includes a term of imprisonment, to the Bureau of Prisons.

(d) Presentence Procedure for an Order of Notice.—Prior to imposing an order of notice pursuant to section 3555, the court shall give notice to the defendant and the Government that it is considering imposing such an order. Upon motion of the defendant or the Government, or on its own motion, the court shall—

(1) permit the defendant and the Government to submit affidavits and written memoranda addressing matters relevant to the imposition of such an order;

(2) afford counsel an opportunity in open court to address orally the appropriateness of the imposition of such an order; and

(3) include in its statement of reasons pursuant to subsection (c) specific reasons underlying its determinations regarding the nature of such an order.

Upon motion of the defendant or the Government, or on its own motion, the court may in its discretion employ any additional procedures that it concludes will not unduly complicate or prolong the sentencing process.

(e) Limited Authority To Impose a Sentence Below a Statutory Minimum.—Upon motion of the Government, the court shall have the authority to impose a sentence below a level established by statute as a minimum sentence so as to reflect a defendant's substantial assistance in the investigation or prosecution of another person who has committed an offense. Such sentence shall be imposed in accordance with the guidelines and policy statements issued by the Sentencing Commission pursuant to section 994 of title 28, United States Code.

(f) Limitation on Applicability of Statutory Minimums in Certain Cases.—Notwithstanding any other provision of law, in the case of an offense under section 401, 404, or 406 of the Controlled Substances Act

(21 U.S.C. 841, 844, 846) or section 1010 or 1013 of the Controlled Substances Import and Export Act (21 U.S.C. 960, 963), the court shall impose a sentence pursuant to guidelines promulgated by the United States Sentencing Commission under section 994 of title 28 without regard to any statutory minimum sentence, if the court finds at sentencing, after the Government has been afforded the opportunity to make a recommendation, that—

(1) the defendant does not have more than 1 criminal history point, as determined under the sentencing guidelines;

(2) the defendant did not use violence or credible threats of violence or possess a firearm or other dangerous weapon (or induce another participant to do so) in connection with the offense;

(3) the offense did not result in death or serious bodily injury to any person;

(4) the defendant was not an organizer, leader, manager, or supervisor of others in the offense, as determined under the sentencing guidelines and was not engaged in a continuing criminal enterprise, as defined in section 408 of the Controlled Substances Act; and

(5) not later than the time of the sentencing hearing, the defendant has truthfully provided to the Government all information and evidence the defendant has concerning the offense or offenses that were part of the same course of conduct or of a common scheme or plan, but the fact that the defendant has no relevant or useful other information to provide or that the Government is already aware of the information shall not preclude a determination by the court that the defendant has complied with this requirement.

APPENDIX C

EXCERPTS FROM THE FEDERAL RULES OF BANKRUPTCY PROCEDURE (EFFECTIVE DECEMBER 1, 2005)

Rule 1001. Scope of Rules and Forms; Short Title

The Bankruptcy Rules and Forms govern procedure in cases under title 11 of the United States Code. The rules shall be cited as the Federal Rules of Bankruptcy Procedure and the forms as the Official Bankruptcy Forms. These rules shall be construed to secure the just, speedy, and inexpensive determination of every case and proceeding.

Rule 1005. Caption of Petition

The caption of a petition commencing a case under the Code shall contain the name of the court, the title of the case, and the docket number. The title of the case shall include the following information about the debtor: name, employer identification number, last four digits of the social security number, any other federal tax identification number, and all other names used by the debtor within six years before filing the petition. If the petition is not filed by the debtor, it shall include all names used by the debtor which are known to petitioners.

Rule 1007. Lists, Schedules and Statements; Time Limits

(a) List of Creditors and Equity Security Holders, and Corporate Ownership Statement

(1) *Voluntary Case.* In a voluntary case, the debtor shall file with the petition a list containing the name and address of each creditor unless the petition is accompanied by a schedule of liabilities. If the debtor is a corporation, other than a governmental unit, the debtor shall file with the petition a corporate ownership statement containing the information described in Rule 7007.1. The debtor shall file a supplemental statement promptly upon any change in circumstances that renders the corporate ownership statement inaccurate.

(2) *Involuntary Case.* In an involuntary case, the debtor shall file within 15 days after entry of the order for relief, a list containing the name and address of each creditor unless a schedule of liabilities has been filed.

(3) *Equity Security Holders.* In a chapter 11 reorganization case, unless the court orders otherwise, the debtor shall file within 15 days after entry of the order for relief a list of the debtor's equity security holders of each class showing the number and kind of interests registered in the name of each holder, and the last known address or place of business of each holder.

(4) *Extension of Time.* Any extension of time for the filing of the lists required by this subdivision may be granted only on motion for cause shown and on notice to the United States trustee and to any trustee, committee elected pursuant to § 705 or appointed pursuant to § 1102 of the Code, or other party as the court may direct.

(b) Schedules and Statements Required.

(1) Except in a chapter 9 municipality case, the debtor, unless the court orders otherwise, shall file schedules of assets and liabilities, a schedule of current income and expenditures, a schedule of executory contracts and unexpired leases, and a statement of financial affairs, prepared as prescribed by the appropriate Official Forms.

(2) An individual debtor in a chapter 7 case shall file a statement of intention as required by § 521(2) of the Code, prepared as prescribed by the appropriate Official Form. A copy of the statement of intention shall be served on the trustee and the creditors named in the statement on or before the filing of the statement.

(c) Time Limits. The schedules and statements, other than the statement of intention, shall be filed with the petition in a voluntary case, or if the petition is accompanied by a list of all the debtor's creditors and their addresses, within 15 days thereafter, except as otherwise provided in subdivisions (d), (e), (f), and (h) of this rule. In an involuntary case, the schedules and statements, other than the statement of intention, shall be filed by the debtor within 15 days after entry of the order for relief. Schedules and statements filed prior to the conversion of a case to another chapter shall be deemed filed in the converted case unless the court directs otherwise. Any extension of time for the filing of the schedules and statements may be granted only on motion for cause shown and on notice to the United States trustee and to any committee elected under § 705 or appointed under § 1102 of the Code, trustee, examiner, or other party as the court may direct. Notice of an extension shall be given to the

United States trustee and to any committee, trustee, or other party as the court may direct.

(d) List of 20 Largest Creditors in Chapter 9 Municipality Case or Chapter 11 Reorganization Case. In addition to the list required by subdivision (a) of this rule, a debtor in a chapter 9 municipality case or a debtor in a voluntary chapter 11 reorganization case shall file with the petition a list containing the name, address and claim of the creditors that hold the 20 largest unsecured claims, excluding insiders, as prescribed by the appropriate Official Form. In an involuntary chapter 11 reorganization case, such list shall be filed by the debtor within 2 days after entry of the order for relief under § 303(h) of the Code.

(e) List in Chapter 9 Municipality Cases. The list required by subdivision (a) of this rule shall be filed by the debtor in a chapter 9 municipality case within such time as the court shall fix. If a proposed plan requires a revision of assessments so that the proportion of special assessments or special taxes to be assessed against some real property will be different from the proportion in effect at the date the petition is filed, the debtor shall also file a list showing the name and address of each known holder of title, legal or equitable, to real property adversely affected. On motion for cause shown, the court may modify the requirements of this subdivision and subdivision (a) of this rule.

(f) Statement of Social Security Number. An individual debtor shall submit a verified statement that sets out the debtor's social security number, or states that the debtor does not have a social security number. In a voluntary case, the debtor shall submit the statement with the petition. In an involuntary case, the debtor shall submit the statement within 15 days after the entry of the order for relief.

(g) Partnership and Partners. The general partners of a debtor partnership shall prepare and file the schedules of the assets and liabilities, schedule of current income and expenditures, schedule of executory contracts and unexpired leases, and statement of financial affairs of the partnership. The court may order any general partner to file a statement of personal assets and liabilities within such time as the court may fix.

(h) Interests Acquired or Arising After Petition. If, as provided by § 541(a)(5) of the Code, the debtor acquires or becomes entitled to acquire any interest in property, the debtor shall within 10 days after the information comes to the debtor's knowledge or within such further time the court may allow, file a supplemental schedule in the chapter 7 liquidation case, chapter 11 reorganization case, chapter 12 family farmer's debt adjustment case, or chapter 13 individual debt adjustment case. If any of the property required to be reported under this subdivision is claimed by the debtor as exempt, the debtor shall

claim the exemptions in the supplemental schedule. The duty to file a supplemental schedule in accordance with this subdivision continues notwithstanding the closing of the case, except that the schedule need not be filed in a chapter 11, chapter 12, or chapter 13 case with respect to property acquired after entry of the order confirming a chapter 11 plan or discharging the debtor in a chapter 12 or chapter 13 case.

(i) Disclosure of List of Security Holders. After notice and hearing and for cause shown, the court may direct an entity other than the debtor or trustee to disclose any list of security holders of the debtor in its possession or under its control, indicating the name, address and security held by any of them. The entity possessing this list may be required either to produce the list or a true copy thereof, or permit inspection or copying, or otherwise disclose the information contained on the list.

(j) Impounding of Lists. On motion of a party in interest and for cause shown the court may direct the impounding of the lists filed under this rule, and may refuse to permit inspection by any entity. The court may permit inspection or use of the lists, however, by any party in interest on terms prescribed by the court.

(k) Preparation of List, Schedules, or Statements on Default of Debtor. If a list, schedule, or statement, other than a statement of intention, is not prepared and filed as required by this rule, the court may order the trustee, a petitioning creditor, committee, or other party to prepare and file any of these papers within a time fixed by the court. The court may approve reimbursement of the cost incurred in complying with such an order as an administrative expense.

(l) Transmission to United States Trustee. The clerk shall forthwith transmit to the United States trustee a copy of every list, schedule, and statement filed pursuant to subdivision (a)(1), (a)(2), (b), (d), or (h) of this rule.

(m) Infants and Incompetent Persons. If the debtor knows that a person on the list of creditors or schedules is an infant or incompetent person, the debtor also shall include the name, address, and legal relationship of any person upon whom process would be served in an adversary proceeding against the infant or incompetent person in accordance with Rule 7004(b)(2).

Rule 1008. Verification of Petitions and Accompanying Papers

All petitions, lists, schedules, statements and amendments thereto shall be verified or contain an unsworn declaration as provided in 28 U.S.C. § 1746.

Rule 2004. Examination

(a) Examination on Motion. On motion of any party in interest, the court may order the examination of any entity.

(b) Scope of Examination. The examination of an entity under this rule or of the debtor under § 343 of the Code may relate only to the acts, conduct, or property or to the liabilities and financial condition of the debtor, or to any matter which may affect the administration of the debtor's estate, or to the debtor's right to a discharge. In a family farmer's debt adjustment case under chapter 12, an individual's debt adjustment case under chapter 13, or a reorganization case under chapter 11 of the Code, other than for the reorganization of a railroad, the examination may also relate to the operation of any business and the desirability of its continuance, the source of any money or property acquired or to be acquired by the debtor for purposes of consummating a plan and the consideration given or offered therefor, and any other matter relevant to the case or to the formulation of a plan.

(c) Compelling Attendance and Production of Documents. The attendance of an entity for examination and the production of documents, whether the examination is to be conducted within or without the district in which the case is pending, may be compelled as provided in Rule 9016 for the attendance of a witness at a hearing or trial. As an officer of the court, an attorney may issue and sign a subpoena on behalf of the court for the district in which the examination is to be held if the attorney is admitted to practice in that court or in the court in which the case is pending.

(d) Time and Place of Examination of Debtor. The court may for cause shown and on terms as it may impose order the debtor to be examined under this rule at any time or place it designates, whether within or without the district wherein the case is pending.

(e) Mileage. An entity other than a debtor shall not be required to attend as a witness unless lawful mileage and witness fee for one day's attendance shall be first tendered. If the debtor resides more than 100 miles from the place of examination when required to appear for an examination under this rule, the mileage allowed by law to a witness shall be tendered for any distance more than 100 miles from the debtor's residence at the date of the filing of the first petition commencing a case under the Code or the residence at the time the debtor is required to appear for the examination, whichever is the lesser.

Rule 2015. Duty to Keep Records, Make Reports, and Give Notice of Case

(a) Trustee or Debtor in Possession. A trustee or debtor in possession shall

(1) in a chapter 7 liquidation case and, if the court directs, in a chapter 11 reorganization case file and transmit to the United States trustee a complete inventory of the property of the debtor within 30 days after qualifying as a trustee or debtor in possession, unless such an inventory has already been filed;

(2) keep a record of receipts and the disposition of money and property received;

(3) file the reports and summaries required by § 704(8) of the Code which shall include a statement, if payments are made to employees, of the amounts of deductions for all taxes required to be withheld or paid for and in behalf of employees and the place where these amounts are deposited;

(4) as soon as possible after the commencement of the case, give notice of the case to every entity known to be holding money or property subject to withdrawal or order of the debtor, including every bank, savings or building and loan association, public utility company, and landlord with whom the debtor has a deposit, and to every insurance company which has issued a policy having a cash surrender value payable to the debtor, except that notice need not be given to any entity who has knowledge or has previously been notified of the case;

(5) in a chapter 11 reorganization case, on or before the last day of the month after each calendar quarter during which there is a duty to pay fees under 28 U.S.C. §1930(a)(6), file and transmit to the United States trustee a statement of disbursements made during that quarter and of any fees payable under 28 U.S.C. § 1930(a)(6) for that quarter.

(b) Chapter 12 Trustee and Debtor in Possession. In a chapter 12 family farmer's debt adjustment case, the debtor in possession shall perform the duties prescribed in clauses (2)-(4) of subdivision (a) of this rule and, if the court directs, shall file and transmit to the United States trustee a complete inventory of the property of the debtor within the time fixed by the court. If the debtor is removed as debtor in possession, the trustee shall perform the duties of the debtor in possession prescribed in this paragraph.

(c) Chapter 13 Trustee and Debtor.

(1) Business Cases. In a chapter 13 individual's debt adjustment case, when the debtor is engaged in business, the debtor shall perform the duties prescribed by clauses (2)-(4) of subdivision (a) of this rule and, if the court directs, shall file and transmit to the United States trustee a complete inventory of the property of the debtor within the time fixed by the court.

(2) Nonbusiness Cases. In a chapter 13 individual's debt adjustment case, when the debtor is not engaged in business, the trustee shall perform the duties prescribed by clause (2) of subdivision (a) of this rule.

(d) Transmission of Reports. In a chapter 11 case the court may direct that copies or summaries of annual reports and copies or summaries of other reports shall be mailed to the creditors, equity security holders, and indenture trustees. The court may also direct the publication of summaries of any such reports. A copy of every report or summary mailed or published pursuant to this subdivision shall be transmitted to the United States trustee.

Rule 3001. Proof of Claim

(a) Form and Content. A proof of claim is a written statement setting forth a creditor's claim. A proof of claim shall conform substantially to the appropriate Official Form.

(b) Who May Execute. A proof of claim shall be executed by the creditor or the creditor's authorized agent except as provided in Rules 3004 and 3005.

(c) Claim Based on a Writing. When a claim, or an interest in property of the debtor securing the claim, is based on a writing, the original or a duplicate shall be filed with the proof of claim. If the writing has been lost or destroyed, a statement of the circumstances of the loss or destruction shall be filed with the claim.

(d) Evidence of Perfection of Security Interest. If a security interest in property of the debtor is claimed, the proof of claim shall be accompanied by evidence that the security interest has been perfected.

(e) Transferred Claim.

(1) Transfer of Claim Other Than for Security Before Proof Filed. If a claim has been transferred other than for security before proof of the claim has been filed, the proof of claim may be filed only by the transferee or an indenture trustee.

(2) Transfer of Claim Other Than for Security After Proof Filed. If a claim other than one based on a publicly traded note, bond, or debenture has been transferred other than for security after the proof of claim has been filed, evidence of the transfer shall be filed by the transferee. The clerk shall immediately notify the alleged transferor by mail of the filing of the evidence of transfer and that objection thereto, if any, must be filed within 20 days of the mailing of the notice or within any additional time allowed by the court. If the alleged transferor files a timely objection and the court finds, after notice and a hearing, that the claim has been transferred other than for security, it shall enter an order substituting the trans-

feree for the transferor. If a timely objection is not filed by the alleged transferor, the transferee shall be substituted for the transferor.

(3) Transfer of Claim for Security Before Proof Filed. If a claim other than one based on a publicly traded note, bond, or debenture has been transferred for security before proof of the claim has been filed, the transferor or transferee or both may file a proof of claim for the full amount. The proof shall be supported by a statement setting forth the terms of the transfer. If either the transferor or the transferee files a proof of claim, the clerk shall immediately notify the other by mail of the right to join in the filed claim. If both transferor and transferee file proofs of the same claim, the proofs shall be consolidated. If the transferor or transferee does not file an agreement regarding its relative rights respecting voting of the claim, payment of dividends thereon, or participation in the administration of the estate, on motion by a party in interest and after notice and a hearing, the court shall enter such orders respecting these matters as may be appropriate.

(4) Transfer of Claim for Security After Proof Filed. If a claim other than one based on a publicly traded note, bond, or debenture has been transferred for security after the proof of claim has been filed, evidence of the terms of the transfer shall be filed by the transferee. The clerk shall immediately notify the alleged transferor by mail of the filing of the evidence of transfer and that objection thereto, if any, must be filed within 20 days of the mailing of the notice or within any additional time allowed by the court. If a timely objection is filed by the alleged transferor, the court, after notice and a hearing, shall determine whether the claim has been transferred for security. If the transferor or transferee does not file an agreement regarding its relative rights respecting voting of the claim, payment of dividends thereon, or participation in the administration of the estate, on motion by a party in interest and after notice and a hearing, the court shall enter such orders respecting these matters as may be appropriate.

(5) Service of Objection or Motion; Notice of Hearing. A copy of an objection filed pursuant to paragraph (2) or (4) or a motion filed pursuant to paragraph (3) or (4) of this subdivision together with a notice of a hearing shall be mailed or otherwise delivered to the transferor or transferee, whichever is appropriate, at least 30 days prior to the hearing.

(f) Evidentiary Effect. A proof of claim executed and filed in accordance with these rules shall constitute prima facie evidence of the validity and amount of the claim.

(g) Evidence of Title. To the extent not inconsistent with the United States Warehouse Act or applicable State law, a warehouse receipt, scale ticket, or similar document of the type routinely issued as evidence of title by a grain storage facility, as defined in section 557 of title 11, shall constitute prima facie evidence of the validity and amount of a claim of ownership of a quantity of grain.

Rule 4002. Duties of Debtor

In addition to performing other duties prescribed by the Code and rules, the debtor shall:

(1) attend and submit to an examination at the times ordered by the court;

(2) attend the hearing on a complaint objecting to discharge and testify, if called as a witness;

(3) inform the trustee immediately in writing as to the location of real property in which the debtor has an interest and the name and address of every person holding money or property subject to the debtor's withdrawal or order if a schedule of property has not yet been filed pursuant to Rule 1007;

(4) cooperate with the trustee in the preparation of an inventory, the examination of proofs of claim, and the administration of the estate, and

(5) file a statement of any change of the debtor's address.

Rule 9011. Signing of Papers; Representations to the Court; Sanctions; Verification and Copies of Papers

(a) Signature. Every petition, pleading, written motion, and other paper, except a list, schedule, or statement, or amendments thereto, shall be signed by at least one attorney of record in the attorney's individual name. A party who is not represented by an attorney shall sign all papers. Each paper shall state the signer's address and telephone number, if any. An unsigned paper shall be stricken unless omission of the signature is corrected promptly after being called to the attention of the attorney or party.

(b) Representations to the Court. By presenting to the court (whether by signing, filing, submitting, or later advocating) a petition, pleading, written motion, or other paper, an attorney or unrepresented party is certifying that to the best of the person's knowledge, information, and belief, formed after an inquiry reasonable under the circumstances,—

(1) it is not being presented for any improper purpose, such as to harass or to cause unnecessary delay or needless increase in the cost of litigation;

(2) the claims, defenses, and other legal contentions therein are warranted by existing law or by a nonfrivolous argument for the extension, modification, or reversal of existing law or the establishment of new law;

(3) the allegations and other factual contentions have evidentiary support or, if specifically so identified, are likely to have evidentiary support after a reasonable opportunity for further investigation or discovery; and

(4) the denials of factual contentions are warranted on the evidence or, if specifically so identified, are reasonably based on a lack of information or belief.

(c) Sanctions. If, after notice and a reasonable opportunity to respond, the court determines that subdivision (b) has been violated, the court may, subject to the conditions stated below, impose an appropriate sanction upon the attorneys, law firms, or parties that have violated subdivision (b) or are responsible for the violation.

(1) How initiated.

(A) By Motion. A motion for sanctions under this rule shall be made separately from other motions or requests and shall describe the specific conduct alleged to violate subdivision (b). It shall be served as provided in Rule 7004. The motion for sanctions may not be filed with or presented to the court unless, within 21 days after service of the motion (or such other period as the court may prescribe), the challenged paper, claim, defense, contention, allegation, or denial is not withdrawn or appropriately corrected, except that this limitation shall not apply if the conduct alleged is the filing of a petition in violation of subdivision (b). If warranted, the court may award to the party prevailing on the motion the reasonable expenses and attorney's fees incurred in presenting or opposing the motion. Absent exceptional circumstances, a law firm shall be held jointly responsible for violations committed by its partners, associates, and employees.

(B) On Court's Initiative. On its own initiative, the court may enter an order describing the specific conduct that appears to violate subdivision (b) and directing an attorney, law firm, or party to show cause why it has not violated subdivision (b) with respect thereto.

(2) Nature of Sanction; Limitations. A sanction imposed for violation of this rule shall be limited to what is sufficient to deter repetition of such conduct or comparable conduct by others similarly situated. Subject to

the limitations in subparagraphs (A) and (B), the sanction may consist of, or include, directives of a nonmonetary nature, an order to pay a penalty into court, or, if imposed on motion and warranted for effective deterrence, an order directing payment to the movant of some or all of the reasonable attorneys' fees and other expenses incurred as a direct result of the violation.

(A) Monetary sanctions may not be awarded against a represented party for a violation of subdivision (b)(2).

(B) Monetary sanctions may not be awarded on the court's initiative unless the court issues its order to show cause before a voluntary dismissal or settlement of the claims made by or against the party which is, or whose attorneys are, to be sanctioned.

(3) Order. When imposing sanctions, the court shall describe the conduct determined to constitute a violation of this rule and explain the basis for the sanction imposed.

(d) Inapplicability to Discovery. Subdivisions (a) through (c) of this rule do not apply to disclosures and discovery requests, responses, objections, and motions that are subject to the provisions of Rules 7026 through 7037.

(e) Verification. Except as otherwise specifically provided by these rules, papers filed in a case under the Code need not be verified. Whenever verification is required by these rules, an unsworn declaration as provided in 28 U.S.C. § 1746 satisfies the requirement of verification.

(f) Copies of Signed or Verified Papers. When these rules require copies of a signed or verified paper, it shall suffice if the original is signed or verified and the copies are conformed to the original.

Rule 9012. Oaths and Affirmations

(a) Persons Authorized to Administer Oaths. The following persons may administer oaths and affirmations and take acknowledgments: a bankruptcy judge, clerk, deputy clerk, United States trustee, officer authorized to administer oaths in proceedings before the courts of the United States or under the laws of the state where the oath is to be taken, or a diplomatic or consular officer of the United States in any foreign country.

(b) Affirmation in Lieu of Oath. When in a case under the Code an oath is required to be taken, a solemn affirmation may be accepted in lieu thereof.

Rule 9017. Evidence

The Federal Rules of Evidence and Rules 43, 44 and 44.1 F.R.Civ.P. apply in cases under the Code.

APPENDIX D

EXCERPTS FROM THE FEDERAL RULES OF EVIDENCE

Rule 101. Scope

These rules govern proceedings in the courts of the United States and before the United States bankruptcy judges and United States magistrate judges, to the extent and with the exceptions stated in rule 1101.

Rule 102. Purpose and Construction

These rules shall be construed to secure fairness in administration, elimination of unjustifiable expense and delay, and promotion of growth and development of the law of evidence to the end that the truth may be ascertained and proceedings justly determined.

Rule 105. Limited Admissibility

When evidence which is admissible as to one party or for one purpose but not admissible as to another party or for another purpose is admitted, the court, upon request, shall restrict the evidence to its proper scope and instruct the jury accordingly.

Rule 603. Oath or Affirmation

Before testifying, every witness shall be required to declare that the witness will testify truthfully, by oath or affirmation administered in a form calculated to awaken the witness' conscience and impress the witness' mind with the duty to do so

APPENDIX E

FORM 1 VOLUNTARY PETITION

(Official Form 1) (10/05)

United States Bankruptcy Court — Voluntary Petition

______________ **District of** ______________

Name of Debtor (if individual, enter Last, First, Middle):	Name of Joint Debtor (Spouse) (Last, First, Middle):
All Other Names used by the Debtor in the last 8 years (include married, maiden, and trade names):	All Other Names used by the Joint Debtor in the last 8 years (include married, maiden, and trade names):
Last four digits of Soc. Sec./Complete EIN or other Tax I.D. No. (if more than one, state all):	Last four digits of Soc. Sec./Complete EIN or other Tax I.D. No. (if more than one, state all):
Street Address of Debtor (No. & Street, City, State): ZIPCODE	Street Address of Joint Debtor (No. & Street, City, and State): ZIPCODE
County of Residence or of the Principal Place of Business:	County of Residence or of the Principal Place of Business:
Mailing Address of Debtor (if different from street address): ZIPCODE	Mailing Address of Joint Debtor (if different from street address): ZIPCODE

Location of Principal Assets of Business Debtor (if different from street address above): ZIPCODE

Type of Debtor (Form of Organization)
(Check **one** box)

- ☐ Individual (include Joint Debtors)
- ☐ Corporation (includes LLC and LLP)
- ☐ Partnership
- ☐ Other (if debtor is not one of the above entities, check this box and provide the information requested below.)
  State type of entity ______________
  ____

Nature of Business
(Check **all** applicable boxes)

- ☐ Health Care Business
- ☐ Single Asset Real Estate as defined in 11 U.S.C. § 101 (51B)
- ☐ Railroad
- ☐ Stockbroker
- ☐ Commodity Broker
- ☐ Clearing Bank
- ☐ Nonprofit Organization qualified under 15 U.S.C. § 501(c)(3)

Chapter or Section of Bankruptcy Code Under Which the Petition is Filed
(Check one box)

- ☐ Chapter 7
- ☐ Chapter 11
- ☐ Chapter 9
- ☐ Chapter 12
- ☐ Chapter 13
- ☐ Chapter 15 Petition for Recognition of a Foreign Main Proceeding
- ☐ Chapter 15 Petition for Recognition of a Foreign Main Proceeding

Nature of Debts (Check one box)

- ☐ Consumer/Non-Business
- ☐ Business

Filing Fee (Check one box)

- ☐ Full Filing Fee attached
- ☐ Filing Fee to be paid in installments (Applicable to individuals only). Must attach signed application for the court's consideration certifying that the debtor is unable to pay fee except in installments. Rule 1006(b). See Official Form No. 3.
- ☐ Filing Fee waiver requested (Applicable to Chapter 7 individuals only). Must attach signed application for the court's consideration. See official Form 3B.

Chapter 11 Debtors

Check one box

- ☐ Debtor is a small business as defined in 11 U.S.C. § 101 (51D).
- ☐ Debtor is not a small business as defined in 11 U.S.C. § 101 (51D).

Check if:

- ☐ Debtor's aggregate noncontingent liquidated debts owed to non-insiders or affiliates are less than $2 million.

Statistical/Administrative Information

- ☐ Debtor estimates that funds will be available for distribution to unsecured creditors.
- ☐ Debtor estimates that, after any exempt property is excluded and administrative expenses paid, there will be no funds available for distribution to unsecured creditors.

Estimated Number of Creditors	1-49	50-99	100-199	200-999	1,000-5,000	5,001-10,000	10,001-25,000	25,001-50,000	50,001-100,000	OVER 100,000
	☐	☐	☐	☐	☐	☐	☐	☐	☐	☐

Estimated Assets

$0 to $50,000	$50,001 to $100,000	$100,001 to $500,000	$500,001 to $1 million	$1,000,001 to $10 million	$10,000,001 to $50 million	$50,000,001 to $100 million	More than $100 million
☐	☐	☐	☐	☐	☐	☐	☐

Estimated Debts

$0 to $50,000	$50,001 to $100,000	$100,001 to $500,000	$500,001 to $1 million	$1,000,001 to $10 million	$10,000,001 to $50 million	$50,000,001 to $100 million	More than $100 million
☐	☐	☐	☐	☐	☐	☐	☐

THIS SPACE IS FOR COURT USE ONLY

(Official Form 1) (10/05) **FORM B1,** Page 2

Voluntary Petition *(This page must be completed and filed in every case)*	Name of Debtor(s):	
Prior Bankruptcy Case Filed within Last 8 Years (If more than one, attach additional sheet)		
Location Where Filed:	Case Number:	Date Filed:
Pending Bankruptcy Case Filed by any Spouse, Partner or Affiliate of this Debtor (If more than one, attach additional sheet)		
Name of Debtor:	Case Number:	Date Filed:
District:	Relationship:	Judge:

Exhibit A

(To be completed if debtor is required to file periodic reports (e.g., forms 10K and 10Q) with the Securities and Exchange Commission pursuant to Section 13 or 15(d) of the Securities Exchange Act of 1934 and is requesting relief under chapter 11.)

☐ Exhibit A is attached and made a part of this petition.

Exhibit B

(To be completed if debtor is an individual whose debts are primarily consumer debts)

I, the attorney for the petitioner named in the foregoing petition, declare that I have informed the petitioner that [he or she] may proceed under chapter 7, 11, 12, or 13 of title 11, United States Code, and have explained, the relief available under each such chapter.

I further certify that I delivered to the debtor the notice required by § 342(b) of the Bankruptcy Code.

X ________________________________

Signature of Attorney for Debtor(s) Date

Exhibit C

Does the debtor own or have possession of any property that poses or is alleged to pose a threat of imminent and identifiable harm to public health or safety?

☐ Yes, and Exhibit C is attached and made a part of this petition.

☐ No

Certification Concerning Debt Counseling by Individual/Joint Debtor(s)

☐ I/we have received approved budget and credit counseling during the 180-day period preceding the filing of this petition.

☐ I/we request a waiver of the requirement to obtain budget and credit counseling prior to filing based on exigent circumstances. (Must attach certification describing.)

Information Regarding the Debtor (Check the Applicable Boxes)

Venue (Check any applicable box)

☐ Debtor has been domiciled or has had a residence, principal place of business, or principal assets in this District for 180 days immediate preceding the date of this petition or for a longer part of such 180 days than in any other District.

☐ There is a bankruptcy case concerning debtor's affiliate, general partner, or Partnership pending in this District.

☐ Debtor is a debtor in a foreign proceeding and has its principal place of business or principal assets in the United States in this District, or has no principal place of business or assets in the United States but is a defendant in an action or proceeding [in a federal or state court] in this District, or the interests of the parties will be served in regard to the relief sought in this District.

Statement by a Debtor Who Resides as a Tenant of Residential Property

Check all applicable boxes.

☐ Landlord has a judgment against the debtor for possession of debtor's residence. (If box checked, complete the following.)

____

(Name of landlord that obtained judgment)

____

(Address of landlord)

☐ Debtor claims that under applicable nonbankruptcy law, there are circumstances under which the debtor would be permitted to cure the entire monetary default that gave rise to the judgment for possession, after the judgment for possession was entered, and

☐ Debtor has included in this petition the deposit with the court of any rent that would become due during the 30-day period after the filing of the petition.

(Official Form I) (10/05)

FORM B1, Page 3

Voluntary Petition
(This page must be completed and filed in every case)

Name of Debtor(s)

Signatures

Signature(s) of Debtor(s)(Individual/Joint)

I declare under penalty of perjury that the information provided in this petition is true and correct.
[If petitioner is an individual whose debts are primarily consumer debts and has chose to file under chapter 7] I am aware that I may proceed under, chapter 7, 11, 12 or 13 of the title 11, United States Code, understand the relief available under each such chapter, and choose to proceed under chapter 7.
[If no attorney represents me and no bankruptcy petition preparer signs the petition] I have obtained and read the notice required by § 342(b) of the Bankruptcy Code

I request relief in accordance with the chapter of title 11, United States Code, specified in this petition.

X ______________________________
Signature of Debtor

X ______________________________
Signature of Joint Debtor

____
Telephone Number (If not represented by attorney)

____
Date

Signature of a Foreign Representative

I declare under penalty of perjury that the information provided in this petition is true and correct, that I am the foreign representative of a debtor in a foreign proceeding, and that I have been authorized to file this petition. (Check only one box.)

☐ I request relief in accordance with chapter 15 of title 11, United States Code, Certified copies of the documents required by § 1515 of title 11 are attached.

☐ Pursuant to § 1511 of title 11, United States Code, I request relief in accordance with the chapter of title 11 specified in this petition. A certified copy of the order granting recognition of the foreign main proceeding is attached.

X ______________________________
(Signature of Foreign Representative)

____
(Printed Name of Foreign Representative)

____
Date

Signature of Attorney

X ______________________________
Signature of Attorney for Debtor(s)

____
Printed Name of Attorney for Debtor(s)

____
Firm Name

____
Address

____

____
Telephone Number

____
Date

Signature of Debtor (Corporation/Partnership)

I declare under penalty of perjury that the information provided in this petition is true and correct, and that I have been authorized to file this petition on behalf of the debtor.
The debtor requests relief in accordance with the chapter of title 11, United States Code, specified in this petition.

X ______________________________
Signature of Authorized Individual

____
Printed Name of Authorized Individual

____
Title of Authorized Individual

____
Date

Signature of Non-Attorney Bankruptcy Petition Preparer

I declare under penalty of perjury that: (1) I am a bankruptcy petition preparer as defined in 11 U.S.C. § 110; (2) I prepared this document for compensation and have provided the debtor with a copy of this document and the notices and information required under 11 U.S.C. §§ 110(b), 110(h), and 342(b); and, (3) if rules or guidelines have been promulgated pursuant to 11 U.S.C. § 110(h) setting a maximum fee for services chargeable by bankruptcy petition preparers, I have given the debtor notice of the maximum amount before preparing any document for filing for a debtor or accepting any fee from the debtor, as required in that section. Official Form 19B is attached.

____
Printed Name and title, if any, of Bankruptcy Petition Preparer

____
Social Security Number (If the bankruptcy petition preparer is not an individual, state the Social Security number of the officer, principal, responsible person or partner of the bankruptcy petition preparer.)(Required by 11 U.S.C. § 110.)

____
Address

____

X ______________________________

____
Date

Signature of Bankruptcy Petition Preparer or officer, principal, responsible person, or partner whose social security number is provided above.

Names and Social Security numbers of all other individuals who prepared or assisted in preparing this document unless the bankruptcy petition preparer is not an individual:

If more than one person prepared this document, attach additional sheets conforming to the appropriate official form for each person.

A bankruptcy petition preparer's failure to comply with the provisions of title 11 and the Federal Rules of Bankruptcy Procedure may result in fines or imprisonment or both 11 U.S.C. §110; 18 U.S.C. §156.

Exhibit "A"

UNITED STATES BANKRUPTCY COURT

______ DISTRICT OF ______

In re ________________ , Case No.________________

Debtor Chapter________________

Exhibit "A" to Voluntary Petition

1. If any of the debtor's securities are registered under Section 12 of the Securities Exchange Act of 1934, the SEC file number is ________________.

2. The following financial data is the latest available information and refers to the debtor's condition on ____________.

a. Total assets $ ____________________________

b. Total debts (including debts listed in 2.c., below) $ ____________________________

c. Debt securities held by more than 500 holders. Approximate number of holders

secured / / unsecured / / subordinated / / $______________ ______________

secured / / unsecured / / subordinated / / $______________ ______________

secured / / unsecured / / subordinated / / $______________ ______________

secured / / unsecured / / subordinated / / $______________ ______________

secured / / unsecured / / subordinated / / $______________ ______________

d. Number of shares of preferred stock ____________________

e. Number of shares common stock ____________________

Comments, if any: ____________________________________

____

____

3. Brief description of debtor's business: ____________________

____

____

4. List the names of any person who directly or indirectly owns, controls, or holds, with power to vote, 5% or more of the voting securities of debtor:

____

Exhibit "B"

UNITED STATES BANKRUPTCY COURT
______ DISTRICT OF ______

"FOR COURT USE ONLY
"Date Petition Filed
"Case Number
"Bankruptcy Judge

"I ________________________, the attorney for the petitioner named in the foregoing petition, declare that I have informed the petitioner that *[he or she]* may proceed under chapter 7 or 13 of title 11, United States Code, and have explained the relief available under each such chapter.

"Executed on ____________________________
"Signature ________________________________
Attorney for Petitioner".

See section 342(b) of the Bankruptcy Code, requiring the clerk, prior to the commencement of a title 11 case by an individual whose debts are primarily consumer debts, to give written notice to such individual indicating each chapter of title 11 under which such individual may proceed.

Exhibit "C"

UNITED STATES BANKRUPTCY COURT

______ DISTRICT OF ______

In re ______________________, Debtor	Case No.______________ Chapter_______________

Exhibit "C" to Voluntary Petition

1. Identify and briefly describe all real or personal property owned by or in possession of the debtor that, to the best of the debtor's knowledge, poses or is alleged to pose a threat of imminent and identifiable harm to the public health or safety (attach additional sheets if necessary):

____

____

____

____

2. With respect to each parcel of real property or item of personal property identified in question 1, describe the nature and location of the dangerous condition, whether environmental or otherwise, that poses or is alleged to pose a threat of imminent and identifiable harm to the public health or safety (attach additional sheets if necessary):

____

____

____

____

APPENDIX F

LIST OF CREDITORS HOLDING 20 LARGEST UNSECURED CLAIMS

UNITED STATES BANKRUPTCY COURT
______ DISTRICT OF ______

In re ________________________, Case No. ___________
Debtor Chapter ____________

LIST OF CREDITORS HOLDING 20 LARGEST UNSECURED CLAIMS

Following is the list of the debtor's creditors holding the 20 largest unsecured claims. The list is prepared in accordance with Fed. R. Bankr. P. 1007(d) for filing in this chapter 11 [*or* chapter 9] case. The list does not include (1) persons who come within the definition of "insider" set forth in 11 U.S.C. § 101, or (2) secured creditors unless the value of the collateral is such that the unsecured deficiency places the creditor among the holders of the 20 largest unsecured claims. If a minor child is one of the creditors holding the 20 largest unsecured claims, indicate that by stating "a minor child" and do not disclose the child's name. See 11 U.S.C. § 112; Fed. R. Bankr. P. 1007(m).

(1) *Name of creditor and complete mailing address including zip code*	(2) *Name, telephone number and complete mailing address, including zip code, of employee, agent, or department of creditor familiar with claim who may be contacted*	(3) *Nature of claim (trade debt, bank loan, government contract, etc.)*	(4) *Indicate if claim is contingent, unliquidated, disputed or subject to setoff*	(5) *Amount of claim [if secured also state value of security]*

Date: ___________

____
Debtor

Declaration Under Penalty of Perjury on Behalf of a Corporation or Partnership

I, [the president *or* other officer *or* an authorized agent of the corporation] [*or* a member *or* an authorized agent of the partnership] named as the debtor in this case, declare under penalty of perjury that I have read the foregoing List of Creditors Holding 20 Largest Unsecured Claims and that it is true and correct to the best of my information and belief.

Date ____________ Signature ____________________

(Print Name and Title) ____________________

APPENDIX G

SCHEDULES

Form 6 – Summary
(10/05)

UNITED STATES BANKRUPTCY COURT
_______ DISTRICT OF _______

In re ______________________ , Debtor	Case No. __________________ (If known)
	Chapter __________________

SUMMARY OF SCHEDULES

Indicate as to each schedule whether that schedule is attached and state the number of pages in each. Report the totals from Schedules A, B, D, E, F, I, and J in the boxes provided. Add the amounts from Schedules A and B to determine the total amount of the debtor's assets. Add the amounts of all claims from Schedules D, E, and F to determine the total amount of the debtor's liabilities. Individual debtors must also complete the "Statistical Summary of Certain Liabilities."

AMOUNTS SCHEDULED					
NAME OF SCHEDULE	ATTACHED (YES/NO)	NO. OF SHEETS	ASSETS	LIABILITIES	OTHER
A – Real Property			$		
B – Personal Property			$		
C – Property Claimed as Exempt					
D – Creditors Holding Secured Claims				$	
E – Creditors Holding Unsecured Priority Claims				$	
F – Creditors Holding Unsecured Nonpriority Claims				$	
G – Executory Contracts and Unexpired Leases					
H – Codebtors					
I – Current Income of Individual Debtor(s)					$
J – Current Expenditures of Individual Debtor(s)					$
Total			$	$	

Form B6B
(10/05)

In re ______________________________, **Case No.** ______________________________
Debtor **(If known)**

SCHEDULE A – REAL PROPERTY

Except as directed below, list all real property in which the debtor has any legal, equitable, or future interest, including all property owned as a co-tenant, community property, or in which the debtor has a life estate. Include any property in which the debtor holds rights and powers exercisable for the debtor's own benefit. If the debtor is married, state whether husband, wife, or both own the property by placing an "H," "W," "J," or "C" in the column labeled "Husband, Wife, Joint, or Community." If the debtor holds no interest in real property, write "None" under "Description and Location of Property."

Do not include interests in executory contracts and unexpired leases on this schedule. List them in Schedule G – Executory Contracts and Unexpired Leases.

If an entity claims to have a lien or hold a secured interest in any property, state the amount of the secured claim. See Schedule D. If no entity claims to hold a secured interest in the property, write "None" in the column labeled "Amount of Secured Claim."

If the debtor is an individual or if a joint petition is filed, state the amount of any exemption claimed in the property only in Schedule C – Property Claimed as Exempt.

DESCRIPTION AND LOCATION OF PROPERTY	NATURE OF DEBTOR'S INTEREST IN PROPERTY	HUSBAND, WIFE, JOINT, OR COMMUNITY	CURRENT VALUE OF DEBTOR'S INTEREST IN PROPERTY, WITHOUT DEDUCTING ANY SECURED CLAIM OR EXEMPTION	AMOUNT OF SECURED CLAIM
		Total?		

(Report also on Summary of Schedules.)

Form B6B– Cont.
(10/05)

In re ____________________________, **Case No.** ____________________________
Debtor **(If known)**

SCHEDULE B - PERSONAL PROPERTY

Except as directed below, list all personal property of the debtor of whatever kind. If the debtor has no property in one or more of the categories, place an "x" in the appropriate position in the column labeled "None." If additional space is needed in any category, attach a separate sheet properly identified with the case name, case number, and the number of the category. If the debtor is married, state whether husband, wife, or both own the property by placing an "H," "W," "J," or "C" in the column labeled "Husband, Wife, Joint, or Community." If the debtor is an individual or a joint petition is filed, state the amount of any exemptions claimed only in Schedule C – Property Claimed as Exempt.

Do not list interests in executory contracts and unexpired leases on this schedule. List them in Schedule G – Executory Contracts and Unexpired Leases.

If the property is being held for the debtor by someone else, state that person's name and address under "Description and Location of Property." In providing the information requested in this schedule, do not include the name or address of a minor child. Simply state "a minor child."

TYPE OF PROPERTY	NONE	DESCRIPTION AND LOCATION OF PROPERTY	HUSBAND, WIFE, JOINT, OR COMMUNITY	CURRENT VALUE OF DEBTOR'S INTEREST IN PROPERTY, WITHOUT DEDUCTING ANY SECURED CLAIM OR EXEMPTION
1. Cash on hand.				
2. Checking, savings or other financial accounts, certificates of deposit, or shares in banks, savings and loan, thrift, building and loan, and homestead associations, or credit unions, brokerage houses, or cooperatives.				
3. Security deposits with public utilities, telephone companies, landlords, and others.				
4. Household goods and furnishings, including audio, video, and computer equipment.				
5. Books; pictures and other art objects; antiques; stamp, coin, record, tape, compact disc, and other collections or collectibles.				
6. Wearing apparel.				
7. Furs and jewelry.				
8. Firearms and sports, photographic, and other hobby equipment.				
9. Interests in insurance policies. Name insurance company of policy and itemize surrender or refund value of each.				
10. Annuities. Itemize and name each issuer.				

Form B6B– Cont.
(10/05)

In re ______________________________, Case No. ______________________________
Debtor (If known)

SCHEDULE B – PERSONAL PROPERTY

(Continuation Sheet)

TYPE OF PROPERTY	NONE	DESCRIPTION AND LOCATION OF PROPERTY	HUSBAND, WIFE, JOINT, OR COMMUNITY	CURRENT VALUE OF DEBTOR'S INTEREST IN PROPERTY, WITHOUT DEDUCTING ANY SECURED CLAIM OR EXEMPTION
11. Interests in an education IRA as defined in 26 U.S.C. § 530(b)(1) or under a qualified State tuition plan as defined in 26 U.S.C. § 529(b)(1). Give particulars. (File separately the record(s) of any such interest(s). 11 U.S.C. § 521(c); Rule 1007(b)).				
12. Interests in IRA, ERISA, Keogh, or other pension or profit sharing plans. Give particulars.				
13. Stock and interests in incorporated and unincorporated businesses. Itemize.				
14. Interests in partnerships or joint ventures. Itemize.				
15. Government and corporate bonds and other negotiable and non-negotiable instruments.				
16. Accounts receivable.				
17. Alimony, maintenance, support, and property settlements to which the debtor is or may be entitled. Give particulars.				
18. Other liquidated debts owing debtor including tax refunds. Give particulars.				
Equitable or future interests, life estates, and rights or powers exercisable for the benefit of the debtor other than those listed in Schedule A—Real Property.				
19. Contingent and noncontingent interests in estate of a decedent, death benefit plan, life insurance policy, or trust.				
20. Other contingent and unliquidated claims of every nature, including tax refunds, counterclaims of the debtor, and rights to setoff claims. Give estimated value of each.				

Form B6B– Cont.
(10/05)

In re ______________________, Case No. ______________________
Debtor (If known)

SCHEDULE B – PERSONAL PROPERTY

(Continuation Sheet)

TYPE OF PROPERTY	NONE	DESCRIPTION AND LOCATION OF PROPERTY	HUSBAND, WIFE, JOINT, OR COMMUNITY	CURRENT VALUE OF DEBTOR'S INTEREST IN PROPERTY, WITHOUT DEDUCTING ANY SECURED CLAIM OR EXEMPTION
21. Patents, copyrights, and other intellectual property. Give particulars. 22. Licenses, franchises, and other general intangibles. Give particulars. 23. Customer lists or other compilations containing personally identifiable information (as defined in 11 U.S.C. § 101 (41A)) provided to the debtor by individuals in connection with obtaining a product or service from the debtor primarily for personal, family, or household purposes. 24. Automobiles, trucks, trailers, and other vehicles and accessories. 25. Boats, motors, and accessories. 26. Aircraft and accessories. 27. Office equipment, furnishings, and supplies. Machinery, fixtures, equipment, and supplies used in business. 28. Inventory. 29. Animals. 30. Crops – growing or harvested. Give particulars. 31. Farming equipment and implements. 32. Farm supplies, chemicals, and feed. 33. Other personal property of any kind not already listed. Itemize.				
________ continuation sheets attached Total ?				$

(Include amounts from any continuation sheets attached. Report total also on Summary of Schedules.)

Form B6B
(10/05)

In re ______________________, Case No. ______________________
Debtor (If known)

SCHEDULE C - PROPERTY CLAIMED AS EXEMPT

Debtor claims the exemptions to which debtor is entitled under:
(Check one box)

☐ 11 U.S.C. § 522(b)(2)
☐ 11 U.S.C. § 522(b)(3)

☐ Check if debtor claims a homestead exemption that exceeds

$125,000.

DESCRIPTION OF PROPERTY	SPECIFY LAW PROVIDING EACH EXEMPTION	VALUE OF CLAIMED EXEMPTION	CURRENT VALUE OF PROPERTY WITHOUT DEDUCTING EXEMPTION

Form B6B
(10/05)

In re ______________________________, **Case No.** ______________________________
Debtor **(If known)**

SCHEDULE D - CREDITORS HOLDING SECURED CLAIMS

State the name, mailing address, including zip code and last four digits of any account number of all entities holding claims secured by property of the debtor as of the date of filing of the petition. The complete account number of any account the debtor has with the creditor is useful to the trustee and the creditor and may be provided if the debtor chooses to do so. List creditors holding all types of secured interests such as judgment liens, garnishments, statutory liens, mortgages, deeds of trust, and other security interests.

List creditors in alphabetical order to the extent practicable. If a minor child is a creditor, indicate that by stating "a minor child" and do not disclose the child's name. See 11 U.S.C. § 112; Fed. R. Bankr. P. 1007(m). If all secured creditors will not fit on this page, use the continuation sheet provided.

If any entity other than a spouse in a joint case may be jointly liable on a claim, place an "X" in the column labeled "Codebtor," include the entity on the appropriate schedule of creditors, and complete Schedule H - Codebtors. If a joint petition is filed, state whether husband, wife, both of them, or the marital community may be liable on each claim by placing an "H," "W," "J," or "C" in the column labeled "Husband, Wife, Joint, or Community."

If the claim is contingent, place an "X" in the column labeled "Contingent." If the claim is unliquidated, place an "X" in the column labeled "Unliquidated." If the claim is disputed, place an "X" in the column labeled "Disputed." (You may need to place an "X" in more than one of these three columns.)

Report the total of all claims listed on this schedule in the box labeled "Total" on the last sheet of the completed schedule. Report this total also on the Summary of Schedules.

☐ Check this box if debtor has no creditors holding secured claims to report on this Schedule D.

CREDITOR'S NAME AND MAILING ADDRESS INCLUDING ZIP CODE AND A ACCOUNT NUMBER (*See Instructions Above*)	CODEBTOR	HUSBAND, WIFE, JOINT, OR COMMUNITY	DATE CLAIM WAS INCURRED, NATURE OF LIEN, AND DESCRIPTION AND VALUE OF PROPERTY SUBJECT TO LIEN	CONTINGENT	UNLIQUIDATED	DISPUTED	AMOUNT OF CLAIM WITHOUT DEDUCTING VALUE OF COLLATERAL	UNSECURED PORTION, IF ANY
ACCOUNT NO.								
			VALUE $					
ACCOUNT NO.								
			VALUE $					
ACCOUNT NO.								
			VALUE $					

_______continuation sheets attached

Subtotal (Total of this page)	$	
Total (Use only on last page)	$	

(Report total also on Summary of Schedules)
(Report total also on Summary of Schedules)

Form B6B– Cont.
(10/05)

In re ______________________________, **Case No.** ______________________________
Debtor **(If known)**

SCHEDULE D - CREDITORS HOLDING SECURED CLAIMS
(Continuation Sheet)

CREDITOR'S NAME AND MAILING ADDRESS INCLUDING ZIP CODE AND A ACCOUNT NUMBER (*See Instructions Above*)	CODEBTOR	HUSBAND, WIFE, JOINT, OR COMMUNITY	DATE CLAIM WAS INCURRED, NATURE OF LIEN, AND DESCRIPTION AND VALUE OF PROPERTY SUBJECT TO LIEN	CONTINGENT	UNLIQUIDATED	DISPUTED	AMOUNT OF CLAIM WITHOUT DEDUCTING VALUE OF COLLATERAL	UNSECURED PORTION, IF ANY
ACCOUNT NO.								
			VALUE $					
ACCOUNT NO.								
			VALUE $					
ACCOUNT NO.								
			VALUE $					
ACCOUNT NO.								
			VALUE $					
ACCOUNT NO.								
			VALUE $					

Sheet no. ___ of ___ continuation sheets attached to Schedule of Creditors Holding Secured Claims	Subtotal (Total of this page)	$
	Total (Use only on last page)	$

Form B6B
(10/05)

In re ______________________________, Case No. ______________________________
Debtor (If known)

SCHEDULE E - CREDITORS HOLDING UNSECURED PRIORITY CLAIMS

A complete list of claims entitled to priority, listed separately by type of priority, is to be set forth on the sheets provided. Only holders of unsecured claims entitled to priority should be listed in this schedule. In the boxes provided on the attached sheets, state the name, mailing address, including zip code, and last four digits of the account number, if any, of all entities holding priority claims against the debtor or the property of the debtor, as of the date of the filing of the petition. Use a separate continuation sheet for each type of priority and label each with the type of priority.

The complete account number of any account the debtor has with the creditor is useful to the trustee and the creditor and may be provided if the debtor chooses to do so. If a minor child is a creditor, indicate that by stating "a minor child" and do not disclose the child's name. See 11 U.S.C. § 112; Fed.R.Bankr.P. 1007(m).

If any entity other than a spouse in a joint case may be jointly liable on a claim, place an "X" in the column labeled "Codebtor," include the entity on the appropriate schedule of creditors, and complete Schedule H-Codebtors. If a joint petition is filed, state whether husband, wife, both of them or the marital community may be liable on each claim by placing an "H," "W," "J," or "C" in the column labeled "Husband, Wife, Joint or Community." If the claim is contingent, place an "X" in the column labeled "Contingent." If the claim is unliquidated, place an "X" in the column labeled "Unliquidated." If the claim is disputed, place an "X" in the column labeled "Disputed." (You may need to place an "X" in more than one of these three columns.)

Report the total of claims listed on each sheet in the box labeled "Subtotal" on each sheet. Report the total of all claims listed on this Schedule E in the box labeled "Total" on the last sheet of the completed schedule. Repeat this total also on the Summary of Schedules.

Report the total of amounts entitled to priority listed on each sheet in the box labeled "Subtotal" on each sheet. Report the total of all amounts entitled to priority listed on this Schedule E in the box labeled "Total" on the last sheet of the completed schedule. In applicable, also report this total on the Means Test form.

☐ Check this box if debtor has no creditors holding unsecured priority claims to report on this Schedule E.

TYPES OF PRIORITY CLAIMS (Check the appropriate box(es) below if claims in that category are listed on the attached sheets)

☐ **Domestic Support Obligations**

Claims for domestic support that are owed to or recoverable by a spouse, former spouse, or child of the debtor, or the parent, legal guardian, or responsible relative of such a child, or a governmental unit to whom such a domestic support claim has been assigned to the extent provided in 11 U.S.C. § 507(a)(1).

☐ **Extensions of credit in an involuntary case**

Claims arising in the ordinary course of the debtor's business or financial affairs after the commencement of the case but before the earlier of the appointment of a trustee or the order for relief. 11 U.S.C. § 507(a)(3).

☐ **Wages, salaries, and commissions**

Wages, salaries, and commissions, including vacation, severance, and sick leave pay owing to employees and commissions owing to qualifying independent sales representatives up to $10,000* per person earned within 180 days immediately preceding the filing of the original petition, or the cessation of business, whichever occurred first, to the extent provided in 11 U.S.C. § 507(a)(4).

☐ **Contributions to employee benefit plans**

Money owed to employee benefit plans for services rendered within 180 days immediately preceding the filing of the original petition, or the cessation of business, whichever occurred first, to the extent provided in 11 U.S.C. § 507(a)(5).

Form B6B
(10/05)

In re ____________________________, Case No. ________________________________
Debtor (If known)

☐ **Certain farmers and fishermen**

Claims of certain farmers or fishermen, up to $4,925* per farmer or fisherman, against the debtor, as provided in 11 U.S.C. § 507(a)(6).

☐ **Deposits by individuals**

Claims of individuals up to $2,225* for deposits for the purchase, lease, or rental of property or services for personal, family, or household use, that were not delivered or provided. 11 U.S.C. § 507(a)(7).

☐ **Taxes and Certain Other Debts Owed to Governmental Units**

Taxes, customs duties, and penalties owing to federal, state, and local governmental units as set forth in 11 U.S.C. § 507(a)(8).

☐ **Commitments to Maintain the Capital of an Insured Depository Institution**

Claims based on commitments to the FDIC, RTC, Director of the Office of Thrift Supervision, Comptroller of the Currency, or Board of Governors of the Federal Reserve System, or their predecessors or successors, to maintain the capital of an insured depository institution. 11 U.S.C. § 507(a)(9).

☐ **Claims for Death or Personal Injury While Debtor Was Intoxicated**

Claims for death or personal injury resulting from the operation of a motor vehicle or vessel while the debtor was intoxicated from using alcohol, a drug, or another substance. 11 U.S.C. § 507(a)(10).

*Amounts are subject to adjustment on April 1, 2007, and every three years thereafter with respect to cases commenced on or after the date of adjustment.

____ continuation sheets attached

Form B6B
(10/05)

In re ______________________________, Case No. ______________________________
Debtor (If known)

SCHEDULE E -
CREDITORS HOLDING UNSECURED PRIORITY CLAIMS

(Continuation Sheet)

TYPE OF PRIORITY ______________________

CREDITOR'S NAME AND MAILING ADDRESS INCLUDING ZIP CODE, AND ACCOUNT NUMBER (*See Instructions*)	CODEBTOR	HUSBAND, WIFE, JOINT, OR COMMUNITY	DATE CLAIM WAS INCURRED AND CONSIDERATION FOR CLAIM	CONTINGENT	UNLIQUIDATED	DISPUTED	AMOUNT OF CLAIM	AMOUNT ENTITLED TO PROIORITY
ACCOUNT NO.								
ACCOUNT NO.								
ACCOUNT NO.								
ACCOUNT NO.								
ACCOUNT NO.								

Sheet no. __ of __ sheets attached to Schedule of Creditors Holding Priority Claims

Subtotal (Total of this page) $

Total $
(Use only on last page of the completed Schedule E.)
(Report total also on Summary of Schedules)

In re ______________________________, **Case No.** ______________________________
Debtor **(If known)**

SCHEDULE F - CREDITORS HOLDING UNSECURED NONPRIORITY CLAIMS

State the name, mailing address, including zip code, and last four digits of any account number, of all entities holding unsecured claims without priority against the debtor or the property of the debtor, as of the date of filing of the petition. The complete account number of any account the debtor has with the creditor is useful to the trustee and the creditor and may be provided if the debtor chooses to do so. If a minor child is a creditor, indicate that by stating "a minor child" and do not disclose the child's name. See 11 U.S.C. § 112; Fed. R. Bankr. P. 1007(m). Do not include claims listed in Schedules D and E. If all creditors will not fit on this page, use the continuation sheet provided.

If any entity other than a spouse in a joint case may be jointly liable on a claim, place an "X" in the column labeled "Codebtor," include the entity on the appropriate schedule of creditors, and complete Schedule H - Codebtors. If a joint petition is filed, state whether husband, wife, both of them, or the marital community may be liable on each claim by placing an "H," "W," "J," or "C" in the column labeled "Husband, Wife, Joint, or Community."

If the claim is contingent, place an "X" in the column labeled "Contingent." If the claim is unliquidated, place an "X" in the column labeled "Unliquidated." If the claim is disputed, place an "X" in the column labeled "Disputed." (You may need to place an "X" in more than one of these three columns.)

Report total of all claims listed on this schedule in the box labeled "Total" on the last sheet of the completed schedule. Report this total also on the Summary of Schedules.

☐ Check this box if debtor has no creditors holding unsecured claims to report on this Schedule F.

CREDITOR'S NAME, MAILING ADDRESS INCLUDING ZIP CODE, AND ACCOUNT NUMBER (*See Instructions above.*)	CODEBTOR	HUSBAND, WIFE, JOINT, OR COMMUNITY	DATE CLAIM WAS INCURRED AND CONSIDERATION FOR CLAIM IF CLAIM IS SUBJECT TO SETOFF, SO STATE	CONTINGENT	UNLIQUIDATED	DISPUTED	AMOUNT OF CLAIM
ACCOUNT NO.							
ACCOUNT NO.							
ACCOUNT NO.							
ACCOUNT NO.							

Continuation sheets attached	Subtotal	$
	Total	$

(Use only on last page of the completed Schedule F.)
(Report total also on Summary of Schedules)

Form B6B
(10/05)

In re ______________________________, Case No. ______________________________
Debtor (If known)

SCHEDULE F - CREDITORS HOLDING UNSECURED NONPRIORITY CLAIMS

(Continuation Sheet)

CREDITOR'S NAME, MAILING ADDRESS INCLUDING ZIP CODE, AND ACCOUNT NUMBER (*See Instructions above.*)	CODEBTOR	HUSBAND, WIFE, JOINT, OR COMMUNITY	DATE CLAIM WAS INCURRED AND CONSIDERATION FOR CLAIM IF CLAIM IS SUBJECT TO SETOFF, SO STATE	CONTINGENT	UNLIQUIDATED	DISPUTED	AMOUNT OF CLAIM
ACCOUNT NO.							
ACCOUNT NO.							
ACCOUNT NO.							
ACCOUNT NO.							
ACCOUNT NO.							

Sheet No. _____ of _____ sheets attached to Schedule of Creditors Holding Unsecured Nonpriority Claims	Subtotal	$
	Total	$
(Use only on last page of the completed Schedule F.) (Report total also on Summary of Schedules)		

In re ____________________________, Case No. ____________________________
Debtor (If known)

SCHEDULE G - EXECUTORY CONTRACTS AND UNEXPIRED LEASES

Describe all executory contracts of any nature and all unexpired leases of real or personal property. Include any timeshare interests. State nature of debtor's interest in contract, i.e., "Purchaser," "Agent," etc. State whether debtor is the lessor or lessee of a lease. Provide the names and complete mailing addresses of all other parties to each lease or contract described. If a minor child is a party to one of the leases or contracts, indicate that by stating "a minor child" and do not disclose the child's name. See 11 U.S.C. § 112; Fed. R. Bankr. P. 1007(m).

☐ Check this box if debtor has no executory contracts or unexpired leases.

NAME AND MAILING ADDRESS, INCLUDING ZIP CODE, OF OTHER PARTIES TO LEASE OR CONTRACT.	DESCRIPTION OF CONTRACT OR LEASE AND NATURE OF DEBTOR'S INTEREST. STATE WHETHER LEASE IS FOR NONRESIDENTIAL REAL PROPERTY. STATE CONTRACT NUMBER OF ANY GOVERNMENT CONTRACT.

In re ______________________________, Case No. ______________________________
Debtor (If known)

SCHEDULE H - CODEBTORS

Provide the information requested concerning any person or entity, other than a spouse in a joint case, that is also liable on any debts listed by debtor in the schedules of creditors. Include all guarantors and co-signers. If the debtor resides or resided in a community property state, commonwealth, or territory (including Alaska, Arizona, California, Idaho, Louisiana, Nevada, New Mexico, Puerto Rico, Texas, Washington, or Wisconsin) within the eight year period immediately proceeding the commencement of the case, identify the name of the debtor's spouse and of any former spouse who resides or resided with the debtor in the community property state, commonwealth, or territory. Include all names used by the nondebtor spouse during the eight years immediately preceding the commencement of this case. If a minor child is a codebtor or a creditor, indicate that by stating "a minor child" and do not disclose the child's name. See 11 U.S.C. § 112; Fed. Bankr. P. 1007(m).

☐ Check this box if debtor has no codebtors.

NAME AND ADDRESS OF CODEBTOR	NAME AND ADDRESS OF CREDITOR

In re ______________________________, Case No. ______________________________
Debtor (If known)

SCHEDULE I - CURRENT INCOME OF INDIVIDUAL DEBTOR(S)

The column labeled "Spouse" must be completed in all cases filed by joint debtors and by a married debtor in a chapter 7, 11, 12 or 13 case whether or not a joint petition is filed, unless the spouses are separated and a joint petition is not filed. Do not state the name of any minor child.

Debtor's Marital Status:	DEPENDENTS OF DEBTOR AND SPOUSE	
	RELATIONSHIP:	AGE:

Employment: Occupation	DEBTOR	SPOUSE
Name of Employer		
How long employed		
Address of Employer		

INCOME: (Estimate of average monthly income)	DEBTOR	SPOUSE
1. Current monthly gross wages, salary, and commissions (Prorate if not paid monthly.)	$__________	$__________
2. Estimated monthly overtime	$__________	$__________
3. SUBTOTAL	$__________	$__________
4. LESS PAYROLL DEDUCTIONS		
a. Payroll taxes and social security	$__________	$__________
b. Insurance	$__________	$__________
c. Union dues	$__________	$__________
d. Other (Specify): ______________________	$__________	$__________
5. SUBTOTAL OF PAYROLL DEDUCTIONS	$__________	$__________
6. TOTAL NET MONTHLY TAKE HOME PAY	$__________	$__________
7. Regular income from operation of business or profession or farm (attach detailed statement)	$__________	$__________
8. Income from real property	$__________	$__________
9. Interest and dividends	$__________	$__________
10. Alimony, maintenance or support payments payable to the debtor for the debtor's use or that of dependents listed above.	$__________	$__________
11. Social security or other government assistance (Specify) ______________________________	$__________	$__________
12. Pension or retirement income	$__________	$__________
13. Other monthly income	$__________	$__________
(Specify) ______________________________	$__________	$__________
______________________________________		

14. SUBTOTAL OF LINES 7 THROUGH 13

15. TOTAL MONTHLY INCOME
(Add amounts shown on lines 6 and 14)

$__________	$__________
$__________	$__________

16. TOTAL COMBINED MONTHLY INCOME $_______________ (Report also on Summary of Schedules)

17. Describe any increase or decrease in income reasonably anticipated to occur within the year following the filing of this document:

____

In re ______________________________, Case No. ________________________________
Debtor (If known)

SCHEDULE J -
CURRENT EXPENDITURES OF INDIVIDUAL DEBTOR(S)

Complete this schedule by estimating the average monthly expenses of the debtor and the debtor's family. Pro rate any payments made bi-weekly, quarterly, semi-annually, or annually to show monthly rate.

☐ Check this box if a joint petition is filed and debtor's spouse maintains a separate household. Complete a separate schedule of expenditures labeled "Spouse."

11. Rent or home mortgage payment (include lot rented for mobile home) $__________
 a. Are real estate taxes included? Yes _______ No _______
 b. Is property insurance included? Yes _______ No _______
2. Utilities a. Electricity and heating fuel $__________
 b. Water and sewer $__________
 c. Telephone $__________
 d. Other ____ $__________
3. Home maintenance (repairs and upkeep) $__________
4. Food $__________
5. Clothing $__________
6. Laundry and dry cleaning $__________
7. Medical and dental expenses $__________
8. Transportation (not including car payments) $__________
9. Recreation, clubs and entertainment, newspapers, magazines, etc. $__________
10. Charitable contributions $__________
11. Insurance (not deducted from wages or included in home mortgage payments)
 a. Homeowner's or renter's $__________
 b. Life $__________
 c. Health $__________
 d. Auto $__________
 e. Other ____ $__________
12. Taxes (not deducted from wages or included in home mortgage payments)
(Specify) ____ $__________
13. Installment payments: (In chapter 12 and 13 cases, do not list payments to be included in the plan)
 a. Auto $__________
 b. Other ____ $__________
 c. Other ____ $__________
14. Alimony, maintenance, and support paid to others $__________
15. Payments for support of additional dependents not living at your home $__________
16. Regular expenses from operation of business, profession, or farm
(attached detailed statement) $__________
17. Other ____ $__________

18. TOTAL MONTHLY EXPENSES (Report also on Summary of Schedules) $__________

19. Describe any increase or decrease in expenditures reasonably anticipated to occur within the year following the filing of this document:

____

20. STATEMENT OF MONTHLY NET INCOME

a. Total projected monthly income from Line 16 of Schedule I $__________

b. Total monthly expenses from Line 18 above $__________

c. Monthly net income (a. minus b.) $__________

In re ______________________, Case No. ______________________
Debtor (If known)

DECLARATION CONCERNING DEBTOR'S SCHEDULES

DECLARATION UNDER PENALTY OF PERJURY BY INDIVIDUAL DEBTOR

I declare under penalty of perjury that I have read the foregoing summary and schedules, consisting of sheets, and that they are true and correct to the best of my knowledge, (*Total shown on summary page plus 1.*) information, and belief.

Date ______________________ Signature ______________________
Debtor

Date ______________________ Signature ______________________
(*Joint Debtor, if any*)
(If joint case, both spouses must sign.)

DECLARATION AND SIGNATURE OF NON-ATTORNEY BANKRUPTCY PREPARER (See 11 U.S.C. § 110)

I declare under penalty of perjury that: (1) I am a bankruptcy petition preparer as defined in 11 U.S.C. § 110; (2) I prepared this document for compensation and have provided the debtor with a copy of this document and the notices and information required under 11 U.S.C. § 110(b), 110(h) and 342(b); and (3) if rules or guidelines have been promulgated pursuant to 11 U.S.C. § 110(h) setting a maximum fee for services chargeable by bankruptcy petition preparers, I have given the debtor notice of the maximum amounts before preparing any document for filing for a debtor or accepting any fee from the debtor, as required by that section.

______________________ ______________________
Printed or Typed Name of Bankruptcy Petition Preparer — Social Security No. (*Required by 11 U.S.C. §110(c).*)

If the bankruptcy petition preparer is not an individuall, state the name, title(if any), address, and social security number of the officer, principal, responsible person, or partner who signs this document.

____

____
Address

X ______________________ ______________________
Signature of Bankruptcy Petition Preparer — Date

Name and Social Security numbers of all other individuals who prepared or assisted in preparing this document, unless the bankruptcy petition preparer is not an individual;

If more than one person prepared this document, attach additional signed sheets conforming to the appropriate Official Form for each person.

A bankruptcy petition preparer's failure to comply with the provisions of title 11 and the Federal Rules of Bankruptcy Procedure may result in fines or imprisonment or both. 11 U.S.C. § 110; 18 U.S.C. § 156.

DECLARATION UNDER PENALTY OF PERJURY ON BEHALF OF A CORPORATION OR PARTNERSHIP

I, the ______________________ [the president or other officer or an authorized agent of the corporation or a member or an authorized agent of the partnership] of the ______________________ [corporation or partnership] named as debtor in this case, declare under penalty of perjury that I have read the foregoing summary and schedules, consisting of sheets, and that they are true and correct to the best of my knowledge, information, and belief. (*Total shown on summary page plus 1.)*

Date ______________________________ Signature ______________________________

____
[Print or type name of individual signing on behalf of debtor.]

[An individual signing on behalf of a partnership or corporation must indicate position or relationship to debtor.]

Penalty for making a false statement or concealing property: Fine of up to $500,000 or imprisonment for up to 5 years or both. 18 U.S.C. §§ 152 and 3571.

APPENDIX H

STATEMENT OF FINANCIAL AFFAIRS

Form 7 Statement of Financial Affairs

Official Form 7
(10/05)

UNITED STATES BANKRUPTCY COURT
_______ DISTRICT OF _______

In re ______________________________, **Case No.** ______________________________
Debtor **(If known)**

STATEMENT OF FINANCIAL AFFAIRS

This statement is to be completed by every debtor. Spouses filing a joint petition may file a single statement on which the information for both spouses is combined. If the case is filed under chapter 12 or chapter 13, a married debtor must furnish information for both spouses whether or not a joint petition is filed, unless the spouses are separated and a joint petition is not filed. An individual debtor engaged in business as a sole proprietor, partner, family farmer, or self-employed professional, should provide the information requested on this statement concerning all such activities as well as the individual's personal affairs. Do not include the name or address of a minor child in this statement. Indicate payments, transfers and the like to minor children by stating "a minor child." See 11 U.S.C. § 112; Fed. R. Bankr. P. 1007(m).

Questions 1 - 18 are to be completed by all debtors. Debtors that are or have been in business, as defined below, also must complete Questions 19 - 25. **If the answer to an applicable question is "None," mark the box labeled "None."** If additional space is needed for the answer to any question, use and attach a separate sheet properly identified with the case name, case number (if known), and the number of the question.

Definitions

"In business." A debtor is "in business" for the purpose of this form if the debtor is a corporation or partnership. An individual debtor is "in business" for the purpose of this form if the debtor is or has been, within six years immediately preceding the filing of this bankruptcy case, any of the following: an officer, director, managing executive, or owner of 5 percent or more of the voting or equity securities of a corporation; a partner, other than a limited partner, of a partnership; a sole proprietor or self-employed full-time or part-time. An individual debtor also may be "in business" for the purpose of this form if the debtor engages in a trade, business, or other activity, other than as an employee, to supplement income from the debtor's primary employment.

"Insider." The term "insider" includes but is not limited to: relatives of the debtor; general partners of the debtor and their relatives; corporations of which the debtor is an officer, director, or person in control; officers, directors, and any owner of 5 percent or more of the voting or equity securities of a corporate debtor and their relatives; affiliates of the debtor and insiders of such affiliates; any managing agent of the debtor. 11 U.S.C. § 101.

---

1. Income from employment or operation of business

None State the gross amount of income the debtor has received from employment, trade, or profession, or from operation of the debtor's business, including part-time activities either as an employee or in independent trade or business, from the beginning of this calendar year to the date this case was commenced. State also the gross amounts received during the **two years** immediately preceding this calendar year. (A debtor that maintains, or has maintained, financial records on the basis of a fiscal rather than a calendar year may report fiscal year income. Identify the beginning and ending dates of the debtor's fiscal year.) If a joint petition is filed, state income for each spouse separately. (Married debtors filing under chapter 12 or chapter 13 must state income of both spouses whether or not a joint petition is filed, unless the spouses are separated and a joint petition is not filed.)

AMOUNT	SOURCE

2. Income other than from employment or operation of business

None State the amount of income received by the debtor other than from employment, trade, profession, operation of the debtor's business? during the **two years** immediately preceding the commencement of this case. Give particulars. If a joint petition is filed, state income for each spouse separately. (Married debtors filing under chapter 12 or chapter 13 must state income for each spouse whether or not a joint petition is filed, unless the spouses are separated and a joint petition is not filed.)

AMOUNT	SOURCE

---

3. Payments to Creditors

Complete a. or b., as appropriate, and c.

None (a) *Individual or joint debtor(s) with primarily consumer debts:* List all payments on loans, installment purchases of goods or services, and other debts to any creditor made within **90 days** immediately preceding the commencement of this case if the aggregate value of all property that constitutes or is affected by such transfer is not less than $600. Indicate with an asterisk (*) any payments that were made to a creditor on account of a domestic support obligation or as part of an alternative repayment schedule under a plan by an approved nonprofit budgeting and creditor counseling agency. (Married debtors filing under chapter 12 or chapter 13 must include payments by either or both spouses whether or not a joint petition is filed, unless the spouses are separated and a joint petition is not filed.)

NAME AND ADDRESS OF CREDITOR PAYMENTS	DATES OF PAID	AMOUNT STILL OWING	AMOUNT

None (b) *Debtor whose debts are not primarily consumer debts:* List each payment or other transfer to any creditor made within **90** days immediately preceding the commencement of the case if the aggregate value of all property that constitutes or is affected by such transfer is less than $5,000. (Married debtors filing under chapter 12 or chapter 13 must include payments and other transfers by either or both spouses whether or not a joint petition is filed, unless the spouses are separated and a joint petition is not filed.)

NAME AND ADDRESS OF CREDITOR	DATES OF PAYMENTS/ TRANSFERS	AMOUNT PAID OR VALUE OF TRANSFERS	AMOUNT STILL OWING

None (c) *All debtors:* List all payments made within **one year** immediately preceding the commencement of this case to or for the benefit of creditors who are or were insiders. (Married debtors filing under chapter 12 or chapter 13 must include payments by either or both spouses whether or not a joint petition is filed, unless the spouses are separated and a joint petition is not filed.)

NAME AND ADDRESS OF CREDITOR AND RELATIONSHIP TO DEBTOR	DATE OF PAYMENT	AMOUNT PAID	AMOUNT STILL OWING

4. Suits and administrative proceedings, executions, garnishments and attachments

None (a) List all suits and administrative proceedings to which the debtor is or was a party within **one year** immediately preceding the filing of this bankruptcy case. (Married debtors filing under chapter 12 or chapter 13 must include information concerning either or both spouses whether or not a joint petition is filed, unless the spouses are separated and a joint petition is not filed.)

CAPTION OF SUIT AND CASE NUMBER	NATURE OF PROCEEDING	COURT OR AGENCY AND LOCATION	STATUS OR DISPOSITION

None (b) Describe all property that has been attached, garnished or seized under any legal or equitable process within **one year** immediately preceding the commencement of this case. (Married debtors filing under chapter 12 or chapter 13 must include information concerning property of either or both spouses whether or not a joint petition is filed, unless the spouses are separated and a joint petition is not filed.)

NAME AND ADDRESS OF PERSON FOR WHOSE BENEFIT PROPERTY WAS SEIZED	DATE OF SEIZURE	DESCRIPTION AND VALUE OF PROPERTY

5. Repossessions, foreclosures and returns

None List all property that has been repossessed by a creditor, sold at a foreclosure sale, transferred through a deed in lieu of foreclosure or returned to the seller of foreclosure or returned to the seller, within **one year** immediately preceding the commencement of this case. (Married debtors filing under chapter 12 or chapter 13 must include information concerning property of either or both spouses whether or not a joint petition is filed, unless the spouses are separated and a joint petition is not filed.)

NAME AND ADDRESS OF CREDITOR OR SELLER	DATE OF REPOSSESSION, FORECLOSURE SALE, TRANSFER OR RETURN	DESCRIPTION AND VALUE OF PROPERTY

6. Assignments and receiverships

None (a) Describe any assignment of property for the benefit of creditors made within **120 days** immediately preceding the commencement of this case. (Married debtors filing under chapter 12 or chapter 13 must include any assignment by either or both spouses whether or not a joint petition is filed, unless the spouses are separated and a joint petition is not filed.)

NAME AND ADDRESS OF ASSIGNEE	DATE OF ASSIGNMENT	TERMS OF ASSIGNMENT OR SETTLEMENT

None (b)List all property which has been in the hands of a custodian, receiver, or court-appointed official within **one year** immediately preceding the commencement of this case. (Married debtors filing under chapter 12 or chapter 13 must include information concerning property of either or both spouses whether or not a joint petition is filed, unless the spouses are separated and a joint petition is not filed.)

NAME AND ADDRESS OF CUSTODIAN	NAME AND LOCATION OF COURT CASE TITLE & NUMBER	DATE OF ORDER	DESCRIPTION AND VALUE OF PROPERTY

7. Gifts

None List all gifts or charitable contributions made within **one year** immediately preceding the commencement of this case except ordinary and usual gifts to family members aggregating less than $200 in value per individual family member and charitable contributions aggregating less than $100 per recipient. (Married debtors filing under chapter 12 or chapter 13 must include gifts or contributions by either or both spouses whether or not a joint petition is filed, unless the spouses are separated and a joint petition is not filed.)

NAME AND ADDRESS OF PERSON OR ORGANIZATION	RELATIONSHIP TO DEBTOR, IF ANY	DATE OF GIFT	DESCRIPTION AND VALUE OF GIFT

8. Losses

None List all losses from fire, theft, other casualty or gambling within **one year** preceding the commencement of this case **or since the commencement of this case**. (Married debtors filing under chapter 12 or chapter 13 must include losses by either or both spouses whether or not a joint petition is filed, unless the spouses are separated and a joint petition is not filed.)

DESCRIPTION AND VALUE OF PROPERTY	DESCRIPTION OF CIRCUMSTANCES AND, IF LOSS WAS COVERED IN WHOLE OR IN PART BY INSURANCE, GIVE PARTICULARS	DATE OF LOSS

9. Payments related to debt counseling or bankruptcy

None List all payments made or property transferred by or on behalf of the debtor to any persons, including attorneys, for consultation concerning debt consolidation, relief under the bankruptcy law or preparation of a petition in bankruptcy within **one year** immediately preceding the commencement of this case.

NAME AND ADDRESS OF PAYEE	DATE OF PAYMENT, NAME OF PAYER IF OTHER THAN DEBTOR	AMOUNT OF MONEY OR DESCRIPTION AND VALUE OF PROPERTY

10. Other transfers

None (a) List all other property, other than property transferred in the ordinary course of the business or financial affairs of the debtor, transferred either absolutely or as security within **two years** immediately preceding the commencement of this case. (Married debtors filing under chapter 12 or chapter 13 must include transfers by either or both spouses whether or not a joint petition is filed, unless the spouses are separated and a joint petition is not filed.)

NAME AND ADDRESS OF TRANSFEREE, RELATIONSHIP TO DEBTOR	DATE	DESCRIBE PROPERTY TRANSFERRED AND VALUE RECEIVED

None (b) List all property transferred by the debtor within **ten years** immediately preceding the commencement of this case to a self-settled trust or similar device of which the debtor is a beneficiary.

NAME OF TRUST OR OTHER DEVICE	DATE(S) OF TRANSFER(S)	AMOUNT OF MONEY OR DESCRIPTION AND VALUE OF PROPERTY OF DEBTOR'S INTEREST IN PROPERTY

11. Closed financial accounts

None List all financial accounts and instruments held in the name of the debtor or for the benefit of the debtor which were closed, sold, or otherwise transferred within **one year** immediately preceding the commencement of this case. Include checking, savings, or other financial accounts, certificates of deposit, or other instruments; shares and share accounts held in banks, credit unions, pension funds, cooperatives, associations, brokerage houses and other financial institutions. (Married debtors filing under chapter 12 or chapter 13 must include information concerning accounts or instruments held by or for either or both spouses whether or not a joint petition is filed, unless the spouses are separated and a joint petition is not filed.)

NAME AND ADDRESS OF INSTITUTION	TYPE OF ACCOUNT, LAST FOUR DIGITS OF ACCOUNT NUMBER, AND AMOUNT OF FINAL BALANCE	AMOUNT AND DATE OF SALE OR CLOSING

12. Safe deposit boxes

None List each safe deposit or other box or depository in which the debtor has or had securities, cash, or other valuables within **one year** immediately preceding the commencement of this case. (Married debtors filing under chapter 12 or chapter 13 must include boxes or depositories of either or both spouses whether or not a joint petition is filed, unless the spouses are separated and a joint petition is not filed.)

NAME AND ADDRESS OF BANK OR OTHER DEPOSITORY	NAMES AND ADDRESSES OF THOSE WITH ACCESS TO BOX OR DEPOSITORY	DESCRIPTION OF CONTENTS	DATE OF TRANSFER OR SURRENDER, IF ANY

13. Setoffs

None List all setoffs made by any creditor, including a bank, against a debt or deposit of the debtor within **90 days** preceding the commencement of this case. (Married debtors filing under chapter 12 or chapter 13 must include information concerning either or both spouses whether or not a joint petition is filed, unless the spouses are separated and a joint petition is not filed.)

NAME AND ADDRESS OF CREDITOR	DATE OF SETOFF	AMOUNT OF SETOFF

14. Property held for another person

None List all property owned by another person that the debtor holds or controls.

NAME AND ADDRESS OF OWNER	DESCRIPTION AND VALUE OF PROPERTY	LOCATION OF PROPERTY

15. Prior address of debtor

None If debtor has moved within **three years** immediately preceding the commencement of this case, list all premises which the debtor occupied during that period and vacated prior to the commencement of this case. If a joint petition is filed, report also any separate address of either spouse.

ADDRESS	NAME USED	DATES OF OCCUPANCY

16. Spouses and Former Spouses

None If the debtor resides or resided in a community property state, commonwealth, or territory (including Alaska, Arizona, California, Idaho, Louisiana, Nevada, New Mexico, Puerto Rico, Texas, Washington, or Wisconsin) within **eight years** immediately preceding the commencement of the case, identify the name of the debtor's spouse and of any former spouse who resides or resided with the debtor in the community property state.

NAME

17. Environmental Information.

For the purpose of this question, the following definitions apply:

"Environmental Law" means any federal, state, or local statute or regulation regulating pollution, contamination, releases of hazardous or toxic substances, wastes or material into the air, land, soil, surface water, groundwater, or other medium, including, but not limited to, statutes or regulations regulating the cleanup of these substances, wastes, or material.

"Site" means any location, facility, or property as defined under any Environmental Law, whether or not presently or formerly owned or operated by the debtor, including, but not limited to, disposal sites.

"Hazardous Material" means anything defined as a hazardous waste, hazardous substance, toxic substance, hazardous material, pollutant, or contaminant or similar term under an Environmental Law.

None (a) List the name and address of every site for which the debtor has received notice in writing by a governmental unit that it may be liable or potentially liable under or in violation of an Environmental Law. Indicate the governmental unit, the date of the notice, and, if known, the Environmental Law:

SITE NAME AND ADDRESS	NAME AND ADDRESS OF GOVERNMENTAL UNIT	DATE OF NOTICE	ENVIRONMENTAL LAW

None (b) List the name and address of every site for which the debtor provided notice to a governmental unit of a release of Hazardous Material. Indicate the governmental unit to which the notice was sent and the date of the notice.

SITE NAME AND ADDRESS	NAME AND ADDRESS OF GOVERNMENTAL UNIT	DATE OF NOTICE	ENVIRONMENTAL LAW

None (c) List all judicial or administrative proceedings, including settlements or orders, under any Environmental Law with respect to which the debtor is or was a party. Indicate the name and address of the governmental unit that is or was a party to the proceeding, and the docket number.

NAME AND ADDRESS OF GOVERNMENTAL UNIT	DOCKET NUMBER	STATUS OR DISPOSITION

18. Nature, location and name of business

None (a) *If the debtor is an individual,* list the names, addresses, taxpayer identification numbers, nature of the businesses, and beginning and ending dates of all businesses in which the debtor was an officer, director, partner, or managing executive of a corporation, partner in a partnership, sole proprietor, or was self-employed in a trade, profession, or other activity either full- or part-time within **six years** immediately preceding the commencement of this case, or in which the debtor owned 5 percent or more of the voting or equity securities within **six years** immediately preceding the commencement of this case.

If the debtor is a partnership, list the names, addresses, taxpayer identification numbers, nature of the businesses, and beginning and ending dates of all businesses in which the debtor was a partner or owned 5 percent or more of the voting or equity securities, within **six years** immediately preceding the commencement of this case.

If the debtor is a corporation, list the names, addresses, taxpayer identification numbers, nature of the businesses, and beginning and ending dates of all businesses in which the debtor was a partner or owned 5 percent or more of the voting or equity securities within **six years** immediately preceding the commencement of this case.

NAME	LAST FOUR DIGITS OF SOC. SEC. NO./ COMPLETE EIN OR OTHER TAXPAYER I.D. NO.	ADDRESS	NATURE OF BUSINESS	BEGINNING AND ENDING DATES

None (b) Identify any business listed in response to subdivision a., above, that is "single asset real estate" as defined in 11 U.S.C. § 101.

NAME	ADDRESS

The following questions are to be completed by every debtor that is a corporation or partnership and by any individual debtor who is or has been, within **six years** immediately preceding the commencement of this case, any of the following: an officer, director, managing executive, or owner of more than 5 percent of the voting or equity securities of a corporation; a partner, other than a limited partner, of a partnership; a sole proprietor or self-employed in a trade, profession, or other activity, either full- or part-time.

(An individual or joint debtor should complete this portion of the statement **only** if the debtor is or has been in business, as defined above, within six years immediately preceding the commencement of this case. A debtor who has not been in business within those six years should go directly to the signature page.)

19. Books, records and financial statements

None (a) List all bookkeepers and accountants who within **two years** immediately preceding the filing of this bankruptcy case kept or supervised the keeping of books of account and records of the debtor.

NAME AND ADDRESS	DATES SERVICES RENDERED

None b. List all firms or individuals who within two years immediately preceding the filing of this bankruptcy case have audited the books of account and records, or prepared a financial statement of the debtor.

NAME	ADDRESS	DATES SERVICES RENDERED

None (c) List all firms or individuals who at the time of the commencement of this case were in possession of the books of account and records of the debtor. If any of the books of account and records are not available, explain.

NAME AND ADDRESS	DATES SERVICES RENDERED

None (d) List all financial institutions, creditors and other parties, including mercantile and trade agencies, to whom a financial statement was issued within **two years** immediately preceding the commencement of this case.

NAME AND ADDRESS	DATE ISSUED

---

20. Inventories

None (a) List the dates of the last two inventories taken of your property, the name of the person who supervised the taking of each inventory, and the dollar amount and basis of each inventory.

DATE OF INVENTORY	INVENTORY SUPERVISOR	DOLLAR AMOUNT OF INVENTORY (Specify cost, market or other basis)

None (b) List the name and address of the person having possession of the records of each of the two inventories reported in a., above.

DATE OF INVENTORY	NAME AND ADDRESSES OF CUSTODIAN OF INVENTORY RECORDS

21. Current Partners, Officers, Directors and Shareholders

None (a) If the debtor is a partnership, list the nature and percentage of partnership interest of each member of the partnership.

NAME AND ADDRESS	NATURE OF INTEREST	PERCENTAGE OF INTEREST

None (b) If the debtor is a corporation, list all officers and directors of the corporation, and each stockholder who directly or indirectly owns, controls, or holds 5 percent or more of the voting or equity securities of the corporation.

NAME AND ADDRESS	TITLE	NATURE AND PERCENTAGE OF STOCK OWNERSHIP

22. Former partners, officers, directors and shareholders

None (a) If the debtor is a partnership, list each member who withdrew from the partnership within **one year** immediately preceding the commencement of this case.

NAME	ADDRESS	DATE OF WITHDRAWAL

None (b) If the debtor is a corporation, list all officers, or directors whose relationship with the corporation terminated within **one year** immediately preceding the commencement of this case.

NAME AND ADDRESS	TITLE	DATE OF TERMINATION

23. Withdrawals from a partnership or distributions by a corporation

None If the debtor is a partnership or corporation, list all withdrawals or distributions credited or given to an insider, including compensation in any form, bonuses, loans, stock redemptions, options exercised and any other perquisite during **one year** immediately preceding the commencement of this case.

NAME & ADDRESS OF RECIPIENT, RELATIONSHIP TO DEBTOR	DATE AND PURPOSE OF WITHDRAWAL	AMOUNT OF MONEY OR DESCRIPTION AND VALUE OF PROPERTY

---

24. Tax Consolidation Group.

None If the debtor is a corporation, list the name and federal taxpayer identification number of the parent corporation of any consolidated group for tax purposes of which the debtor has been a member at any time within **six years** immediately preceding the commencement of the case.

NAME OF PARENT CORPORATION	TAXPAYER IDENTIFICATION NUMBER (EIN)

---

25. Pension Funds.

None If the debtor is not an individual, list the name and federal taxpayer identification number of any pension fund to which the debtor, as an employer, has been responsible for contributing at any time within **six years** immediately preceding the commencement of the case.

NAME OF PENSION FUND	TAXPAYER IDENTIFICATION NUMBER (EIN)

APPENDIX I

PROOF OF CLAIM

(If completed by an individual or individual and spouse)

I declare under penalty of perjury that I have read the answers contained in the foregoing statement of financial affairs and any attachments thereto and that they are true and correct.

Date ________________________________ Signature ____________________________
of Debtor

Date ________________________________ Signature ____________________________
of Joint Debtor (if any)

[If completed on behalf of a partnership or corporation]

I, declare under penalty of perjury that I have read the answers contained in the foregoing statement of financial affairs and any attachments thereto and that they are true and correct to the best of my knowledge, information and belief.

Date ________________________________ Signature ____________________________

____
Print Name and Title

[An individual signing on behalf of a partnership or corporation must indicate position or relationship to debtor.]

____continuation sheets attached

Penalty for making a false statement: Fine of up to $500,000 or imprisonment for up to 5 years, or both. 18 U.S. C. § 152 and 3571

DECLARATION OF SIGNATURE OF NON-ATTORNEY BANKRUPTCY PETITION PREPARER (See 11 U.S.C. § 110)

I declare under penalty of perjury that: 1) I am a bankruptcy petition preparer as defined in 11 U.S.C. § 110; (2) I prepared this document for compensation and have provided the debtor with a copy of this document and the notices and information required under 11 U.S.C. §§ 110(b), 110(h), and 342(b); and, (3) if rules or guidelines have been promulgated pursuant to 11 U.S.C. § 110(h) setting a maximum fee for services chargeable by bankruptcy petition preparers, I have given the debtor notice of the maximum amount before preparing any document for filing for a debtor or accepting any fee from the debtor, as required by that section.

________________________________ ________________________________

Printed or Typed Name and Title, if any, of Bankruptcy Petition Preparer

Social Security No. (Required by 11 U.S.C. § 110.)

If the bankruptcy petition preparer is not an individual, state the name, title (if any), address and social security number of the officer, principal, responsible person, or partner who signs this document.

____

____

Address

x __________________________________ _______________________________________

Signature of Bankruptcy Petitioner Preparer Date

Names and Social Security numbers of all other individuals who prepared or assisted in preparing this document unless the bankruptcy petition preparer is not an individual:

If more than one person prepared this document, attach additional signed sheets conforming to the appropriate Official Form for each person.

A bankruptcy petition preparer's failure to comply with the provisions of title II and the Federal Rules of Bankruptcy Procedure may result in fines or imprisonment or both. 18 U.S.C. §156.

FORM B10 (Official Form 10) (10/05)

<table>
<tr><td colspan="2">UNITED STATES BANKRUPTCY COURT DISTRICT OF</td><td rowspan="4">PROOF OF CLAIM

THIS SPACE IS FOR COURT USE ONLY</td></tr>
<tr><td>Name of Debtor</td><td>Case Number</td></tr>
<tr><td colspan="2">NOTE: This form should not be used to make a claim for an administrative expense arising after the commencement of the case. A "request" for payment of an administrative expense may be filed pursuant to 11 U.S.C. § 503.</td></tr>
<tr><td>Name of Creditor (The person or other entity to whom the debtor owes money or property)

Name and Address Where Notices Should be Sent</td><td>☐ Check box if you are aware that anyone else has filed a proof of claim relating to your claim. Attach copy of statement giving particulars.
☐ Check box if you have never received any notices from the bankruptcy court in this case.
☐ Check box if the address differs from the address on the envelope sent to you by the court.</td></tr>
<tr><td>Last four digits of account or other number by which creditor identifies debtor:

083805</td><td colspan="2">Check here ☐ replaces

if this claim ☐ amends previously filed claims dated: ____________________</td></tr>
</table>

1. Basis for Claim

- ☐ Goods sold
- ☐ Services performed
- ☐ Money loaned
- ☐ Personal injury/wrongful death
- ☐ Taxes
- ☐ Other:
- ☐ Retiree benefits as defined in 11 U.S.C. § 1114(a)
- ☐ Wages, salaries and compensation (fill out below)

Last four digits of your SS#:_____________

Unpaid compensation for services performed

from _____________to________________

(date) (date)

2. **Date debt was incurred:**	3. **If court judgment, date obtained:**

4. **Classification of Claim.** Check the appropriate box or boxes that best describe your claim and state the amount of the claims at the time case filed

See reverse side for important explanations.

Unsecured Nonpriority Claim:
See Attached Supplement

☐ Check this box if: a) there is not collateral or lien securing your claim, or b) your claim exceeds the value of the property securing it, or if c) none or only part of your claim is entitled to priority.

Secured Claim

☐ Check this box if your claim is secured by collateral (including a right of setoff)

Brief Description of Collateral:

☐ Real Estate ☐ Motor Vehicle ☐ Other ______

Value of Collateral: $____________

Amount of arrearage and other charges at time case filed included in

Secured claim, if any: $ ______________________

Unsecured Priority Claim

☐ Check this box if you have an unsecured priority claim, all or part of which is entitled to priority.

Amount entitled to priority $ ___________
Specify the priority of the claim:

☐ Domestic support obligation under 11 U.S.C. § 507(a)(I)(A) or (a)(I)(B)

☐ Up to $2,225* of deposits toward purchase, lease, or rental of property or services for personal, family, or household use – 11 U.S.C. § 507(a)(7).

☐ Wages, salaries, or commissions (up to $10,000), * earned within 180 days before filing of the bankruptcy petition or cessation of the debtor's business, whichever is earlier – 11 U.S.C. § 507(a)(4).

☐ Taxes or penalties owed to governmental units – 11 U.S.C. § 507(a)(8).

☐ Contributions to an employee benefit plan – 11 U.S.C. § 507(a)(5).

☐ Other – Specify applicable paragraph of 11 U.S.C. § 507(a)(____).

**Amounts are subject to adjustment on 4/1/07 and every 3 years thereafter with respect to cases commenced on or after the date of adjustment.*

5.	**Total Amount of Claim at Time Case Filed:**	$_______ (unsecured)	$_______ (secured)	$_______ (priority)	$_______ (Total)

❒ Check this box if claim includes interest or other charges in addition to the principal amount of the claim. Attach itemized statement of all interest or additional charges.

6. **Credits:** The amount of all payments on this claim has been credited and deducted for the purpose of making this proof of claim. 7. **Supporting Documents:** *Attach copies of supporting documents,* such as promissory notes, purchase orders, invoices, itemized statements of running accounts, contracts, court judgments, mortgages, security agreements, and evidence of perfection of lien. DO NOT SEND ORIGINAL DOCUMENTS. If the documents are not available, explain. If the documents are voluminous, attach a summary. 8. **Date Stamped Copy:** To receive an acknowledgment of the filing of your claim, enclose a stamped, self-addressed envelope and copy of this proof of claim.	THIS SPACE IS FOR COURT USE ONLY
Date Sign and print the name and title, of any, of the creditor or other person authorized to file this claim (attach copy of power of attorney, if any): By: ____________________________ Its:	

Penalty for presenting fraudulent claim: Fine of up to $500,000 or imprisonment for up to 5 years, or both. 18 U.S.C. §§ 152 and 3571.

APPENDIX J

EXCERPTS FROM THE ABA MODEL RULES OF PROFESSIONAL CONDUCT

RULE 1.2 - SCOPE OF REPRESENTATION

(a) A lawyer shall abide by a client's decisions concerning the objectives of representation, subject to paragraphs (c), (d) and (e), and shall consult with the client as to the means by which they are to be pursued. A lawyer shall abide by a client's decision whether to accept an offer of settlement of a matter. In a criminal case, the lawyer shall abide by the client's decision, after consultation with the lawyer, as to a plea to be entered, whether to waive jury trial and whether the client will testify.

(b) A lawyer's representation of a client, including representation by appointment, does not constitute an endorsement of the client's political, economic, social or moral views or activities.

(c) A lawyer may limit the objectives of the representation if the client consents after consultation.

(d) A lawyer shall not counsel a client to engage, or assist a client, in conduct that the lawyer knows is criminal or fraudulent, but a lawyer may discuss the legal consequences of any proposed course of conduct with a client and may counsel or assist a client to make a good faith effort to determine the validity, scope, meaning or application of the law.

(e) When a lawyer knows that a client expects assistance not permitted by the rules of professional conduct or other law, the lawyer shall consult with the client regarding the relevant limitations on the lawyer's conduct.

Comment

Scope of Representation

Both lawyer and client have authority and responsibility in the objectives and means of representation. The client has ultimate authority to determine the purposes to be served by legal representation, within the limits imposed by law and the lawyer's professional obligations. Within those limits, a client also has a right to consult with the lawyer about the means to be used in pursuing those objectives. At the same time, a lawyer is not required to pursue objectives or employ means simply because a client may wish that the lawyer do so. A clear distinction between objectives and means sometimes cannot be drawn, and in many cases the client-lawyer relationship partakes of a joint undertaking. In questions of means, the lawyer should assume responsibility for technical and legal tactical issues, but should defer to the client regarding such questions as the expense to be incurred and concern for third persons who might be adversely affected. Law defining the lawyer's scope of authority in litigation varies among jurisdictions.

In a case in which the client appears to be suffering mental disability, the lawyer's duty to abide by the client's decisions is to be guided by reference to Rule 1.14.

Independence from Client's Views or Activities

Legal representation should not be denied to people who are unable to afford legal services, or whose cause is controversial or the subject of popular disapproval. By the same token, representing a client does not constitute approval of the client's views or activities.

Services Limited in Objectives or Means

The objectives or scope of services provided by a lawyer may be limited by agreement with the client or by the terms under which the lawyer's services are made available to the client. For example, a retainer may be for a specifically defined purpose. Representation provided through a legal aid agency may be subject to limitations on the types of cases the agency handles. When a lawyer has been retained by an insurer to represent an insured, the representation may be limited to matters related to the insurance coverage. The terms upon which representation is undertaken may exclude specific objectives or means. Such limitations may exclude objectives or means that the lawyer regards as repugnant or imprudent.

An agreement concerning the scope of representation must accord with the Rules of Professional Conduct and other law. Thus, the client may not be asked to agree to representation so limited in scope as to violate Rule 1.1, or to surrender the right to terminate the lawyer's services or the right to settle litigation that the lawyer might wish to continue.

Criminal, Fraudulent and Prohibited Transactions

A lawyer is required to give an honest opinion about the actual consequences that appear likely to result from a client's conduct. The fact that a client uses advice in a course of action that is criminal or fraudulent does not, of itself, make a lawyer a party to the course of action. However, a lawyer may not knowingly assist a client in criminal or fraudulent conduct. There is a critical distinction between presenting an analysis of legal aspects of questionable conduct and recommending the means by which a crime or fraud might be committed with impunity.

When the client's course of action has already begun and is continuing, the lawyer's responsibility is especially delicate. The lawyer is not permitted to reveal the client's wrongdoing, except where permitted by Rule 1.6. However, the lawyer is required to avoid furthering the purpose, for example, by suggesting how it might be concealed. A lawyer may not continue assisting a client in conduct that the lawyer originally supposes is legally proper but then discovers is criminal or fraudulent. Withdrawal from the representation, therefore, may be required.

Where the client is a fiduciary, the lawyer may be charged with special obligations in dealings with a beneficiary.

Paragraph (d) applies whether or not the defrauded party is a party to the transaction. Hence, a lawyer should not participate in a sham transaction; for example, a transaction to effectuate criminal or fraudulent escape of tax liability. Paragraph (d) does not preclude undertaking a criminal defense incident to a general retainer for legal services to a lawful enterprise. The last clause of paragraph (d) recognizes that determining the validity or interpretation of a statute or regulation may require a course of action involving disobedience of the statute or regulation or of the interpretation placed upon it by governmental authorities.

Model Code Comparison

Paragraph (a) has no counterpart in the Disciplinary Rules of the Model Code. EC 7-7 stated: "In certain areas of legal representation not affecting the merits of the cause or substantially prejudicing the rights of a client, a lawyer is entitled to make decisions on his own. But otherwise the authority to make decisions is exclusively that of the client. . . ." EC 7-8 stated that "[I]n the final analysis, however, the . . . decision whether to forego legally available objectives or methods because of nonlegal factors is ultimately for the client. . . . In the event that the client in a nonadjudicatory matter insists upon a course of conduct that is contrary to the judgment and advice of the lawyer but not prohibited by Disciplinary Rules, the lawyer may withdraw from the employment." DR 7-101(A)(1) provided that a lawyer "shall not intentionally . . . fail to seek the lawful objectives of his client through reasonably available means permitted by law. . . . A lawyer does not violate this Disciplinary Rule, however, by . . . avoiding offensive tactics. . . ."

Paragraph (b) has no counterpart in the Model Code.

With regard to Paragraph (c), DR 7-101(B)(1) provided that a lawyer may, "where permissible, exercise his professional judgment to waive or fail to assert a right or position of his client."

With regard to Paragraph (d), DR 7-102(A)(7) provided that a lawyer shall not "counsel or assist his client in conduct that the lawyer knows to be illegal or fraudulent." DR 7-102(A)(6) provided that a lawyer shall not "participate in the creation or preservation of evidence when he knows or it is obvious that the evidence is false." DR 7-106 provided that a lawyer shall not "advise his client to disregard a standing rule of a tribunal or a ruling of a tribunal . . . but he may take appropriate steps in good faith to test the validity of such rule or ruling." EC 7-5 stated that a lawyer "should never encourage or aid his client to commit criminal acts or counsel his client on how to violate the law and avoid punishment therefor."

With regard to Paragraph (c), DR 2-110(C)(1)(c) provided that a lawyer may withdraw from representation if a client "insists" that the lawyer engage in "conduct that is illegal or that is prohibited under the Disciplinary Rules." DR 9-101(C) provided that "a lawyer shall not state or imply that he is able to influence improperly . . . any tribunal, legislative body or public official."

RULE 1.6 - CONFIDENTIALITY OF INFORMATION

(a) A lawyer shall not reveal information relating to the representation of a client unless the client gives informed consent, the disclosure is impliedly authorized in order to carry out the representation or the disclosure is permitted by paragraph (b).

(b) A lawyer may reveal such information relating to the representation of a client to the extent the lawyer reasonably believes necessary:

(1) to prevent reasonably certain death or substantial bodily harm;

(2) to prevent the client from committing a crime or fraud that is reasonably certain to result in substantial injury to the financial interests or property of another and in furtherance of which the client has used or is using the lawyer's services;

(3) to prevent, mitigate or rectify substantial injury to the financial interests or property of another that is reasonably certain to result or has resulted from the client's commission of a crime or fraud in furtherance of which the client has used the lawyer's services;

(4) to secure legal advice about the lawyer's compliance with these Rules;

(5) to establish a claim or defense on behalf of the lawyer in a controversy between the lawyer and the client, to establish a defense to a criminal charge or civil claim against the lawyer based upon conduct in which the client was involved, or to respond to allegations in any proceeding concerning the lawyer's representation of the client; or

(6) to comply with other law or a court order.

Comment

[1] This Rule governs the disclosure by a lawyer of information relating to the representation of a client during the lawyer's representation of the client. See Rule 1.18 for the lawyer's duties with respect to information provided to the lawyer by a prospective client, Rule 1.9(c)(2) for the lawyer's duty not to reveal information relating to the lawyer's prior representation of a former client and Rules 1.8(b) and 1.9(c)(1) for the lawyer's duties with respect to the use of such information to the disadvantage of clients and former clients.

[2] A fundamental principle in the client-lawyer relationship is that, in the absence of the client's informed consent, the lawyer must not reveal information relating to the representation. See Rule 1.0(e) for the definition of informed consent. This contributes to the trust that is the hallmark of the client-lawyer relationship. The client is thereby encouraged to seek legal assistance and to communicate fully and frankly with the lawyer even as to embarrassing or legally damaging subject matter. The lawyer needs this information to represent the client effectively and, if necessary, to advise the client to refrain from wrongful conduct. Almost without exception, clients come to lawyers in order to determine their rights and what is, in the complex of laws and regulations, deemed to be legal and correct. Based upon experience, lawyers know that almost all clients follow the advice given, and the law is upheld.

[3] The principle of client-lawyer confidentiality is given effect by related bodies of law: the attorney-client privilege, the work product doctrine and the rule of confidentiality established in professional ethics. The attorney-client privilege and work-product doctrine apply in judicial and other proceedings in which a lawyer may be called as a witness or otherwise required to produce evidence concerning a client. The rule of client-lawyer confidentiality applies in situations other than those where evidence is sought from the lawyer through compulsion of law. The confidentiality rule, for example, applies not only to matters communicated in confidence by the client but also to all information relating to the representation, whatever its source. A lawyer may not disclose

such information except as authorized or required by the Rules of Professional Conduct or other law. See also Scope.

[4] Paragraph (a) prohibits a lawyer from revealing information relating to the representation of a client. This prohibition also applies to disclosures by a lawyer that do not in themselves reveal protected information but could reasonably lead to the discovery of such information by a third person. A lawyer's use of a hypothetical to discuss issues relating to the representation is permissible so long as there is no reasonable likelihood that the listener will be able to ascertain the identity of the client or the situation involved.

Authorized Disclosure

[5] Except to the extent that the client's instructions or special circumstances limit that authority, a lawyer is impliedly authorized to make disclosures about a client when appropriate in carrying out the representation. In some situations, for example, a lawyer may be impliedly authorized to admit a fact that cannot properly be disputed or to make a disclosure that facilitates a satisfactory conclusion to a matter. Lawyers in a firm may, in the course of the firm's practice, disclose to each other information relating to a client of the firm, unless the client has instructed that particular information be confined to specified lawyers.

Disclosure Adverse to Client

[6] Although the public interest is usually best served by a strict rule requiring lawyers to preserve the confidentiality of information relating to the representation of their clients, the confidentiality rule is subject to limited exceptions. Paragraph (b)(1) recognizes the overriding value of life and physical integrity and permits disclosure reasonably necessary to prevent reasonably certain death or substantial bodily harm. Such harm is reasonably certain to occur if it will be suffered imminently or if there is a present and substantial threat that a person will suffer such harm at a later date if the lawyer fails to take action necessary to eliminate the threat. Thus, a lawyer who knows that a client has accidentally discharged toxic waste into a town's water supply may reveal this information to the authorities if there is a present and substantial risk that a person who drinks the water will contract a life-threatening or debilitating disease and the lawyer's disclosure is necessary to eliminate the threat or reduce the number of victims.

[7] Paragraph (b)(2) is a limited exception to the rule of confidentiality that permits the lawyer to reveal information to the extent necessary to enable affected persons or appropriate authorities to prevent the client from commit-

ting a crime or fraud, as defined in Rule 1.0(d), that is reasonably certain to result in substantial injury to the financial or property interests of another and in furtherance of which the client has used or is using the lawyer's services. Such a serious abuse of the client-lawyer relationship by the client forfeits the protection of this Rule. The client can, of course, prevent such disclosure by refraining from the wrongful conduct. Although paragraph (b)(2) does not require the lawyer to reveal the client's misconduct, the lawyer may not counsel or assist the client in conduct the lawyer knows is criminal or fraudulent. See Rule 1.2(d). See also Rule 1.16 with respect to the lawyer's obligation or right to withdraw from the representation of the client in such circumstances, and Rule 1.13(c), which permits the lawyer, where the client is an organization, to reveal information relating to the representation in limited circumstances.

[8] Paragraph (b)(3) addresses the situation in which the lawyer does not learn of the client's crime or fraud until after it has been consummated. Although the client no longer has the option of preventing disclosure by refraining from the wrongful conduct, there will be situations in which the loss suffered by the affected person can be prevented, rectified or mitigated. In such situations, the lawyer may disclose information relating to the representation to the extent necessary to enable the affected persons to prevent or mitigate reasonably certain losses or to attempt to recoup their losses. Paragraph (b)(3) does not apply when a person who has committed a crime or fraud thereafter employs a lawyer for representation concerning that offense.

[9] A lawyer's confidentiality obligations do not preclude a lawyer from securing confidential legal advice about the lawyer's personal responsibility to comply with these Rules. In most situations, disclosing information to secure such advice will be impliedly authorized for the lawyer to carry out the representation. Even when the disclosure is not impliedly authorized, paragraph (b)(4) permits such disclosure because of the importance of a lawyer's compliance with the Rules of Professional Conduct.

[10] Where a legal claim or disciplinary charge alleges complicity of the lawyer in a client's conduct or other misconduct of the lawyer involving representation of the client, the lawyer may respond to the extent the lawyer reasonably believes necessary to establish a defense. The same is true with respect to a claim involving the conduct or representation of a former client. Such a charge can arise in a civil, criminal, disciplinary or other proceeding and can be based on a wrong allegedly committed by the lawyer against the client or on a wrong alleged by a third person, for example, a person claiming to have been defrauded by the lawyer and client acting together. The lawyer's right to respond arises when an assertion of such complicity has been made. Paragraph (b)(5)

does not require the lawyer to await the commencement of an action or proceeding that charges such complicity, so that the defense may be established by responding directly to a third party who has made such an assertion. The right to defend also applies, of course, where a proceeding has been commenced.

[11] A lawyer entitled to a fee is permitted by paragraph (b)(5) to prove the services rendered in an action to collect it. This aspect of the rule expresses the principle that the beneficiary of a fiduciary relationship may not exploit it to the detriment of the fiduciary.

[12] Other law may require that a lawyer disclose information about a client. Whether such a law supersedes Rule 1.6 is a question of law beyond the scope of these Rules. When disclosure of information relating to the representation appears to be required by other law, the lawyer must discuss the matter with the client to the extent required by Rule 1.4. If, however, the other law supersedes this Rule and requires disclosure, paragraph (b)(6) permits the lawyer to make such disclosures as are necessary to comply with the law.

[13] A lawyer may be ordered to reveal information relating to the representation of a client by a court or by another tribunal or governmental entity claiming authority pursuant to other law to compel the disclosure. Absent informed consent of the client to do otherwise, the lawyer should assert on behalf of the client all nonfrivolous claims that the order is not authorized by other law or that the information sought is protected against disclosure by the attorney-client privilege or other applicable law. In the event of an adverse ruling, the lawyer must consult with the client about the possibility of appeal to the extent required by Rule 1.4. Unless review is sought, however, paragraph (b)(6) permits the lawyer to comply with the court's order.

[14] Paragraph (b) permits disclosure only to the extent the lawyer reasonably believes the disclosure is necessary to accomplish one of the purposes specified. Where practicable, the lawyer should first seek to persuade the client to take suitable action to obviate the need for disclosure. In any case, a disclosure adverse to the client's interest should be no greater than the lawyer reasonably believes necessary to accomplish the purpose. If the disclosure will be made in connection with a judicial proceeding, the disclosure should be made in a manner that limits access to the information to the tribunal or other persons having a need to know it and appropriate protective orders or other arrangements should be sought by the lawyer to the fullest extent practicable.

[15] Paragraph (b) permits but does not require the disclosure of information relating to a client's representation to accomplish the purposes specified in paragraphs (b)(1) through (b)(6). In exercising the discretion conferred by this Rule, the lawyer may consider such factors as the nature of the lawyer's rela-

tionship with the client and with those who might be injured by the client, the lawyer's own involvement in the transaction and factors that may extenuate the conduct in question. A lawyer's decision not to disclose as permitted by paragraph (b) does not violate this Rule. Disclosure may be required, however, by other Rules. Some Rules require disclosure only if such disclosure would be permitted by paragraph (b). See Rules 1.2(d), 4.1(b), 8.1 and 8.3. Rule 3.3, on the other hand, requires disclosure in some circumstances regardless of whether such disclosure is permitted by this Rule. See Rule 3.3(c).

Acting Competently to Preserve Confidentiality

[16] A lawyer must act competently to safeguard information relating to the representation of a client against inadvertent or unauthorized disclosure by the lawyer or other persons who are participating in the representation of the client or who are subject to the lawyer's supervision. See Rules 1.1, 5.1 and 5.3.

[17] When transmitting a communication that includes information relating to the representation of a client, the lawyer must take reasonable precautions to prevent the information from coming into the hands of unintended recipients. This duty, however, does not require that the lawyer use special security measures if the method of communication affords a reasonable expectation of privacy. Special circumstances, however, may warrant special precautions. Factors to be considered in determining the reasonableness of the lawyer's expectation of confidentiality include the sensitivity of the information and the extent to which the privacy of the communication is protected by law or by a confidentiality agreement. A client may require the lawyer to implement special security measures not required by this Rule or may give informed consent to the use of a means of communication that would otherwise be prohibited by this Rule.

Former Client

[18] The duty of confidentiality continues after the client-lawyer relationship has terminated. See Rule 1.9(c)(2). See Rule 1.9(c)(1) for the prohibition against using such information to the disadvantage of the former client

Model Code Comparison

Rule 1.6 eliminates the two-pronged duty under the Model Code in favor of a single standard protecting all information about a client "relating to representation." Under DR 4-101, the requirement applied to information protected by the attorney-client privilege and to information "gained in" the professional relationship that "the client has requested be held inviolate or the disclosure of which would be embarrassing or would be likely to be detrimental to the client." EC 4-4 added that the duty differed from the evidentiary privilege in that it existed "without regard to the nature or source of information or the fact that others share the knowledge." Rule 1.6 imposes confidentiality on information relating to the representation even if it is acquired before or after the relationship existed. It does not require the client to indicate information that is to be confidential, or permit the lawyer to speculate whether particular information might be embarrassing or detrimental.

Paragraph (a) permits a lawyer to disclose information where impliedly authorized to do so in order to carry out the representation. Under DR 4-101(B) and (C), a lawyer was not permitted to reveal "confidences" unless the client first consented after disclosure.

Paragraph (b) redefines the exceptions to the requirement of confidentiality. Regarding paragraph (b)(1), DR 4-101(C)(3) provided that a lawyer "may reveal [t]he intention of his client to commit a crime and the information necessary to prevent the crime." This option existed regardless of the seriousness of the proposed crime.

With regard to paragraph (b)(2), DR 4-101(C)(4) provided that a lawyer may reveal "[c]onfidences or secrets necessary to establish or collect his fee or to defend himself or his employers or associates against an accusation of wrongful conduct." Paragraph (b)(2) enlarges the exception to include disclosure of information relating to claims by the lawyer other than for the lawyer's fee; for example, recovery of property from the client.

RULE 1.13 - ORGANIZATION AS CLIENT

(a) A lawyer employed or retained by an organization represents the organization acting through its duly authorized constituents.

(b) If a lawyer for an organization knows that an officer, employee or other person associated with the organization is engaged in action, intends to act or refuses to act in a matter related to the representation that is a violation of a legal obligation to the organization, or a violation of law that reasonably might be imputed to the organization, and is likely to result in substantial injury to the organization, then the lawyer shall proceed as is reasonably necessary in the best interest of the organization. Unless the lawyer reasonably believes that it is not necessary in the best interest of the organization to do so, the lawyer shall refer the matter to higher authority in the organization, including, if warranted by the circumstances to the highest authority that can act on behalf of the organization as determined by applicable law:

(c) Except as provided in paragraph (d), if

(1) despite the lawyer's efforts in accordance with paragraph (b) the highest authority that can act on behalf of the organization insists upon or fails to address in a timely and appropriate manner an action, or a refusal to act, that is clearly a violation of law, and
(2) the lawyer reasonably believes that the violation is reasonably certain to result in substantial injury to the organization,

then the lawyer may reveal information relating to the representation whether or not Rule 1.6 permits such disclosure, but only if and to the extent the lawyer reasonably believes necessary to prevent substantial injury to the organization.

(d) Paragraph (c) shall not apply with respect to information relating to a lawyer's representation of an organization to investigate an alleged violation of law, or to defend the organization or an officer, employee or other constituent associated with the organization against a claim arising out of an alleged violation of law.

(e) A lawyer who reasonably believes that he or she has been discharged because of the lawyer's actions taken pursuant to paragraphs (b) or (c), or who withdraws under circumstances that require or permit the lawyer to take action under either of those paragraphs, shall proceed as the lawyer reasonably believes necessary to assure that the organization's highest authority is informed of the lawyer's discharge or withdrawal.

(f) In dealing with an organization's directors, officers, employees, members, shareholders or other constituents, a lawyer shall explain the identity of the client when the lawyer knows or reasonably should know that the organization's interests are adverse to those of the constituents with whom the lawyer is dealing.

(g) A lawyer representing an organization may also represent any of its directors, officers, employees, members, shareholders or other constituents, subject to the provisions of Rule 1.7. If the organization's consent to the dual representation is required by Rule 1.7, the consent shall be given by an appropriate official of the organization other than the individual who is to be represented, or by the shareholders.

Comment

The Entity as the Client

[1] An organizational client is a legal entity, but it cannot act except through its officers, directors, employees, shareholders and other constituents. Officers, directors, employees and shareholders are the constituents of the corporate organizational client. The duties defined in this Comment apply equally to unincorporated associations. "Other constituents" as used in this Comment means the positions equivalent to officers, directors, employees and shareholders held by persons acting for organizational clients that are not corporations.

[2] When one of the constituents of an organizational client communicates with the organization's lawyer in that person's organizational capacity, the communication is protected by Rule 1.6. Thus, by way of example, if an organizational client requests its lawyer to investigate allegations of wrongdoing, interviews made in the course of that investigation between the lawyer and the client's employees or other constituents are covered by Rule 1.6. This does not mean, however, that constituents of an organizational client are the clients of the lawyer. The lawyer may not disclose to such constituents information relating to the representation except for disclosures explicitly or impliedly authorized by the organizational client in order to carry out the representation or as otherwise permitted by Rule 1.6.

[3] When constituents of the organization make decisions for it, the decisions ordinarily must be accepted by the lawyer even if their utility or prudence is doubtful. Decisions concerning policy and operations, including ones entailing serious risk, are not as such in the lawyer's province. Paragraph (b) makes clear, however, that when the lawyer knows that the organization is likely to be substantially injured by action of an officer or other constituent that violates a legal obligation to the organization or is in violation of law that might be imputed to the organization, the lawyer must proceed as is reasonably necessary in the best interest of the organization. As defined in Rule 1.0(f), knowledge can be inferred from circumstances, and a lawyer cannot ignore the obvious.

[4] In determining how to proceed under paragraph (b), the lawyer should give due consideration to the seriousness of the violation and its consequences, the responsibility in the organization and the apparent motivation of the person involved, the policies of the organization concerning such matters, and any other relevant considerations. Ordinarily, referral to a higher authority would be necessary. In some circumstances, however, it may be appropriate for the lawyer to ask the constituent to reconsider the matter; for example, if the circumstances involve a constituent's innocent misunderstanding of law and subse-

quent acceptance of the lawyer's advice, the lawyer may reasonably conclude that the best interest of the organization does not require that the matter be referred to higher authority. If a constituent persists in conduct contrary to the lawyer's advice, it will be necessary for the lawyer to take steps to have the matter reviewed by a higher authority in the organization. If the matter is of sufficient seriousness and importance or urgency to the organization, referral to higher authority in the organization may be necessary even if the lawyer has not communicated with the constituent. Any measures taken should, to the extent practicable, minimize the risk of revealing information relating to the representation to persons outside the organization. Even in circumstances where a lawyer is not obligated by Rule 1.13 to proceed, a lawyer may bring to the attention of an organizational client, including its highest authority, matters that the lawyer reasonably believes to be of sufficient importance to warrant doing so in the best interest of the organization.

[5] Paragraph (b) also makes clear that when it is reasonably necessary to enable the organization to address the matter in a timely and appropriate manner, the lawyer must refer the matter to higher authority, including, if warranted by the circumstances, the highest authority that can act on behalf of the organization under applicable law. The organization's highest authority to whom a matter may be referred ordinarily will be the board of directors or similar governing body. However, applicable law may prescribe that under certain conditions the highest authority reposes elsewhere, for example, in the independent directors of a corporation.

Relation to Other Rules

[6] The authority and responsibility provided in this Rule are concurrent with the authority and responsibility provided in other Rules. In particular, this Rule does not limit or expand the lawyer's responsibility under Rules 1.8, 1.16, 3.3 or 4.1. Paragraph (c) of this Rule supplements Rule 1.6(b) by providing an additional basis upon which the lawyer may reveal information relating to the representation, but does not modify, restrict, or limit the provisions of Rule 1.6(b)(1) - (6). Under paragraph (c) the lawyer may reveal such information only when the organization's highest authority insists upon or fails to address threatened or ongoing action that is clearly a violation of law, and then only to the extent the lawyer reasonably believes necessary to prevent reasonably certain substantial injury to the organization. It is not necessary that the lawyer's services be used in furtherance of the violation, but it is required that the matter be related to the lawyer's representation of the organization. If the lawyer's services are being used by an organization to further a crime or fraud by

the organization, Rules 1.6(b)(2) and 1.6(b)(3) may permit the lawyer to disclose confidential information. In such circumstances Rule 1.2(d) may also be applicable, in which event, withdrawal from the representation under Rule 1.16(a)(1) may be required.

[7] Paragraph (d) makes clear that the authority of a lawyer to disclose information relating to a representation in circumstances described in paragraph (c) does not apply with respect to information relating to a lawyer's engagement by an organization to investigate an alleged violation of law or to defend the organization or an officer, employee or other person associated with the organization against a claim arising out of an alleged violation of law. This is necessary in order to enable organizational clients to enjoy the full benefits of legal counsel in conducting an investigation or defending against a claim.

[8] A lawyer who reasonably believes that he or she has been discharged because of the lawyer's actions taken pursuant to paragraph (b) or (c), or who withdraws in circumstances that require or permit the lawyer to take action under either of these paragraphs, must proceed as the lawyer reasonably believes necessary to assure that the organization's highest authority is informed of the lawyer's discharge or withdrawal.

Government Agency

[9] The duty defined in this Rule applies to governmental organizations. Defining precisely the identity of the client and prescribing the resulting obligations of such lawyers may be more difficult in the government context and is a matter beyond the scope of these Rules. See Scope [18]. Although in some circumstances the client may be a specific agency, it may also be a branch of government, such as the executive branch, or the government as a whole. For example, if the action or failure to act involves the head of a bureau, either the department of which the bureau is a part or the relevant branch of government may be the client for purposes of this Rule. Moreover, in a matter involving the conduct of government officials, a government lawyer may have authority under applicable law to question such conduct more extensively than that of a lawyer for a private organization in similar circumstances. Thus, when the client is a governmental organization, a different balance may be appropriate between maintaining confidentiality and assuring that the wrongful act is prevented or rectified, for public business is involved. In addition, duties of lawyers employed by the government or lawyers in military service may be defined by statutes and regulation. This Rule does not limit that authority. See Scope.

Clarifying the Lawyer's Role

[10] There are times when the organization's interest may be or become adverse to those of one or more of its constituents. In such circumstances the lawyer should advise any constituent, whose interest the lawyer finds adverse to that of the organization of the conflict or potential conflict of interest, that the lawyer cannot represent such constituent, and that such person may wish to obtain independent representation. Care must be taken to assure that the individual understands that, when there is such adversity of interest, the lawyer for the organization cannot provide legal representation for that constituent individual, and that discussions between the lawyer for the organization and the individual may not be privileged.

[11] Whether such a warning should be given by the lawyer for the organization to any constituent individual may turn on the facts of each case.

Dual Representation

[12] Paragraph (g) recognizes that a lawyer for an organization may also represent a principal officer or major shareholder.

Derivative Actions

[13] Under generally prevailing law, the shareholders or members of a corporation may bring suit to compel the directors to perform their legal obligations in the supervision of the organization. Members of unincorporated associations have essentially the same right. Such an action may be brought nominally by the organization, but usually is, in fact, a legal controversy over management of the organization.

[14] The question can arise whether counsel for the organization may defend such an action. The proposition that the organization is the lawyer's client does not alone resolve the issue. Most derivative actions are a normal incident of an organization's affairs, to be defended by the organization's lawyer like any other suit. However, if the claim involves serious charges of wrongdoing by those in control of the organization, a conflict may arise between the lawyer's duty to the organization and the lawyer's relationship with the board. In those circumstances, Rule 1.7 governs who should represent the directors and the organization.

Model Code Comparison

There was no counterpart to this Rule in the Disciplinary Rules of the Model Code. EC 5-18 stated that a "lawyer employed or retained by a corporation or similar entity owes his allegiance to the entity and not to a stockholder, director, officer, employee, representative, or other person connected with the entity. In advising the entity, a lawyer should keep paramount its interests and his professional judgment should not be influenced by the personal desires of any person or organization. Occasionally, a lawyer for an entity is requested by a stockholder, director, officer, employee, representative, or other person connected with the entity to represent him in an individual capacity; in such case the lawyer may serve the individual only if the lawyer is convinced that differing interests are not present." EC 5-24 stated that although a lawyer "may be employed by a business corporation with non-lawyers serving as directors or officers, and they necessarily have the right to make decisions of business policy, a lawyer must decline to accept direction of his professional judgment from any layman." DR 5-107(B) provided that a lawyer "shall not permit a person who . . . employs . . . him to render legal services for another to direct or regulate his professional judgment in rendering such legal services."

RULE 3.3 - CANDOR TOWARD THE TRIBUNAL

(a) A lawyer shall not knowingly:

(1) make a false statement of material fact or law to a tribunal;
(2) fail to disclose a material fact to a tribunal when disclosure is necessary to avoid assisting a criminal or fraudulent act by the client;
(3) fail to disclose to the tribunal legal authority in the controlling jurisdiction known to the lawyer to be directly adverse to the position of the client and not disclosed by opposing counsel; or
(4) offer evidence that the lawyer knows to be false. If a lawyer has offered material evidence and comes to know of its falsity, the lawyer shall take reasonable remedial measures.

(b) The duties stated in paragraph (a) continue to the conclusion of the proceeding, and apply even if compliance requires disclosure of information otherwise protected by Rule 1.6.

(c) A lawyer may refuse to offer evidence that the lawyer reasonably believes is false.

(d) In an ex parte proceeding, a lawyer shall inform the tribunal of all material facts known to the lawyer which will enable the tribunal to make an informed decision, whether or not the facts are adverse.

Comment

The advocate's task is to present the client's case with persuasive force. Performance of that duty while maintaining confidences of the client is qualified by the advocate's duty of candor to the tribunal. However, an advocate does not vouch for the evidence submitted in a cause; the tribunal is responsible for assessing its probative value.

Representations by a Lawyer

An advocate is responsible for pleadings and other documents prepared for litigation, but is usually not required to have personal knowledge of matters asserted therein, for litigation documents ordinarily present assertions by the client, or by someone on the client's behalf, and not assertions by the lawyer. Compare Rule 3.1. However, an assertion purporting to be on the lawyer's own knowledge, as in an affidavit by the lawyer or in a statement in open court, may properly be made only when the lawyer knows the assertion is true or believes it to be true on the basis of a reasonably diligent inquiry. There are circumstances where failure to make a disclosure is the equivalent of an affirmative misrepresentation. The obligation prescribed in Rule 1.2(d) not to counsel a client to commit or assist the client in committing a fraud applies in litigation. Regarding compliance with Rule 1.2(d), *see* the Comment to that Rule. *See* also the Comment to Rule 8.4(b).

Misleading Legal Argument

Legal argument based on a knowingly false representation of law constitutes dishonesty toward the tribunal. A lawyer is not required to make a disinterested exposition of the law, but must recognize the existence of pertinent legal authorities. Furthermore, as stated in paragraph (a)(3), an advocate has a duty to disclose directly adverse authority in the controlling jurisdiction which has not been disclosed by the opposing party. The underlying concept is that legal argument is a discussion seeking to determine the legal premises properly applicable to the case.

False Evidence

When evidence that a lawyer knows to be false is provided by a person who is not the client, the lawyer must refuse to offer it regardless of the client's wishes.

When false evidence is offered by the client, however, a conflict may arise between the lawyer's duty to keep the client's revelations confidential and the duty of candor to the court. Upon ascertaining that material evidence is false, the lawyer should seek to persuade the client that the evidence should not be offered or, if it has been offered, that its false character should immediately be disclosed. If the persuasion is ineffective, the lawyer must take reasonable remedial measures.

Except in the defense of a criminal accused, the rule generally recognized is that, if necessary to rectify the situation, an advocate must disclose the existence of the client's deception to the court or to the other party. Such a disclosure can result in grave consequences to the client, including not only a sense of betrayal but also loss of the case and perhaps a prosecution for perjury. But the alternative is that the lawyer cooperate in deceiving the court, thereby subverting the truth-finding process which the adversary system is designed to implement. *See* Rule 1.2(d). Furthermore, unless it is clearly understood that the lawyer will act upon the duty to disclose the existence of false evidence, the client can simply reject the lawyer's advice to reveal the false evidence and insist that the lawyer keep silent. Thus the client could in effect coerce the lawyer into being a party to fraud on the court.

Perjury by a Criminal Defendant

Whether an advocate for a criminally accused has the same duty of disclosure has been intensely debated. While it is agreed that the lawyer should seek to persuade the client to refrain from perjurious testimony, there has been dispute concerning the lawyer's duty when that persuasion fails. If the confrontation with the client occurs before trial, the lawyer ordinarily can withdraw. Withdrawal before trial may not be possible, however, either because trial is imminent, or because the confrontation with the client does not take place until the trial itself, or because no other counsel is available.

The most difficult situation, therefore, arises in a criminal case where the accused insists on testifying when the lawyer knows that the testimony is perjurious. The lawyer's effort to rectify the situation can increase the likelihood of the client's being convicted as well as opening the possibility of a prosecution for perjury. On the other hand, if the lawyer does not exercise control over the proof, the lawyer participates, although in a merely passive way, in deception of the court.

Three resolutions of this dilemma have been proposed. One is to permit the accused to testify by a narrative without guidance through the lawyer's questioning. This compromises both contending principles; it exempts the lawyer from the duty to disclose false evidence but subjects the client to an implicit disclosure of information imparted to counsel. Another suggested resolution, of relatively recent origin, is that the advocate be entirely excused from the duty to reveal perjury if the perjury is that of the client. This is a coherent solution but makes the advocate a knowing instrument of perjury.

The other resolution of the dilemma is that the lawyer must reveal the client's perjury if necessary to rectify the situation. A criminal accused has a right to the assistance of an advocate, a right to testify and a right of confidential communication with counsel. However, an accused should not have a right to assistance of counsel in committing perjury. Furthermore, an advocate has an obligation, not only in professional ethics but under the law as well, to avoid implication in the commission of perjury or other falsification of evidence. *See* Rule 1.2(d).

Remedial Measures

If perjured testimony or false evidence has been offered, the advocate's proper course ordinarily is to remonstrate with the client confidentially. If that fails, the advocate should seek to withdraw if that will remedy the situation. If withdrawal will not remedy the situation or is impossible, the advocate should make disclosure to the court. It is for the court then to determine what should be done — making a statement about the matter to the trier of fact, ordering a mistrial or perhaps nothing. If the false testimony was that of the client, the client may controvert the lawyer's version of their communication when the lawyer discloses the situation to the court. If there is an issue whether the client has committed perjury, the lawyer cannot represent the client in resolution of the issue, and a mistrial may be unavoidable. An unscrupulous client might in this way attempt to produce a series of mistrials and thus escape prosecution. However, a second such encounter could be construed as a deliberate abuse of the right to counsel and as such a waiver of the right to further representation.

Constitutional Requirements

The general rule — that an advocate must disclose the existence of perjury with respect to a material fact, even that of a client — applies to defense counsel in criminal cases, as well as in other instances. However, the definition of the lawyer's ethical duty in such a situation may be qualified by constitutional provisions for due process and the right to counsel in criminal cases. In some jurisdictions these provisions have been construed to require that counsel present an accused as a witness if the accused wishes to testify, even if counsel knows the testimony will be false. The obligation of the advocate under these Rules is subordinate to such a constitutional requirement.

Duration of Obligation

A practical time limit on the obligation to rectify the presentation of false evidence has to be established. The conclusion of the proceeding is a reasonably definite point for the termination of the obligation.

Refusing to Offer Proof Believed to Be False

Generally speaking, a lawyer has authority to refuse to offer testimony or other proof that the lawyer believes is untrustworthy. Offering such proof may reflect adversely on the lawyer's ability to discriminate in the quality of evidence and thus impair the lawyer's effectiveness as an advocate. In criminal cases, however, a lawyer may, in some jurisdictions, be denied this authority by constitutional requirements governing the right to counsel.

Ex Parte Proceedings

Ordinarily, an advocate has the limited responsibility of presenting one side of the matters that a tribunal should consider in reaching a decision; the conflicting position is expected to be presented by the opposing party. However, in an *ex parte* proceeding, such as an application for a temporary restraining order, there is no balance of presentation by opposing advocates. The object of an *ex parte* proceeding is nevertheless to yield a substantially just result. The judge has an affirmative responsibility to accord the absent party just consideration. The lawyer for the represented party has the correlative duty to make disclosures of material facts known to the lawyer and that the lawyer reasonably believes are necessary to an informed decision.

Model Code Comparison

Paragraph (a)(1) is substantially identical to DR 7-102(A)(5), which provided that a lawyer shall not "knowingly make a false statement of law or fact."

Paragraph (a)(2) is implicit in DR 7-102(A)(3), which provided that "a lawyer shall not . . . knowingly fail to disclose that which he is required by law to reveal."

Paragraph (a)(3) is substantially identical to DR 7-106(B)(1).

With regard to paragraph (a)(4), the first sentence of this subparagraph is similar to DR 7-102(A)(4), which provided that a lawyer shall not "knowingly use" perjured testimony or false evidence. The second sentence of paragraph (a)(4) resolves an ambiguity in the Model Code concerning the action required of a lawyer who discovers that the lawyer has offered perjured testimony or false evidence. DR 7-102(A)(4), quoted above, did not expressly deal with this situation, but the prohibition against "use" of false evidence can be construed to preclude carrying through with a case based on such evidence when that fact has become known during the trial. DR 7-102(B)(1), also noted in connection with Rule 1.6, provided that a lawyer "who receives information clearly establishing that . . . [h]is client has . . . perpetrated a fraud upon . . . a tribunal shall [if the client does not rectify the situation] . . . reveal the fraud to the . . . tribunal. . . ." Since use of perjured testimony or false evidence is usually regarded as "fraud" upon the court, DR 7-102(B)(1) apparently required disclosure by the lawyer in such circumstances. However, some states have amended DR 7-102(B)(1) in conformity with an ABA-recommended amendment to provide that the duty of disclosure does not apply when the "information is protected as a privileged communication." This qualification may be empty, for the rule of attorney-client privilege has been construed to exclude communications that further a crime, including the crime of perjury. On this interpretation of DR 7-102(B)(1), the lawyer had a duty to disclose the perjury.

Paragraph (c) confers discretion on the lawyer to refuse to offer evidence that the lawyer "reasonably believes" is false. This gives the lawyer more latitude than DR 7-102(A)(4), which prohibited the lawyer from offering evidence the lawyer "knows" is false.

There was no counterpart in the Model Code to paragraph (d).

APPENDIX K

EXCERPTS FROM THE U.S. SENTENCING GUIDELINES MANUAL, AS AMENDED AND EFFECTIVE NOVEMBER 1, 2004

§2B1.1. ***Larceny, Embezzlement, and Other Forms of Theft; Offenses Involving Stolen Property; Property Damage or Destruction; Fraud and Deceit; Forgery; Offenses Involving Altered or Counterfeit Instruments Other than Counterfeit Bearer Obligations of the United States***

(a) Base Offense Level:

(1) **7**, if (A) the defendant was convicted of an offense referenced to this guideline; and (B) that offense of conviction has a statutory maximum term of imprisonment of 20 years or more; or

(2) **6**, otherwise.

(b) Specific Offense Characteristics

(1) If the loss exceeded $5,000, increase the offense level as follows:

Loss (Apply the Greatest)		*Increase in Level*
(A)	$5,000 or less	no increase
(B)	More than $5,000	add **2**
(C)	More than $10,000	add **4**
(D)	More than $30,000	add **6**
(E)	More than $70,000	add **8**
(F)	More than $120,000	add **10**
(G)	More than $200,000	add **12**
(H)	More than $400,000	add **14**
(I)	More than $1,000,000	add **16**
(J)	More than $2,500,000	add **18**
(K)	More than $7,000,000	add **20**
(L)	More than $20,000,000	add **22**
(M)	More than $50,000,000	add **24**
(N)	More than $100,000,000	add **26**

(O)	More than $200,000,000	add **28**
(P)	More than $400,000,000	add **30**.

(2) (Apply the greatest) If the offense—

(A) (i) involved 10 or more victims; or (ii) was committed through mass-marketing, increase by **2** levels;

(B) involved 50 or more victims, increase by **4** levels; or

(C) involved 250 or more victims, increase by **6** levels.

(3) If the offense involved a theft from the person of another, increase by **2** levels.

(4) If the offense involved receiving stolen property, and the defendant was a person in the business of receiving and selling stolen property, increase by **2** levels.

(5) If the offense involved misappropriation of a trade secret and the defendant knew or intended that the offense would benefit a foreign government, foreign instrumentality, or foreign agent, increase by **2** levels.

(6) If the offense involved theft of, damage to, or destruction of, property from a national cemetery, increase by **2** levels.

(7) If the offense involved (A) a misrepresentation that the defendant was acting on behalf of a charitable, educational, religious, or political organization, or a government agency; (B) a misrepresentation or other fraudulent action during the course of a bankruptcy proceeding; (C) a violation of any prior, specific judicial or administrative order, injunction, decree, or process not addressed elsewhere in the guidelines; or (D) a misrepresentation to a consumer in connection with obtaining, providing, or furnishing financial assistance for an institution of higher education, increase by **2** levels. If the resulting offense level is less than level **10**, increase to level **10**.

(8) If (A) the defendant relocated, or participated in relocating, a fraudulent scheme to another jurisdiction to evade law enforcement or regulatory officials; (B) a substantial part of a fraudulent scheme was committed from outside the United States; or (C) the offense otherwise involved sophisticated means, increase by **2** levels. If the resulting offense level is less than level **12**, increase to level **12**.

(9) If the offense involved (A) the possession or use of any device-making equipment; (B) the production or trafficking of any unauthorized access device or counterfeit access device; or (C)(i) the unauthorized transfer or use of any means of identification unlawfully to produce or obtain any other means of identification; or (ii) the possession of 5 or more means of identification that unlawfully were produced from, or obtained by the use of, another means of identification, increase by **2** levels. If the resulting offense level is less than level **12**, increase to level **12**.

(10) If the offense involved an organized scheme to steal vehicles or vehicle parts, and the offense level is less than level **14**, increase to level **14**.

(11) If the offense involved (A) the conscious or reckless risk of death or serious bodily injury; or (B) possession of a dangerous weapon (including a firearm) in connection with the offense, increase by **2** levels. If the resulting offense level is less than level **14**, increase to level **14**.

(12) (Apply the greater) If—

(A) the defendant derived more than $1,000,000 in gross receipts from one or more financial institutions as a result of the offense, increase by **2** levels; or

(B) the offense (i) substantially jeopardized the safety and soundness of a financial institution; (ii) substantially endangered the solvency or financial security of an organization that, at any time during the offense, (I) was a publicly traded company; or (II) had 1,000 or more employees; or

(iii) substantially endangered the solvency or financial security of 100 or more victims, increase by **4** levels.

(C) The cumulative adjustments from application of both subsections (b)(2) and (b)(12)(B) shall not exceed **8** levels, except as provided in subdivision (D).

(D) If the resulting offense level determined under subdivision (A) or (B) is less than level **24**, increase to level **24**.

(13) (A) (Apply the greatest) If the defendant was convicted of an offense under:

(i) 18 U.S.C. § 1030, and the offense involved (I) a computer system used to maintain or operate a critical infrastructure, or used by or for a government entity in furtherance of the administration of justice, national defense, or national security; or (II) an intent to obtain personal information, increase by **2** levels.

(ii) 18 U.S.C. § 1030(a)(5)(A)(i), increase by **4** levels.

(iii) 18 U.S.C. § 1030, and the offense caused a substantial disruption of a critical infrastructure, increase by **6** levels.

(B) If subdivision (A)(iii) applies, and the offense level is less than level **24**, increase to level **24**.

(14) If the offense involved—

(A) a violation of securities law and, at the time of the offense, the defendant was (i) an officer or a director of a publicly traded company; (ii) a registered broker or dealer, or a person associated with a broker or dealer; or (iii) an investment adviser, or a person associated with an investment adviser; or

(B) a violation of commodities law and, at the time of the offense, the defendant was (i) an officer or a director of a futures commission merchant or an introducing broker; (ii) a commodities trading advisor; or (iii) a commodity pool operator, increase by **4** levels.

(c) Cross References

(1) If (A) a firearm, destructive device, explosive material, or controlled substance was taken, or the taking of any such item was an object of the offense; or (B) the stolen property received, transported, transferred, transmitted, or possessed was a firearm, destructive device, explosive material, or controlled substance, apply §2D1.1 (Unlawful Manufacturing, Importing, Exporting, or Trafficking (Including Possession with Intent to Commit These Offenses); Attempt or Conspiracy), §2D2.1 (Unlawful Possession; Attempt or Conspiracy), §2K1.3 (Unlawful Receipt, Possession, or Transportation of Explosive Materials; Prohibited Transactions Involving Explosive Materials), or §2K2.1 (Unlawful Receipt, Possession, or Transportation of Firearms or Ammunition; Prohibited Transactions Involving Firearms or Ammunition), as appropriate.

(2) If the offense involved arson, or property damage by use of explosives, apply §2K1.4 (Arson; Property Damage by Use of Explosives), if the resulting offense level is greater than that determined above.

(3) If (A) neither subdivision (1) nor (2) of this subsection applies; (B) the defendant was convicted under a statute proscribing false, fictitious, or fraudulent statements or representations generally (e.g., 18 U.S.C. § 1001, § 1341, § 1342, or § 1343); and (C) the conduct set forth in the count of conviction establishes an offense specifically covered by another guideline in Chapter Two (Offense Conduct), apply that other guideline.

(4) If the offense involved a cultural heritage resource, apply §2B1.5 (Theft of, Damage to, or Destruction of,

Cultural Heritage Resources; Unlawful Sale, Purchase, Exchange, Transportation, or Receipt of Cultural Heritage Resources), if the resulting offense level is greater than that determined above.

§2B4.1. *Bribery in Procurement of Bank Loan and Other Commercial Bribery*

(a) Base Offense Level: **8**

(b) Specific Offense Characteristics

(1) If the greater of the value of the bribe or the improper benefit to be conferred (A) exceeded $2,000 but did not exceed $5,000, increase by **1** level; or (B) exceeded $5,000, increase by the number of levels from the table in §2B1.1 (Theft, Property Destruction, and Fraud) corresponding to that amount.

(2) (Apply the greater) If—

(A) the defendant derived more than $1,000,000 in gross receipts from one or more financial institutions as a result of the offense, increase by **2** levels; or

(B) the offense substantially jeopardized the safety and soundness of a financial institution, increase by **4** levels. If the resulting offense level determined under subdivision (A) or (B) is less than level **24**, increase to level **24**.

(c) Special Instruction for Fines – Organizations

(1) In lieu of the pecuniary loss under subsection (a)(3) of §8C2.4 (Base Fine), use the greatest of: (A) the value of the unlawful payment; (B) the value of the benefit received or to be received in return for the unlawful payment; or (C) the consequential damages resulting from the unlawful payment.

§2F1.1. [Deleted]

§2J1.3. ***Perjury or Subornation of Perjury; Bribery of Witness***

(a) Base Offense Level: **14**

(b) Specific Offense Characteristics

(1) If the offense involved causing or threatening to cause physical injury to a person, or property damage, in order to suborn perjury, increase by **8** levels.

(2) If the perjury, subornation of perjury, or witness bribery resulted in substantial interference with the administration of justice, increase by **3** levels.

(c) Cross Reference

(1) If the offense involved perjury, subornation of perjury, or witness bribery in respect to a criminal offense, apply §2X3.1 (Accessory After the Fact) in respect to that criminal offense, if the resulting offense level is greater than that determined above.

(d) Special Instruction

(1) In the case of counts of perjury or subornation of perjury arising from testimony given, or to be given, in separate proceedings, do not group the counts together under §3D1.2 (Groups of Closely Related Counts).

§3A1.1. ***Hate Crime Motivation or Vulnerable Victim***

(a) If the finder of fact at trial or, in the case of a plea of guilty or nolo contendere, the court at sentencing determines beyond a reasonable doubt that the defendant intentionally selected any victim or any property as the object of the offense of conviction because of the actual or perceived race, color, religion, national origin, ethnicity, gender, disability, or sexual orientation of any person, increase by **3** levels.

(b) (1) If the defendant knew or should have known that a victim of the offense was a vulnerable victim, increase by **2** levels.

(2) If (A) subdivision (1) applies; and (B) the offense involved a large number of vulnerable victims, increase the offense level determined under subdivision (1) by **2** additional levels.

(c) Special Instruction

(1) Subsection (a) shall not apply if an adjustment from §2H1.1(b)(1) applies.

§3A1.2. *Official Victim*

(a) If (1) the victim was (A) a government officer or employee; (B) a former government officer or employee; or (C) a member of the immediate family of a person described in subdivision (A) or (B); and (2) the offense of conviction was motivated by such status, increase by **3** levels.

(b) If, in a manner creating a substantial risk of serious bodily injury, the defendant or a person for whose conduct the defendant is otherwise accountable—

(1) knowing or having reasonable cause to believe that a person was a law enforcement officer, assaulted such officer during the course of the offense or immediate flight therefrom; or

(2) knowing or having reasonable cause to believe that a person was a prison official, assaulted such official while the defendant (or a person for whose conduct the defendant is otherwise accountable) was in the custody or control of a prison or other correctional facility, increase by **3** levels.

§3A1.3. *Restraint of Victim*

If a victim was physically restrained in the course of the offense, increase by **2** levels.

§3B1.1. *Aggravating Role*

Based on the defendant's role in the offense, increase the offense level as follows:

(a) If the defendant was an organizer or leader of a criminal activity that involved five or more participants or was otherwise extensive, increase by **4** levels.

(b) If the defendant was a manager or supervisor (but not an organizer or leader) and the criminal activity involved five or more participants or was otherwise extensive, increase by **3** levels.

(c) If the defendant was an organizer, leader, manager, or supervisor in any criminal activity other than described in (a) or (b), increase by **2** levels.

§3B1.3. *Abuse of Position of Trust or Use of Special Skill*

If the defendant abused a position of public or private trust, or used a special skill, in a manner that significantly facilitated the commission or concealment of the offense, increase by **2** levels. This adjustment may not be employed if an abuse of trust or skill is included in the base offense level or specific offense characteristic. If this adjustment is based upon an abuse of a position of trust, it may be employed in addition to an adjustment under §3B1.1 (Aggravating Role); if this adjustment is based solely on the use of a special skill, it may not be employed in addition to an adjustment under §3B1.1 (Aggravating Role).

§3C1.1. *Obstructing or Impeding the Administration of Justice*

If (A) the defendant willfully obstructed or impeded, or attempted to obstruct or impede, the administration of justice during the course of the investigation, prosecution, or sentencing of the instant offense of conviction, and (B) the obstructive conduct related to (i) the defendant's offense of conviction and any relevant conduct; or (ii) a closely elated offense, increase the offense level by **2** levels.

§4A1.3. *Departures Based on Inadequacy of Criminal History Category (Policy Statement)*

(a) UPWARD DEPARTURES.—

(1) STANDARD FOR UPWARD DEPARTURE.—If reliable information indicates that the defendant's criminal history category substantially under-represents the seriousness of the defendant's criminal history or the likelihood that the defendant will commit other crimes, an upward departure may be warranted.

(2) TYPES OF INFORMATION FORMING THE BASIS FOR UPWARD DEPARTURE.—The information described in subsection (a) may include information concerning the following:

(A) Prior sentence(s) not used in computing the criminal history category (e.g., sentences for foreign and tribal offenses).

(B) Prior sentence(s) of substantially more than one year imposed as a result of independent crimes committed on different occasions.

(C) Prior similar misconduct established by a civil adjudication or by a failure to comply with an administrative order.

(D) Whether the defendant was pending trial or sentencing on another charge at the time of the instant offense.

(E) Prior similar adult criminal conduct not resulting in a criminal conviction.

(3) PROHIBITION.—A prior arrest record itself shall not be considered for purposes of an upward departure under this policy statement.

(4) DETERMINATION OF EXTENT OF UPWARD DEPARTURE.—

(A) IN GENERAL.—Except as provided in subdivision (B), the court shall determine the extent of a departure under this subsection by using, as a reference, the criminal history category applicable to defendants whose criminal history or likelihood to recidivate most closely resembles that of the defendant's.

(B) UPWARD DEPARTURES FROM CATEGORY VI.—In a case in which the court determines that the extent and nature of the defendant's criminal history, taken together, are sufficient to warrant an upward departure from Criminal History Category VI, the court should structure the departure by moving incrementally down the sentencing table to the next higher offense level in Criminal History Category VI until it finds a guideline range appropriate to the case.

(b) DOWNWARD DEPARTURES.—

(1) STANDARD FOR DOWNWARD DEPARTURE.—If reliable information indicates that the defendant's criminal history category substantially over-represents the seriousness of the defendant's criminal history or the likelihood that the defendant will commit other crimes, a downward departure may be warranted.

(2) PROHIBITIONS.—

(A) CRIMINAL HISTORY CATEGORY I.—A departure below the lower limit of the applicable guideline range for Criminal History Category I is prohibited.

(B) ARMED CAREER CRIMINAL AND REPEAT AND DANGEROUS SEX OFFENDER.—A downward departure under this subsection is prohibited for (i) an armed career criminal within the meaning of §4B1.4 (Armed Career Criminal); and (ii) a repeat and dangerous sex offender against minors within the meaning of §4B1.5 (Repeat and Dangerous Sex Offender Against Minors).

(3) LIMITATIONS.—

(A) LIMITATION ON EXTENT OF DOWNWARD DEPARTURE FOR CAREER OFFENDER.—The extent of a downward departure under this subsection for a career offender within the meaning of §4B1.1 (Career Offender) may not exceed one criminal history category.

(B) LIMITATION ON APPLICABILITY OF §5C1.2 IN EVENT OF DOWNWARD DEPARTURE TO CATEGORY I.—A defendant whose criminal history category is Category I after receipt of a downward departure under this subsection does not meet the criterion of subsection (a)(1) of §5C1.2 (Limitation on Applicability of Statutory Maximum Sentences in Certain Cases) if, before receipt of the downward departure, the defendant had more than one criminal history point under §4A1.1 (Criminal History Category).

(c) WRITTEN SPECIFICATION OF BASIS FOR DEPARTURE.—In departing from the otherwise applicable criminal history category under this policy statement, the court shall specify in writing the following:

(1) In the case of an upward departure, the specific reasons why the applicable criminal history category substantially under-represents the seriousness of the defendant's criminal history or the likelihood that the defendant will commit other crimes.

(2) In the case of a downward departure, the specific reasons why the applicable criminal history category substantially over-represents the seriousness of the defendant's criminal history or the likelihood that the defendant will commit other crimes.

§5B1.1. *Imposition of a Term of Probation*

(a) Subject to the statutory restrictions in subsection (b) below, a sentence of probation is authorized if:

(1) the applicable guideline range is in Zone A of the Sentencing Table; or
(2) the applicable guideline range is in Zone B of the Sentencing Table and the court imposes a condition or combination of conditions requiring intermittent confinement, community confinement, or home detention as provided in subsection (c)(3) of §5C1.1 (Imposition of a Term of Imprisonment).

(b) A sentence of probation may not be imposed in the event:

(1) the offense of conviction is a Class A or B felony, 18 U.S.C. § 3561(a)(1);
(2) the offense of conviction expressly precludes probation as a sentence, 18 U.S.C. § 3561(a)(2);
(3) the defendant is sentenced at the same time to a sentence of imprisonment for the same or a different offense, 18 U.S.C. § 3561(a)(3).

§5B1.3. *Conditions of Probation*

(a) Mandatory Conditions—

(1) for any offense, the defendant shall not commit another federal, state or local offense (see 18 U.S.C. § 3563(a));
(2) for a felony, the defendant shall (A) make restitution, (B) give notice to victims of the offense pursuant to 18 U.S.C. § 3555, or (C) reside, or refrain from residing, in a specified place or area, unless the court finds on the record that extraordinary circumstances exist that would make such a condition plainly unreasonable, in which event the court shall impose one or more of the

discretionary conditions set forth under 18 U.S.C. § 3563(b) (see 18 U.S.C. § 3563(a)(2));

Note: Section 3563(a)(2) of Title 18, United States Code, provides that, absent unusual circumstances, a defendant convicted of a felony shall abide by at least one of the conditions set forth in 18 U.S.C. § 3563(b)(2), (b)(3), and (b)(13). Before the enactment of the Antiterrorism and Effective Death Penalty Act of 1996, those conditions were a fine ((b)(2)), an order of restitution ((b)(3)), and community service ((b)(13)). Whether or not the change was intended, the Act deleted the fine condition and renumbered the restitution and community service conditions in 18 U.S.C. § 3563(b), but failed to make a corresponding change in the referenced paragraphs under 18 U.S.C. § 3563(a)(2). Accordingly, the conditions now referenced are restitution ((b)(2)), notice to victims pursuant to 18 U.S.C. § 3555 ((b)(3)), and an order that the defendant reside, or refrain from residing, in a specified place or area ((b)(13)).

(3) for any offense, the defendant shall not unlawfully possess a controlled substance (see 18 U.S.C. § 3563(a));

(4) for a domestic violence crime as defined in 18 U.S.C. § 3561(b) by a defendant convicted of such an offense for the first time, the defendant shall attend a public, private, or non-profit offender rehabilitation program that has been approved by the court, in consultation with a State Coalition Against Domestic Violence or other appropriate experts, if an approved program is available within a 50-mile radius of the legal residence of the defendant (see 18 U.S.C. § 3563(a));

(5) for any offense, the defendant shall refrain from any unlawful use of a controlled substance and submit to one drug test within 15 days of release on probation and at least two periodic drug tests thereafter (as determined by the court) for use of a controlled substance, but the condition stated in this paragraph may be ameliorated or suspended by the court for any indi-

vidual defendant if the defendant's presentence report or other reliable information indicates a low risk of future substance abuse by the defendant (see 18 U.S.C. § 3563(a));

(6) the defendant shall (A) make restitution in accordance with 18 U.S.C. §§ 2248, 2259, 2264, 2327, 3663, 3663A, and 3664; and (B) pay the assessment imposed in accordance with 18 U.S.C. § 3013;

(7) the defendant shall notify the court of any material change in the defendant's economic circumstances that might affect the defendant's ability to pay restitution, fines, or special assessments (see 18 U.S.C. § 3563(a));

(8) if the court has imposed a fine, the defendant shall pay the fine or adhere to a court-established payment schedule (see 18 U.S.C. § 3563(a));

(9) a defendant convicted of a sexual offense as described in 18 U.S.C. § 4042(c)(4) shall report the address where the defendant will reside and any subsequent change of residence to the probation officer responsible for supervision, and shall register as a sex offender in any State where the person resides, is employed, carries on a vocation, or is a student;

(10) the defendant shall submit to the collection of a DNA sample from the defendant at the direction of the United States Probation Office if the collection of such a sample is authorized pursuant to section 3 of the DNA Analysis Backlog Elimination Act of 2000 (42 U.S.C. § 14135a).

(b) The court may impose other conditions of probation to the extent that such conditions (1) are reasonably related to (A) the nature and circumstances of the offense and the history and characteristics of the defendant; (B) the need for the sentence imposed to reflect the seriousness of the offense, to promote respect for the law, and to provide just punishment for the offense; (C) the need for the sentence imposed to afford adequate deterrence to criminal conduct; (D) the need to protect the public from further crimes of the defendant; and (E) the need to provide the defendant with needed educational or vocational training, medical care, or other correctional treatment in the most effective manner; and (2) involve only such deprivations of liberty or property as are reasonably necessary for the purposes of sentencing indicated in 18 U.S.C. § 3553(a) (see 18 U.S.C. § 3563(b)).

(c) (Policy Statement) The following "standard" conditions are recommended for probation. Several of the conditions are expansions of the conditions required by statute:

(1) the defendant shall not leave the judicial district or other specified geographic area without the permission of the court or probation officer;

(2) the defendant shall report to the probation officer as directed by the court or probation officer and shall submit a truthful and complete written report within the first five days of each month;

(3) the defendant shall answer truthfully all inquiries by the probation officer and follow the instructions of the probation officer;

(4) the defendant shall support the defendant's dependents and meet other family responsibilities (including, but not limited to, complying with the terms of any court order or administrative process pursuant to the law of a state, the District of Columbia, or any other possession or territory of the United States requiring payments by the defendant for the support and maintenance of any child or of a child and the parent with whom the child is living);

(5) the defendant shall work regularly at a lawful occupation unless excused by the probation officer for schooling, training, or other acceptable reasons;

(6) the defendant shall notify the probation officer at least ten days prior to any change of residence or employment;

(7) the defendant shall refrain from excessive use of alcohol and shall not purchase, possess, use, distribute, or administer any controlled substance, or any paraphernalia related to any controlled substance, except as prescribed by a physician;

(8) the defendant shall not frequent places where controlled substances are illegally sold, used, distributed, or administered, or other places specified by the court;

(9) the defendant shall not associate with any persons engaged in criminal activity, and shall not associate with any person convicted of a felony unless granted permission to do so by the probation officer;

(10) the defendant shall permit a probation officer to visit the defendant at any time at home or elsewhere and shall permit confiscation of any contraband observed in plain view by the probation officer;

(11) the defendant shall notify the probation officer within seventy-two hours of being arrested or questioned by a law enforcement officer;

(12) the defendant shall not enter into any agreement to act as an informer or a special agent of a law enforcement agency without the permission of the court;

(13) as directed by the probation officer, the defendant shall notify third parties of risks that may be occasioned by the defendant's criminal record or personal history or characteristics, and shall permit the probation officer to make such notifications and to confirm the defendant's compliance with such notification requirement;

(14) the defendant shall pay the special assessment imposed or adhere to a court-ordered installment schedule for the payment of the special assessment.

(d) (Policy Statement) The following "special" conditions of probation are recommended in the circumstances described and, in addition, may otherwise be appropriate in particular cases:

(1) *Possession of Weapons*

If the instant conviction is for a felony, or if the defendant was previously convicted of a felony or used a firearm or other dangerous weapon in the course of the instant offense — a condition prohibiting the defendant from possessing a firearm or other dangerous weapon.

(2) *Debt Obligations*

If an installment schedule of payment of restitution or a fine is imposed — a condition prohibiting the defendant from incurring new credit charges or opening additional lines of credit without approval of the probation officer unless the defendant is in compliance with the payment schedule.

(3) *Access to Financial Information*

If the court imposes an order of restitution, forfeiture, or notice to victims, or orders the defendant to pay a fine — a condition requiring the defendant to provide the probation officer access to any requested financial information.

(4) *Substance Abuse Program Participation*

If the court has reason to believe that the defendant is an abuser of narcotics, other controlled substances or alcohol — a condition requiring the defendant to participate in a program approved by the United States Probation Office for substance abuse, which program may include testing to determine whether the defendant has reverted to the use of drugs or alcohol.

(5) *Mental Health Program Participation*

If the court has reason to believe that the defendant is in need of psychological or psychiatric treatment — a condition requiring that the defendant participate in a mental health program approved by the United States Probation Office.

(6) *Deportation*

If (A) the defendant and the United States entered into a stipulation of deportation pursuant to section 238(c)(5) of the Immigration and Nationality Act (8 U.S.C. § 1228(c)(5)*); or (B) in the absence of a stipulation of deportation, if, after notice and hearing pursuant to such section, the Attorney General demonstrates by clear and convincing evidence that the alien is deportable — a condition ordering deportation by a United States district court or a United States magistrate judge.

(7) *Sex Offenses*
If the instant offense of conviction is a sex offense, as defined in §5D1.2 (Term of Supervised Release) — a condition requiring the defendant to participate in a program approved by the United States Probation Office for the treatment and monitoring of sex offenders.

*So in original. Probably should be 8 U.S.C. § 1228(d)(5).

(e) Additional Conditions (Policy Statement)
The following "special conditions" may be appropriate on a case-by-case basis:

(1) *Community Confinement*
Residence in a community treatment center, halfway house or similar facility may be imposed as a condition of probation.

(2) *Home Detention*
Home detention may be imposed as a condition of probation but only as a substitute for imprisonment. See §5F1.2 (Home Detention).

(3) *Community Service*
Community service may be imposed as a condition of probation. See §5F1.3 (Community Service).

(4) *Occupational Restrictions*
Occupational restrictions may be imposed as a condition of probation. See §5F1.5 (Occupational Restrictions).

(5) *Curfew*
A condition imposing a curfew may be imposed if the court concludes that restricting the defendant to his place of residence during evening and nighttime hours is necessary to provide just punishment for the offense, to protect the public from crimes that the defendant might commit during those hours, or to assist in the rehabilitation of the defendant. Electronic monitoring may be used as a means of surveillance to ensure compliance with a curfew order.

(6) *Intermittent Confinement*
Intermittent confinement (custody for intervals of time) may be ordered as a condition of probation during the first year of probation.

§5D1.1. Imposition of a Term of Supervised Release

(a) The court shall order a term of supervised release to follow imprisonment when a sentence of imprisonment of more than one year is imposed, or when required by statute.
(b) The court may order a term of supervised release to follow imprisonment in any other case.

§5E1.1. *Restitution*

(a) In the case of an identifiable victim, the court shall –

(1) enter a restitution order for the full amount of the victim's loss, if such order is authorized under 18 U.S.C. § 1593, § 2248, § 2259, § 2264, § 2327, § 3663, or § 3663A, or 21 U.S.C. § 853(q); or
(2) impose a term of probation or supervised release with a condition requiring restitution for the full amount of the victim's loss, if the offense is not an offense for which restitution is authorized under 18 U.S.C. § 3663(a)(1) but otherwise meets the criteria for an order of restitution under that section.

(b) *Provided*, that the provisions of subsection (a) do not apply –

(1) when full restitution has been made; or
(2) in the case of a restitution order under 18 U.S.C. § 3663; a restitution order under 18 U.S.C. § 3663A that pertains to an offense against property described in 18 U.S.C. § 3663A(c)(1)(A)(ii); or a condition of restitution imposed pursuant to subsection (a)(2) above, to the extent the court finds, from facts on the record, that (A) the number of identifiable victims is

so large as to make restitution impracticable; or (B) determining complex issues of fact related to the cause or amount of the victim's losses would complicate or prolong the sentencing process to a degree that the need to provide restitution to any victim is outweighed by the burden on the sentencing process.

(c) If a defendant is ordered to make restitution to an identifiable victim and to pay a fine, the court shall order that any money paid by the defendant shall first be applied to satisfy the order of restitution.

(d) In a case where there is no identifiable victim and the defendant was convicted under 21 U.S.C. § 841, § 848(a), § 849, § 856, § 861, or § 863, the court, taking into consideration the amount of public harm caused by the offense and other relevant factors, shall order an amount of community restitution not to exceed the fine imposed under §5E1.2.

(e) A restitution order may direct the defendant to make a single, lump sum payment, partial payments at specified intervals, in-kind payments, or a combination of payments at specified intervals and in-kind payments. See 18 U.S.C. § 3664(f)(3)(A). An in-kind payment may be in the form of (1) return of property; (2) replacement of property; or (3) if the victim agrees, services rendered to the victim or to a person or organization other than the victim. See 18 U.S.C. § 3664(f)(4).

(f) A restitution order may direct the defendant to make nominal periodic payments if the court finds from facts on the record that the economic circumstances of the defendant do not allow the payment of any amount of a restitution order and do not allow for the payment of the full amount of a restitution order in the foreseeable future under any reasonable schedule of payments.

(g) Special Instruction

(1) This guideline applies only to a defendant convicted of an offense committed on or after November 1, 1997. Notwithstanding the provisions of §1B1.11 (Use of Guidelines Manual in Effect on Date of Sentencing),

use the former §5E1.1 (set forth in Appendix C, amendment 571) in lieu of this guideline in any other case.

§5E1.2. ***Fines for Individual Defendants***

(a) The court shall impose a fine in all cases, except where the defendant establishes that he is unable to pay and is not likely to become able to pay any fine.

(b) The applicable fine guideline range is that specified in subsection (c) below. If, however, the guideline for the offense in Chapter Two provides a specific rule for imposing a fine, that rule takes precedence over subsection (c) of this section.

(c) (1) The minimum of the fine guideline range is the amount shown in column A of the table below.

(2) Except as specified in (4) below, the maximum of the fine guideline range is the amount shown in column B of the table below.

(3) Fine Table

Offense Level	A Minimum	B Minimum
3 and below	$100	$5,000
4-5	$250	$5,000
6-7	$500	$5,000
8-9	$1,000	$10,000
10-11	$2,000	$20,000
12-13	$3,000	$30,000
14-15	$4,000	$40,000
16-17	$5,000	$50,000
18-19	$6,000	$60,000
20-22	$7,500	$75,000
23-25	$10,000	$100,000
26-28	$12,500	$125,000
29-31	$15,000	$150,000
32-34	$17,500	$175,000

(4) Subsection (c)(2), limiting the maximum fine, does not apply if the defendant is convicted under a statute authorizing (A) a maximum fine greater than $250,000, or (B) a fine for each day of violation. In such cases, the court may impose a fine up to the maximum authorized by the statute.

(d) In determining the amount of the fine, the court shall consider:

(1) the need for the combined sentence to reflect the seriousness of the offense (including the harm or loss to the victim and the gain to the defendant), to promote respect for the law, to provide just punishment and to afford adequate deterrence;
(2) any evidence presented as to the defendant's ability to pay the fine (including the ability to pay over a period of time) in light of his earning capacity and financial resources;
(3) the burden that the fine places on the defendant and his dependents relative to alternative punishments;
(4) any restitution or reparation that the defendant has made or is obligated to make;
(5) any collateral consequences of conviction, including civil obligations arising from the defendant's conduct;
(6) whether the defendant previously has been fined for a similar offense;
(7) the expected costs to the government of any term of probation, or term of imprisonment and term of supervised release imposed; and
(8) any other pertinent equitable considerations.

The amount of the fine should always be sufficient to ensure that the fine, taken together with other sanctions imposed, is punitive.

(e) If the defendant establishes that (1) he is not able and, even with the use of a reasonable installment schedule, is not likely to become able to pay all or part of the fine required by the preceding provisions, or (2) imposition of a fine would unduly burden the defendant's dependents, the court may impose a lesser fine or waive the fine. In these circumstances, the court shall consider alternative sanctions in lieu of all or a portion of the fine, and must still impose a total combined sanction that is punitive. Although any additional sanction not proscribed by the guidelines is permissible, community service is the generally preferable alternative in such instances.

(f) If the defendant establishes that payment of the fine in a lump sum would have an unduly severe impact on him or his dependents, the court should establish an installment schedule for payment of the fine. The length of the installment schedule generally should not exceed twelve months, and shall not exceed the maximum term of probation authorized for the offense. The defendant should be required to pay a substantial installment at the time of sentencing. If the court authorizes a defendant sentenced to probation or supervised release to pay a fine on an installment schedule, the court shall require as a condition of probation or supervised release that the defendant pay the fine according to the schedule. The court also may impose a condition prohibiting the defendant from incurring new credit charges or opening additional lines of credit unless he is in compliance with the payment schedule.

(g) If the defendant knowingly fails to pay a delinquent fine, the court shall resentence him in accordance with 18 U.S.C. § 3614.

§5F1.1. ***Community Confinement***

Community confinement may be imposed as a condition of probation or supervised release.*

*Note: Section 3583(d) of title 18, United States Code, provides that "[t]he court may order, as a further condition of supervised release...any condition set forth as a discretionary condition of probation in section 3563(b)(1) through (b)(10) and (b)(12) through (b)(20), and any other condition it considers to be appropriate." Subsection (b)(11) of section 3563 of title 18, United States Code, is explicitly excluded as a condition of supervised release. Before the enactment of the Antiterrorism and Effective Death Penalty

Act of 1996, the condition at 18 U.S.C. § 3563(b)(11) was intermittent confinement. The Act deleted 18 U.S.C. § 3563(b)(2), authorizing the payment of a fine as a condition of probation, and redesignated the remaining conditions of probation set forth in 18 U.S.C. § 3563(b); intermittent confinement is now set forth at subsection (b)(10), whereas subsection (b)(11) sets forth the condition of residency at a community corrections facility. It would appear that intermittent confinement now is authorized as a condition of supervised release and that community confinement now is not authorized as a condition of supervised release.

However, there is some question as to whether Congress intended this result. Although the Antiterrorism and Effective Death Penalty Act of 1996 redesignated the remaining paragraphs of section 3563(b), it failed to make the corresponding redesignations in 18 U.S.C. § 3583(d), regarding discretionary conditions of supervised release.

§5F1.2. ***Home Detention***

Home detention may be imposed as a condition of probation or supervised release, but only as a substitute for imprisonment.

§5F1.3. ***Community Service***

Community service may be ordered as a condition of probation or supervised release.

§5H1.1. ***Age*** **(Policy Statement)**

Age (including youth) is not ordinarily relevant in determining whether a sentence should be outside the applicable guideline range. Age may be a reason to impose a sentence below the applicable guideline range when the defendant is elderly and infirm and where a form of punishment such as home confinement might be equally efficient as and less costly than incarceration. Physical condition, which may be related to age, is addressed at §5H1.4 (Physical Condition, Including Drug or Alcohol Dependence or Abuse).

§5K1.1. ***Substantial Assistance to Authorities*** **(Policy Statement)**

Upon motion of the government stating that the defendant has provided substantial assistance in the investigation or prosecution of another person who has committed an offense, the court may depart from the guidelines.

(a) The appropriate reduction shall be determined by the court for reasons stated that may include, but are not limited to, consideration of the following:

(1) the court's evaluation of the significance and usefulness of the defendant's assistance, taking into consideration the government's evaluation of the assistance rendered;
(2) the truthfulness, completeness, *and* reliability of any information or testimony provided by the defendant;
(3) the nature and extent of the *defendant's* assistance;
(4) any injury suffered, or any *danger* or risk of injury to the defendant or his family resulting from his assistance;
(5) the timeliness of the *defendant's* assistance.

TABLE OF AUTHORITIES

Cases

Baltimore City Department of Social Services v. Bouknight, 493 U.S. 549 (1990)

Bartkus v. United States, 21 F.2d 425 (7th Cir. 1927)

Bartlett v. United States, 354 F.2d 745 (8th Cir. 1966)

Begier v. I.R.S., 496 U.S. 53 (1990)

Bennett v. Berg, 685 F.2d 1053 (8th Cir. 1981)

Blakely v. Washington, 542 U.S. 296 (2004)

Braswell v. United States, 487 U.S. 99 (1988)

Bronston v. United States, 409 U.S. 352 (1973)

Bryson v. United States, 396 U.S. 64 (1969)

Citibank, N.A. v. Andros, 666 F.2d 1192 (8th Cir. 1981)

City of Philadelphia v. Westinghouse Electric Corp., 210 F. Supp. 483 (E.D. Pa.)

Coghlan v. United States, 147 F.2d 233 (8th Cir. 1945)

Colero-Toledo v. Pearson Yacht Leasing Co., 416 U.S. 663 (1974)

Commodity Futures Trading Comm'n. v. Weintraub, 471 U.S. 343 (1986)

Diversified Indus., Inc. v. Meredith, 572 F.2d 596 (8th Cir. 1977)

Doe v. United States, 487 U.S. 201 (1988)

Duggins v. Heffron, 128 F.2d 546 (9th Cir. 1942)

Dunn v. United States, 442 U.S. 100 (1979)

Edwards v. United States, 265 F.2d 302 (9th Cir. 1959)

Eisenberg v. Gagnon, 766 F.2d 770 (3d Cir. 1985)

Fisher v. United States, 425 U.S. 391 (1976)

General Electric Co. v. Kilpatrick, 312 F.2d 742 (3d Cir. 1962)

Geoff v. Oklahoma (In re Geoff), 159 B.R. 33 (Bankr. N.D. Okla. 1993)

Gretsch v. United States, 242 F. 897 (3d Cir. 1917)

Hammer v. United States, 271 U.S. 620 (1926)

Harper Row Publishers, Inc. v. Decker, 423 F.2d 487 (7th Cir. 1970), *aff'd.*, 400 U.S. 348 (1971)

Henderson v. United States, 815 F.2d 1189 (8th Cir. 1987)

Hoffman v. United States, 341 U.S. 479 (1951)

Holt v. United States, 218 U.S. 245 (1910)

In re Ahead By A Length, 78 B.R. 708 (Bankr. S.D.N.Y. 1987)

In re Bevill, Bresler & Schulman Asset Management Corp., 805 F.2d 120 (3d Cir. 1986)

In re Chaplin, 179 B.R. 123 (Bankr. E.D. Wis. 1995)

In re Connelly, 59 B.R. 421 (Bankr. N.D. Ill. 1986)

In re Grand Jury Proceedings, 119 B.R. 945 (E.D. Mich. 1990)

In re Grand Jury Subpoena Duces Tecum, 722 F.2d 981 (2d Cir. 1983)

In re Harris, 221 U.S. 274 (1911)

In re Heinsohn, 231 B.R. 48 (Bankr. E.D. Tenn. 1999)

In re Holder, 207 B.R. 574 (Bankr. M.D. Tenn. 1997)

In re Johns Manville Corp., 60 B.R. 612 (Bankr. S.D.N.Y. 1986)

In re Masterson, 280 N.Y.S.2d 936 (N.Y. 1967)

In re Moreno, 892 F.2d 417 (5th Cir. 1990)

In re Ross, 156 B.R. 272 (Bankr. D. Idaho 1993)

In re Scott, 172 F.3d 959 (7th Cir. 1999)

In re Slocum, 22 F.2d 282 (2d Cir. 1927)

In re: Sattler's, Inc., 73 B.R. 780 (S.D.N.Y. 1987)

In re Sheehan, 187 B.R. 669 (Bankr. D. Ariz. 1995)

In re Stockbridge Funding Corp., 153 B.R. 654 (Bankr. S.D.N.Y. 1993)

Kanner v. United States, 21 F.2d 285 (2d Cir. 1927)

Kastigar v. United States, 406 U.S. 441 (1972)

Kolender v. Lawson, 461 U.S. 352 (1983)

Kungys v. United States, 485 U.S. 759 (1988)

Lefkowitz v. Cunningham, 431 U.S. 801 (1977)

Levinson v. United States, 263 F. 257 (3d Cir. 1920)

Local Loan Co. v. Hunt, 292 U.S. 234 (1934)

Lurie v. United States, 20 F.2d 589 (6th Cir. 1927)

Martin-Trigona v. Belford (*In re Martin-Trigona*), 732 F.2d 170 (2d Cir. 1984)

Meagher v. United States, 36 F.2d 156 (9th Cir. 1929)

Metheany v. United States, 365 F.2d 90 (9th Cir. 1966)

Metheany v. United States, 390 F.2d 559 (9th Cir. 1968)

Nilson Van & Storage Co. v. Marsh, 755 F.2d 362 (4th Cir. 1985)

Norwest Bank Neb., N.A. v. Tveten, 848 F.2d 871 (8th Cir. 1988)

Nye & Nissen v. United States, 336 U.S. 613 (1949)

Pallett v. United States, 228 F.2d 671 (5th Cir. 1956)

Parklane Hosiery Co. v. Shore, 439 U.S. 322 (1979)

Pereira v. United States, 347 U.S. 1 (1954)

Powell v. United States, 352 F.2d 705 (D.C. Cir. 1965)

Raiford v. Abney (*In re Raiford*), 695 F.2d 521 (11th Cir. 1983)

Roviaro v. United States, 353 U.S. 53 (1957)

Rudin v. United States, 254 F.2d 45 (6th Cir. 1958)

Sachs v. Ryan (*In re Ryan*), 15 B.R. 514 (Bankr. D. Md. 1981)

Sedima v. Imrex Co., Inc., 473 U.S. 479 (1985)

Sinclair v. United States, 279 U.S. 263 (1929)

Somberg v. United States, 71 F.2d 637 (7th Cir. 1934)

Standefer v. United States, 447 U.S. 10 (1980)

States v. Kramer, 73 F.3d 1067 (11th Cir. 1996)

Stuhley v. Hyatt, 667 F.2d 807 (9th Cir. 1982)

Sultan v. United States, 249 F.2d 385 (5th Cir. 1957)

Toussie v. United States, 397 U.S. 112 (1970)

U.S. v. Bailey, 123 F.3d 1381 (11th Cir. 1997)

U.S. v. Kimler, 167 F.3d 889 (5th Cir. 1999)

U.S. v. Sullivan, 255 F.3d 1256 (10th Cir. 2001)

U.S. v. Bertoli, 40 F.3d 1384 (3d Cir. 1994)

U.S. v. Coyle, 154 Fed.Appx. 173 (11th Cir. 2005)

U.S. v. Eddy, 102 Fed.Appx. 643 (10th Cir. 2004)

U.S. v. Feldhacker, 849 F.2d 293 (8th Cir. 1988)

U.S. v. Lewis, 235 F. 3d 215 (4th Cir. 2000)

U.S. v. Ortland, 109 F.3d 539 (9th Cir. 1997)

U.S. v. Regan, 989 F.2d 44 (1st Cir. 1993)

U.S. v. Vivit, 214 F.3d 908 (7th Cir. 2000)
United States v. James Daniel Goode Real Property, 510 U.S. 43 (1993)
United States v. Aguilar, 21 F.3d 1475 (9th Cir. 1994)
United States v. Allen, 13 F.3d 105 (4th Cir. 1993)
United States v. Arch Trading Co., 987 F.2d 1087 (4th Cir. 1993)
United States v. Arge, 418 F.2d 721 (10th Cir. 1969)
United States v. Ballard, 779 F.2d 287 (5th Cir. 1986)
United States v. Bane, 583 F.2d 832 (6th Cir. 1978)
United States v. Banks, 942 F.2d 1576 (11th Cir. 1991)
United States v. Beacon Brass Co., 344 U.S. 43 (1952)
United States v. Beery, 678 F.2d 856 (10th Cir. 1982)
United States v. Blanchard, 9 F.3d 22 (6th Cir. 1993)
Kastigar v. United States
United States v. Booker, 543 U.S. 220 (2005)
United States v. Bosby, 675 F.2d 1174 (11th Cir. 1982)
United States v. Bradstreet, 135 F.3d 46 (1st Cir.)
United States v. Bramblett, 348 U.S. 503 (1955)
United States v. Brown, 188 F.3d 519 (10th Cir. 1999)
United States v. Brown, 943 F.2d 1246 (10th Cir. 1991)
United States v. Buffalano, 727 F.2d 50 (2d Cir. 1989)
United States v. Burns, 104 F.3d 529 (2d Cir. 1997)
United States v. Bushert, 997 F.2d 1343 (11th Cir. 1992)
United States v. Calandrella, 605 F.2d 236 (6th Cir. 1979)
United States v. Cardall, 885 F.2d 656 (10th Cir. 1989)
United States v. Casel, 995 F.2d 1299 (5th Cir. 1993)
United States v. Center, 853 F.2d 568 (7th Cir. 1988)
United States v. Chaplin, 25 F.3d 1373 (7th Cir. 1994)
United States v. Cherek, 734 F.2d 1248 (7th Cir. 1984)
United States v. Cluck, 143 F.3d 174 (5th Cir. 1998)
United States v. Cluck, 87 F.3d 138 (5th Cir. 1996)
United States v. Cohan, 46 F.2d 310 (M.D. Pa. 1931)
United States v. Collins, 424 F. Supp. 465 (E.D. Ky. 1977)
United States v. Connery, 867 F.2d 929 (6th Cir. 1989)

United States v. Cote, 456 F.2d 142 (8th Cir. 1972)

United States v. Crockett, 534 F.2d 589 (5th Cir. 1976)

United States v. Cueto, 151 F.3d 620 (7th Cir. 1998)

United States v. Curran, 20 F.3d 560 (3d Cir. 1994)

United States v. Daddano, 432 F.2d 1119 (7th Cir. 1970)

United States v. Davis, 533 F.2d 921 (5th Cir. 1976)

United States v. Defazio, 899 F.2d 626 (7th Cir. 1990)

United States v. DiCaro, 772 F.2d 1314 (7th Cir. 1985)

United States v. Diorio, 451 F.2d 21 (2d Cir. 1971)

United States v. DiSantillo, 615 F.2d 128 (3d Cir. 1980)

United States v. Doe, 465 U.S. 605 (1984)

United States v. Dolan, 120 F.3d 856 (8th Cir. 1997)

United States v. Dolan, 120 F.3d 856 (8th Cir. 1997)

United States v. Dolt, 27 F.3d 235 (6th Cir. 1994)

United States v. Egenberg, 441 F.2d 441 (2d Cir. 1971)

United States v. Falcone, 544 F.2d 607 (2d Cir. 1976)

United States v. Faudman, 640 F.2d 20 (6th Cir. 1981)

United States v. Filiberti, 353 F. Supp. 252 (D. Conn. 1973)

United States v. Fornaro, 894 F.2d 508 (2d Cir. 1990)

United States v. Fraidin, 63 F. Supp. 271 (D. Md. 1945)

United States v. Frankhauser, 80 F.3d 641 (1st Cir. 1996)

United States v. Friedman, 649 F.2d 199 (3d Cir. 1981)

United States v. Frost, 125 F.3d 346 (6th Cir. 1997)

United States v. Fulbright, 69 F.3d 1468 (9th Cir. 1995)

United States v. Gaudin, 515 U.S. 506 (1995)

United States v. Gellene, 182 F.3d 578 (7th Cir. 1999)

United States v. Gilbert, 136 F.3d 1451 (11th Cir. 1998)

United States v. Gleave, 786 F. Supp. 258 (W.D.N.Y. 1992)

United States v. Goodstein, 883 F.2d 1362 (7th Cir. 1989)

United States v. Gordon, 379 F.2d 788 (2d Cir. 1967)

United States v. Grady, 544 F.2d 598 (2d Cir. 1976)

United States v. Graham, 60 F.3d 463 (8th Cir. 1995)

United States v. Grant, 971 F.2d 799 (1st Cir. 1992)

United States v. Green, 745 F.2d 1205 (9th Cir. 1984)

United States v. Guglielmini, 425 F.2d 439 (2d Cir. 1970)

United States v. Gunderson, 55 F.3d 1332 (7th Cir. 1995)

United States v. Hamilton, 931 F.2d 1046 (5th Cir. 1991)

United States v. Harris, 79 F.3d 223 (2d Cir. 1996)

United States v. Harriss, 347 U.S. 612 (1954)

United States v. Hernandez, 160 F.3d 661 (11th Cir. 1998)

United States v. Hewes, 729 F.2d 1302 (11th Cir. 1984)

United States v. Hsia, 176 F.3d 517 (D.C. Cir. 1999)

United States v. Hubbard, 514 U.S. 695 (1995)

United States v. Hvass, 355 U.S. 570 (1958)

United States v. Indelicato, 865 F.2d 1370 (2d Cir. 1989)

United States v. Ismail, 97 F.3d 50 (4th Cir. 1996)

United States v. Johnson, 971 F.2d 562 (10th Cir. 1992)

United States v. Kenny, 973 F.2d 339 (4th Cir. 1992)

United States v. Key, 859 F.2d 1257 (7th Cir. 1988)

United States v. Keys, 95 F.3d 874 (9th Cir. 1996)

United States v. King, 169 F.3d 1035 (6th Cir. 1999)

United States v. Knoll, 16 F.3d 1313 (2d Cir. 1994)

United States v. Kubrick, 205 F.3d 1117 (9th Cir. 1999)

United States v. Ladum, 141 F.3d 1328 (9th Cir. 1998)

United States v. Lanier, 520 U.S. 259 (1997)

United States v. Lester, 363 F.2d 68 (6th Cir. 1966)

United States v. Levine, 457 F.2d 1186 (10th Cir. 1972)

United States v. Levine, 970 F.2d 681 (10th Cir. 1992)

United States v. Lindholm, 24 F.3d 1078 (9th Cir. 1994)

United States v. Linville, 10 F.3d 630 (9th Cir. 1993)

United States v. Littleton, 76 F.3d 614 (4th Cir. 1996)

United States v. Lloyd, 142 B.R. 866 (Bankr. E.D. Ark. 1992)

United States v. Lloyd, 947 F.2d 339 (8th Cir. 1991)

United States v. Local 560, 780 F.2d 267 (3d Cir. 1985)

United States v. Lynch, 11 F.2d 298 (W.D. La. 1926)

United States v. Maloney, 71 F.3d 645 (7th Cir. 1995)

United States v. Margolis, 138 F.2d 1002 (3d Cir. 1943)

United States v. Martin, 408 F.2d 949 (7th Cir. 1969)

United States v. Mathies, 203 F. Supp. 797 (W.D. Pa. 1962)

United States v. Maultasch, 596 F.2d 19 (2d Cir. 1979)

United States v. Mazzei, 700 F.2d 85 (2d Cir. 1983)

United States v. McAffee, 8 F.3d 1010 (5th Cir. 1993)

United States v. McCormick, 72 F.3d 1404 (9th Cir. 1995)

United States v. McIntosh, 124 F.3d 1330 (10th Cir. 1997)

United States v. Melton, 763 F.2d 401 (11th Cir. 1985)

United States v. Messner, 107 F.3d 1448 (10th Cir. 1997)

United States v. Micciche, 525 F.2d 544 (8th Cir. 1975)

United States v. Mohammad, 53 F.3d 1426 (7th Cir. 1995)

United States v. Moody, 923 F.2d 341 (5th Cir. 1991)

United States v. Moore, 613 F.2d 1029 (D.C. Cir. 1980)

United States v. Moss, 562 F.2d 155 (2d Cir. 1977)

United States v. Nazifpour, 944 F.2d 472 (9th Cir. 1991)

United States v. Neiswender, 590 F.2d 1269 (4th Cir. 1979)

United States v. Neuman, 474 U.S. 242 (1986)

United States v. Nill, 518 F.2d 793 (5th Cir. 1975)

United States v. Nofziger, 878 F.2d 442 (D.C. Cir. 1989)

United States v. O'Neill, 463 F. Supp. 1205 (E.D. Pa. 1979)

United States v. Overmyer, 867 F.2d 937 (6th Cir. 1989)

United States v. Palmisano, 185 B.R. 476 (D. Vt. 1995)

United States v. Pfingst, 477 F.2d 177 (2d Cir. 1973)

United States v. Phillips, 606 F.2d 884 (9th Cir. 1979)

United States v. Piervinazi, 23 F.3d 670 (2d Cir. 1994)

United States v. Ramsey, 785 F.2d 184 (7th Cir. 1986)

United States v. Rasheed, 663 F.2d 843 (9th Cir. 1981)

United States v. Robbins, 997 F.2d 390 (8th Cir. 1993)

United States v. Roberts, 783 F.2d 767 (9th Cir. 1985)

United States v. Robinson, 763 F.2d 778 (6th Cir. 1985)

United States v. Robinson, 8 F.3d 398 (7th Cir. 1993)

United States v. Rodgers, 466 U.S. 475 (1984)

United States v. Rowe, 144 F.3d 15 (1st Cir. 1998)
United States v. Sarihifard, 155 F.3d 301 (4th Cir. 1998)
United States v. Savage, 67 F.3d 14350 (9th Cir. 1995)
United States v. Schireson, 116 F.2d 881 (3d Cir. 1940)
United States v. Shadduck, 112 F.3d 523 (1st Cir. 1997)
United States v. Shapiro, 101 F.2d 375 (7th Cir. 1939)
United States v. Singleton, 702 F.2d 1159 (D.C. Cir. 1983)
United States v. Smith, 39 F.3d 119 (6th Cir. 1994)
United States v. Sternback, 402 F.2d 353 (7th Cir. 1968)
United States v. Stull, 743 F.2d 439 (6th Cir. 1984)
United States v. Tackett, 113 F.3d 603 (6th Cir. 1997)
United States v. Tashjian, 660 F.2d 829 (1st Cir. 1981)
United States v. Thomas, 916 F.2d 647 (11th Cir. 1990)
United States v. Tobias, 863 F.2d 685 (9th Cir. 1988)
United States v. Turkette, 452 U.S. 576 (1981)
United States v. Van Dyke, 605 F.2d 220 (6th Cir. 1979)
United States v. Vanderburg, 358 F.2d 6 (7th Cir. 1966)
United States v. Wagner, 382 F.3d 598 (6th Cir. 2004)
United States v. Waldemar, 98 F.3d 306, *rev'd*, 106 F.3d 729 (7th Cir. 1996)
United States v. Walgren, 885 F.2d 1417 (9th Cir. 1989)
United States v. Walker, 415 F.2d 530 (9th Cir. 1969)
United States v. Webster, 125 F.3d 1024 (7th Cir. 1997)
United States v. Weinstein, 834 F.2d 1454 (9th Cir. 1988)
United States v. Weiss, 168 F. Supp. 728 (W.D. Pa. 1958)
United States v. Welch, 103 F.3d 906 (9th Cir. 1996)
United States v. Westine, 1994 WL 88831 (6th Cir. 1994)
United States v. White, 950 F.2d 426 (7th Cir. 1991)
United States v. Whiting Pools, Inc., 462 U.S. 198 (1983)
United States v. Willey, 57 F.3d 1374 (5th Cir. 1995)
United States v. Worthington, 822 F.2d 315 (2d Cir. 1987)
United States v. Yagow, 953 F.2d 427 (8th Cir. 1992)
United States v. Yasser, 114 F.2d 558 (3d Cir. 1940)
United States v. Yermian, 468 U.S. 63 (1984)

United States v. Zang, 703 F.2d 1186 (10th Cir. 1982)

United States v. Zehrbach, 47 F.3d 1252 (3d Cir. 1995)

United States v. Zimmerman, 943 F.2d 1204 (10th Cir. 1991)

United States v. Zisblatt, 78 F. Supp. 9 (S.D.N.Y. 1948)

United States v. Zolin, 491 U.S. 554 (1989)

Upjohn Co. v. United States, 449 U.S. 383 (1981)

Weiler v. United States, 323 U.S. 606 (1945)

Wilson v. United States, 221 U.S. 361 (1911)

Wonneman v. Stratford Securities Co., 23 F.R.D. 281 (S.D.N.Y. 1959)

GENERAL STATUTORY MATERIALS

United States Code

Title 11

§ 101
§ 103
§ 105
§ 109
§ 110
§ 154
§ 324
§ 327
§ 328
§ 329
§ 330
§ 331
§ 341
§ 344
§ 362
§ 363
§ 502
§ 503
§ 521
§ 523
§ 524
§ 526
§ 541
§ 542
§ 543
§ 545
§ 546
§ 547
§ 548
§ 549
§ 727
§ 1102
§ 1103
§ 1104
§ 1106
§ 1107
§ 1109
§ 1111
§ 1125
§ 1129
§ 1141

Title 18

§ 2
§ 3
§ 4
§ 151
§ 152
§ 153
§ 154
§ 155
§ 156
§ 157
§ 201
§ 364
§ 371
§ 401
§ 645
§ 664
§ 981
§ 1001
§ 1014
§ 1032
§ 1114
§ 1341
§ 1343
§ 1344
§ 1503
§ 1519
§ 1603
§ 1621
§ 1622
§ 1623
§ 1911
§ 1956
§ 1961
§ 1962
§1963
§ 1964
§ 1965
§ 1966
§ 1967
§ 1968
§ 2314
§ 2315
§ 2516
§ 3057
§ 3161
§ 3282
§ 3284
§ 3284
§ 3553
§ 3563
§ 3571
§ 3613
§ 3663
§ 6003

Title 21

§ 881

Title 28

§ 515
§ 516
§ 586
§ 1746

United States Constitution

Art. I
Amed. IV
Amed. V
Amed. VI

U.S. Sentencing Guidelines

§ 1B1.11
§ 2B1.1
§ 2F1.1
§ 3B1.2
§ 3D1.2
§ 3E1.1
§ 4A1.1
§ 4A1.3
§ 5B1.1
§ 5B1.3
§ 5D1.1
§ 5E1.1
§ 5E1.4
§ 5E1.5
§ 5F1.1
§ 5F1.2
§ 5F1.3
§ 5H1.1
§ 5H1.2
§ 5H1.3
§ 5H1.4
§ 5H1.5
§ 5H1.6
§ 5H1.7
§ 5H1.8
§ 5H1.9
§ 5H1.10
§ 5H1.11
§ 5H1.12
§ 5K1.1
§ 6B1.4
§ 7B1.1
§ 8A1.1
§ 8B1.1
§ 8B1.3
§ 8C2.3
§ 8C4.1
§ 2J1.3
§ 2B4.2
§ 3A1.1
§ 3B1.1
§ 3B1.3
§ 3C1.1

Federal Rules of Criminal Procedure

Rule 5.1
Rule 6
Rule 7
Rule 8
Rule 11
Rule 12
Rule 18
Rule 58

Federal Rules of Bankruptcy Procedure

Rule 1007
Rule 1008
Rule 2004
Rule 2014
Rule 2015
Rule 2016
Rule 7003

Federal Rules of Evidence

Rule 101
Rule 501
Rule 603

Model Rules

Rule 1.1
Rule 1.13
Rule 1.2(d)
Rule 1.3
Rule 1.6
Rule 1.7
Rule 1.9
Rule 3.3
Rule 3.7

INDEX

A

abetting. *See* aiding and abetting
Abington Discount, 96–97
accessory after fact, 99–100, 208, 258, 366
accountant, definition of, 216
accounts
  false, 24, 35, 37, 56
  versus recorded information, 23, 67, 69–70, 73, 76, 203, 259
administrative claims, 51
adversary proceeding, and self-incrimination privilege, 58, 175–176, 286
adverse interest, 74–77, 213, 260
advice of counsel, 157–158, 166–167
affiliate, definition of, 216
affirmations, 293
affirmative defenses, 157–158
age, and sentencing guidelines, 190, 368
aggravating role, sentencing guidelines, 190, 368
agreements
  conspiratorial, 100–101
  farmout, 223
  fee, 260–261
  plea, 200–201
  repurchase, 113, 223, 231
  swap, 224, 234–236
aiding and abetting, 95–100
Allen, Lawrence, 112
ambiguities
  in Bankruptcy Code, 16, 25
  as defense, 158
American bankruptcy law, history of, 6–9
American Bar Association Model Rules of Professional Conduct, 339–359
  candor toward tribunal, 354–358
  confidentiality, 342–347
  conflict of interest, 353
  organizational clients, 348–353
  scope of representation, 339–341
Anderson, David R. 104–106
appeal, right to, waiver of, 201, 357
Arochem, 120
asset(s)
  borrowing of, 72
  camouflaging of, 29, 33
  disclosure (*See* disclosure), 34–39
  equitable distribution of, 19, 56
  exempt, 188, 206
  failure to list, 29
  forfeiture, and choice of statutory provision, 94
  transfers, ethical issues with, 215
asset concealment
  and appointment of trustee, 33, 74, 156, 310
  Bankruptcy Code provisions 15, 19
  Bankruptcy Criminal Code provisions, 15, 19
  as continuing offense, 37
  definition of, 28
  examples of, 37–39
  forms of, 29
  and intent issues, 30–31
  and materiality, 33–34
  overlap with other sections, 34–37
  and property issues, 31–33
asset planning
  common devices used in, 206–208
  negligent, 208
asset sales. *See* bankruptcy sales

assistance to authorities, substantial, sentencing guidelines, 193, 384–385
Atlantis International, Ltd. 98
attorney(s). *See also* United States attorneys
accessory issues, 100, 208, 258
advice of, 2
aiding and abetting, 95–100
compensation, 79
and conflict of interest issues, 131, 212–215
conduct of (*See* professional conduct)
confidentiality (*See also* attorney-client privilege)
ABA model rules, 339–359
conflict of interest
ABA model rules, 353
conspiracy charges against, 35, 104–105
corporate (*See* corporate counsel)
definition of, 3
indirect responsibility of, 102
Attorney General, definition of, 277
attorney-client privilege, 169–174
corporate, 171–172
ethical issues, 205–215
exceptions to, 172–173
trustee's control of, 172
waiver of, 172
Avery, Kathryn, 112
avoidance litigation, 47

B

Bacon, Kimberly, 114
bad faith, 20
Ballard, 173–174, 389
bank fraud, 4, 92, 94, 119–120, 265
bank loan, procurement, bribery in, 365
bankruptcy [term], derivation of, 5
Bankruptcy Abuse Prevention and Consumer Protection Act of 2005, 86, 250
Bankruptcy Act of 1898, 6, 28, 31, 40
bankruptcy cases, volume of, 1
bankruptcy clause, to Constitution, 6
Bankruptcy Code, 54–63
ambiguities in, 16, 25
asset sale provisions, 59, 75, 159–160, 243
chapter 9 overview, 17–27
civil *versus* criminal laws, 202–205
claim definition, 50–51
confirmation of plan, 57, 176, 180, 252–257
debtor eligibility, 21, 46
debtor's duties, 22, 37, 175, 245–250
definitions, 16, 21–22
disclosure, 23–24, 34–39, 76
excerpts, 216–258
immunity, 150–151, 241
meetings of creditors and equity security holders, 240–241
objectives, 182
postpetition disclosure and solicitation, 251–252
professional compensation, 80
property of estate, 159
self-incrimination, 241
transfer definition, 63–64, 236–237
trustee provisions, 241–245
use, sale, or lease of property, 241–245
Bankruptcy Commission, 6–8
Bankruptcy Criminal Code
accessory after fact, 99–100, 208, 258, 366
adverse interest, 74–77, 213, 260
asset concealment, 15–19
bank fraud, 4, 92, 94, 119–120, 265
versus Bankruptcy Code, 8, 16
bankruptcy fraud, 10–13, 88, 146, 264
bribery, 18, 54–62
and chapter 7 discharge, 204
conduct of officers, 74–77
conflict of interest, 212–215
conspiracy, 61–64, 101–107
crop insurance, 262–263
definitions, 16, 21–22
discounts, 262–263
embezzlement, 34, 72–73, 172, 186–187, 189, 274, 276
excerpts, 216–257
false claims, 50–53, 112
false oaths, 24, 35, 39–49, 131, 161, 259, 271
fee agreements, 78–81, 260–261
frauds, 10–13, 88, 146, 264
influencing or injuring officer or juror, 265–266

intent, 54–62
investigations, 2, 68, 149, 152, 266, 273, 275, 277
loan and credit applications, 262–263, 271
misprision, 95–100, 208, 258
money laundering, 4, 94, 120, 124,140–145, 197
overlap with Federal Criminal Code, 91, 94
principals, 64–65, 171, 213, 258
receiverships, 6, 8, 78–81, 147, 260–261, 277, 326
renewals, 262–263
sentencing, 182–194
statements or entries generally, 262
swindles, 264
transfer definition, 63–64, 236–237
wire, radio, or television fraud, 87, 89, 94, 116–120, 139, 274
bankruptcy fraud
definition of, 4, 88, 92, 94, 119–120, 265
intent issues, 89
mail fraud statute, 116, 118–119
under RICO, 120
sentencing guidelines, 4, 17, 182–194, 201, 279–280, 282, 361–385
bankruptcy mill schemes, 83, 88
bankruptcy nexus, insufficient, 159
bankruptcy petition preparer
definition of, 82
fraud, 8, 82–86
bankruptcy planning. *See* asset planning
Bankruptcy Reform Act of 1978, 8, 23
Bankruptcy Rules and Forms. *See also specific form*
instruction violations, sentencing guidelines, 186, 189, 365
bankruptcy sales, 11–12
bid bribery in, 59–62
to court officers, 260
looting schemes with, 12
procedures for, 11–12
bankruptcy system
fundamental policy of, 17–19
historical summary of, 5–9
integrity of, 49, 67, 75, 214
purpose of, 2–3
base offense levels, 186–187
adjustments to
bribery of witness, 366
fraud/deceit/forgery/counterfeiting, 146, 271, 274
larceny/embezzlement/theft, 360–365
perjury, 126–134
bid bribery, 59–62
bid protection orders, 12
Black's Law Dictionary, false statement definition, 109
Bleedout, 10–11
Borah, William E., 78
Borah Act, 6, 8, 78
borrowing, of estate assets
Breindel, Robert, 103
bribery
in bank loan procurement, 365
bid, 59–62
of public officials, 146
sentencing guidelines, 186, 189, 365
of witnesses, 146
bright line test
for bankruptcy integral to fraud, 89–90
for property concealment, 28–39
Bronston, Samuel, 133
Bronston Productions, Inc., 133
Brown, Tom, 102–104
bustout scheme, 64, 88, 120,
Buycrus-Erie Company, 131

C

candor toward tribunal, 354
capital punishment, 5, 373, 383–384
cash collateral, 55, 189, 241–242
Cassani, Robert, 112
Cassani, Shirley, 112
Cassani Electrical Service, 112
causing
and aiding and abetting issues, 95–100
mailing, 117
Center, Mark, 44
Chaplin, 130–131
chapter 7 (liquidation)

bid bribery, 54–55, 57–58
conversion of chapter 11 to, 176
debtor eligibility, 21, 46
discharge, 114, 143, 164
duties of debtor or trustee, 291
false oaths/declarations, 24, 35, 39–49, 131, 161, 259, 271
false statements, 111–112, 114
misprision and accessory, 100
money laundering, 4, 94, 120, 124,140–145, 197
property transfer, 54, 227
and self-incrimination privilege, 175–176, 178
trustee appointment, 22–23
chapter 9 (municipalities)
debtor eligibility, 21, 46
list of creditors, 301
statutory overlap, 91–94
chapter 11 (reorganization)
aiding and abetting, 95–100
appointment of trustee, 22–23, 31
bribery, 54–55, 57–58
claim issues, 51–52
concealment, 70
conversion to chapter 7, 164
creditors committees, 149
debtor eligibility, 21, 46
disclosure, 36
duties of debtor or trustee, 291
false oaths/declarations, 24, 35, 39–49, 131, 161, 259, 271
list of creditors, 301
money laundering, 94, 120, 124,140–145, 197
perjury, 133–134
property transfer, 54, 227, 327
self-incrimination privilege, 175–176, 178
statute of limitations, 127, 157, 162–165
trustee appointment, 22–23, 31
chapter 12 (family farmers)
debtor eligibility, 21, 46
duties of debtor or trustee, 291
trustee appointment, 22–23
chapter 13 (wage earner plans)
debtor eligibility, 21, 46
duties of debtor or trustee, 291
trustee appointment, 22–23
charge offense sentencing, 183
charitable institution, misrepresentation involving, 361
child support debt, definition of, 206, 375
circumstantial evidence
and conspiracy, 101–106
and perjury, 129
civil compliance, 160–161
civil penalties, 3, 86
civil proceedings, relationship between criminal proceedings and, 202–204
claim(s)
administrative, 50–51
community, 217–218
for debts paid by third party, 53
definitions, 50
false, 50–53
and intent, 52–53
overstating of, 51
prepetition, payment of, 55
prioritization of, 310–311
proof of (*See* proof of claim)
secured, 52, 254–256
transferred, 289
unsecured
nonpriority, 301–302
priority, 301–302
client loyalty, 214
co-conspiracy, 61, 68, 101–107
Code of Professional Responsibility. *See* professional conduct
Codebtors, 302, 308, 310, 313, 316
Cohen, Bernard, 129–130
collateral estoppel, 202, 204
commercial bribery, sentencing guidelines, 186, 365
commercial real estate, skimming schemes with, 12, 44, 88
Commission on the Bankruptcy Laws of the United States, 6
Committee on the Judiciary, United States House of Representatives, 150

commodity broker, definition of, 217
common interest privilege, 170
community claim, definition of, 217–218
community confinement, 193–194
community service, 193–194, 373, 378
company cars, fraud prosecutions involving, 32, 105, 319
compensation. *See also* fee(s)
  of counsel
    and conflict of interest issues, 131, 212–215
  and mill schemes, 83–88
  of officers, 78
  of trustees, 72, 78, 244
Comprehensive Crime Control Act of 1984, Title II, 182
concealment
  of assets (*See* asset concealment), 28–40
  and conspiracy charges, 102
  indictment for, 155
  loss amount determination, 187
  and money laundering, 141
  and multiplicity, 92
  prebankruptcy, 63–67
  of proceeds of bankruptcy sales, 11
  of records, 67–70, 259, 266, 271
  statute of limitations, 162–165
conduct. *See also* obstruction of justice
  of court officers, 122
  egregious, 26, 39, 143
  professional (*See* professional conduct), 339–359
  prohibited under RICO, 138–139
confidentiality. *See also* attorney-client privilege
  ABA model rules, 339–359
  timeframe, 208–215
confirmation of plan, 252–257
conflict of interest, 131, 212–215
ABA model rules
    General, 339–359
    prohibited transactions, 339–359
  potential sources of, 339–359
  undisclosed, 339–359
Congress, 6, 7, 14, 42, 49
Connery, Edmund, 52–53
conspiracy
  statute of limitations, 162–165
Constitution
  bankruptcy clause, 6
  infractions, 157
  and legal ethics, 205–215
  rights under, 157–158
consumer bankruptcy filings, 83
consumer debt, 8, 82–83, 86, 216–217
contingency fee arrangements, 144
continuing offense, concealment as, 37, 92, 162, 210
control test, for corporate privilege, 171
corporate counsel
  ABA model rules, 205–215, 339–359
  Confidentiality, 208–212
  conflict of interest, 212–215
corporate officers, aiding and abetting by, 63
corporate privilege, 171–172
corporate transactions, bleedout schemes with, 11
corporation
  definition of, 137, 164, 217–218
  and self-incrimination privilege, 86, 175
corruptly, definition of, 113, 121–122, 261
counsel. *See* attorney(s)
counterfeiting
  sentencing guidelines, 271
court approval
  prior, 160
  of professional persons, 79
  retroactive, 160
court order
  for appointment of trustee, 22–23
  for disclosure, 23–24, 76
  for inspection, 74
  obstruction of, 76–77
  violation of, 188–189
credit applications, 262–263
credit industry, 82
credit union, insured, definition of, 223
creditors
  definition of, 218
  equitable asset distribution among, 56
  holding secured claims, 302, 308–309

holding unsecured claims
nonpriority, 302, 313
priority, 302, 310
lists of
meetings of, 41, 240–241, 246–248
crime control, 136, 182–183
Criminal Enforcement Tracking System, 150
Criminal Enforcement Unit, 147, 150
criminal history, and sentencing guidelines, 184, 191–194
criminal intent. *See* intent
criminal proceedings, relationship between civil proceedings and, 202–204
crop insurance, 262–263
culpability
for bankruptcy integral to fraud, 90
degrees of, for sentencing, 184
culpability scorecurative acts, 159–160
curfew, 378–379
custodian, definition of, 74

D

death penalty, 5, 373, 383–384
debt
child support, 206, 375
consumer, 8, 82–83, 86, 216–217, 240, 296–297, 299, 324
definition of, 22
paid by third party, claims for, 53
and probation, 193–194
unlawful, 135, 276
debt relief agency, 86, 219
debtor(s)
current expenditures of, 23
current income of, 302, 317
default, 248, 286
definition of, 22
duties of, 291
eligibility as, 21
examination of, 287
debtor in possession
displacement by trustee, 74
debtor partnerships, 285
deceit
loss amount determination, 186–189
sentencing guidelines, 192–194
declarations. *See also* false declarations
unsworn, *versus* oaths, 23–24, 286, 293
decriminalization of bankruptcy, 9
defenses
advice of counsel, 166–168
affirmative, 157–158
ambiguities as, 16, 25
civil compliance, 160–161
curative acts, 159–160
factual, 166
ignorance of law as, 60, 80, 84–85
intent, 158
joint, 170
materiality, 161
to perjury, 132–133
safe harbor, 160–161
defraud, definition of, 89
Department of Justice (DOJ), Operation Total Disclosure, 1–2, 147
departures, sentencing, 194
deportation, 377–378
depository institution, insured, definition of, 228
derivative actions, and corporate counsel, 353
derivative use immunity, 178
destruction
of estate documents, 73
of records, 67–70
diminished capacity, 158
discharge
under chapter 7, 112, 114, 143, 164
granting of, 17, 163
disclosure
and attorney-client privilege, 169–174
and confidentiality, 342–348
of conflict of interest, 353
court-directed, 357
defenses based on, 159–160
failure of (*See* asset concealment; concealment; nondisclosure)
full and accurate, importance of, 18, 37
of informant identity, prevention of, 151, 275
postpetition, 251–257

prior, 160
of security holders list, 286
and self-incrimination privilege, 58, 175–176, 286
disclosure statement
asset exemption on, 33–34, 307
fraud on, 173
discounts, 262–263
discovery, 29, 35, 67–68
disgorgement, 17, 42, 159
disinterested person, definition of, 79, 219–220
dismissal
and fraud schemes, 10–13
pretrial motion for, 157, 166
and self-incrimination privilege, 58, 175–176, 286
and statute of limitations, 162–165
document(s)
production of, and self-incrimination privilege, 76
versus recorded information, 67, 69–70, 73, 76, 203, 246
secretion/destruction of, 67–70
document for filing, definition of, 82
documentary material, definition of, 277
Dolan, Gary L., 104
double jeopardy, 125, 155, 157–158
Drizos Investments, Inc., 60
dual representation, by corporate counsel, 349, 353
due process, 14–16

E

Edict of Padua, 5
egregious conduct, 26
embezzlement
by court officers, 146, 260
from employee benefit plan, 146
from escrow accounts, 72
of filing fees, 72
loss amount determination, 187–189
of property of estate, 71–73
sentencing guidelines, 184–187
employee benefit plan, embezzlement or theft from, 146
Employee Retirement Income Security Act of 1974 (ERISA), 247
English bankruptcy laws, 5–6
enterprise, definition of, 137, 276
entity, definition of, 137, 216, 220, 350–351
equity security, definition of, 220
equity security holders
definition of, 220
lists of, 283–284
meetings of, 240–241
equity skimming, 12, 88
escrow accounts, embezzlement from, 72
estate
definition of, 24–25, 31–33
officer of (*See* officer of court; trustees)
property of (*See* property of estate)
estate assets. *See* asset(s)
estate planning. *See* asset planning
ethics. *See* professional conduct
evidence. *See also* testimony
circumstantial
and conspiracy, 101
and perjury, 219
and confidentiality issues, 170, 172–173, 208–212
false, and legal ethics, 205–215
limited admissibility, 294
and proof of claim, 50–53, 289, 334–335
evidentiary standard, for perjury, 129
ex parte proceedings, 354, 358
Ex Post Facto Clause, 184–185
ex post facto crimes, prohibition of, 14
examination, 241, 265, 277, 286–287
examiner, removal for cause, 74
executive branch, 16, 111, 352
executory contracts, 284, 302–303
exemption, asset, 33–34, 307
expenditures, current, of individual debtors, 23, 43, 245–246, 284, 319–320

F

factual defense, 166
failure to charge offense, 157
fair market value, for loss amount determination, 187

fair warning, 14, 16
faith. *See* bad faith; good faith
false accounts, 56
false claims, 50–53, 112
false declarations
with concealment, 92
and intent, 42–43
and materiality, 45–49, 161
versus perjury, 127–128
recantation, 132–133
and receipt of property, 136
statute of limitations, 162–165, 212–215
false evidence, and legal ethics, 205–215
false identification, 264
false oaths. *See also* perjury
with concealment, 271
and intent, 42–43
and materiality, 45–49, 161
versus perjury, 127–128
recantation, 132–133
false statements, *See also* perjury
definition of, 108–109
to FBI, 108, 111, 114
to governmental agency, 108–110
false swearing statute, 127, 131
falsity, establishment of, 109–110, 127, 132, 354
family farmers. *See also* chapter 12 (family farmers)
definition of, 220–221
with regular annual income, definition of, 221–222
family limited partnerships, 206–207
farming operation, definition of, 222
farmout agreement, definition of, 223
Federal Bankruptcy Commissioner, 7
Federal Bureau of Investigation (FBI), 3, 38, 61, 91, 111, 114, 123, 151–152
Federal Criminal Code
overlap with Bankruptcy Criminal Code, 91, 94
reporting obligations under, 147–149
Federal Deposit Insurance Corporation (FDIC), 223–224, 237–238, 263
federal depository institutions regulatory agency, definition of, 223
Federal Rules of Bankruptcy Procedure, 261, 283–293
Federal Rules of Criminal Procedure, 153, 398
Federal Rules of Evidence, 294, 398
federal sentencing guidelines. *See* sentencing guidelines
fee(s)
contingency, 144
filing, embezzlement of, 72
professional (*See also* compensation)
allowance and payment of, 151
fee agreements, 78–81
fee caps, mutual, 81
fee fixing, prohibition of, 6, 8, 78
Fifth Amendment
right to due process, 175–181
right to grand jury, 153–154
self-incrimination privilege, 86, 177
filing. *See* petition filing
financial affairs, statement of, 323–333
Financial Crimes Enforcement Network, 152, 269,
financial institution
crimes affecting, 116
definition of, 223
fine(s). *See also* loss amount
and ability to pay, 195–196
organizational, 17, 28, 40, 50, 54, 71, 87, 194, 380
paid in installments, 198–199
and plea agreements, 201
sentencing guidelines, 192–194
fine table, 381
foreclosure, bankruptcy filing to stay, 84
foreign bank accounts, used for concealment, 98, 187
foreign proceeding, definition of, 224
foreign representative, definition of, 224
forfeiture
civil, 94, 197–198
criminal, 197–199
effect of automatic stay, 13
trustee's avoidance of asset forfeiture, 94

turnover of forfeited property, 198
forgery, sentencing guidelines, 360–385
forward contract, definition of, 224–225
forward contract merchant, definition of, 225
Foxcliff, Inc., 44–45
fraud. *See also specific type of fraud*
Bankruptcy Criminal Code provisions, 16
bankruptcy integral to, 89–90
common schemes, 8, 10–13
incidence of, 1
loss amount determination, 187–189
sentencing guidelines, 182–194
fraudulent intent
versus deception, 42
fraudulent action, 188–189
defenses that seek to negate, 158
definition of, 42
and false oaths, accounts, and declarations, 40–42
and perjury, 127–128
and receipt of property, 136
Friedman, Lawrence A., 150, 164, 390

G

Galaxy, 129–130
Garnigan, 64–65
Gellene, John, 42–43, 48–49, 127–128, 131, 160, 190, 212–213, 390
general federal perjury statute, 111, 126–128
Gleave, Ted, 163–164, 174, 390
good faith
and bid bribery, 60
definition of, 61
and mail/wire fraud, 118
Goodstein, 160, 390
government employee, as victim, sentencing guidelines, 33
government misconduct, in investigation, 158
governmental agencies. *See also specific agency*
false statements made to, 109–111, 114
involved in investigations, 123
representation of, 352
governmental unit, definition of, 225
grand jury
indictment by (*See* indictment)
irregularities, 157
pending investigation by, 122
right to, 157–158
subpoenas issued by, 124, 152
witness tampering, 125
Grant, John, 32–34, 38–39
guilty plea, 200, 204

H

Hand, Learned, 96
hate crime motivation, sentencing guidelines, 366–367
Hernandez, 187, 391
home detention, 192–194, 372, 378, 384
horizontal dimension, 55–56
Hornaday, Albert, 114–115
Hubbard, John Bruce, 110–112, 391

I

identification, false, 274, 362
ignorance of law, as defense, 60, 84, 212
immunity
Bankruptcy Code, 150–151
for trustees, 150–151, 178–179
impounding, of security holders list, 286
in camera review, 174
incarceration. *See also* sentencing
determination of range, 184, 384
intermittent, 192–193
income, current, of individual debtors, 23–24
incriminatory, definition of, 176
indenture, definition of, 226
indenture trustee, definition of, 226
indictment
for concealment, 259, 263
dismissal of (*See* dismissal)
joinder of offenses in, 91
return of, 153–154
superseding, and statue of limitations, 112, 164
technical requirements for, 154
venue for, 155–156
individual with regular income, definition of, 226
informants, identity disclosure, 151
information
joinder of offenses in, 91
innocence, consciousness of, 158
insanity, 158

insider, definition of, 226
insider transactions, 11, 149
insolvent, definition of, 227
inspection
court-directed, 74–77, 286
refusal to permit, 77
institution-affiliated party, definition of, 227–228
intellectual property, definition of, 228
intent, 22–23. *See also* knowing; willfulness
and aiding and abetting, 95–100
and bankruptcy fraud, 139, 144
and claim presentation, 52–53
and concealment, 259
and conflict of interest, 212–215
in conspiracy, 101–107
defenses that seek to negate, 157–161
and false oaths, accounts, and declarations, 40–42
and false statements, 108–109
fraudulent (*See* fraudulent intent)
and mail/wire fraud, 117–119
and money laundering, 140–143
and obstruction of justice, 121–123
and perjury, 126–130
intermittent confinement, 193–194, 372, 379
Internal Revenue Service (IRS), 124, 149, 152, 173, 198
interstate wire communication, 119
investigations
government misconduct in, 158
pending, by grand jury, 148
racketeering, definition of, 277
rights of trustees in, 150–151

J

joinder of offenses, in same indictment, 91
joint defense, 170
judicial branch, 16, 23, 108, 110, 182, 262
judicial lien, definition of, 228
judicial process violation, sentencing guidelines, 186, 188–189
jurisdiction
and false statements, 108–109
lack of, 198
over forfeited property, 198
jurors, influencing or injuring of, 265–266
just dessert principle, 183

K

Key, Bobby, 47–49, 391
Key, Jeraldine, 47–49, 391
kickback schemes, 143
Knoll, David, 98–99, 163–164, 208
knowing
and aiding and abetting, 95–100
under Bankruptcy Criminal Code, 139, 144, 213–214
and concealment, 259
and intent defenses, 157–161
and money laundering, 140–143
and perjury, 126–131
and receipt of property, 59, 136

L

Ladum, Robert, 124–125
larceny, sentencing guidelines, 361–364
law enforcement privilege, 151
leases, unexpired, 285, 302–303
leave of court, 153
legal arguments, misleading, 355
legal compliance, 158
legality, 14, 16, 61
lenity
for administrative claimants, 14–16, 51
and withholding of recorded information, 70
Levine, Gary, 37, 67–68
Levine, Marcee, 37, 67–68
liability
limiting, 75, 159, 161, 212, 263
malpractice, 208
lien
definition of, 228
fine or restitution as, 197
judicial, definition of, 234
statutory, definition of, 234
liquidation. *See* chapter 7 (liquidation)
lists, of creditors and equity security holders, 283–284
literal truth, 133–134
literary rights, 219, 272

litigation
  acquisition of interest in, 135
  avoidance, 47, 257
  conflict of interest issues, 212–215, 353
loan applications
    bribery issues, 114–115
local rule violations, 85
looting, 11–12
loss amount. *See also* fine(s)
  determination of, 186–189
  fraud/deceit/forgery/counterfeiting, 186–189
  larceny/embezzlement/theft, 186–189

M

mail fraud
  and multiplicity, 94
  under RICO, 120, 139
  statute, 116, 118–119
mailing, causing, 117
malpractice liability, 208
margin payment, definition of, 228
mask work, definition of, 229
material evidence, and confidentiality issues, 209
materiality
  and concealment, 33, 45
  defenses based on, 161
  determination of, 45
  and false oaths/declarations, 161
  and false statements, 46, 48, 161
  and perjury, 128–129, 131–132
  and receipt of property, 59, 136
McIntosh, 144
media rights, 76, 126–127, 275
meetings, of creditors and equity security holders, 240
Megra Properties, 93
mens rea
  lack of, 158
  for mail/wire fraud, 118
  for obstruction of justice, 122
mental health program participation, 377
mental state. *See also* intent; knowing; willfulness
  and advice of counsel, 166
  and aiding and abetting, 96
  of counsel, and professional responsibility, 205
Mervis, 60–61
Micciche, 64–65
Mileage, 64–65
Misprision, 95, 100, 208
misrepresentation
  affirmative, 355
  of charitable institution, 186
  of governmental agency, 186
money laundering
  and forfeiture, 197
  proof of, 142
  and RICO, 197
  transportation, 141
Moody, Shearn, 65
morality, and bankruptcy system, 9
mortgage refinancing, 83
multiple representation, and conflict of interest, 214
multiple victim enhancement, 186
multiplicity. *See also* overcharging
  sentencing guidelines, 191
multiplier, 194
municipality. *See also* chapter 9 (municipalities)
  definition of, 229
mutual fee caps, 81
MWI Land, Inc, 114

N

negotiation
  fraudulent (*See* bribery), 58
  legitimate, *versus* bribery, 58
nolo contendere, 200–201, 366
nondisclosure. *See also* concealment
  and advice of counsel, 167–168
  and looting schemes, 12
no-shop provisions, 11
notice, right to, 14

O

oaths. *See also* false oaths; perjury
  affirmation in lieu of, 293

oral examination under, and self-incrimination privilege, 175
versus unsworn declarations, 41
objective test, for invoking advice of counsel, 166
obstruction of court order, 123, 188, 343, 375–376
sentencing adjustments, 189
occupational restrictions, 378
officer of court
compensation of, 78
conduct of, 122
definition of, 265
embezzlement by, 146
influencing or injuring of, 265
self-incrimination implications, 176
official victim, sentencing guidelines, 367
offshore accounts, 98
omnibus clause, 122–125
Operation Total Disclosure, 1–2, 147
oral examination under oath, and self-incrimination privilege, 175
order of notice, presentence procedure, 281
ordinary course standard, 55
organizations
fines paid by, 194
representation (*See* corporate counsel), 211
sentencing of, 194
Organized Crime Control Act of 1970
overcharging
and false statements, 112
and level of punishment, 94
Overmyer, Daniel, 52
overt act, in conspiracy, 106, 156, 165

P

Palmisano, Joseph, 112
papers
signing of, 291, 293
verification of, 286, 293
parties in interest
definition of, 81
and fee agreements, 80
partnership, debtor, 21, 159, 227, 285, 297, 330
pension funds, bleedout schemes with, 11
perjury. *See also* false oaths; false statements
in bankruptcy case, 131, 175
defense to, 132–133
elements of, 94, 128
evidentiary standard for, 129
versus false oaths/declarations, 24, 37
and legal ethics, 213–214
legal history of, 8–9
sentencing guidelines, 186, 189
person, definition of, 21, 28–29, 40–41, 50, 54
personal bankruptcy, 2, 83
personal property, schedule B, 302
petition(s)
caption of, 283
definition of, 82, 230
interests acquired after, 285
involuntary, 64
verification of, 286
voluntary, 295
petition filing
false identification information on, 274
time limits for, 284
volume of, 230
petition filing fees, embezzlement of, 72–73
Pinkney, Charles, 6
plan of confirmation, contest, 176
plea agreements, 200
prebankruptcy concealment, 208
prebankruptcy transfers, fraudulent, 63–65
predicate acts, 136–137, 139
prepetition claims, payment of, 55
pretrial motion to dismiss, 166
principals, 64–65, 258
probable cause, 148, 154, 157, 174
probation
conditions, 193
and payment of restitution, 195
sentencing guidelines, 278, 281
upon payment of fines, 196–197
production payment, definition of, 230
professional conduct
ABA model rules, 168, 341
dispute concerning, 356
resolution framework, 214

professional persons, court approval of, 79
prohibited transactions, conflict of interest rules, 271, 340, 364
proof, standard of, in civil *versus* criminal proceedings, 202–203
proof of claim
  filing of, 50–53
  form for, 289
property. *See also* property of estate
  of debtor, 18
  definition of, 327–331, 333, 336–337
  exempt, 20
  mismanagement by receiver, 22
  personal, 20, 30, 35
  real, 34, 303
  receipt with intent to defeat Bankruptcy Code, 54
  stolen, sentencing guidelines, 361, 364
  transfer, prebankruptcy, 63
  use, sale, or lease, Bankruptcy Code provisions, 55, 241
property of estate
  and concealment, 28–29
  defenses based on, 157, 160
  definition of, 327–331, 333, 336–337
  embezzlement of, 70–71
  versus property of debtor, 327
prosecution
  procedures governing, 153
  selective, 158
  vindictive, 158
prosecutorial discretion, exercise of, 3
public officials, bribery of, 146
public perception, of bankruptcy system, 169, 178, 180, 344
public records doctrine, 177
purchaser, definition of, 230

R

Racketeer Influenced and Corrupt Organizations Act (RICO)
  elements for prosecution, 136
  forfeiture, 197
  prohibited conduct, 138
racketeering activity, 138
  definition of, 136
  pattern of, 138
racketeering investigation, definition of, 277
racketeering investigator, definition of, 277
radio fraud, 116–117, 264
railroad, definition of, 230
ratification, 159–160
reachback periods, 47
real estate
  commercial, skimming schemes, 12, 88
  single asset, definition of, 233
real offense sentencing, 183
real property, schedule A, 43, 233, 303
reasonable basis, 148
recantation, 132, 159–160
receiverships
  fee agreements under, 78–79, 260
  property mismanagement under, 326
recorded information
  concealment/destruction of, 67, 69
  definition of, 67
  versus documents and accounts, 67, 76
  integrity of, 67
  withholding of, 69–70
refiling, prohibitions on, 89
relative, definition of, 230
religious institution, misrepresentation involving, 186
relitigation, 204
remedial measures, and legal ethics, 209–211, 357
renewals, 262
Reno, Janet, 2
Renoja, 138–139
rental income, skimming of, 12, 88
reorganization. *See* chapter 11 (reorganization), 8, 21, 67, 138, 147, 224, 254, 277, 285, 287
repo participant, definition of, 231–232
reporting, of suspected bankruptcy crimes, 147, 151
reports, transmission of, 289
representation. *See also* misrepresentation
  dual, by corporate counsel, 211
  multiple, and conflict of interest, 131, 212

scope of, 339
reprisal, fear of, 125
repurchase agreement, definition of, 231
responsibility, acceptance, downward adjustment for, 190
restitution
and ability to pay, 195
calculation of, 195
and debt obligations, 377
and plea agreements, 200
sentencing guidelines, 190
restraint of victim, sentencing guidelines, 367
RICO. *See* Racketeer Influenced and Corrupt Organizations Act
right to, 50, 150, 154, 157–158, 200–201, 217, 223, 287, 239
Robinson, 138–139
Rosenberg, Arthur, 59
Rosenberg Bros, 59
Rowe, Robert, 43
rule of law. *See* legality, 14, 16

S

safe harbor defense, 161
Salmon & Co, 130
Sam Houston Bank, 114
Sanctions, 9, 13, 176, 291–293
Sarbanes-Oxley Act, 68
Schedules
A-real property, 29, 43, 303
B-personal property, 304–306
C-property claimed as exempt, 303–304, 307
D-creditors holding secured claims, 308–309
declaration concerning, 321
E-creditors holding unsecured priority claims, 302, 310, 312
failure to list assets on, 29
F-creditors holding unsecured nonpriority claims, 314
G-executory contracts and unexpired leases, 284, 302, 304, 315
H-codebtors, 310
I-current income of individual debtors, 302, 317
J-current expenditures of individual debtors, 302, 319
summary of, 302
Schireson, 35, 156
Schwartz, David, 102–104
search and seizure, unreasonable, right against, 157
search warrants, 152
secretion, of estate documents, 71
Securities and Exchange Commission (SEC), 129, 232–233, 296
securities clearing agency, definition of, 232
security, definition of, 220, 232–233
security agreement, definition of, 233
security interest, definition of, 233
Seidman, Bernice, 130
selective prosecution, 158
self-dealing, by court officers, 74–75
self-incrimination privilege
civil consequences of, 86
elements necessary for, 175–176
sentencing, 223–237. *See also* sentencing guidelines
Bankruptcy Criminal Code provisions, 4
base offense levels (*See* base offense levels), 186
criminal history factors in, 184, 191–192, 282
departures, 192, 194
determination of, 192
enhancements, 188–190
fines (*See* fine(s)), 136, 196
forfeiture, 136, 197
fundamental approach of, 183
honesty in, 182
loss amounts, 201
mandatory guidelines for, 192–193
for multiple counts, 191
and offender characteristics, 192
of organizations, 194
and plea agreements, 200
policy objectives, 182
proportionality in, 183
purpose of, 54, 87–88, 119
uniformity in, 183

sentencing guidelines
abuse of position of trust, 189–190
age issues, 192
aggravating role, 189–190
bribery, 54–58
counterfeiting, 146, 271
criminal history adjustments, 192–193, 282
deceit, 186, 360
fines, 136, 195
forgery, 275, 360
fraud360
hate crime motivation/vulnerable victim, 366
larceny, 360
obstruction of justice, 121
official victim, 367
perjury, 126
probation, 191–192
restitution, 193
restraint of victim, 367–368
special skill use, 368
stolen property, 120, 275, 360
and substantial assistance to authorities, 384–385
theft, 183, 270–272, 360–361, 364
for violation of judicial process, 146
and waiver of right to appeal, 201
Sentencing Reform Act of 1984, 182, 184
separation of powers, 14, 16
serial filer schemes, 88
serious bodily injury, reckless risk of, 186, 362
settlement payment, definition of, 233
Shadylane Farms, Inc., 114
sham transaction, 53, 341
signature, 41, 83, 154, 291, 296–297, 301, 321
silence, right to, 212
single asset real estate, definition of, 233
skimming, 10, 12, 88, 139
Slingerland, 64–65
small business, definition of, 233
Social Security Administration, 2, 152
Sofa Gallery, Inc., 102
Solicitation, 251–252
special skill enhancement, 190
specificity, requirement of, 155
speedy trial, right to, 157
standard of reasonable care, 207
state, definition of, 234
state of mind. *See* intent; knowing; mental state; willfulness, 19, 118, 130
state tax stamps, fraudulent, 146
statement of financial affairs, 23, 41, 323
statements. *See also* false statements
definition of, 262
statute(s)
equitable distribution mandates, 19
interpretation of, 14
overlap of, 91
statute of limitations
for aiding and abetting, 163
for concealment, 163
for conspiracy, 165
exceptions to, 172
for false declarations, 39, 92, 128, 131
starting date of, 186
and superseding indictment, 164–165
tolling of, 164
statutory lien, definition of, 234
stay of case, 38
stealth, 19, 58
stockbroker, definition of, 234
stolen goods
sale or receipt of, 146
sentencing guidelines, 360
transportation of, 146
strict construction rule, 15
subjective test, for invoking advice of counsel, 166
subpoenas, grand jury, 178
substance abuse program participation, 377
Summit City Utilities, Inc., 44
supervised release, 39, 192, 194, 196, 201, 278, 378–379
Supreme Court
attorney-client privilege rulings, 169–170
false statements ruling, 109
immunity ruling, 179
obstruction of justice ruling, 121, 123
perjury rulings, 133
swap agreement, definition of, 234
swap participant, definition of, 236
swindles, 264

T

take-down phase, 88
tax fraud, 11
tax stamps, fraudulent, 146
Taylorcraft Aviation Corporation, 60
telephone communications, interception of, 152
television fraud, 116–117, 264–265
term overriding royalty, definition of, 236
termination fee, 11–12
testimonial, definition of, 176
testimony
  of counsel, for advice of counsel defense, 168
  failure to give, 24
  false (*See* false oaths; perjury), 47, 128, 130, 358–359
  immunity for, 178–179
  misleading, 133
theft. *See also* stolen goods
  from employee benefit plan, 146
  sentencing guidelines, 183
timeshare plan, definition of, 236
Tobias, 132–133
transactional immunity, 179
Transamerica Premium Insurance, 130
transfer
  of assets, ethical issues with, 18, 26, 208
  of claim, 289–290
  definition of, 63–64, 236–237
  property, 57
  voidable, 47
transportation money laundering, 141
trial by jury, right to, 183
trust funds, bleedout schemes with, 11
trustees. *See also* United States trustee(s)
  appointment of, 22, 31, 74, 156
    and confidentiality issues, 208–210, 342
    court order for, 22, 31, 74, 77
    to displace debtor in possession, 74
    and self-incrimination privilege, 86, 175–176
  compensation of, 23, 72, 149
  control of attorney-client privilege by, 172
  definition of, 239
  duties of, 22, 246–247
  embezzlement of funds by, 72–73
  immunity conferred upon, 150
  indenture, definition of, 226
  monitoring of, 7–8
  removal for cause, 177
  reporting of suspected crimes to, 23
  rights in investigations, 150
  selection by United States trustee, 31
  self-incrimination, 176
trusts, 20, 190, 207
turnover, 76, 158, 198
two-witness rule, 129–130

U

United States attorneys
  authority to prosecute, 3
  reporting of suspected crimes to, 148, 150
  role of, 147, 150
United States Court of Appeals
  for District of Columbia, 15
  for First Circuit, 185
  for Second Circuit, 96–97, 99, 109, 122, 129
  for Third Circuit, 35, 61
  for Fourth Circuit, 113, 122
  for Fifth Circuit, 92, 122, 173
  for Sixth Circuit, 37, 117, 122
  for Seventh Circuit, 36, 42, 48–49, 122, 130–131, 173
  for Eighth Circuit, 93
  for Ninth Circuit, 122, 125, 132
  for Tenth Circuit, 103–104, 107, 115, 143
  for Eleventh Circuit, 119, 129, 204
United States Postal Inspection Service, 2, 152
United States Sentencing Commission, 182, 282
United States Sentencing Guidelines Manual, excerpts, 360
United States trustee(s)
  criminal referral coordinators established by, 72, 91, 151
  investigations by, 148–149
  refusal to permit inspection by, 77
  reporting of suspected crimes to, 23

reporting requirements for, 23
selection of trustee by, 31
United States v. Booker, 182–183
use immunity, 178–179

V

vehicles, fraud prosecutions involving, 32
venue, for indictment, 155–156
vertical dimension, 55
Victim and Witness Protection Act, 124
victim-related adjustments, 189
vindictive prosecution, 158
void for vagueness, 14–15
voidable transfers, 47
voluntary compliance, importance of, 18
vulnerable victim, sentencing guidelines, 366–367

W

wage earner plans. *See* chapter 13 (wage earner plans), 21
Ward, 64–65, 79
weapon, dangerous, possession of, 186–187, 282, 376
Weiner, 96–97
Willey, Doyle Marshall, 114
willfully blind, 30
willfulness
and aiding and abetting, 95
in conspiracy, 106
and intent defenses, 98, 110, 166
and perjury, 126
wire fraud
and money laundering, 4, 94, 120
and multiplicity, 120
and RICO, 120
statute, 87, 120
wire tapping, 152
witness
bribery of, 58
right to confront, 158, 175
trustees as, 149–150
witness tampering, 125

Y

Yagow, Merlyn, 38

Z

Zimmerman, Steven, 102–103

Printed in the United States
145586LV00002B/7/A